# LEADING WELL FROM WITHIN

A Neuroscience and Mindfulness-Based
Framework for Conscious Leadership

## DANIEL FRIEDLAND, MD

SuperSmartHealth®

Published by SuperSmartHealth Publishing.

Grateful acknowledgment is made to the following for permission to reprint or reference previously published material:

Figures 1.1, 1.2, 1.3, 1.4, 1.5, and 3.2 are referenced and reprinted with the permission of The Leadership Circle.

Excerpt from "The Guest House" in its entirety by Jalal al-Din Rumi, translated by Coleman Barks, published in *The Essential Rumi* (San Francisco: HarperSanFrancisco, 1997). Reprinted by permission of Coleman Barks.

ISBN: 978-0-9978538-0-3

SuperSmartHealth
P.O. Box 910286
San Diego, CA 92191-0286
United States of America
Telephone: 858.481.2393
E-mail: Support@SuperSmartHealth.com

For Sue, Zach, and Dyl

# Table of Contents

# The Case for Conscious Leadership

It was sunrise on a clear-blue-sky Sunday morning in June, the type of morning here in San Diego when I'd usually go surfing. But it was not about to be a day of fun and relaxation. Little did I know I would soon face a crisis of leadership and one of the greatest tests of my life.

Tension had already been brewing for about a week between myself and my fourteen-year-old son, Zach. His summer vacation had begun, and he'd been spending late nights out with his friends. Zach and I have a close relationship and have even written a book together called *The Big Decision,* about how to make good decisions in life. But all week he'd seemed distant and irritable in our conversations, which had caused me frustration.

This morning Zach and my wife Sue were leaving for a weekend away at a lacrosse tournament. When Zach and I say goodbye each day, whether before school or longer trips away, we have a ritual of hugging heart to heart, which we've done since he was eight years old. But as I reached out to say goodbye this morning, he barely made eye contact and walked past me, mumbling something incomprehensible as he left.

It was a painful moment. For the first time, I felt dismissed and invisible in his life. I feared I had reached the time I had heard other parents talk about, where they feel they've lost connection and influence with their teenager.

As CEO of SuperSmartHealth, I train business and healthcare leaders in Conscious Leadership, where they learn to master their thoughts and feelings so they can act in alignment with their vision, purpose, and values—and inspire others to do the same. In other words, I teach people to lead well from within so they can lead well in the world. Had I lost my ability to lead in one of the most important relationships in my life?

My ego and survival-oriented mind reeled, feeling threatened by what I perceived to be a lack of respect. I felt angry and irritated. I began to fantasize about the conversation I was going to have with him when he returned. I thought about the consequences I could threaten him with to regain a sense of control.

Yet my true crisis of leadership still lay ahead.

After my attempt to say goodbye to Zach, I got into the car to drive to a board meeting. About eight months before, I had taken on the role of board chair of the Academy of Integrative Health and Medicine (AIHM). Assuming this leadership role with AIHM felt like a blessed opportunity to work with the current and next generation of leaders to transform healthcare, as well as to learn and grow personally, to walk my talk based on what I teach about Conscious Leadership.

Today was the second day of a combined board meeting with another leading organization in integrative health to formalize our upcoming collaboration. My fellow leader of our collaborating organization had led the first day well. We'd left yesterday evening inspired by a shared vision of the difference our organizations could make together.

All the way to the meeting, my survival-oriented brain kindled with anger and irritation from my interaction with Zach. As I became aware of my negative thoughts and feelings, I began to feel intense self-doubt, realizing I was not embodying the kind of Conscious Leadership I teach to others, which brought to the surface the self-doubt I'd already been carrying as a leader of AIHM. How had I landed in this role, leading such an esteemed group of healthcare leaders? Was I good enough? Would I be exposed as an imposter? With these unsettling questions in mind and a painful sense of incongruence, I walked into the meeting with my ego threatened and feeling raw.

After we all sat down around the table, my fellow leader opened the meeting by expressing heartfelt appreciation for what we'd achieved the day before, picking up on the group's previous thread of goodwill and cohesion. He then began to outline his vision for how we could structure a partnership to make a difference together.

As he spoke, I became troubled that the vision he was sharing seemed very different from what I thought our task force, which had spent months working on this partnership, had shared with me. This was not what we had agreed to!

I looked around the table. Everybody, including my board members, seemed enraptured by his vision. My baseline anxiety from the morning spiked. Somebody had to say something about the incongruence I was hearing! I had reached that moment as a leader where you hope someone else will jump in— and you realize that someone is you.

I abruptly interrupted my fellow leader. "I have to stop you!" I exclaimed. "This is not my understanding of what our task force discussed!"

He responded, "What don't you understand?" with what I sensed was complete surprise, followed by a threatening edge of irritation.

Twenty board members from both organizations felt our tension. All eyes locked on us in anticipation of a duel.

My heart thumped in my chest. A sweat broke out on my forehead. What did I just do? Did I prevent a terrible mistake or just create one? My mind scrambled for clarity and an eloquent response, neither of which manifested. Instead, the tone of my voice flattened, matching the look on my face, which betrayed the stress I was feeling.

I stammered, "I still don't understand. What exactly are we talking about here?" The vagueness of my question only seemed to add to the confusion and heighten the tension.

I then reached out to one of our task force members. "This wasn't what we discussed during our Executive Committee call, was it?" He responded that his memory of events was entirely different from mine.

I felt betrayed and alone and pressed further, insisting, "I still don't understand the arrangement you're proposing and cannot move forward with this until we are all clear."

Needless to say, my pressing did not come from a place of calm and decisive strength. It came from fear. Even beyond the words I declared, all in the room could sense my anxiety. I, in turn, felt my colleague's ire and exasperation when he said, "I don't understand what you don't understand!"

I counterattacked, looking to establish my power and control: "Here's what I have a problem with . . ." but my brain scrambled in fear. Consequently, I failed to state my case clearly, which I sensed further eroded trust for me in the room, intensifying my heightened feelings of self-doubt.

I was now operating on survival instinct alone. My heart felt like it was going to jump out of my chest, and I could feel the pulse in my ears as adrenaline surged in my blood. This was no longer about me serving as a leader. This was now all about me saving face. Eyes darted uncomfortably between board members around the room. I then heard somebody at the top of the table whisper, "Please make this stop!"

My fellow leader then called for a break and was about to gather with a couple of task force members on my board to debrief. I felt intensely disoriented and nauseated. Every fiber of my being wanted to take flight, isolate myself, and find some time alone to regroup and regain my composure.

In the space of ten minutes, I had just singlehandedly derailed a partnership that had been months in the making. I had also undone much of the trust I had built up as board chair. Had my worst fears been realized? What had just happened?

Fortunately, I knew exactly what had just happened. The survival part of my brain had taken over, and I was in a highly reactive state. My brain had done exactly what it was programmed to do under the circumstances, and I was now at a crossroads: was I going to allow the survival part of my brain continue to run the show, or was I going to put my "internal CEO," the higher part of my brain, back in charge?

Thanks to my years of mindfulness practice, I was able to find some internal reserve to gather myself. My awareness of the moment returned, and I could consciously observe what was happening to me. I saw how I was in the grip of fear, uncertainty, and self-doubt.

I began to shift from a reactive state to conscious awareness. Instead of becoming more stressed about being stressed, I was able to recognize how my amped-up energy was simply mobilizing resources to help me best deal with this significant challenge. Extending myself a touch of compassion and summoning all the courage I could muster, I leaned into the challenge. I caught my fellow leader and task force members before they slipped away and asked to meet with them on the patio to see if we could work this out.

Once outside, they expressed their anger and frustration with me about the vision and momentum I'd thwarted. They also helped clarify the issues I had been struggling to understand. As we began to wrap up our conversation, my fellow leader said it had felt like a dark energy had descended and caused the warrior in him to draw his sword. He felt that I'd damaged the spirit of collaboration and drained the energy from the room. He then asked what I was going to do to fix this. I was painfully aware of my responsibility and said I'd like to address the group when we went back in.

As I walked back towards the conference room by myself, a mix of thoughts and feelings swirled in my mind. Part of me felt tense, and another part of me felt angry and misunderstood. Yet another part of me felt sad and fearful that I'd irrevocably lost the trust of the group to be an effective leader. I felt lonely and isolated. I recognized how ironic it was that my day job was spent working with leaders of other organizations about how to consciously lead in times of stress, yet here I had been reacting unconsciously, overwhelmed by stress, fighting for control at the edge of falling apart, one step away from a panic attack.

Yet, at the same moment, I also knew it was "go time"—that this big challenge was a pivotal moment of growth. The next moment would determine whether I could effectively lead and serve my organization moving forward.

I took a couple of minutes before I walked into the room to settle down and center myself. I began to calm myself with a number of slow, deep, heart-centered breaths and brought a sense of tenderness and kindness to the tension I felt in my body. I then silently prayed for guidance, asking how I could best serve the group.

Once we had reconvened, my fellow leader announced that I'd like to address the events of the morning.

As he turned the floor over to me, I settled down further, and my energy felt more focused. I found my way back to a place of grounding, stillness, congruence, and clarity. Without knowing what I was about to say, the words seemed to move though me.

"Outside we were talking about a darkness that has descended into the room. Sometimes when we face darkness, it's best just to call it out. For my part, I am sorry that my fear got the best of me and for inviting this darkness into the room.

"Yesterday we spoke about the importance of constructively engaging each other, speaking our truth, and avoiding the pitfalls of destructive conflict or, worse yet, artificial harmony.

"Well, here we are in this moment of conflict. More important than any of the issues we face is how we will constructively engage each other right now to find healing and trust in the face of our conflict."

More than the words I spoke, my tone and expression communicated my shift. My demeanor softened, and the tone of my voice, which had previously been flat and tense, had regained its prosody.

I took responsibility for not having checked in with my task force before the meeting to find out where the latest discussions were or ask how I could best support the process moving forward. Next I explained that, more than anything, I wanted clarity about whether we were all aligned in moving forward and that I now felt clearer after the discussion I'd just had with my fellow leader on the patio. I then went around to check in with each member of our task force to make sure each one also felt good about the direction of the vision.

As I spoke, the shift in our collective mood was palpable. Energy came back into the room as lightness rippled in to reclaim the dark.

Continuing to lean into my challenge with self-compassion and feeling connected to something larger than myself, I felt my ego release its grip. I regained a sense of my higher self, connected to service and purpose. With a greater lightness of being and the clarity I'd been seeking, I could now rest assured that the direction my fellow leader had proposed indeed best served our collaboration and all the stakeholders we serve. I stated I could now support the new direction.

My fellow leader graciously thanked me; the silence in the room was replaced with relief, laughter, and chatter, reflecting on what had just happened. Someone said she had never seen anything addressed like this in a board meeting. Another, who had just written a blog post on courageous leadership, said it took bravery to take responsibility and speak the truth about what was happening.

One of the other leaders in the room noted that the light often attracts the dark. We reflected in awe on how we'd been tested by the dark and were able to come back together as a group, stronger than before.

A couple of days later, I had the opportunity to connect again with my fellow leader. I apologized to him for letting my fear thwart the process. He apologized to me for drawing his sword. As strangers, we had become intimately linked in a spiral of reactivity, triggering each other's defenses. Having come through this experience, we are no longer strangers. Our relationship was, in fact, strengthened by this event, and we emerged knowing we can heal from intense challenges, while valuing and respecting each other and trusting we'll do good work together.

When Zach returned from his trip, we also had a chance to sit down and have a heart-to-heart talk (free of the ego-driven fantasies of consequences and control I had when I was angry). I told him how I missed him and felt sad we had not spent much time connecting over the prior couple of weeks. I also shared that I had felt hurt and dismissed when he hadn't said goodbye.

He said, "I'm really sorry, Dad. I've just had a lot on my mind and was just very tired when I left." I felt touched by the genuine warmth and caring in his response and thanked him for his apology. I then asked him what had been on his mind, and in just one conversation, we were able to share our feelings, truly hear each other, and fully reconnect.

In retrospect, I have come to truly appreciate this crisis of leadership. As painful as it was at the time, it was what I needed to learn. It transformed my theoretical understanding of what I teach about Conscious Leadership into a truly lived, real-world experience critical to my own development.

I've shared this story at length with you in hopes of reminding you of when you too may have been reactive as a leader. There is gold to be found in our stories, particularly those that reflect the most difficult times. In the next section we'll unpack what this story has to teach.

## Lessons Learned: A Tale of Two Mindsets

During my crisis of leadership, you may have noticed a movement between two polarities:

1. One involves a *reactive mindset,* where we feel threatened with fear, stress, self-doubt, ego, and conflict; where an unconscious and reflexive series of protective responses can dominate our psyche and ripple through our actions, activating similar experiences in others that can instantly drain energy and fragment teams as well as families.

2. The other involves a *creative mindset,* where with conscious awareness, self-compassion, and courage, we can lean in and grow, even in our most challenging circumstances. Inspiration, energy, and empathy are present, and innovation can flourish, enabling a team to work well together with transparency and trust and become aligned in a shared vision to more fully focus its collective energy to serve others and something larger than themselves.

Leaders, and their ability to be aware of and navigate stress, uncertainty, and self-doubt in any given situation, can profoundly influence which mindset dominates.

When I use the term *mindset,* I realize that people may define it differently. Some think of a mindset as a fixed set of beliefs and others as an inclination or even mood.[1] Many say our mindsets can be changed. For the purposes of this book, I'm using the term *mindset* to represent a more dynamic state of mind.

On this particular Sunday morning, when I arrived at our meeting, our group was operating from a *creative mindset.* I could sense the goodwill in my fellow leader and the room, and the group was well aligned, consciously and creatively working in service of something larger than themselves.

However, my frame of mind was initially in a *reactive mindset.* I was in survival mode, experiencing a threat response to the stress of my morning interaction with my son and then, on my drive over, to my feelings of self-doubt as a leader.

Consequently, I was not prepared to lead well from within at the meeting, where my threatening feelings of stress and self-doubt only intensified. That morning my ego, seeking power and fighting for control, was in the driver's seat. And this reactive mindset would soon find its way into the room—and affect everyone in it—taking our collaboration to the brink of dissolution.

Had I simply asked for clarification from my colleagues, free of fear and in service of our larger mission, I have no doubt my misunderstanding would have been easily resolved and we would have been able to move forward without a hitch.

Thankfully, when I became mindfully aware of what was going on inside of me, I was able to use specific skills and practices (which you'll learn more about in this book) to transform my stress into a healthier response.

The key is to understand that stress is not inherently bad. It's simply energy that can be used in both positive and negative ways. Instead of being swept away by harmful and threatening feelings of fight-or-flight, I was able to *refocus and leverage this energy of stress* to proactively engage the challenge at hand. By leaning into the stress and viewing it as an energy source I could direct, I extended compassion towards myself and others with the intention of turning the conflict around. This shift in perspective enabled me to regain a sense of mental clarity, communicate more effectively, and adopt a more creative mindset.

That creative mindset was not only evident in the words I spoke. The shift in the tone of my voice, facial expression, and posture of my body also conveyed to the group that I was no longer a threat and they were safe. Together we could refocus on our collaboration and the larger good.

As a leader—whether of a large organization, a division, a team, a volunteer group, or your family—can you think of a time when you felt threatened by stress or self-doubt and your reactive mindset triggered stress, uncertainty, and self-doubt in others, which resulted in a breakdown in the dynamic of your team or your family?

Can you also think of a time when, as a leader, you faced a stressful and challenging situation, and your conscious and creative mindset had a beneficial effect on your team or your family?

I suspect you recognize which mindset has generally been more effective for you. Research has shown that the characteristics of a creative mindset not only result in high-performance leadership and increased organizational effectiveness, but they also protect against the symptoms of burnout, which we'll cover in more detail in chapter 1. Mastering this ability to shift from a reactive to creative mindset has never been more crucial.

Also, from my work with business leaders and healthcare providers, I know that we can shift between the conscious states of creativity and the unconscious states of reactivity in an instant, depending on the degree of fear and threat we feel. Even leaders who are trained (or who train others) in Conscious Leadership can be triggered by stress and self-doubt and become unconsciously reactive—just as I did during the joint board meeting.

Can you relate? Can you think of a situation where you were completely in the groove, feeling energized, loving what you were doing, and knowing you were making a difference in someone's life, and then, BOOM—some threatening event triggers overwhelming stress or self-doubt that completely takes the wind out of your sails and risks sinking you? It could be a mistake you made or a client or patient complaint or a fight with your spouse.

If so, hopefully my story also conveys that it is possible to reengage a creative mindset in short order. By becoming conscious of your reactivity, showing compassion toward yourself and others, and transforming your view of stress from "threat" to "challenge," you have the capacity to reengage your creative mindset, promote healing in your relationships, and inspire creativity in others, too.

The key is, once you are triggered, feel threatened, and become reactive, how quickly can you reorient towards a conscious and creative mindset?

In this book, I'll be sharing with you a practical framework to give you the skills and practices to more fully engage your capacity for Conscious Leadership and a creative mindset, regardless of the amount of stress you're under in the moment. More than just learning how to manage stress, you will learn how to leverage it as creative fuel to achieve even higher levels of performance than you would without any stress at all!

# My "Why" for This Work

With credit to Simon Sinek's book *Start with Why*,[2] before I share further about *how* to shift towards Conscious Leadership, I'd love to share with you *why* I am so passionate about this work. In its simplest terms, this book is about learning how to consciously navigate stress and self-doubt to focus on what matters most in life. I found my purpose for learning, practicing, and teaching this work through the gift of having fallen apart during medical school at the University of California, San Francisco (UCSF). I understand firsthand how stress, uncertainty, and self-doubt can fragment you and how learning to embrace these feelings and focus on what is truly important can restore to you a sense of feeling whole again.

In my second year of medical school, I spiraled into a depression after a painful breakup with a girlfriend. Six months into much-needed therapy, my counselor said to me, "It sounds to me like you have flipped your lid."

In that moment, everything changed. In my mind, I saw two sides of a lid. On one side, I saw myself before I immigrated to America from South Africa. I had spent my entire life driven by ego and achievement to prove my self-worth and to overcome my underlying feelings of self-doubt. In my striving, I became one of the top students at university and sought out a circle of friends who validated me. The most dangerous aspect was the delusion and pride I experienced in believing I had somehow "arrived" at a place where I believed I had no self-doubt. Ominously, my sense of self-acceptance was contingent on this measure of self-esteem.

On the other side of the lid, I saw how immigrating to the United States and then attending medical school with a group of overachievers humbled me and exposed me to unbearable feelings of self-doubt. The breakup with my girlfriend and my ensuing feelings of self-doubt brought me to my knees with panic attacks and depression. So when my counselor told me I had "flipped my lid," I saw this lid flipped over, so that my stress and self-doubt, which had once been on the underside of the lid, concealed and protected by my achievements and drive to prove my self-worth, were now painfully exposed. When the "lid" flipped, I became highly reactive and panicked. I did not have the resources to accept myself with these feelings.

In my revelation about my delusion with self-doubt, I could clearly see how self-doubt had always run my life, even when I believed I did not have it. Subconsciously, it drove me to prove my self-worth and avoid anything that could have potentially triggered further self-doubt. It prevented me from reaching out to make new connections, being vulnerable and truly intimate in my relationships, or taking risks to explore and pursue what was truly meaningful to me.

Seeing for the first time just how much self-doubt I had, I arrived at a critical branch point. I had a conscious decision to make. I could go back on my path of denial, reacting to my underlying feelings of self-doubt by driving myself further to prove my self-worth. Or, I could learn how to embrace and navigate my feelings of stress and self-doubt, learn from what they had to teach, and consciously choose to align my decisions and actions around what was truly important to me and how I could best serve others.

I knew that the path of overcoming self-doubt was limiting, exhausting, and unsustainable, and I set my course, determined to learn how to do the latter as best I could.

Later, I also began to more fully appreciate how the threat of stress and self-doubt not only affected me, but others, too. I became acutely aware how the patients we were seeing suffered as well. I also sensed how our attending physicians were overwhelmed with feelings of stress, uncertainty, and self-doubt. On medical rounds, some seemed cynical, distant, or aloof with patients. Their struggles seemed to strain the compassion from their care and led many into a cycle of burnout.

Initially, in medical school, I thought everyone else seemed so well adjusted. When I came to class, I felt like an outsider, watching everyone happily interacting with each other in groups. I told my counselor I felt like a loser, struggling alone with my feelings of stress and self-doubt.

He reassured me I was by no means alone and that more than half of my class was in counseling. That completely blew me away. Here I was, attending one of the top medical schools, surrounded by overachievers pursuing one of the most competitive and demanding careers in the world. And half of us were in counseling! No one was talking about it, but many of us were suffering in a culture of silence, believing we could not show any weakness and yet fearful we were falling apart.

I decided to reach out to my classmates. With one phone call, I founded the UCSF Medical Student Network. Together, with a group of my fellow fourth-year medical students, we signed up almost the entire medical school into this network. We formed twenty-five "families" of support groups. Each group included all four years of medical students who were led by the fourth-year students.

At the age of twenty-six, I presented my first leadership seminar to my fellow fourth-year students, in which I shared the story of my struggles and encouraged them to share their stories with their support groups, too. To model this, I gave a front-page interview in the *Synapse,* our university's newspaper, to share the story of my emotional crisis and the vision for the network.

I sensed if we, as students, could become more aware of our vulnerabilities, care for ourselves with those vulnerabilities, share them, and then listen compassionately to the stories of others, we could transform our culture. Further, this process would enable us to more fully listen and connect with the suffering of our patients and inoculate ourselves from the effects of the stress that had strained the compassion from some of our attending physicians. In leaning into and learning from our stressful challenges with self-compassion, we could mitigate burnout, cultivate resiliency, grow, and more fully engage in the compassionate delivery of healthcare.

As I made meaning from my pain and heard the stories fellow students shared about how meaningful the network was to their transformation, I knew I wanted to dedicate my life to this work.

Then I took what I initially thought was a detour. After my medical residency, I was asked to become the first teaching fellow at UCSF. Although I knew I wanted to dedicate myself to helping physicians navigate stress and become more resilient so they could stay focused on what matters most, I was advised that this pursuit would not be a good choice and that I should "rather focus on something more academic."

So I pursued my second choice, which was to train the faculty at UCSF on something called evidence-based medicine (EBM). This choice led me to authoring one of the first textbooks on this process, which is how doctors are now all trained to apply the best available scientific research to medical decisions with their patients.

I then spent the next decade training tens of thousands of physicians in almost every state in America about how to leverage scientific information to make better decisions and better care for their patients.

But about eight years ago, I became intensely restless. To me, EBM is about the "mind of medicine," and I was deeply missing this work that I view as the "heart of healthcare," as well as conscious business.

Armed now with the science-based skills of evidence-based medicine, I rededicated myself to the work I'm most passionate about—helping people navigate stress and self-doubt and align themselves with what's truly most important in their lives.

On this quest, I conducted a study of over three hundred people about their experiences with self-doubt and immersed myself in the literature in the areas of brain science, cognitive behavioral therapy, positive psychology, and the practice of mindfulness. I looked for the best available skills and practices I could find for you to support yourself in rewiring your brain to more effectively navigate stress and self-doubt and to engage a creative mindset to thrive in your health, relationships, and at work.

I have digested all of this information and created a practical and integrated system to help you shift from the mindset of reactivity to creativity. This system is called *The 4 in 4 Framework™ to Engage Conscious Leadership,* so named because it has four primary steps and then four components in each of the steps. The four steps of this framework will frame much of our journey through this book together.

## The Road Ahead

If you are a high-achieving, highly responsible leader looking for an edge, and you sometimes feel overwhelmed with stress or self-doubt (or even fear you could fall apart), I want you to know that you're not alone. That's exactly why I'm sharing my stories with you and why I've written this book: you don't have to suffer in silence. There is a path back toward wholeness and high-level performance from exactly where you stand—even as you face tremendous responsibility and stress daily.

While my inspiration for writing this book is highly personal, the framework you'll learn in this book is far from soft. It's based upon a solid, four-layer foundation that's important to cover in detail, which is what we'll do in part 1. Each foundational layer builds upon the previous one.

First, chapter 1 provides the "why" of Conscious Leadership: here you'll learn more about the science of leadership that explains the practical, bottom-line impact of both reactive and creative mindsets and why learning to shift to a creative mindset is so crucial for leaders today. Chapter 2 will build upon that foundation of evidence-based results with brain science, and you'll gain a deeper understanding about how your brain works so you can identify the keys to shifting your mindset. Chapter 3 further builds upon that foundation of brain science with a key practice called mindfulness that enables you to work your brain even better. Then, in chapter 4, I'll share with you an overview of the 4 in 4 Framework for Engaging Conscious Leadership, which will provide you with the four key steps to shifting from a reactive to a creative mindset at will. This framework will then serve as our foundation for the remainder of the book.

In part 2 of the book, you'll learn how to apply the 4 in 4 Framework so you can lead well from within. Chapters 5 through 8 will take you through each of the four steps of the 4 in 4 Framework, teaching you the specific neuroscience and mindfulness-based skills and practices you can use right now to navigate stress and self-doubt and identify and stay aligned with what matters most in your life.

Once you've learned how to leverage stress and shift from a reactive to a creative mindset for yourself, in part 3 you'll discover how to apply the 4 in 4 Framework to lead well in the world. In chapter 9, you'll learn how cycles of reactivity and creativity impact your relationships, both at work and at home, and in chapter 10, you'll learn how to apply the 4 in 4 Framework to transform those reactive cycles into creative cycles by resolving conflicts and nurturing your most important relationships. Similarly, chapter 11 explains how cycles of reactivity and creativity show up in cultures—again, both at work and at home. Chapter 12 then shows you how the 4 in 4 Framework can be applied to transform families, organizations, communities, and even the world.

We will conclude by simplifying the four steps into one simple step that engages all the other steps and then summarizing all the skills and practices you have learned for lifelong learning and ongoing transformation.

A few years ago, on my quest to learn how to shift from a reactive mindset to a creative mindset—from fragmentation to wholeness—I crystallized a simple mission for my life: "I vow to live my life from home; when I get lost, I find my way back and inspire others to live from home, too." I trust the stories and science that have culminated in the 4 in 4 Framework will empower you to learn from your own stories and thrive at home within yourself, too, especially when you find yourself overwhelmed, lost, or fragmented with stress and self-doubt.

So, are you ready to learn a whole new way of leading well?

Let's get started!

# Part 1

## The Foundation for
## Engaging Conscious Leadership

# CHAPTER 1

# Evidence and Inspiration for Engaging Conscious Leadership

When I begin my workshops on Engaging Conscious Leadership, I typically ask participants to think about the most inspiring leader they know. I'd like to invite you to do the same.

Bring to mind for a moment, as vividly as you can, the most inspiring leader you have ever encountered. Perhaps it was someone who mentored you or raised you or a leader you have met or followed from afar. Or it may be a leader you've been inspired by in history.

As you bring this leader to your mind as vividly as you can, reflect on this: what qualities most inspire you?

Now go ahead and write these qualities below under the heading "High-Performance Leaders."

**High-Performance Leaders:**


Now, in contrast, reflect on the qualities of low-performance leaders you have encountered. These individuals may have made your life miserable or cause you to bristle when you think about them. Go ahead and write down their qualities under the heading "Low-Performance Leaders."

**Low-Performance Leaders:**

When I ask participants in my workshops to share these qualities, here are the typical responses I get:

*High-performance leaders* have vision and purpose, are strategically focused, are decisive and get things done, care about and relate well to people, are humble and compassionate, are courageous and have integrity, are emotionally intelligent, and can see the big picture. These leaders tend to be highly passionate and innovative. And when you come right down to it, high-performance leaders lead from their highest selves and are in service of something larger than themselves.

*Low-performance leaders,* in contrast, tend to lead with ego and intimidation, are territorial, micromanage, judge, criticize and blame others, and may be wishy-washy and expedient. They are emotionally labile and cannot be trusted. These leaders may fight for power and control to prove their self-worth or alternatively take flight from their responsibility or what personally threatens them. In short, these leaders lead from ego in service of themselves.

In 2010, IBM conducted over 1,500 face-to-face interviews with CEOs from companies of all sizes across 60 countries, representing 33 industries, asking leaders what they thought was the most important quality leaders need to navigate the increasingly complex environment in which business is conducted. The number one quality they pointed to was *creativity.*[1]

As we'll see below, creativity means more than just innovative thinking and expression. It also means having a greater awareness of yourself, others, and the system in which you operate; connecting authentically and well with others; and achieving meaningful results.

This definition may be more akin to *proactivity*: using our knowledge and creativity to anticipate situations and seizing them as opportunities to affect the outcome.

In his book *Man's Search for Meaning,* Viktor Frankl, an Austrian neurologist and psychiatrist who survived the Holocaust, captures the essence of being proactive, which is to take responsibility for your life rather than reacting to outside circumstances or other people. This is especially important in high-stakes, stressful situations.

Frankl stresses the importance of courage, perseverance, individual responsibility, awareness of our choices, and conscious and deliberate engagement in those choices, which enable us to more fully contribute to the lives of others and provide our sense of meaning.[2]

The qualities listed above for high-performance leaders typically reflect this kind of *creative* mindset. In contrast, the qualities listed for low-performance leaders tend to reflect a *reactive* mindset.

The Leadership Circle,[3] a leading organization in the area of leadership assessment, has created a well-validated 360-degree assessment[4] to evaluate these reactive and creative leadership qualities and their relationship to leadership effectiveness for over 60,000 leaders.[5] It specifically evaluates the reactivity and creativity of leaders using the following domains and subdomains:[6]

### *The Creative Leadership Competencies*

### Relating

- Caring Connection
- Fosters Team Play
- Collaborator
- Mentoring and Developing
- Interpersonal Intelligence

### Self-Awareness

- Selfless Leader
- Composure
- Balance
- Personal Learner

### Authenticity

- Integrity
- Courageous Authenticity

21

## Systems Awareness

- Community Concern
- Sustainable Productivity
- Systems Thinker

## Achieving

- Strategic Focus
- Purposeful and Visionary
- Achieves Results
- Decisiveness

### *The Reactive Leadership Tendencies*

## Complying

- Conservative (i.e., playing it safe)
- Pleasing
- Belonging (i.e., conforming)
- Passive

## Protecting

- Arrogant
- Critical
- Distant

## Controlling

- Perfectionist
- Driven (i.e., to prove self-worth)
- Ambitious (i.e., to get ahead of other people)
- Autocratic

To summarize, the Leadership Circle finds that leaders with a creative leadership style relate well to people, are authentic, are both systems aware and self-aware, and are achievement oriented. Referencing the work of highly regarded psychologist Karen Horney, they find that leaders with a reactive leadership style focus on protecting their ego with a stance of being overly compliant, protective, or controlling.

How many of these creative and reactive qualities did you identify in the high-performance and low-performance leaders you have encountered?

Most of us would say that the creative mindset does seem to result in high-performance leadership, just as the reactive mindset seems to result in low-performance leadership. But is there any real evidence?

In their 360-degree assessments, in addition to asking questions to quantify the leader's level of creativity and reactivity, the Leadership Circle also asks the following five questions about leadership effectiveness to comprise a Leadership Effectiveness Scale:

1. I am satisfied with the quality of leadership that he/she provides.

2. He/she is the kind of leader that others should aspire to become.

3. He/she is an example of an ideal leader.

4. His/her leadership helps this organization to thrive.

5. Overall, he/she provides very effective leadership.

With their large database of completed assessments, the Leadership Circle has correlated this measure of leadership effectiveness with the leaders' composite scores for creativity and reactivity. Here is what they found:

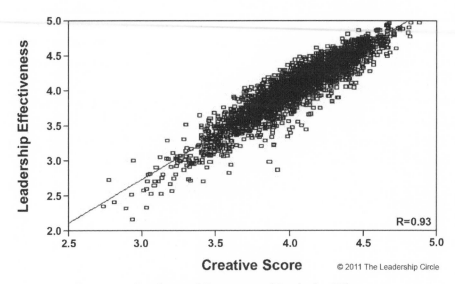

*Figure 1.1. Correlation of Creativity and Leadership Effectiveness*

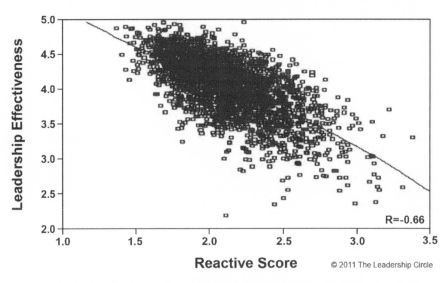

*Figure 1.2. Correlation of Reactivity and Leadership Effectiveness*

These graphs show that the more reactive your mindset is, the less effective a leader you are viewed to be. Conversely, the more creative your mindset is, the more effective a leader you are viewed to be.

While the impact of creative and reactive mindsets on leadership effectiveness may be important, you might also be wondering about the bottom line: does a leader's mindset have a measurable impact on organizational performance?

The Leadership Circle went further to conduct a study of approximately five hundred leaders to evaluate the relationship of leadership effectiveness on an index of business performance success criteria, which included the following:[7]

- Sales/revenue growth
- Market share
- Profitability/return on assets
- Quality products/services
- New product development
- Overall performance

The graph below shows what they found:

*Figure 1.3. Correlation of Leadership Effectiveness and Business Performance*

This graph shows a clear correlation between leadership effectiveness and business performance.

The Leadership Circle further explored the aggregate Leadership Circle Profiles of the fifty leaders whose businesses were in the top 10 percent, versus the fifty leaders whose businesses were in the bottom 10 percent.

Here's what the aggregate profile for the fifty top leaders looks like:

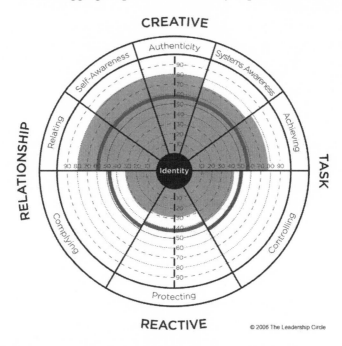

*Figure 1.4. Aggregate Leadership Circle Profile Scores for Top Fifty Leaders*

To explain what you are looking at, the shading in the circle represents the results of the 360-degree reviews for each domain of creativity and reactivity by percentile. So, for example, on the Relating domain in the left upper quadrant, these leaders were assessed by others to be at the 80th percentile of Relating in relation to the Leadership Circle's large norm database. The bold lines represent how the leaders assessed themselves.

As you can see, these top-performing leaders were assessed by others to be much more creative than reactive. Further, the bolded lines seem to indicate they assessed themselves with some humility, rating themselves to be less creative and more reactive than others viewed them.

Why might this be? A creative mindset is a growth mindset, a concept made popular by Carol Dweck's bestselling book *Mindset: The New Psychology of Success.*[8] Dweck defines a growth mindset as the belief that qualities such as intelligence and personality can be cultivated through effort—as opposed to a fixed mindset that believes such qualities are set in stone. People with a growth mindset don't see failure as failure. They are able to embrace their failure as a challenge and see it as learning.[9] In other words, because people with a growth mindset believe they are always learning, they know they don't have all the answers and they never will. Such a perspective results in a sense of humility, which makes them less likely to overrate these positive qualities. They know, in their quest for learning, there's always more to learn.

By contrast, here's the aggregate profile of the leaders whose businesses' performance were evaluated to be in the bottom 10 percent:

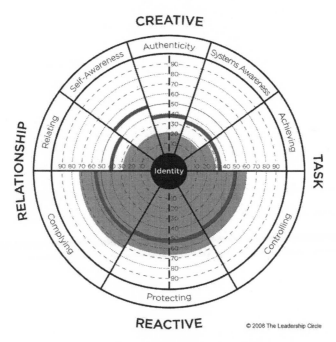

*Figure 1.5. Aggregate Leadership Circle Profile Scores for Bottom Fifty Leaders*

What you can see is that these leaders were assessed by others to be more reactive than creative. Further, they appeared to be more generous to themselves than the top performing leaders were, assessing themselves to be more creative and less reactive than others viewed them.

In contrast to a growth mindset, a reactive mindset tends to be a fixed mindset, defined by Dweck as the belief that our qualities are fixed and permanent. In other words, you're either capable, intelligent, or successful, or you're not—and as Dweck says, "failure means you're not."[10] Failure is threatening and unacceptable. Thus, it's not surprising to see reactive leaders overestimate their abilities. It's hard to admit you're struggling if you believe you can't improve.

In summary, this research shows that high-performance leadership is indeed correlated with a creative mindset and low-performance leadership with a reactive mindset.

Leaders who are able to adopt a creative mindset become aware of, take responsibility for, and regulate their internal responses to stress, uncertainty, and self-doubt. Through their awareness, their compassion for themselves and others, and their capacity to harness and embrace stress and challenge, these leaders embody resiliency and strength. They promote healing and inspire trust by reengaging and realigning their team with the overall mission and purpose of the enterprise, especially when faced with adversity or when things go off track. They can then take wise action to engage and inspire their team to manifest a shared vision that serves all stakeholders. This is the essence of Conscious Leadership and leading well from within.

## The Impact of Mindset on Burnout and Resiliency

The skills and practices that allow us to shift from a reactive to a creative mindset, or stay in a creative mindset under pressure, have never been more crucial, since the circumstances and stress we face today feel more threatening than ever.

The US military uses a term that succinctly describes the challenges inherent to what all leaders are facing today. It's called *VUCA,* which stands for Volatility, Uncertainty, Complexity, and Ambiguity.[11] VUCA perfectly describes the daily reality of business and healthcare today, where we see leaders breaking down and cultures buckling, feeling overwhelmed and threatened by this stress. And the all-too-common downstream effect of the reactive response to this stress is *burnout.*

A 2013 study by Dr. Srinivasan Pillay, an international expert in burnout, stress, and anxiety at Harvard Medical School, found that 96 percent of senior leaders reported some degree of burnout. One-third described their burnout as extreme.[12]

Burnout is an ominous triad of symptoms in which individuals experience emotional exhaustion, feel disconnected in their relationships, and experience a reduced sense of personal accomplishment in their work.[13] Dealing with burnout is not only debilitating for the leader, but the leader's stress can ripple through an organization, eroding the culture and significantly impacting employee engagement and the bottom line. (We'll be exploring the financial impact of employee disengagement later in the book.)

In healthcare, 54 percent of physicians experience symptoms of burnout,[14] which has been linked to medical errors and physician dissatisfaction.[15] In turn, physician dissatisfaction is linked to patient dissatisfaction and increased malpractice risk.[16]

What's sadly ironic is that 75–90 percent of patients present to their primary care doctors with stress-related concerns,[17] only to be seen by a doctor who is often more stressed out than they are. How can physicians effectively heal patients unless they are better able to navigate their own stress and heal themselves first?

Furthermore, we have a large body of research telling us just how dangerous stress is for our health. For example, a study published in 2012 of almost 70,000 people found that even low levels of stress were associated with a 20 percent increased risk of death. Moderate levels and extreme levels of stress were associated with a 43 percent and 94 percent increased risk, respectively. (The deaths were largely due to cardiovascular disease, cancer, accidents, and injuries.)[18]

Data such as this compels doctors to communicate how toxic stress is for your health, which, ironically, only ends up making you feel more stressed about being stressed, making the problem worse!

As you will see later in the book, the harmful effects of stress are only part of the story on stress and, in fact, have a lot to do with your *mindset* about stress: whether you view it as harmful or helpful.

When you learn how to *engage stress as an asset,* you can not only improve your health, but promote personal growth and enhance your performance as well.

Part of the solution to burnout involves learning skills and practices to cultivate *resiliency*—to learn how to engage stress more effectively and reengage with what matters most in your life.

The good news is that these are the same skills you need for a creative mindset and Conscious Leadership in both healthcare and business, which you'll learn in this book.

It is also crucial to support and coach the development of Conscious Leaders in every context, so they can create optimal environments and resilient cultures within which employees and practitioners can heal themselves and thrive, to serve their clients and patients well. The peril of not doing so is that low-performance leaders can be threatening to their employees and lead them into burnout.

For example, one study, by Dr. Roy Poses from Alpert Medical School at Brown University, highlights the damage a healthcare leader can have on the psyche of physicians. He surveyed 287 family medicine and general internal medicine respondents (with a 68.3 percent response rate), assessing their level of burnout against a Perceived Leadership Integrity Index (PLII). They were asked to rate leaders on qualities congruent with Conscious Leadership, including whether the leader:

- Supported the physician's core values
- Prioritized quality over costs
- Positively responded when the physician raised quality issues
- Demonstrated interest in patient care above self-interest
- Was honest

The study found that a low PLII was significantly correlated with physician burnout (p = 0.0001) and the physicians' intention to leave (p = 0.026).[19]

This study is further supported by a more recent study of almost 3,000 physicians in the Mayo Clinic system that found the composite leadership scores of immediate supervisors, as well as the ratings of the respective division or department chairs, strongly correlated with physician burnout.[20]

These studies speak to the vital importance of cultivating Conscious Leadership in healthcare. But this need is just as great in the business world as well. Leaders who are unaware and/or ill-equipped to deal with their reactions to stress and self-doubt are predisposed to act from a reactive mindset, especially in VUCA environments. These leaders are prone to act from a place of personal power and self-interest, rather than the common good, where financial interests hold sway over core values, social interests, and the delivery of quality and value. All of these can erode a sense of meaning and purpose and increase the risk of burnout within a culture.

Conscious Leaders can effectively navigate and leverage stress and self-doubt and shift from a reactive to a creative mindset in the most challenging of circumstances. These leaders are resilient and can hold themselves and others on track to find innovative and creative solutions that inoculate all against stress and burnout in a VUCA environment.

Fortunately, the qualities of Conscious Leadership (or a creative mindset) that enable you to navigate stress and transform burnout into resiliency are the same qualities that yield high-performance leadership.

Conscious, high-performing leaders embody the antithesis of burnout. They thrive under stress and engage it in alignment with their vision and purpose to exude passion and vitality. They connect with and inspire others and take all stakeholders into account. And they experience fulfillment and significance in knowing they are serving and contributing value to the greater good. These qualities not only transform the leader, but all they serve.

The benefits of learning to leverage your stress and consciously shift from a reactive to a creative mindset don't just apply to leaders in government, business, and healthcare. They apply to all leaders, whether a healer, parent, teacher, coach, spouse, or anyone wanting to better navigate stress, lead more consciously, and contribute more fully to the lives of others.

Considering that two-thirds of adults are either moderately or extremely stressed on a daily basis,[21] our need for these skills and an approach to cultivate a creative mindset and high-performance Conscious Leadership is clear.

Fortunately, there are a number of worldviews to inspire the engagement of Conscious Leadership, both in business and healthcare. Here are two examples. Each has much to contribute to the other in the development of Conscious Leaders.

## Inspiration from the World of Business: Conscious Capitalism

In 2012, I had the privilege to present my Framework for Engaging Conscious Leadership to a remarkable organization, Conscious Capitalism. This organization was founded by and collaborates with leaders of some of the most highly regarded companies today. Just think of their corporate cultures as I mention them: Starbucks, Whole Foods, Zappos, Trader Joe's, Best Buy, Patagonia, the Container Store, and Southwest Airlines—just to name a few.

Conscious Capitalism sees the congruence and power in integrating consciousness and capitalism. Their purpose is to facilitate greater awareness in order to create thriving and sustainable enterprises that elevate humanity.

They have declared four principles to be crucial in achieving this mission:[22]

1. **Higher Purpose.** The first principle acknowledges that a higher purpose is needed to effectively drive any enterprise.

   "While making money is essential for the vitality and sustainability of a business, it is not the only or even the most important reason a business exists. Conscious businesses focus on their purpose beyond profit."

   Borrowing from a metaphor in healthcare, one of their trustees, Darden School of Management professor Ed Freeman, explains:

   "We need red blood cells to live (the same way a business needs profits to live), but the purpose of life is more than to make red blood cells (the same way the purpose of business is more than simply to generate profits)."

The organization further states, "By focusing on its deeper Purpose [beyond profits], a Conscious Business inspires, engages, and energizes its stakeholders. Employees, customers, and others trust and even love companies that have an inspiring purpose."

2. **Stakeholder Orientation.** The second principle ensures all stakeholders in the system—clients, employees, vendors, shareholders, affected communities as well as the environment, etc.—are valued and considered.

   All too often, leaders focus only on shareholders or their financial stake in the company. It's only by recognizing the interdependence of all stakeholders and seeking to create win-win-win solutions that you can sustain a healthy ecosystem within which everyone thrives.

3. **Conscious Leadership.** The third principle acknowledges the vital importance of Conscious Leadership as we've defined it in this book.

   The Conscious Capitalism organization states that "Conscious Leaders focus on 'we,' rather than 'me.' They inspire, foster transformation, and bring out the best in those around them. They understand that their role is to serve the purpose of the organization, to support the people within the organization, and to create value for all of the organization's stakeholders. They recognize the integral role of culture and purposefully cultivate a Conscious Culture of trust and care."

   At its root, Conscious Leadership is servant leadership inspired by purpose. It's inspired leadership, leading from your highest self in service of something larger than yourself.

4. **Conscious Culture.** Conscious Leadership, in turn, is the key to driving the vital force of Conscious Culture, where leaders, employees, and all stakeholders consciously and actively engage in the communication and collective action that embodies the principles and values of the company and thus allows it to manifest its purpose.

   The environment of safety, trust, and caring that leaders facilitate is crucial to creating a culture of active engagement, where employees are willing to go above and beyond, investing discretionary resources into the company and all whom they serve. Collectively, these employees perform at their highest levels to provide value and outstanding customer service, which results in a thriving enterprise.

The principles of Conscious Capitalism apply not only to business, but to healthcare organizations, too. The skills and practices of Conscious Leadership can help healthcare leaders enhance their capacity to lead with vision and purpose, ensure all stakeholders are considered, and create truly healing, resilient, and thriving cultures that deliver high-quality, compassionate, and patient-centered care.

## Inspiration from the World of Healthcare: Integrative Health and Medicine

Not only can healthcare learn from the world of business, business can also learn much from the world of healthcare. You could say that much of the philosophy of Conscious Capitalism focuses on creating healthy leaders who can create healthy organizations that deliver value.

If business and other leaders know where to look within the world of healthcare, they can discover how to more fully create physical, mental, emotional, and even spiritual health that can serve them well as they become Conscious Leaders.

As I mentioned in the introduction, I feel blessed to serve as a leader of the Academy of Integrative Health and Medicine (AIHM), one of the leading organizations working to advance the creation of health through the global field of integrative healthcare.

AIHM defines integrative health and medicine as a field of healthcare that "reaffirms the importance of the relationship between practitioner and patient, focuses on the whole person, is informed by evidence, and makes use of all appropriate therapeutic approaches, healthcare professionals, and professions to achieve optimal health and healing."[23]

At AIHM, our vision is to establish a new paradigm of healthcare for humanity and the planet.

"We too have a dream where

- Healthcare is about health and available to all;
- Prevention is our foundation and mechanical fixes are embraced when we need them;
- Environmental sustainability is integrated into our culture, practice, and training, and
- All healthcare providers work collaboratively to heal body, mind, and spirit."[24]

In establishing a new paradigm of health, we are committed to redefining the common perception that "health" is simply the "absence of disease" and to more fully embrace this word's etymology. The root of the word "health" comes from the Old English *hal,* which means "whole."[25]

Of note, the root of the word "patient" comes from the Latin *patiens,* from *patior,* which means "to suffer."[26]

So the healing journey of healthcare is this: Patients suffer from fragmentation of mind, body, and spirit. The role of the healer is to support patients in reconnecting with their essential wholeness—i.e., health.

Consequently, AIHM defines "optimal health" as "the conscious pursuit of the highest level of functioning and balance of the physical, environmental, mental, emotional, social, and spiritual aspects of human experience, resulting in a dynamic state of being fully alive."[27]

Using the language of Conscious Capitalism, you can think of all of these aspects of optimal health as our *internal* stakeholders, whose wholeness we consciously pursue by learning to lead well from within.

The movement from a reactive to a creative mindset in leadership— representing low-performance and high-performance leadership states, respectively—is also essentially a shift from fragmentation to wholeness (or, as I mentioned in the introduction, a sense of "home" within ourselves).

On one hand, our experience of stress and self-doubt can fragment us and lead us astray, damaging our health, relationships, and ability to focus on what matters most in our work. On the other hand, learning to engage stress more effectively and lead more consciously can help us find our way back to feel more integrated and whole, which contributes to our sense of optimal health.

When we feel whole, we are more able to fully engage in our relationships and connect with our highest selves, where we are best able to create truly healthy organizations that purposefully serve and make a meaningful difference in the lives of others.

The world of healthcare offers specific fields of study that can support this shift from a reactive to creative mindset, which can be leveraged in healthcare as well as business. These fields include neuroscience, cognitive behavioral therapy, positive psychology, and mindfulness (with all due respect to the wisdom of the spiritual traditions from which mindfulness-based applications in healthcare have been derived). I've integrated these fields for you into the 4 in 4 Framework to Engage Conscious Leadership, which you'll be learning about chapter 4.

In summary, research has clearly documented the impact of our mindset upon bottom-line performance: a reactive mindset diminishes leadership performance, organizational effectiveness, and resiliency against burnout, while a creative mindset (or Conscious Leadership) improves them. The approach of Conscious Leadership is also equally effective across industries, from business to healthcare and to life at home and beyond.

Since our mindset begins and ends in our brain, let's now shift to the second foundational layer of Conscious Leadership: brain science. In chapter 2, you'll learn more about how your brain works so you can better work your brain to become a more Conscious Leader.

# CHAPTER 2

# Learn How Your Brain Works to Better Work Your Brain

Recall the list of qualities you wrote down for low-performance leaders and high-performance leaders in the previous chapter. If you did not make your own list, take a moment to reflect on the list of qualities of reactive and creative leadership I shared from the Leadership Circle Profile Assessment.[1]

## REACTIVITY
### Low-Performance Leader

**Complying**
- Conservative
- Pleasing
- Belonging
- Passive

**Protecting**
- Arrogant
- Critical
- Distant

**Controlling**
- Perfectionist
- Driven
- Ambitious
- Autocratic

## CREATIVITY
### High-Performance Leader

**Relating**
- Caring Connection
- Fosters Team Play
- Collaborator
- Mentoring and Developing
- Interpersonal Intelligence

**Self-Awareness**
- Selfless Leader
- Composure
- Balance
- Personal Learner

**Authenticity**
- Integrity
- Courageous Authenticity

**Systems Awareness**
- Community Concern
- Sustainable Productivity
- Systems Thinker

**Achieving**
- Strategic Focus
- Purposeful and Visionary
- Achieves Results
- Decisiveness

Now let me ask you a question. Can you relate to both sets of reactive and creative qualities?

If you answered yes, you are in good company. I ask the same question during my workshops, and typically all participants raise their hands. Many acknowledge they not only experience both sets of qualities, but they may oscillate between them on the same day, especially in times of stress.

In addition to experiencing this short-term oscillation between reactive and creative states, have you also experienced more prolonged periods of stress-driven reactivity that resulted in burnout—where you feel emotionally exhausted, disconnected in your relationships, and a reduced sense of accomplishment or significance in what you are doing?

If so, you're also not alone. But if you have experienced periods of burnout, can you also recall other times of your life where you felt more creative, energized, and resilient, experiencing vitality, heartfelt connection in your relationships, and a sense of significance in the way you lead at work or at home?

So why is it that we can all relate to low-performance and high-performance leadership qualities, as well as the capacity to experience burnout and resiliency?

The answer is that the reactive and creative qualities of both leadership performance and resiliency relate to patterns of activity in specific networks and regions in the brain that we all have.

As you will discover, the state of reactivity associated with low-performance leadership generally includes the more reflexive and inflexible patterns of behavior influenced by the lower, survival-oriented regions of the brain, which are focused on self-preservation or self-gain. Prolonged periods of reactivity can predispose you to feeling drained of energy and burned out.

In contrast, the state of creativity associated with high-performance leadership is largely driven by your higher cortical circuits, and the front part of your brain in particular, which facilitate awareness, social cooperation, and the cognitive flexibility to envision, strategize, and achieve your desired results. These high-performance states enable you to optimize your vitality, relationships, productivity, and well-being, which help inoculate you from stress and cultivate your resilience.

So although we all have the capacity for low-performance leadership and burnout, we also all have the capacity for high-performance leadership and resiliency. The key is to have a *reliable system* to help you get out of the downward spiral caused by feeling threatened and overwhelmed with stress, so you can recover more quickly and optimally manage and refocus your energy to get back to doing what you do best. Then you can shift from feeling reactive, depleted, and burned out to being more creative, energized, and resilient. In short, you can shift from being a low-performance leader to a high-performance leader.

How do you make this shift? Well, you have to start where all your fear, stress, and doubt originates—in your brain.

In this chapter, I want to give you a brief foundational overview of how your brain works so you can leverage the best of what it has to offer and know there's nothing wrong with you when you feel stressed. Your brain's stress response to a perceived threat is simply a result of how your brain is programmed—not just from childhood, but from millennia of evolutionary history. We are hardwired to fight or take flight to protect ourselves from threat and harm. This response is adaptive, especially in the face of short-term stressors, like being chased by a predator. Our brains still operate very similarly to the way they did in prehistoric times. But we now have different types of stressors that are more prolonged, such as worrying about our finances or difficult people in our lives, where our fight-or-flight threat responses over the long term can do more harm than good.

The good news is that we now also have the science to better understand the brain and manage modern stress. We now know there are other types of stress responses that are far more helpful than fight-or-flight when dealing with these prolonged stressors. So if your brain is your prehistoric-age operating system, these neuroscientific discoveries are your new software updates that will help you not only handle greater levels of stress, but actually leverage more adaptive stress responses to more effectively harness this energy to sustain higher levels of performance.

So think of this chapter as a user's guide for your brain to optimize your energy and performance. It will tell you what's going on in your brain when you're feeling threatened, reassuring you that your reactions are understandable and normal, not weak or flawed. You'll learn why your brain feels scrambled when you get overwhelmed by stress, why an ongoing threat response predisposes you to burnout, and why the transition between work and home can be the most treacherous time of the day.

You'll also learn which part of your brain best serves as its CEO to maximize your brain's ability to manage and leverage stress, allowing you to proactively shift between reactivity and creativity and to transform burnout into resiliency. As a bonus, you'll also discover how you can avoid stepping on a stress-laden landmine when you get home from work.

Now, more than a decade out from the "Decade of the Brain,"[2] and with advances in neuroimaging and an explosion of neuroscience research, we have come a long way in the science of understanding this phenomenally powerful and complex organ and how it can be optimized for us to lead well from within.

Still, we're humbled by how much we do not yet understand. And there are some things we may never understand. There's a saying: "If the human brain were so simple that we could understand it, we would be so simple that we couldn't!"[3]

With that said, let's step into your brain and explore how it's designed.

## How Your Brain Is Organized

Although there are a number of ways to describe the organizational structure of the brain, and despite the controversies around specific aspects of this model, one of the simplest and most helpful concepts to provide a basic understanding of the brain is that of the *triune brain*.[4] This organizational framework was developed in the 1960s by Dr. Paul MacLean, a physician, neuroscientist, and former director of the Laboratory of Brain Evolution and Behavior at the National Institute of Mental Health (NIMH).

The term "triune" implies that we don't only have one brain; we have three brains in one. Based on his research at Yale Medical School and NIMH, MacLean proposed an evolutionary model of the brain in which more recent and complex levels of brain development have been layered on earlier, more primitive structures. In essence, the brain has developed from the bottom up and from the back forward. This framework highlights a number of important brain regions.

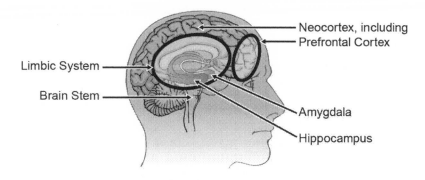

*Figure 2.1. Key Regions in Your Brain*

### *The Brain Stem and Basal Ganglia*

According to MacLean, the first part of the triune brain is the *reptilian brain.* It is crucial to your most primitive survival needs and includes both the brain stem and the basal ganglia.

The brain stem contains those vital life centers responsible for controlling your respiration, blood pressure, and heart rate. It regulates sleep/wake transitions and levels of arousal and attention. It is also involved in defensive fight-or-flight behaviors.[5]

The basal ganglia play an important role in the way you move and form and express habits.[6] (For example, the unconscious movements you employ typing, playing a musical instrument, or riding a bicycle are stored here.) Further, your basal ganglia are involved in motivation, reward, and pleasure, as well as cravings and addiction.[7] And according to MacLean, it's also engaged in aggression, dominance, and territoriality.[8]

### *The Limbic System*

Now, unlike reptiles that lay their eggs and skedaddle, we mammals do something different. We suckle and nurture our young. According to MacLean, these behaviors led to the evolution of the next region of the triune brain—a collection of structures known as the *paleomammalian* ("old-mammal") *brain,* or the *limbic system.*

The limbic system engages your primal drives, especially related to feeding, sex, and bonding in intimate relationships. Most notably, it also plays a key role in your memory and emotions.[9] Two structures within the limbic system are especially important here.

First, the *hippocampus* helps regulate your emotions and is involved in the storage of long-term memories that are autobiographical in nature, such as your memory of names, places, and events.[10] For example, your hippocampus helps you remember what happened with your clients last week.

In front of the hippocampus is a structure called the *amygdala,* which is involved with the way you store emotional memories.[11] While your hippocampus remembers your interactions with your clients, the amygdala helps you to remember whether you liked your clients or not!

Your amygdala is also primarily responsible for keeping you safe. It's connected to your fear and threat circuits, as well as your reward circuits, and is forever scanning your environment, asking, "Am I safe or not safe? Is this person or event a reward or a threat?"

Because your amygdala is designed to keep you safe, it's said to be "Velcro" for threatening or bad experiences and "Teflon" for good experiences.[12] In other words, it predisposes you to look for problems or danger, rather than savoring joyful moments. It has a hair trigger for threatening experiences.

If a person or event matches for threat, the amygdala sends signals directly to your brain stem and your hypothalamus to mobilize your fight-or-flight responses throughout your body so you can fend off your attacker or get away now.[13] These structures were vital to keeping your ancestors alive when encountering dangerous animals and rival clans in prehistoric times.

All together, the reptilian brain and the limbic system are primitive, sub-cortical, subconscious structures that are critical to your basic survival needs. But if they were the only parts of your brain, you might be nothing more than a highly impulsive animal, reflexively moving towards pleasure and away from pain, fighting or taking flight to protect yourself from physical as well as psychological threats. And sometimes you may feel as if they are the only parts of your brain!

Although our primary stressors may be psychological rather than physical, they represent a threat to our safety just the same, primarily in the form of self-doubt, and we still respond with our prehistoric fight-or-flight programming. For example, when we feel threatened by stress and self-doubt as we wrestle over our mortgages, our overwhelming to-do lists, keeping up with others, or how to stay ahead, we may find ourselves consumed, mindlessly fighting for control or self-worth, or taking flight from anything that triggers stress and self-doubt—leaving us feeling out of control.

Consequently, while these subconscious regions of our brain developed to protect us from physical harm, they may also be responsible for some of the low-performance leadership qualities described above, where we may become highly controlling, protective, or overly compliant.

### *The Neocortex*

This brings us to the third part of the triune brain: the *neomammalian* ("new-mammal") *brain,* which consists of the cerebral *neocortex.* The neocortex wraps over the top of the first two parts and is vital to your conscious awareness and to engaging high-performance, Conscious Leadership. It enables you to weigh the present, imagine a better future, and strategize and take wise action to get you there.

The neocortex is divided into right and left hemispheres and then into a number of lobes.[14] If you take another look at figure 2.1, starting at the back of the neocortex, the first lobes are the *right and left occipital lobes,* which are important for how you visually perceive the world.

The next lobes up from the back are the *parietal lobes,* which allow you to orient yourself in space as well as experience sensation.

Then, overlying the limbic system on either side of the brain are the *temporal lobes,* which play a vital role in your hearing, smell, and memory.

Finally, coming over the top towards the front of the brain are the *frontal lobes,* which are crucial for moving different parts of your body and for your cognitive abilities.

Before we talk more about the frontal lobes, I want to mention a fifth lobe that is also very important. Tucked away on either side of your brain in a crevice between the temporal, parietal, and frontal lobes is the *insular cortex.* The insular cortex integrates and relays a highway of information coming up from all areas of your body, including the gut (or what's known as your "gut instinct") and your heart (or your "heart intelligence," or "knowing what's in your heart"). All this information comes up into the insular cortex to be sent throughout the brain. The insular cortex also plays a role in intuition, empathy, compassion, love, or disgust.[15]

Now let's return to the frontal lobes. Right at the anterior portion of the frontal lobe, behind your forehead, is a very important region called the *prefrontal cortex.* The prefrontal cortex (PFC) regulates and integrates information from all the other parts of the brain. If you were to hire a CEO to effectively run your brain, the PFC would be the one for the job! It's the key player in your ability to lead well from within.

The PFC has a number of very important functions.[16] The first is emotional regulation, which relates to its proximity to and relationship with the amygdala. For example, certain fibers called *GABAergic projections* travel directly from the PFC to the amygdala. In one of his presentations, well-renowned UCLA psychiatrist Dan Siegel called these projections "GABA goo," meaning that this part of the brain acts as a "goo" to help calm down your stress response within seconds.

Another function of the PFC is to integrate all of the information coming up through the insular cortex (including your gut instinct and your heart intelligence), engaging your capacity for social awareness, empathy, compassion, and morality.

The PFC is also involved in your short-term memory, executive functions, judgment, planning, abstraction, decision making, and the willpower to follow through on the decisions you make.[17]

Finally, another very important function of the PFC is meta-cognition, or meta-awareness,[18] where you can step back and observe the thoughts, sensations, and feelings passing through your awareness and pause before you act. With meta-cognition, you can step back and say, "Boy, there goes a damn crazy thought—perhaps I won't act on that one!"

So, as you can see, the PFC has a number of very important functions that relate to high-performance leadership, including your ability to strategize, make good decisions, achieve your desired results, connect well with others, and maintain self-awareness and self-composure in times of stress. In short, it enables you to lead well from within so you can become creative and innovative and thrive with a sense of significance.

Now, let's connect a few dots. In the next section, I'll explain how this triune structure relates to what we discussed in the previous chapter: the states of reactivity and creativity, low- and high-performance leadership, burnout, and cultivating resilience.

## Your Brain: A Multilayered System Designed to Meet a Hierarchy of Needs

The brain is an elegantly designed system adaptively designed to both keep us safe as well as provide great cognitive flexibility, which has enabled us to socially cooperate and innovate as a species.

To simplify our discussion of the triune brain, you can think of your brain in three highly networked layers, as represented by figure 2.2 below.

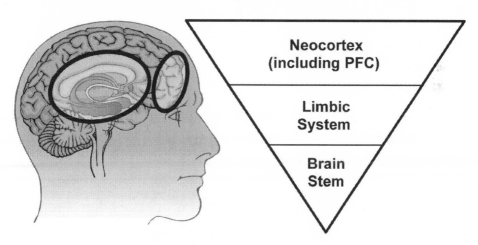

*Figure 2.2. Your Brain as a Multilayered System*

In this representation, the brain stem lies at the base of the inverted triangle, the limbic system at the next level up, and the neocortex, including the PFC, at the top.

Each level can directly express a behavioral response. However, because they're designed to protect us from harm, the lower levels of the brain stem and the limbic system work at far greater processing speeds than the neocortex.

When sensory information reaches your brain, it is first filtered through your brain stem and limbic system, which are always reflecting on the most basic of questions: "Can I eat it, will it eat me, and can I have sex with it?"[19] If you find yourself face to face with something your amygdala registers as a threat, your limbic system reacts with a fight-or-flight response—even before the highest layer of your brain is engaged and you are fully aware of what you are responding to.[20]

This is what happens when a colleague at work or a loved one criticizes you. You reflexively blurt out an angry and cutting response, and then, a moment later, you realize you went too far and think, "I can't believe I just said that!"

When you experience fear, threat, and stress, the lower, survival-oriented regions of your brain automatically direct all of your attention.

However, if your brain perceives the environment to be safe, it can then more fully engage the highest level of the system—your neocortex (including the PFC)—which integrates all levels below. In doing so, this level layers on greater cognitive flexibility.

For example, when you feel safe and trust others, you are more likely to open yourself up and be intimate, loving, vulnerable, or comfortable sharing your creative ideas. When you have access to your higher cortical circuits, you actually feel smarter, as if you have gained IQ points. Conversely, it's also why you may feel like a bumbling fool around someone who intimidates you.

This three-layered structure of the brain, and its prioritization of safety over love/belonging and self-actualization, essentially explains Maslow's Hierarchy of Needs, an adaption of which is shown in figure 2.3 below.

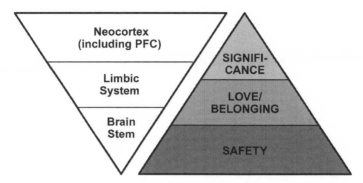

*Figure 2.3. Your Triune Brain Mapped to an Adaption of Maslow's Hierarchy of Needs*

In this hierarchy, Maslow places our need to satisfy our physiological and safety needs first (represented as "safety" in the diagram), our love and belonging needs next, and then our needs for self-esteem and self-actualization, which I've lumped together here as the need for significance.[21]

This hierarchy of needs maps beautifully with the successive levels of the triune brain, where our physiological and safety needs correspond with our brain stem and parts of our limbic system, our love and belonging needs correspond with parts of our limbic system and neocortex, and our significance needs correspond to our ability to fully engage other parts of our neocortex, especially our PFC.

When you feel safe, you have more to give and feel more productive. You can more fully engage your capacity for empathy, love, and compassion. And you can think more creatively and put yourself in a position to self-actualize your full potential and experience greater meaning and significance in your life.

With this understanding, we can now also begin to map the brain and the needs it fulfills to the three components of burnout that we mentioned in chapter 1.[22]

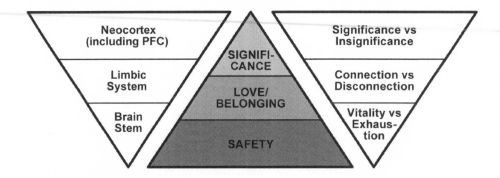

*Figure 2.4. Your Brain and Its Relationship to Your Hierarchy of Needs and Burnout*

Here, in figure 2.4, we can see that if we are wrestling with feeling unsafe and we're not having our physiological and safety needs met, we are continually drawing upon resources from the survival-oriented parts of our brain—which can leave us in a state of *exhaustion*.

Further, as we pour resources into our safety and survival circuits, we forego meeting our love and belonging needs and can experience a sense of *disconnection*.

Finally, as we simultaneously withdraw our resources away from or otherwise disrupt the circuits in the cortex and PFC that enable us to experience self-esteem and self-actualization, we can be left with a reduced sense of personal accomplishment or feeling of *insignificance*.

Essentially, when you experience a prolonged period of not meeting your hierarchy of needs, you feel burned out.

On the other hand, when you are able to meet your physiological and safety needs, you can experience a sense of *vitality*. When you meet your love and belonging needs, you can experience a sense of *connection*. And when you meet your needs for self-esteem and are able to self-actualize, you can experience a great sense of accomplishment and *significance* in your life.

In other words, when you satisfy your hierarchy of needs, you flourish and feel more resilient.

So, then, what determines whether your brain sinks into a spiral of reactivity and burnout or cultivates creativity and resiliency? To answer this question, you need to understand how mental activity flows dynamically through the layers of your brain.

## How Mental Activity Flows in Your Brain

It's important to appreciate that all of the various components, regions, and layers of the brain we've just discussed rarely act in isolation, but rather as coordinated networks.

Think of your brain as your network of connections on Facebook, where one post can go viral and rapidly generate a thread of activity all across the world. If that post is inspiring, positivity can ripple throughout your network. Conversely, if that post is negative, it can drag everyone down.

The same is true for your brain: what happens in one area affects the whole.

Our brain is a collection of numerous interconnected networks that each serve specific functions. For example, two of the main networks are known as the *default mode network* (DMN) and the *task positive network* (TPN).

The DMN includes connections between the middle underside part of your PFC (i.e., your ventromedial PFC) and the posterior portion of your cingulate cortex, near the back of your brain. This network is active when your brain is not involved in focusing on anything in particular. The DMN is involved in memory retrieval, daydreaming, thinking of the future, and conceiving of the perspective of others—as well as reflecting on your relationship with yourself and others, which can lead you into a state of rumination and worry.[23] This self-reflective processing commonly feels like an inner critic spawning thoughts and feelings of self-doubt.

The TPN includes the side region near the top of your PFC (i.e., your doroslateral PFC), your insular cortex, and the part of your motor cortex that controls your body's movement. Your TPN serves to focus your attention on engaging a task at hand.[24]

These two networks dynamically switch between each other.[25] When you go on task, your TPN becomes active while the activity in your DMN diminishes and vice versa. This may explain why, when you are just hanging out, not doing anything in particular, you may sometimes find yourself worrying for no good reason and then feel compelled to go on task with e-mails or other to-dos as a way to silence your ruminating thoughts.

What then is the primary driver that directs much of the mental activity between the various components, regions, layers, and networks of your brain?

It's your *mind*. Learning how to use your mind is how you can better work your brain to fully leverage its intelligence, and to that end, we'll be talking more about the practice of mindfulness in the next chapter.

But first, what exactly *is* your mind?

This has been an age-old philosophical debate. Amongst numerous perspectives, some consider the mind to be distinct from the brain (the view of *dualism*), while others consider it to be representative of the activity of the brain (the view of *materialism*).

Dr. Dan Siegel, the UCLA psychiatrist mentioned earlier who is also the founding co-director of the Mindful Awareness Research Center, convened a group of forty scientists across diverse fields from anthropology to neuroscience that met over the course of four years to discuss the relationship between the brain and mind. Their conclusions represent a dualistic viewpoint: they agreed that the mind was indeed distinct from the brain. For this group, defining the brain was the easy part: it's that three-pound gelatinous mass of one hundred billion nerve cells sitting inside your skull. Defining the mind posed a far greater challenge.

While it's nearly impossible to get scientists, even in the same field, to agree on anything, the esteemed group finally and unanimously arrived at the following definition: "The mind is an embodied and relational process that regulates the flow of energy and information within the brain and between brains."[26]

This definition implies that the thoughts, emotions, and experiences in your mind, which arise out of the brain, play a major role in directing the flow of energy and information in the system of your brain.[27] Further, the system in which the energy flows is not a closed system; it interacts with other brain systems as well, through circuits of social contagion. (We will be exploring this idea further in part 3.)

In contrast to this group of scientists, Arne Dietrich, a leading expert on creativity and the author of *How Creativity Happens in the Brain,* takes a materialistic perspective. He suggests that many of the thoughts you have arise from countless subconscious neural networks that are continuously forming and reforming coalitions that compete for your awareness and behavior. Further, your conscious, higher-level thinking can affect the firing activity of nerves in various subconscious networks to influence the subsequent stream of thoughts you have.[28]

However it happens on a neurological level, your mind plays a vital role in directing your flow of mental energy into states of reactivity or creativity. As shown in figure 2.5 below, two main streams of mental activity influence whether you move toward reactivity or creativity: stress and self-doubt, or inspiration.

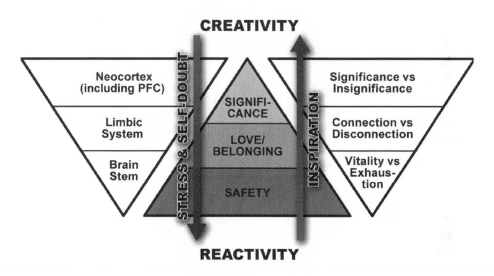

*Figure 2.5. Two Main Streams of Mental Activity in Your Brain*

Let's take a closer look at these two streams, including how they are also mediated by your *autonomic nervous system,* which is comprised of two components: your *sympathetic nervous system* and your *parasympathetic nervous system.*

## Stress, Self-Doubt, and Reactivity

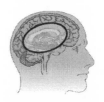

**REACTIVITY**

*Fight or Flight*

**Low-Performance
Leadership**

When I get stressed and reactive, my wife likes to remind me that I've "gone limbic!"

What she is referring to is the fact that my limbic system has just jumped in the driver's seat of my brain in reaction to the stress I'm experiencing.

When your limbic system takes over, your amygdala triggers your *sympathetic nervous system* to release adrenaline and noradrenaline from your adrenal glands, which revs you up, like stepping on a car's accelerator. The consequence is a rapid shift from the *parasympathetic* "rest and digest" functions into a physiology that prepares you to fight or flee. Your heart races, your palms sweat, you get a pit in your stomach, and you may get tunnel vision, where your thinking constricts as you focus solely on whatever it will take for you to survive.

What triggers this sympathetic response and ensuing reactivity is *perceived threat.* While this threat may be *physical,* such as risk to life and limb, extremes of hot and cold, and starvation, nowadays it's more commonly the *psychological* threats of stress and self-doubt.

Although most of us know stress and self-doubt when we experience it, let's take a moment to define both. Stress has been defined in a number of ways. Hans Selye, who coined the term in 1936, defined it as "the non-specific response of the body to any demand for change."[29] In short, stress asks the question, "Can I handle it?" When you fear you can't handle the challenge or you'll fail, you feel overwhelmed or stressed out. *Self-doubt* can be a subset of this kind of stress, where we further ask, "And how will I value myself in the process of handling this stressful situation?" Conversely, your feelings of self-doubt can also cause more stress by threatening your self-identity and thus making you feel unsafe too (you'll find out why self-doubt feels dangerous in chapter 6).

A number of researchers point out that we feel threatened when the *demands* we experience exceed the *resources* we have to handle them. Demands involve danger, uncertainty, novel situations, and the amount of effort required to engage the situation. Your resources include your knowledge, ability, and disposition (for example, your degree of optimism, sense of control, self-esteem, and perception that you can handle the situation), as well as the amount of external support you can mobilize to assist you.[30]

Whenever your perceived demands exceed your perceived resources and you feel unsafe as you experience stress or self-doubt, this triggers your *threat response,* which activates a specific type of sympathetic nervous system reaction that drives your flow of mental activity into your survival circuits and creates a state of reactivity. (In the next section, you'll see there is another type of sympathetic response, too.)

The input that triggers this kind of psychological stress or self-doubt could be an external threat, arising from sensory information flowing up through your brain stem and limbic system, such as when you encounter someone who intimidates you. Or the threat could be internal, resulting from your inner critic in the default mode network in the higher levels of your brain. For example, you might lie awake at night, anxiously ruminating over past or future events (including mistakes you've made or could make), driving all your mental activity from your higher cortical circuits down into your survival circuits.

Dietrich points out that your brain is a predictive machine, continuously running simulations to anticipate the safest and best possible actions for our future.[31] Much of the simulations we run are fear-based, "what if," worst-case, danger scenarios that can provoke a fair amount of anxiety, which activates our survival brain.

Regardless of whether the threat is external or internal, your subconscious, survival-based coalitions of networks that drive your threat response (i.e., your fight-or-flight behaviors) now dominate, outcompete, and may draw resources away from your higher cortical circuits that engage in empathy and compassion, as well as good decision making and responsiveness.

Sometimes, when you get triggered, your sympathetic response may be so intense that for a moment you feel like you have lost your mind. And you may well have, or at least a crucial part of it in that moment. When you experience intense stress, it can result in "amygdala highjack,"[32] where your limbic response drives the flow of mental activity down into your survival circuits to such an extent that it completely disrupts your higher PFC-related circuits of awareness—so that in that very moment you are not even *aware* that you are "flipping out" and potentially wreaking havoc!

I carry a havoc-wreaking lesson from an interaction I had with my younger son, Dylan, when he was at the tender age of six. It was about ten o'clock, way past his bedtime, and I was battling to get him to stay in his bed and go to sleep. On his third time jumping up out of bed, I said, "Dyl, I feel my blood boiling. I need you to listen to me and get back into bed." On his fourth time up, I flipped my lid and completely lost it. I screamed at him with an intensity he had never before experienced in me: "GET BACK INTO BED RIGHT NOW!" He looked at me in complete shock, then trembled, started crying, and fearfully crawled back into bed, turning his back to me under the covers.

I left the room to calm myself down. As my PFC came back online, I became aware of what I had done. A wave of regret washed over me. I felt horrible, like a bad dad. I returned to his room to see how he was doing and began to offer a heartfelt apology. I then tried to reach out, asking if he would like a hug goodnight.

Painfully, he was frozen, immobilized, with his hands over his ears.

I gently said, "Dyl, I'm trying to talk to you, but it doesn't seem like you can hear me."

He responded, "I can't hear you. My brain is shut down."

My heart still breaks when I think of it. In that moment of anger, my limbic system had hijacked my PFC, and I'd lost my mind and my self-control in the way I dealt with Dyl. In turn, I had hijacked his amygdala and shut down his still-young and budding PFC, taking offline any capacity he had to connect with me.

This was also what happened to my brain during my crisis of leadership where I felt like my brain was scrambled and I'd lost my mind. Based on what we have learned about the brain, I hadn't as much lost it as it had been hijacked by my limbic system.

Can you relate? Can you think of times at home or at work where your limbic system hijacked your higher cortical circuits, or even when you lost your temper as a result, hijacking someone else's higher brain circuits and disrupting his or her ability to think clearly and to connect?

There is another common way your PFC gets taken offline, leaving you vulnerable to shifting from creativity into reactivity. At the beginning of this chapter, I mentioned that the most treacherous time of day is when we transition between work and home. Many people say they are most likely to get irritated and respond abrasively to circumstances between four and six, near the end of the workday and just before dinner. Why? The reason is that your PFC, a more-recently evolved part of your brain, more easily fatigues and is no match for the power of your more primitive, low-road limbic system, which is well muscled for survival.

By the end of the day, after making hundreds of decisions and constantly regulating your emotions in response to difficult people and challenging circumstances, your PFC may be spent, which means your resources may be relatively diminished to handle the demands you are about to encounter. Further, your blood sugar may be low, especially if you missed lunch, so your PFC is not only fatigued but also low on fuel.

You then walk into your home at six, before dinner, greeted by piles of "crap" lying on the floor—an issue that now feels like a national emergency. Without the counterbalance of a well-functioning PFC, your capacity for engaging creatively is diminished, and you find yourself more predisposed to feeling threatened and shifting into a state of reactivity.

For this reason, this is probably not the best time to "talk" to your kids about the mess, have a crucial conversation with your spouse, or make a vital, strategic decision at work. These activities may best be reserved for when internal resources are more optimized and your PFC is nourished, rested, rejuvenated, and fully back online.

In summary, whenever the demands you face exceed your internal resources and your PFC fails to regulate your limbic reactivity, you may feel threatened and unsafe. Consequently, your subconscious, survival-based circuits may outcompete or draw resources away from your higher cortical circuits, keeping you from being fully able to connect well with others and experience significance as a high-performance, creative leader. And when your subconscious survival circuits drive you into reactivity on a persistent basis, causing you to regularly forgo these Maslowian needs, you can become predisposed to burnout.

However, it's also important to avoid suggesting that reactivity is always "bad" and creativity is always "good." Reactivity can have many adaptive advantages, especially in short-term situations.

For example, if someone is physically threatening you or your loved ones, your rapidly acting limbic system is exactly what you want driving your fight-or-flight threat response. This response may well be more adaptive than taking precious time to analyze the situation.

Further, people train many hours to prepare for emergency situations and to develop mastery in any endeavor, in order to hardwire their skills into their subcortical basal ganglia. This way, when they find themselves in the moment of stress or challenge, they may react both rapidly and skillfully in the heat of the moment. Here too a reactive command-and-control style of leadership may be most effective to get the best outcome.

On the other hand, if you are in a high-stakes negotiation and dealing with difficult people at the table, getting edgy and going into a reactive mode of fight or flight can do more harm than good. Here, your broader awareness and ability to lean into and leverage your stress with more adaptive and agile responses, harnessing the wisdom and discernment of a clear-thinking PFC, will likely result in better decisions and more creative solutions.

Let's now explore the stream of inspiration leading to the state of creativity.

## Awareness, Inspiration, and Creativity

### CREATIVITY
*Fulfillment*
### High-Performance
### Leadership

When my wife tells me that I'm "going limbic," I sometimes respond, "Would you rather I go full frontal?" What I mean, of course, is that I am offering to regulate my reactivity with my PFC and enter a more flexible state of creativity.

With conscious and purposeful awareness, your mind can proactively regulate and harness the energy of stress with your PFC, the CEO of your brain, leading. Here you have access to your capacities of emotional regulation, shifting and focusing attention, self- and social awareness, empathy and compassion, morality, the executive functions of visioning, strategic planning, decision making, and innovative thinking and expression, all of which are key to creativity and high-performance leadership (which is why I have highlighted this area with the oval in the image above).

You can also think of your PFC as Grand Central Station for the information arriving from throughout your brain. Your PFC effectively regulates and/or integrates both the left and right side of your neocortex and all the layers below it, including the limbic system and brain stem.

That means creativity is not isolated to the PFC. *Creativity is a whole-brain phenomenon.*

Creativity feeds on the flow of inspiration, which requires a mindset shift, especially in the face of stress. In contrast to Selye's definition of stress—which hinges on whether we can cope with demands—Kelly McGonigal, a health psychologist at Stanford University and the author of *The Upside of*

*Stress,* provides us with another way of defining stress, one that feels far more empowering. She states, "Stress is what arises when something you care about is at stake."[33]

As such, stress can simply be viewed as energy that helps you to mobilize internal resources to focus on the outcomes that matter most to you.

In addition to the fight-or-flight *threat response,* Jim Blascovich, a professor of psychology at the University of California, Santa Barbara, and his colleagues point to another type of a stress response where your resources are more than sufficient to meet the demands at hand. It's called the *challenge response.*[34] Shelley Taylor, a professor of social psychology at the University of California, Los Angeles, further highlights yet another type of stress response that enables you to mobilize your resources of social support—the *tend-and-befriend* response.[35]

Unlike the threat response that drives reactivity, your challenge and tend-and-befriend responses facilitate creativity. Your challenge response enables you to lean into your challenges, seek creative solutions, and embrace the stressful situation as an opportunity for growth and learning. Your tend-and-befriend response encourages you to reach out to connect with family, friends, and colleagues for support and to collaborate well with others, especially in times of stress.

Simply shifting your mindset about stress can have profoundly positive results. In Dietrich's terms, it changes the firing activity of your subconscious neural networks and, therefore the thoughts that manifest in your conscious awareness.

When you view your stress as dangerous, you're more likely to avoid stress or resent people who trigger it, causing well-grooved reactive responses. On the other hand, when you're able to view your stress as an asset, you release yourself from becoming stressed about being stressed. You are able to think in a more inspired way, connect more fully with others, and engage with more adaptive and creative stress responses.

In contrast to the threat response, your challenge response and tend-and-befriend response reverse the flow of mental energy in your brain and how you engage your hierarchy of needs. As you can see in figure 2.5, the tend-and-befriend response serves to engage your love and belonging needs, and your challenge response serves your need for self-actualization and significance. (You'll also learn more about the challenge and tend-and-befriend responses in part 2.)

Hence, when you view stress as an asset, it fuels the stream of inspiration, feeding the state of creativity.

This state of creativity is mediated by your autonomic nervous system.

Blascovich and colleagues' studies in humans[36] build on the animal studies of Richard Dienstbier,[37] the former chair of psychology at the University of Nebraska, to show how the challenge response is physiologically distinct from the threat response. The challenge response is actually an even more efficient and well-optimized sympathetic response. In the challenge response, like the threat response, the sympathetic nervous system activates the adrenals to release adrenaline and norepinephrine and the hypothalamus and pituitary to release cortisol, which with chronic elevation can lead to a host of stress-related diseases.

However, unlike the threat response, in the challenge response, there is a lower baseline level of arousal, a more delayed release of cortisol, and a faster onset and stronger release of adrenaline and epinephrine to a stimulating event. This causes the challenge response to have a relatively greater dilation of peripheral blood vessels, lower peripheral blood vessel resistance, and a higher cardiac output, which leads to even better energy utilization in the brain and muscles. (According to Blascovich, it is the same cardiovascular pattern of activation you get from aerobic exercise.[38]) Further, the production of adrenaline, norepinephrine, and cortisol switches off more quickly when they are no longer needed, and your body has a greater capacity to sustain their use when they are needed. The net result is greater focus, increased energy use, increased performance, and better effect on your health, as compared to the threat response.

The second component of the autonomic nervous system, the *parasympathetic nervous system* (PNS), may help drive the quicker recovery from the sympathetic activation in the challenge response. In the challenge response, Blascovich and co-author Mendes note that a strong PNS response accompanies the challenge response, which overshoots its baseline, which may lead to the rapid recovery.[39]

Your PNS acts as a brake to counterbalance your sympathetic nervous system, the accelerator that also drives your fight-or-flight reactions.[40] Thus, when you tap the brake with your PNS, you are able to shift your physiology and patterns of behaviors from a state of "fight or flight" back to states of "rest and digest," "feed and breed," "stay and play," or "pause and plan"—whichever parasympathetic alternative you prefer. (You'll also learn more about facilitating this shift in part 2.)

Your *tend-and-befriend response,* which helps you to marshal external resources and support in times of stress, is also physiologically distinct from both your threat and challenge response in that your PNS is generally more active throughout.[41] Of note, a fairly robust body of research shows that higher levels of PNS activation are also associated with higher levels of self-esteem, both of which enable you to engage your internal resources that buffer against the demands of threatening stressors.[42]

It is important to emphasize that, like your threat response, your challenge and tend and befriend responses also include sympathetic arousal. However, with parasympathetic engagement, your autonomic nervous system may be more balanced, so that you might find yourself in a higher-performance state of "jive and thrive" or "excite and delight," a relatively more engaged *and* more relaxed state of alertness than "fight or flight."

Your PFC also plays key roles in facilitating your tend-and-befriend and challenge responses. Your PFC activates your PNS, which, as we have mentioned above, engages your tend-and-befriend response and puts the brake on your threat response and your challenge response (when it's no longer needed). Further, research has shown that distinct patterns of activation in the PFC predict whether you will manifest a threat or challenge response in the face of a strong stressor.

Kristina Koslov, a social psychologist and former Associate Director of the Emotion, Health, and Psychophysiology Lab at the University of California, San Francisco, conducted a study on eighty-four women to measure their response to a stressful situation.[43] She first used electroencephalograms to determine the baseline patterns of activation in their PFC. She then randomly chose certain women to experience a modified version of one of the most anxiety-provoking tests you can perform in the laboratory: the Trier Social Stress task. In this test, participants were instructed to give a five-minute speech and then answer five minutes of questions in a mock interview with researchers trained to give nonverbal cues of disapproval, such as shaking their heads, frowning, leaning back, and appearing to dislike the participant's performance. While delivering the speech, the participants were also hooked up to non-invasive monitors that assessed their cardiac output and peripheral vascular resistance, to identify whether they were having a threat or a challenge response to this stressor.

To provide a little more context, in the study, Koslov refers to numerous other studies that show left prefrontal cortical activation is associated with a relatively greater ability to regulate negative emotions, an increased motivation to approach potentially rewarding things in your life, and a higher level of well-being. Conversely, right PFC activation is associated with stress-related avoidant experiences, such as social anxiety and depression.

In line with their hypothesis, Koslov and her colleagues discovered that subjects who had higher left PFC activation relative to their right PFC were indeed more likely to experience a challenge than a threat response, as assessed by their cardiovascular responses. Her study was the first to show this connection.

What's even more exciting is that in the next chapter you will learn about a foundational practice that can help you shift your baseline activity from your right PFC towards your left PFC and sustain these changes on an enduring basis. According to Koslov's study, this practice, which cultivates greater awareness, will help you better deal with your most challenging stressors and transform many of your stress responses from threat to challenge.

In summary, the physiology of your autonomic nervous system, as it is influenced by your PFC and manifests as the tend-and-befriend or challenge responses, in various ways drives your flow of energy up Maslow's Hierarchy of Needs. It allows you to direct your mental activity up into the higher layers of your brain so you can connect more fully with others and optimize your decision making, cognitive flexibility, and capacity for creativity.

As mentioned in chapter 1, according to the Leadership Circle framework, creativity involves self-awareness, systems awareness, an ability to relate well with others, and an ability to achieve results.

When it comes to results, creativity has also been defined more specifically as the ability to produce something *novel* and *useful*.[44] A number of theories have been offered around this perspective on creativity.[45] One of the most widely referenced is that offered by Joy Paul Guilford, a pioneer in the area of creativity. He proposed that the creative process includes two types of thinking:[46]

1. *Divergent thinking,* or thinking outside of the box, where you generate a variety of many *novel* ideas, including those that seem wild and crazy, which sometimes yield explosive gains or breakthroughs

2. *Convergent thinking,* where you narrow things down and select among various possibilities to incrementally refine and implement at least one *useful* idea

Again, while your PFC plays a key role in this creative process, *all* levels of your brain may be involved. And sometimes two heads are better than one.

Many people think that the success of Disneyland was due to the vision and creative genius of Walt Disney. But Disneyland and its related businesses would never have been manifested without the participation of Walt's brother, Roy Disney, who was largely responsible for executing and operationalizing Walt's vision.

Walt and Roy embody the two types of creative thinking to generate *novel* and *useful* ideas. On the one hand, Walt was the consummate divergent thinker in the Disney team, a true visionary with an abundance of novel ideas. Roy was the convergent thinker who was key to refining and practically implementing Walt's ideas. (It's not surprising that you see this type of teamwork in many innovative companies. Think of Gates and Allen, and Jobs and Wozniak, for instance.)

So how can our understanding of the brain help us engage both divergent thinking to generate novelty and convergent thinking to select, refine, and implement a useful idea?

Novelty can be generated externally or internally. Externally, we can draw on inspiration from all of our senses (think of Newton's revelations about gravity while watching an apple drop or your own brainstorming with others).

Internally, new ideas can arise under the influence of powerful limbic emotions (such as the stirring paintings of Van Gogh or the poetry of John Butler Yeats, Elizabeth Barrett Browning, or Dylan Thomas). Or we can draw from our knowledge stores distributed throughout the neocortex (think of all the ideas generated by NASA engineers to bring Apollo 13 safely back to earth or Edison's "thousand failures" in inventing the light bulb).

Novelty can also be generated by your default mode network[47] where, in addition to running fear-based simulations to keep you safe, you can daydream and run success-based simulations about various solutions to creative problems.

You can also generate novelty in your dreams as you sleep. When you dream, your PFC is relatively inactive and information streams uninhibitedly into your awareness, often in seemingly bizarre ways, from other parts of your brain.[48] Examples are Kekule's discovery of the Benzene ring by dreaming of a snake coil back on itself to eat its tail and Paul McCartney recounting how he woke up one morning in 1964 with the tune of "Yesterday," voted the number one pop song of all time in 2000, in his head.[49] Here's how McCartney described his experience:

> I woke up with a lovely tune in my head. I thought, "That's great, I wonder what that is?" There was an upright piano next to me, to the right of the bed by the window. I got out of bed, sat at the piano, found G, found F sharp minor 7th—and that leads you through then to B to E minor, and finally back to E. It all leads forward logically. I liked the melody a lot, but because I'd dreamed it, I couldn't believe I'd written it. I thought, "No, I've never written anything like this before." But I had the tune, which was the most magic thing![50]

Sometimes the generation of novelty is spontaneous and effortless, arriving unbidden in your dreams or through flashes of insight (such as Archimedes's moment of "Eureka!"). Other times, it is deliberate and effortful (again, think of Edison's systematic process of discovery).[51]

Whatever way novelty is generated, typically your best ideas need to be selected and further refined. Even after Edison systematically worked through all the possibilities to arrive at the light bulb, over the years it has been further refined to last longer, shine brighter, and become even more useful. Newton no doubt iterated on his initial source of inspiration to converge on his Law for Universal Gravity. And McCartney worked for months to complete the lyrics for "Yesterday." His initial placeholder for the opening verse was "Scrambled eggs, oh, my baby how I love your legs."[52]

This convergent aspect of creativity draws on the resources of the PFC, where your novel ideas can be further refined in working memory and decisions can be made about what would be most useful to others and how your contribution can best be expressed.

The PFC also plays a key role in the moment of creative expression and peak performance. A study of the "brain on jazz" reveals an important part of the puzzle. But not what you might expect.

Charles Limb, a trained jazz saxophonist and associate professor of head and neck surgery at Johns Hopkins, and his colleague Allen Braun, from the National Institutes of Health, enrolled jazz pianists to improvise on a special keyboard without any metal parts while lying in an MRI scanner.[53] They found that the side of the PFC (the dorsolateral PFC) involved in effortful problem solving, conscious self-monitoring, and focused attention had become extensively *deactivated*.

This deactivation enables spontaneous composition, as well as unplanned associations, sudden insights, or realizations, to arise, providing the ability to express oneself without inhibition.

At the same time, the jazz pianist's most anterior portion of the PFC (the frontopolar PFC) was active. This area is thought to be associated with self-expression and individuality, such as when you tell a story about yourself. Limb shares, "What we think is happening is when you're telling your own musical story, you're shutting down impulses that might impede the flow of novel ideas." And so, personalized and beautifully improvised music is expressed.[54]

This moment of peak performance expression is a "Maslow moment" of self-actualization, or what Mihaly Csikszentmihalyi has described as a state of *flow,* "an almost automatic, effortless, yet highly focused state of consciousness."[55]

According to Csikszentmihalyi, any mental or physical activity can produce flow if it absorbs you in a challenging task where the goals are clear, feedback is immediate, and your capacity or level of skill is well matched to the opportunity or challenge at hand.

Dietrich explains how one of the key ways of entering the flow state is through leveraging the executive attention network, involving the PFC, to narrow one's focus of attention so much that it creates a hypofrontal state.[56] Consequently, vast areas of the PFC become deactivated.

In so doing, the self-consciousness, effortful deliberation, and slower processing speed of the PFC makes way for the highly rapid and efficient processing speeds in the lower subconscious levels of your brain, including the well-practiced habits of skill and excellence stored in the basal ganglia, which leads to a smoother and higher level of performance.[57] You can see this in high-level athletes, who perform their best when they "think" less and just "do" what they do best.

So when it comes to your creative brain, we are speaking about a whole-brain process that in many ways your PFC orchestrates, even while at moments the PFC itself is dynamically activated or deactivated. This process may include both divergent and convergent thinking to create and refine novel and useful ideas, which may also be beautifully expressed in moments of peak performance.

More broadly, your PFC also enables you to pause before you reflexively respond; integrate higher-level processes such as insight, intuition, empathy, morality; see the big picture to make better decisions; and take wiser action—all of which are key to your creative, high-performance leadership state. Further, your ability to soothe your threat response, engage a challenge or tend-and-befriend response to better relate to others, and align with what's meaningful and significant in your life (note the resonance with Maslow's Hierarchy of Needs here) inoculates you against burnout and cultivates greater resiliency.

This flow of inspiration, creativity, and high-performance leadership, often in service of others and something larger than oneself, provide a counterbalance to the ego-driven forces in service of oneself that exert a strong pull towards the sometimes harmful state of reactivity and low-performance leadership.

## A Fine Balance: Your Reactivity-Creativity Equilibrium

At the beginning of this chapter, I asked if you could relate to experiencing both reactivity and creativity, which represent low-performance and high-performance leadership states respectively. I also shared how most people in my workshops not only say they do, but say they experience both multiple times a day.

Now you see why. These states map to specific patterns of thinking related to various parts of our brain that we all have. Each of us has the capacity for reactivity and creativity at any moment. We tend to flip-flop back and forth between these states in a dynamic *reactivity-creativity equilibrium,* as shown in figure 2.8 below.

*Figure 2.6. The Dynamic Equilibrium of Reactivity and Creativity*

For example, imagine the joy and fulfillment you might feel while putting together what you felt was an inspired vision and strategic plan at work (creativity), only then to have it criticized by your colleagues. You immediately feel threatened, thwarted, deflated, angry, and defensive (reactivity). Then, once you get over the initial criticism, drawing on your internal resources to extend yourself some kindness and self-compassion, you are willing to lean in and take up the challenge to explore the feedback given, reengage, refocus, make changes, and present a radically improved plan (creativity).

Or imagine you are having a special moment, engaged in the creative flow of connecting with one of your friends. You're laughing and having a good time, and then something shifts. Your friend teases you about something. Rather than being funny, it feels like your friend is taking a jab at you. In a flash, you feel threatened, go limbic, and become sarcastic and edgy. You catch yourself, extend yourself some self-compassion with a few deep, calming breaths, and find the courage to share how that hurt you. Now you are both apologizing and again "tending and befriending" each other. You feel reassured by the social support, and your feelings of stress and self-doubt subside. You laugh at what just happened, feel good about bravely navigating this challenge, and get back into the creative groove, feeling connected as friends again.

Or imagine you're on stage, giving a keynote presentation or addressing your organization. You feel in command and in a high-performance moment of creative flow—all until your computer crashes and you lose your slides. With the impending threat of embarrassment or potential humiliation—a sudden unexpected spike in demand—you feel threatened and sense you are about to become reactive. Just before your brain scrambles completely and you lose it—an impending low-performance state—you tap into your inner resources to catch yourself, breathe, and lean into the challenge. You make a joke, adjust to the moment, and find your composure to proceed and make the most of it.

I had just such a moment while presenting a keynote at an international conference for leaders in the wellness industry. I was speaking on the brain science of imagination and innovation when I lost my slides. After my initial "YIKES!," I took a couple of deep breaths and, looking back at the blank screen, found the wherewithal to say, "Oh, well, since the theme of this conference is imagination, let's all just imagine there is a slide here!" With that, the audience broke into laughter and expressed their support with applause. The rest of the presentation went off without a hitch—perhaps even better with the snafu that bonded us through our laughter together.

This is the dynamic interplay between reactivity and creativity. As you learned earlier, your mind's flow between these states is largely mediated by the external demands you face and your thoughts and autonomic nervous system, which can help you to marshal your internal and external resources to meet these demands.

When your demands exceed your perceived resources to cope, you feel threatened, and you mobilize your physiological fight-or-flight responses with the characteristic autonomic sympathetic nervous system activity that accompanies the threat response.

When your perceived resources exceed the demands you face, you may engage in a challenge response, which further optimizes your sympathetic nervous system, cardiovascular physiology, and mental focus to more effectively deal with the situation at hand. Alternatively, you may engage in a tend-and-befriend response, which brings internal parasympathetic balance and external social support to help you deal with your demands.

Either way, the tend-and-befriend and challenge responses bring a greater sense of clarity and calm, or relaxed alertness, than the threat response, allowing energy and information to flow more freely into your conscious cortical circuits.[58] Now your brain can more flexibly dedicate resources to being more thoughtful in your responses and satisfying your higher levels of needs in Maslow's hierarchy. Here your neocortex enables you to see the bigger picture; more fully experience empathy, love, and compassion to engage more skillfully in relationships; and think more creatively to actualize your full potential.

Therefore, as you can see in figure 2.6 above, the two factors that impact the amount of time you tend to spend in reactivity versus creativity include:

1. The impact of *stress and self-doubt:* How much of a stress load, or demand, you experience from your environment, and how adaptively you can mobilize your internal and external resources to meet your demands. (As you will discover in subsequent chapters, and especially chapter 6, a large part of mobilizing your resources involves your mindset and resiliency regarding stress and self-doubt—whether you are able to view and leverage it as an asset.)

2. The impact of *inspiration:* Your willingness and capacity to identify, focus on, and act upon what inspires and matters to you the most.

Think about how much time you spend in a state of reactivity versus a state of creativity and how quickly you can shift from reactivity to creativity. What if your equilibrium set point was spending 60 percent of your time, on average, in reactivity and 40 percent in creativity? What if you could spend even 10 percent more of your time in a creative state and shift between these states more rapidly in the heat of the moment? What would it mean to your health and vitality, the quality of your relationships, or your productivity and capacity to lead?

If you sense it could make a significant difference in your life, you are ready to ask the big question.

## How Can You Enhance Your Capacity to Shift from Reactivity to Creativity at Will?

To lead well from within, you need to ensure you have the best driver in the driver's seat to meet life's demands. For truly life-threatening situations, where rapid fight-or-flight responses make the difference between life and death, it is most adaptive for your instinctive limbic system to drive.

However, for daily living, regulating or leveraging stress with challenge and tend-and-befriend responses, and making decisions about what matters most, such as your health, relationships, and productivity, you'd want to be more fully resourced, with the CEO of your brain—your PFC—driving. Furthermore, you'd want your CEO to be well trained to ensure it does not get led astray and you get the best results, especially in times of stress.

When your limbic system and your PFC (your brain's CEO) pull in different directions, you can experience a sense of inner fragmentation. For example, when your limbic system causes you to blurt out some epithet you regret or when you overeat or drink too much alcohol and wish you hadn't, you experience inner conflict. On the other hand, when you feel aligned and act in accordance with your highest values, experiencing emotions that are congruent and motivating, you feel a sense of coherence, wholeness, and power. Your CEO is driving, with your limbic system serving. In short, you feel at home within yourself.

Brain science has made astounding progress in teaching us how we can lead well with the CEO of our brain. For example, we now know what skills and practices influence our parasympathetic nervous system, which can help regulate our sympathetic nervous system's fight-or-flight responses. The brain-imaging techniques (like functional MRIs) that detect where blood flows in the brain, as well as electroencephalograms (EEGs) that register brain-wave activity, have enabled us to identify the behaviors, skills, and practices that can shift electrical activity and blood flow between various brain regions and elevate our level of performance.

Research has also shown how *you can regulate the activity in your subconscious limbic system with your PFC*[59] to rapidly recover from stress and reactivity. Further, research reveals how you can set up the ideal conditions for divergent and convergent thinking and your creative expression, to optimize your creative process. (You'll learn more about this in chapter 7.)

In our earlier discussion of the Koslov study, I also alluded to research I'll mention in the next chapter that suggests certain practices can create enduring changes in the PFC that predispose you to experiencing a challenge rather than a threat response.

These enduring brain changes relate to a broader area of scientific discovery over the last two decades that has changed everything we thought we knew about the brain.

When I went through medical school, I was taught that by the age of five, you have all the brain cells (neurons) you're ever going to have and that individual parts of your brain, with their specific functions, are static and resistant to change. We were also taught that if your brain was damaged, by trauma or otherwise, it was unlikely to recover its functioning.

What we now know is that the brain can grow new neurons (a process called *neurogenesis*) and continually rewire and reshape itself, not only in young, developing brains, but throughout your life span—into your eighties and even your nineties! The brain is moldable, or "plastic." Consequently, this process has been called *neuroplasticity.*[60]

And here's what's truly phenomenal and most encouraging. You have the power to rewire your own brain in what has been called *"self-directed neuroplasticity.*"[61] You can learn to more fully engage your PFC and rewire your brain to more effectively navigate and leverage stress so you can think more clearly, creatively, and proactively.

*You can consciously build a more resilient brain to live a more creative and meaningful life.*

One of the most powerful ways to rewire your own brain is through the thoughts you have. Just like working out in the gym builds muscle, certain ways of thinking can strengthen your brain, especially the circuits in important areas of your neocortex.

So, how can you change your mindset and the thoughts you have to build a more resilient brain?

The foundation is *conscious awareness.* Conscious awareness enables you to *notice* the thoughts and feelings you're having in any given moment, as well as to more skillfully focus your attention on anything you choose. Where you focus your attention ultimately affects your effectiveness as a leader and the impact you have on everyone around you.

Fortunately, there is a practice that empowers your conscious awareness. It's known as *mindfulness.* Mindfulness plays a key role in helping you to more effectively marshal your internal resources and meet the demands you face, as well as focus on what inspires and matters to you the most. It enhances your capacity to shift from states of reactivity to creativity, from burnout to resiliency, and from low-performance to high-performance leadership. It is the core practice of Conscious Leadership and harnessing the CEO of your brain to lead well from within, so that you can lead well in the world.

In the next chapter, you will discover the third layer of our foundation for Conscious Leadership—the power of mindfulness to better work your brain. Then, in the subsequent chapter, you will see how it serves as the foundational practice of the 4 in 4 Framework, which will empower you with the specific steps to shift from reactivity to creativity at will.

## CHAPTER 3

# How to Better Work Your Brain with Mindfulness

In the previous chapter, we discussed how our mind plays a key role in directing the flow of energy and information within our brain. Yet our brain tends to have a mind of its own. In fact, it can mindlessly sweep us away with a host of cravings, stressors, self-doubts, uncertainties, worries, and the countless stories we tell ourselves.

This kind of mindlessness can lead you straight into a state of low-performance leadership, as well as burnout, where you feel emotionally exhausted, disconnected, and insignificant.[1]

To successfully navigate back to high-performance leadership, you need to both more consciously work your brain to enhance your internal resources and develop your resilience to stay on the path of high performance, especially when external and internal demands of stress, uncertainty, or self-doubt threaten to derail you.

The solution is *mindfulness*. Mindfulness is a practice that enables you to be more aware and present, less prone to being swept away by pain and distraction, and more purposeful in focusing your energy and attention on what is truly most meaningful in your life. It empowers your mind to direct the flow of energy and information in your brain from the state of reactivity to the state of creativity more quickly and may even protect against triggering reactivity in the first place.

It has a long and rich history.

## The History of Mindfulness

Various forms of mindfulness have been practiced for thousands of years in many of the wisdom traditions. Major threads can be traced back to the yogic teachings in Hinduism as far back as 1500 BCE, the contemplation of existence within Daoism in the sixth century BCE, Buddhism in 535 BCE, the Christian contemplative practices arising in communal monasteries in 530 CE, and the mysticism of Sufism and the Kabala arising within Islam and Judaism in the ninth and tenth centuries respectively.[2] The mindfulness practice we will be referring to most closely relates to the "insight" meditative practices of Buddhism, but without any aspect of religiosity.

Jon Kabat-Zinn, who founded the Mindfulness-Based Stress Reduction (MBSR) Program at the Center for Mindfulness at the University of Massachusetts Medical Center, is largely responsible for the secular dissemination of this mental training practice in the West. He began teaching mindfulness in 1979 as a way to support patients who could not be fully cared for by the healthcare system, to help them deal with their suffering from pain and chronic illness. As of last count, the MBSR program is now taught in over seven hundred hospitals worldwide.[3] It is not only offered to patients, but to healthcare providers who are stressed out, too!

While deep respect was paid to the Buddhist origins of mindfulness, the MBSR program makes little reference to the spiritual teaching or the culture of Buddhism itself. This was by design. Had mindfulness been taught as a religion or spiritual practice while the MBSR program was being developed at the University of Massachusetts Medical Center, it might have conflicted with patients' spiritual practices or beliefs and posed a barrier to their engaging in its therapeutic benefits. Likewise, it would have limited the spreading of this practice across the healthcare system at large and in other secular settings, such as schools and the business world.

Kabat-Zinn was careful to point out that mindfulness is simply a mental training practice and way of being that no one can patent.

Beyond the healthcare setting, mindfulness has also gone mainstream. Programs are being embraced by those in the military, by judges and lawyers, and by those who are in law enforcement and are incarcerated.

It has also found its way into government. US Congressman Tim Ryan, author of *A Mindful Nation,* hosts a meditation group on Capitol Hill called the Quiet Time Caucus.[4]

Mindfulness has become common practice in the business world. Steve Jobs helped to raise the awareness of its value, as he attributed much of his innovation and success to his Zen mindfulness practices. Many more corporations, including Google, General Mills, and Intel, are now offering mindfulness training to help leaders and employees better handle stress and sustain high levels of performance.

In a 2014 *Huffington Post* article, Otto Scharmer, a senior lecturer at MIT and co-founder of the Presencing Institute, reported that since it was first introduced in 2012, mindfulness has become one of the most popular topics at the World Economic Forum in Davos.[5] In 2014, almost all of the mindfulness-related events had been oversubscribed, with attendees sitting on the floor or standing against the wall.

Scharmer quoted the CEO of a private equity fund, who after an evening mindfulness session shared, "This night was a turning point for me. I realized that as a leader and a human being I not only need to engage in training and practices that keep up my physical fitness, but I can also engage in training and practices that develop and keep up my quality of mindfulness. This has been my most important experience in Davos this year."

Scharmer names three drivers behind the rise of mindfulness:

- "New tech: our hyperconnectivity and fast-paced lives have caused us to disconnect more and more from ourselves.

- "New challenges: leaders are facing more situations that require them to access their self-awareness and emotional intelligence in order to be successful.

- "New science: the past ten years have brought breakthrough research in cognition science, particularly about the impact of mindfulness on brain plasticity." (We'll be talking more about this later in the chapter.)

The rise of mindfulness has also found its way into the mainstream media. In addition to the *Huffington Post,* numerous articles have been published in the *New York Times, Washington Post,* and other media outlets. Signaling a tipping point, in February 2014, Time magazine featured the practice of mindfulness on its cover. The title read, "The Mindful Revolution: The Science of Finding Focus in a Stressed-Out Multitasking Culture."[6]

In December 2014, Anderson Cooper did a feature on mindfulness for the television show *60 Minutes.* Cooper chronicled the week that he spent on a mindfulness retreat with Jon Kabat-Zinn at Mount Madonna in the Santa Cruz Mountains.[7]

I have memories of my own life-changing experience with Kabat-Zinn on this very same retreat more than a decade ago. It was an immersion in the MBSR program to learn not only the science and how the eight-week program is delivered, but also to directly experience its core practices: mindfulness meditation, yoga, and a body awareness practice called the "Body Scan." This immersion also included a thirty-six-hour period of complete silence to facilitate a deeper experience of present-moment awareness.

Of note, there were no clocks in the room during the retreat, and everyone was asked to surrender their cell phones upon arriving. I recall how, at the outset, Kabat-Zinn had warned us that if any of us were tempted to ask what the time was, we would get only one answer: "The time is now!"

## The Science of Mindfulness

There is a large body of research supporting the benefits of mindfulness. The most rigorous review so far on this topic identified over 18,000 articles.[8] What set this review apart is that the researchers specifically looked for studies that were randomized, controlled trials where the comparison group received a comparable amount of time, attention, and expectation of benefit as the intervention group. (An example of such a control group would be those who received an educational program to better deal with stress.)

What they found in the 47 trials that met their inclusion criteria was that mindfulness-based meditation programs had evidence supporting its benefit for anxiety, depression, and pain, as well as for stress, distress, and mental-health-related quality of life. Benefits for other areas in this review, such as positive mood, attention, substance use, eating habits, sleep, and weight were inconclusive.

While there was an absence of evidence showing benefits for some of the areas above, it should also be noted that many of these studies are relatively small in numbers, and these findings do not prove the absence of benefit itself.

Further research supports the benefits of mindfulness for a broad range of conditions such as ADHD,[9] eating disorders,[10] addiction,[11] irritable bowel syndrome,[12] psoriasis,[13] fibromyalgia,[14] obesity,[15] as well as better cardiovascular health from smoking less, exercising more, and having a significantly lower fasting glucose level and body mass index.[16]

Research further suggests that mindfulness training can also help your brain to perform better, improving cognitive skills like memory and concentration that may lead to an improvement in academic results.[17]

Part of how mindfulness works to help you lead and heal well from within is by transforming your body's physiology. Tonya Jacobs, a postdoctoral researcher at the University of California, Davis Center for Mind and Brain, studied people attending a three-month meditation retreat and found that an increase in mindfulness was associated with a decrease in the levels of the stress hormone cortisol.[18]

In another study, she found that the meditation retreat also increased the level of telomorase, the enzyme that maintains and increases telomere length, which is considered to be a marker for cellular aging.

What was fascinating about the results of this study was that a greater sense of *life purpose* from the meditation practice played the key role in decreasing stress and negative emotions and increasing the telomorase levels.[19] This raises a profound question: could it be that living your life on purpose extends your life, giving you more time to express your purpose?

As we discussed in the last chapter, meeting your needs for significance and a life of purpose cultivates resiliency and prevents burnout. So it is also not a surprise that a randomized clinical trial of seventy-four practicing physicians in the Department of Medicine at the Mayo Clinic in Rochester, Minnesota, found that a nine-month mindfulness-based program, in which clinicians met one hour every other week, reduced burnout as well as increased engagement at work. These results were sustained at one year after the study.[20]

Mindfulness-based programs can also have a significant impact on the bottom line. A study of 4,452 patients who participated in a mindfulness-based program at the Benson-Henry Institute for Mind-Body Medicine at Massachusetts General Hospital to enhance their relaxation response and resiliency with stress had a 43 percent reduction in healthcare utilization at one year, including a decrease in clinical encounters with healthcare providers, lab testing, imaging studies, and emergency department visits.[21]

Aetna, one of the largest health insurance and benefits companies with over 50,000 employees, estimates that since instituting its mindfulness program, it has saved about $2,000 per employee in healthcare costs and gained about $3,000 per employee in productivity.[22]

What has made the science of mindfulness especially compelling is the research looking at the effects of mindfulness on your brain.

Specifically, brain imaging suggests mindfulness may rewire your limbic system and PFC, enabling you to become more resilient in the face of stress. In a study by Britta Holzel, twenty-six stressed but otherwise healthy individuals enrolled in an eight-week MBSR program and were evaluated with baseline and post-program MRI scans to identify changes that took place in their brain. She found that the training shrank the grey-matter density of the participant's stress response–inducing amygdalae and that these changes were correlated with a reduction in their perception of stress.[23]

Some of the most intriguing findings come from studies of Buddhist monks with tens of thousands of hours of meditation practice. Brain imaging and EEG findings have discovered brain changes related to emotional regulation, attention, and empathy, the magnitude of which correlate with the number of lifelong hours they'd spent meditating.[24] One monk, Mattieu Riccard, was found to have such dramatic changes in his brain that he has been dubbed as the happiest man in the world.[25]

And here is the study I alluded to in the last chapter, a powerful companion to the Koslov study, which showed individuals with higher left prefrontal cortical activation relative to their right were more likely to respond to stress with a challenge response than a threat response. A study conducted by Richard Davidson, Jon Kabat-Zinn, and colleagues also examined electroencephalogram brain changes, but in twenty-five newbies to mindfulness from a biotechnology company in Wisconsin who engaged in the eight-week MBSR program. A group of sixteen of their colleagues, who were waiting to go through the training later, served as a control. In the experimental group, they found that eight weeks of mindfulness increased the activity in the left PFC (which, as mentioned in the last chapter, is associated with more engaging, approach-oriented behavior and increased well-being) relative to the right PFC (which is associated with stress-related, avoidant behaviors).[26]

In summary, this research suggests that mindfulness can help you reshape your brain to better manage stress, transform your stress response from threat to challenge, shift from a reactive to a creative mindset, and live a healthier, more engaged, joyful, and productive life! (We'll be expanding more on the implications of these studies in the next chapter.)

Now let's take a closer look at how mindfulness works.

## How Mindfulness Works

According to Jon Kabat-Zinn, "Mindfulness means paying attention in a particular way: on purpose, in the present moment, and nonjudgmentally."[27]

In a review on the "mechanism of mindfulness," Shapiro and colleagues highlight three aspects of this definition.[28]

1. *"On purpose"* refers to one's intention in practicing mindfulness. Shapiro points out, "When Western psychology attempted to extract the essence of mindfulness practice from its original religious/cultural roots, we lost, to some extent, the aspect of intention, which for Buddhism was enlightenment and compassion for all beings." In this definition, "purpose" preserves a reminder to be mindful of your intent. It provides you with motivation and a guiding vision, your "why" for investing yourself in practicing in the first place, which will allow you to stick with your practice over time.

Your purpose may also change over time. For example, you may start with the intent to better deal with your stress, then to further explore your values, and then to open your heart, connect more fully with others, and lead more effectively. In a study of meditation practitioners, the length of practice was found to correlate with the primary reasons for practicing. These reasons progressed along a continuum from emotional regulation to self-exploration to self-liberation (i.e., liberating oneself from one's ego to be able to more fully engage in compassionate service of others).[29] As you contemplate engaging in mindfulness practice, take a moment to reflect on your purpose for doing so.

Of note, the first principle of Conscious Capitalism, which we discussed in chapter 1, is that higher purpose serves as the key driver in conscious organizations. You may reflect on how your personal purpose for mindfulness practice aligns with your higher purpose for your organization. In other words, how can your purpose in your practice enable you to lead well from within, so you can lead well in manifesting your purpose in the world?

2. *"Paying attention"* refers to the way you learn to direct and redirect your focus of attention on the contents of your consciousness, moment by moment, in the present moment.

In the Cherokee legend of "The Two Wolves," an elderly Cherokee chief is teaching his grandson about life.[30]

"A fight is going on inside me," he said to the boy. "It is a terrible fight, and it is between two wolves. One is evil—he is anger, envy, sorrow, regret, greed, arrogance, self-pity, guilt, resentment, inferiority, lies, false pride, superiority, self-doubt, and ego. The other is good—he is joy, peace, love, hope, serenity, humility, kindness, benevolence, empathy, generosity, truth, compassion, and faith. This same fight is going on inside you—and inside every other person, too."

The grandson thought about it for a minute and then asked his grandfather, "Which wolf will win?"

The old chief simply replied, "The one you feed."

In other words, the one you pay attention to. (You may have also noticed that the two wolves reflect some of the key qualities of low- and high-performance leadership.)

This habit of mindfully paying attention engages neuroplastic brain change in a couple of key ways that dictate the quality and meaning of your life.

First, your habit of consciously shifting your attention strengthens your brain's ability to shift your attention as needed. Later in this chapter, you'll learn about a study that shows when you repeatedly shift your attention from a state of mind-wandering to your breath, your brain becomes more efficient in making this shift. Likewise, as you enhance your ability to shift your attention, it becomes easier for you to shift your focus from pain and distraction to more meaningful tasks and experiences at hand.

Also, whatever you repeatedly focus your attention on wires itself in your brain, too. For example, research suggests that when you commit to a practice of gratitude, such as writing down five things you are grateful for at the end of each day for a couple of weeks, you will feel more appreciative and your sense of happiness and well-being increases. The research also shows that when you feel grateful, you may also be more likely to provide emotional support to others or help them with a personal problem—further providing positive spillover effects that can enhance the joy and significance of your life.[31]

In other words, what you pay attention to grows.

Likewise, when you repeatedly focus your attention on the qualities of high-performance leadership, such leaning in to express yourself with courageous authenticity or maintaining your composure by mindfully regulating your emotions in times of stress, you will develop the neural changes and associated habits of high-performance leadership that enable you to lead well in the world.

3. *"In a particular way"* speaks to the attitude or the qualities of mindfulness you bring to your practice.

When you bring a cold, analytical, or judgmental quality to the lens of your awareness, these qualities can lead to a hard-driving and self-critical way of being.

On the other hand, when you set an intention of goodwill for yourself and others and bring the nonjudgmental qualities of openness, curiosity, and kindness, these qualities promote a sense of equanimity and ease.

Each of these approach-oriented qualities is key to transforming your relationship with stress. Since stress tends to be uncomfortable, we tend to want to avoid it and close the door on it. However, since stress also commonly arises around things we most care about, when we close the door on stress, we also risk missing the opportunity to work through important issues and engage with what brings our lives greatest meaning.

*Openness* literally opens the door to exploring what you most deeply care about. *Curiosity,* then, causes you to lean in through the door to engage your challenge response to stress and benefit from the growth and learning that ensues. And *kindness* engages your tend-and-befriend response to provide you with self-compassion and courage to embrace your exploration and discoveries and connect well with others.

These qualities also facilitate your ability to meet your Maslowian Hierarchy of Needs: kindness helps you meet your love and belonging needs, and curiosity supports your growth mindset towards self-actualization and significance.

Amplifying specific individual qualities can also be very helpful under certain circumstances. For example, the quality of curiosity is key to learning and growth when facing challenges or when creativity and innovation is called for. Kindness is especially important for facilitating resiliency in times of painful self-doubt or any other form of suffering. (We'll be expanding on this below and in subsequent chapters, particularly chapter 6.)

When you bring these qualities of openness, curiosity, and kindness to your practice, you experience a healthy state of mind—a sense of wholeness—that integrates qualities of both mind *and* heart.

In Japanese kanji, mindfulness, or *nen,* is represented by the following character:

The top element, which looks like a peaked roof, signifies presence, or this moment now. The elements below the peak represent the combination of heart and mind.[32] This character beautifully captures the very essence of mindfulness, bringing conscious awareness with your heart and mind to your moment of now.

One of the best ways to understand the power of mindfulness is to experience it for yourself. I'd like to invite you now to learn about and experience a brief practice.

## A Brief Mindfulness Practice

In summary, mindfulness is the practice of paying purposeful attention with a sense of openness, curiosity, and kindness for whatever is arising in the present moment.

At its foundation, mindfulness is simply a way of being. You can cultivate this way of being informally by simply bringing your awareness to whatever you are doing or to whatever is arising in the present moment, whether you are washing dishes, brushing your teeth, playing with your kids, or working out.

You can also cultivate mindfulness formally through a specific practice. Formal mindfulness practice is often done lying down, sitting, standing, walking, or as an integral part of yoga.

There are two main elements to mindfulness practice. One involves the simple practice of "open awareness" of whatever is arising. Another element is "concentrated awareness," where you *aim* and *sustain* your focus of attention to a specific object in your field of awareness, such as your breathing, your body, sounds, or even the ebb and flow of your thoughts and feelings.

The foundational practice I am about to introduce to you involves both elements, beginning with open awareness. It then engages the element of concentration, where I will invite you to focus your attention on your breath.

Set aside five to ten minutes to do this practice. You can either read through these instructions first and then begin, record yourself reading aloud these instructions so you can listen to them as you practice, or go to SuperSmartHealth.com/BookBonus and download the mp3 of these instructions that I have recorded for you. (If you have practiced mindfulness before, I encourage you to approach this exercise with "beginner's mind.")

So let's begin:

1.  Allow yourself to lie down on your back, with your arms at your sides, or assume a comfortable sitting posture with your spine straight and your shoulders relaxed, letting your hands rest gently in your lap in whatever way feels natural to you. Either close your eyes or softly focus them in front of you.

2.  More important than your external posture is the internal posture you bring to your practice. Bring with you an intention to sit with a light touch of openness, curiosity, and kindness for whatever arises in you, moment by moment.

3.  There is no need to modify, fix, or suppress any sensations, thoughts, or feelings. Simply notice whatever sensations, thoughts, and feelings are arising in and passing through your awareness.

4.  Now, bring your attention to your breath, wherever you notice your breath most strongly. This may be the rise and fall of your belly or the sensation of air moving in and out at the rim of your nostrils or the gentle rise and fall of the center of your chest.

5.  Imagining that your breath is flowing in and out through the center of your chest—your heart center—can be a powerful way of amplifying the heart quality in your practice and co-mingling a sense of kindness and compassion for yourself while breathing.

6.  Observe where the sensation of your breathing feels most noticeable, natural, and centering for you, breathing in your normal, resting rhythm with a soft belly that expands as you breathe in and recedes as you breathe out.

7.  Continue being with your breathing, just noticing it, following it, and flowing with it, without trying to change what feels natural for you.

8. As you do this, you may notice that your mind may wander and that your focus on your breathing can be swept away by thoughts, sensations, or emotions. This is natural, and it can happen within a breath or two.

9. The moment you become aware that your attention has shifted off your breath or notice any number of thoughts, sensations, or emotions, acknowledge and appreciate that you are now aware that your mind has wandered and gently and firmly bring your awareness back to your breath.

10. Thoughts, sensations, and emotions may naturally continue to arise and repeatedly cause your mind to wander from your focus on your breath. There is no need to suppress, change, or fix your thoughts or emotions—simply notice how they ebb and flow without resisting them. As soon as you become aware that your attention has wandered off your breath, *shift your focus back to your breath*—over and over again.

11. As you continue to bring your awareness back to your breath, see if you can notice how your awareness is distinct from your thoughts and emotions and how, in your awareness, you can shift your focus of attention back to your breath.

12. Take as much time as is helpful to you, resting in awareness with your focus of attention on your breath. When you notice your mind wandering, acknowledge and appreciate your awareness of this wandering and gently and firmly bring your attention back to your breath, over and over again.

13. Then when you feel ready, if your eyes are closed, allow them to open.

## Reflecting on Your Mindfulness Experience

So what was this experience like for you?

Were you able to notice your thoughts, sensations, and emotions from a place of openness, curiosity, and kindness? Or did you bring a judgmental quality to what you were experiencing? Did you feel tempted to suppress, fix, or modify your thoughts and feelings? If you did, see if you can simply, kindly, and nonjudgmentally notice that you were doing so.

This meditative practice is not about trying to empty or still your mind (a tall order at best), but simply observing whatever arises and passes through your field of awareness.

A number of metaphors have been used to describe this form of open awareness. One is that of a waterfall, where the flow of water represents your passing sensations, thoughts, and feelings, and you are standing behind the waterfall, watching this flow.

Another metaphor is that your sensations, thoughts, and feelings are like clouds passing across the sky, with the sky representing your awareness itself. While the clouds and weather may change, the sky is forever constant.

The metaphor I find most useful is the one offered by Dan Siegel. He describes mindfulness using the image of a "Wheel of Awareness."[33] I have adapted his wheel to produce a graphic I find helpful for our purposes.

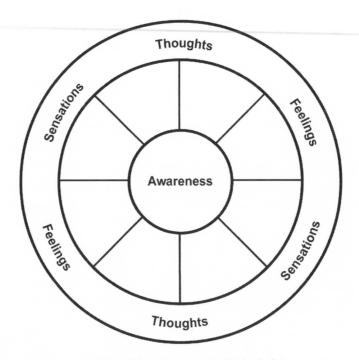

*Figure 3.1. Adapted from Dan Siegel's "Wheel of Awareness"*

In this construct, the hub of the wheel represents your awareness, and the rim of the wheel represents anything you can be aware of, such as your sensations, thoughts, and feelings. Spokes radiate from the hub to the rim, representing your focus of attention.

As with all of the metaphors above, where you believe you are positioned—here, whether you perceive yourself at the rim or the hub of the wheel—profoundly affects your experience.

Many individuals identify with their experience at the rim, saying things like, "I am angry"; "I am anxious"; "I am sad"; or "I am worthless." In essence, they overidentify with their thoughts, sensations, and feelings.

As you engage in mindfulness practice, your core identity begins to shift more towards the hub of awareness itself. You'll be more likely to say things like, "I'm *noticing* that I'm having angry, anxious, or sad feelings." Or "I am *noticing* I'm having thoughts of self-doubt."

And this makes all the difference in the world. Instead of being swept away and reflexively reacting to stress-related feelings by *being* angry, sad, or fearful, gripped by these experiences that often cause more harm than good until they subside, mindfulness enables you to be aware that you are simply *having* anxious, angry, or fearful thoughts and feelings.

Victor Frankl said, "Between stimulus and response there is a space. In that space is our power to choose our response. In our response lies our growth and our freedom."[34] This element of open awareness opens a space in which you are able to pause before you act and take this time to consciously choose the best possible action to take. In other words, it provides you with a greater stability of mind from which to pivot.

Awareness is stable, whole, and complete. With practice, as your identity becomes more attuned to the hub, you begin to appreciate that you are not your sensations, thoughts, and feelings, which all too often can leave you feeling fragmented. Instead, from the hub of awareness, noticing with curiosity, kindness, and acceptance that you are simply having an ever-changing stream of experience through your stable field of awareness conveys an experience of wholeness, a foundational sense that you are complete and enough as you are, or that you simply just "are."

The element of concentration in this mindfulness practice—bringing your attention to your breath over and over—serves another purpose, which we mentioned earlier in the chapter. In my workshops, I often ask how many people felt like their mind wandered off their breath as many as one hundred times. A number of hands always go up, some sheepishly so. I then ask if they felt like this reflected a "bad" meditation or they had just got an F for this practice. Some do. I then share how, to the contrary, this experience actually represents a very helpful meditation.

If your mind wanders one hundred times from your breath during this practice, reflect for a moment on how it also means you must have shifted your attention back to your breath one hundred times. This shifting is exactly what transforms the brain.

Again, just like working out in the gym strengthens your muscles, returning your attention to your object of focus in the concentrative element of your meditation strengthens the neurological "muscle" that enables you to shift your attention within your field of awareness.

In a study by Wendy Hasenkamp at Emory University, fourteen meditation practitioners performed a breath-focused meditation—very similar to the one you just experienced—while undergoing fMRI brain scanning. The moment participants became aware their mind had wandered, they pressed a button in the scanner and shifted their focus to the breath.

The researchers found that when the participants' minds had wandered, key structures in the default mode network of their brains were active. When they shifted their focus to back to their breath, the activity in their brain shifted to the dorsolateral PFC, a key structure in their task-positive network.

What's more, it appeared that more experienced practitioners were able to disengage more effectively from mind wandering and shift with greater speed and efficiency onto their breath, which was the task at hand.[35]

Remember, whatever you focus on grows. Whatever your brain does repetitively strengthens those circuits. Nerve networks develop a greater density of connections, and the insulation around the nerves, known as myelination, also further develops, increasing the speed and efficiency of nerve conduction.

Thus, as you repeatedly shift your attention to your breath over and over, standing at the hub of your Wheel of Awareness, you are strengthening your inner resources—your ability to direct your spoke of attention towards any point on the rim that you choose.

## Applying Mindfulness to Thrive as a Resilient and Effective Leader

Your ability to notice all of what is on your rim, and focus your energy and attention accordingly, has significant implications for reversing burnout, cultivating resiliency, thriving with well-being, and improving your effectiveness as a leader—in short, for leading well from within so you can lead well in the world.

In chapter 1, we discussed the Leadership Circle's research about how the Creative and Reactive domains are positively and negatively associated with leadership effectiveness respectively. I then showed you the Leadership Circle's Leadership Profile, the diagram they use to report the results of leaders' 360 reviews.[36]

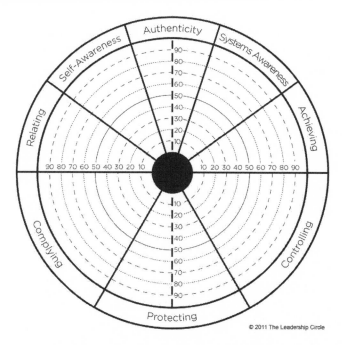

*Figure 3.2. The Leadership Circle's Leadership Profile Diagram*

Do you notice a similarity between this diagram and the Wheel of Awareness above? The Creative and Reactive domains of leadership—representing our thoughts, feelings, and sensations—are mapped out on the rim of the wheel, and your awareness is represented by the hub at the center.

But here we need to make an important point about what's on the rim of your wheel. In the context of leadership, many people tend to assume that creativity is always "good" and reactivity is always "bad." But as we saw in the last chapter, in many ways reactivity can also be highly adaptive and protect you from harm.

As leaders, we have all of these creative *and* reactive qualities within us. In the last chapter, we discussed why: these qualities map to specific regions of our brain that we all have.

Just like a wheel is a complete circle, the Wheel of Awareness and the Leadership Circle diagram reveal the wholeness of who you are. There is no need to deny parts of who you are; every part of yourself is important and serves as a teaching tool.

Denying parts of yourself causes you to go to war within yourself, where your shadow characteristics can take over and further drive you into stress and burnout. By acknowledging the totality of your entire wheel of awareness, you can rest in your essential wholeness.

We have no need to slice, dice, or deny parts of who we are. Rather, we can accept all of our dimensions, and then, using our ability to shift our attention, we can more skillfully shift between our reactive and creative dimension and intentionally focus our attention on whatever part of the rim we choose.

In simplest terms, mindfulness is the power to *notice* and *choose*. Your mind's ability to notice and choose engages your PFC, the CEO of your brain. And at your hub of awareness, with your mind engaging the CEO of your brain, you are truly centered and have tremendous power to marshal your inner resources to meet any demand. You are both an energy generator and energy conductor. You can renew your energy, enhance your energy, and set an intention to bring your good energy to your interactions. You can observe your reactive and creative dimensions, and through the lens of openness, curiosity, kindness, and nonjudgment, you can purposefully focus and direct your energy and attention on whatever you choose.

For example, with mindfulness, you can optimize your energy by mindfully noticing what depletes your energy and what enhances it and redirect your focus accordingly. If you notice that your energy is being depleted by focusing on the reactive dimension—such as fearful thoughts of the future, regrets of the past, or fight-or-flight-based behaviors—from your hub of awareness in the moment of now, you can reset and redirect your attention toward the creative dimension. You might reflect on what your challenge has to teach you, soothe yourself with self-compassion, rest if needed, or connect more fully with others and/or your source of inspiration. You can further consider the outcomes and results you would like to work toward or consider how you can best express yourself in serving others.

When you come right down to it, your ability to shift your attention in the moment is what ultimately determines the quality of your health, relationships, and work and the success, happiness, and fulfillment you create in your life. It is what allows you to lead well from within.

Further, because whatever we repeatedly choose to focus our attention on grows, the habit of repeatedly pivoting from a reactive to a creative mindset hardwires in the qualities of high-performance creative leadership. This process continually enhances growth in your leadership effectiveness, which results in increasing performance both at work and at home.

With knowledge comes understanding. However, it is *practicing* that knowledge that facilitates transformation. So the key here is to practice mindfulness as a habit, not merely understand its benefits.

To cultivate your practice, I invite you to engage in the formal mindfulness breathing practice outlined above for at least five to fifteen minutes, twice a day. As mentioned, I have posted the audio guiding you through the practice at SuperSmartHealth.com/BookBonus. You can download the audio to your smartphone and use it during your daily practice or any time you experience stress.

Further, I invite you to more informally integrate mindfulness throughout your day by bringing mindful awareness to whatever you are doing at least for a few moments each hour, starting now. You can set a reminder on your phone or bring mindful awareness to a specific routine in your day, such as each time you walk through a doorway frame, enter your office, log onto your computer, brush your teeth, take a shower, wash the dishes, or exercise.

In moments of stress during the day, it can be helpful to remember to pause and take three heart-centered, soft-belly breaths to shift from a reactive to a more creative state in the moment. We'll be coming back to this suggestion in part 2 as well.

The practice of mindfulness is a powerful tool for the Conscious Leader. However, as foundational as it is, it is not enough. Shifting from a reactive to a creative mindset is challenging. First of all, the sheer number of stress and self-doubt triggers we all face in today's world can be overwhelming. Second, reactivity is inherently subconscious, which means that much of the reactive behavior we may wish to shift away from lies within the blind spots of our consciousness, so we often don't even know what is triggering our reactive behavior. Third, even if we are able to navigate our way through our blind spots and our abundance of triggers, we may not fully know what's truly most important to navigate towards. And fourth, even if we have clarified what is truly important, life's natural challenges and stressors can make it challenging to stay aligned with our vision and purpose.

What we also need is a *framework* that includes the skills and practices to further enhance our inner resources both to navigate stress and to stay on track with what's truly meaningful in our lives.

In the next chapter, we'll build upon the foundations of the research supporting Conscious Leadership, brain science, and mindfulness with an introduction to a system for doing so: *The 4 in 4 Framework to Engage Conscious Leadership.*

# CHAPTER 4

# Introducing the 4 in 4 Framework to Engage Conscious Leadership

Now that we have set the foundation of the research supporting Conscious Leadership, brain science, and the key practice of mindfulness, we are well positioned to introduce the 4 in 4 Framework to Engage Conscious Leadership.

This four-step framework can help you to mindfully shift from reactivity to creativity and to experience a life less dominated by the threat of stress and more led by inspiration, wellness, and well-being.

## How the 4 in 4 Framework Cultivates Resiliency and Peak Performance

Before we learn more about the 4 in 4 Framework, let me ask you a couple of questions.

How well are you functioning in your life regarding your health, your relationships, and your productivity at work or at home? Do you feel like you are thriving, operating at peak performance in these areas, or below your peak?

If you don't feel you are functioning consistently at your peak in any of these areas, what do you feel is standing in your way? (Take a few moments to reflect on this question before you read further.)

When I ask my workshop participants or coaching clients this question, the answers typically fall into two buckets.

On one hand, some say they frequently feel overwhelmed with the threat of stress or self-doubt. For example, they feel stressed about having too much to do and not enough time to do it. They fear what others may think and are afraid to fully express themselves. They feel limited by fear of failure and self-doubt and avoid pursuing what they really want to do. They feel that stress clouds their thinking, making it hard to make good decisions and perform well.

On the other hand, others say what most limits them is a lack of focus, vision, or sense of purpose. They don't feel they've identified or fully tapped into what inspires them the most. Or, if they do know what inspires them, they don't feel like they have a clear enough strategy or skills to prioritize well and optimize their performance. Or they have trouble finding sufficient motivation, commitment, or willpower to lean into their challenges and take the necessary action to achieve the results they envision for their life.

Does any of this resonate with you? If so, take heart. You are by no means alone. You can also surmount these challenges.

The 4 in 4 Framework is a system that enables you to effectively navigate and harness your stress and self-doubt to focus your attention on what matters most to you. It helps you clarify your purpose and vision and implement strategies to optimize your health and vitality, your relationships with yourself and others, and your productivity and impact at work and at home.

This approach also cultivates *resiliency* to prevent burnout in high-stress environments. According to research, two broad skill sets have been identified as being crucial to building resilience:[1]

1. The ability to recover rapidly from the distress of stress
2. The ability to engage stress to sustain growth in the face of adversity

These skills of resiliency are also key to achieving and sustaining peak performance. Here's why. Many people think that the relationship between stress and performance is linear—that is, you perform at your best when your stress is lowest, and your performance decreases as your stress level increases.

But this is not so. In the early 1900s, psychologists Robert Yerkes and John Dodson discovered the relationship between stress (arousal) and performance,[2] which is represented by the bell-shaped curve shown below.

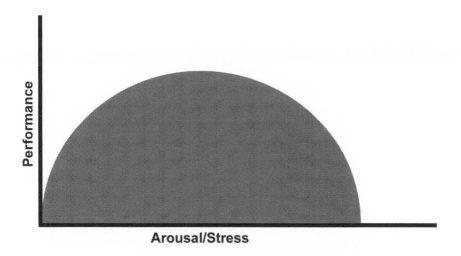

*Figure 4.1. The Yerkes-Dodson Stress and Performance Curve*

This stress and performance curve indicates that there is a level of stress where a person performs at his or her peak. It has been described as "eustress," or "good stress." It's a place where you feel fully engaged, integrated, and whole within yourself. It's a state where you sense you have sufficient resources to meet your challenging demands, your autonomic system is optimized, and you feel fully engaged in heart and mind in what you are doing. You're in a relatively relaxed state of alertness, where you're well balanced mentally and emotionally. You have full awareness, focus, and mental clarity, which is optimal for problem solving and decision making. At the same time, you feel perfectly coordinated both mentally and physically, in the sweet spot of your rhythm. As you might recall from chapter 2, this state of eustress and engagement is also what Mihaly Csikszentmihalyi calls "flow."[3]

At the peak of the bell curve, where your resources are able to match your demands, you are "eustressed" and "in the zone." However, as you become increasingly overwhelmed with stress ("distressed")—for example, having bitten off more than you can chew for a project or a deadline—you begin to shift to the right of the peak on the curve. Here, with increasing stress and anxiety at not having enough time or skill (i.e., internal resources to meet the demands and expectations of your task), you feel threatened with thoughts about potential failure and find it increasingly difficult to focus and concentrate. You may also feel frazzled and drained of energy. The resources in your brain shift into survival mode and away from the executive functions, cognitive flexibility, and creativity of your higher brain circuits. Consequently, your performance rapidly descends from the peak down the right side of the curve.

Alternatively, if you don't experience any stress at all—for example, if you feel apathetic, disengaged, unfocused, or bored, without much desire to engage the internal resources you have—you can find yourself to the left of the peak on the curve. Here you're in a low energy state. The higher cortical circuits of your mind aren't fully engaged; your heart just isn't in it; and you're not performing very well either.

Learning skills within the two domains of resiliency—the ability to recover from the distress of stress *and* to leverage a healthy level of stress to cultivate growth at the edge of your capabilities—is the key to optimizing your energy and navigating toward the peak of your performance curve.

Specifically, learning skills to navigate and reduce the overwhelming threat of stress and self-doubt moves you up the *right* side of the bell curve toward peak performance. Learning skills that help you lean in to meaningful challenges that sustain your growth moves you up the *left* side of the bell curve toward peak performance, as shown in figure 4.2.

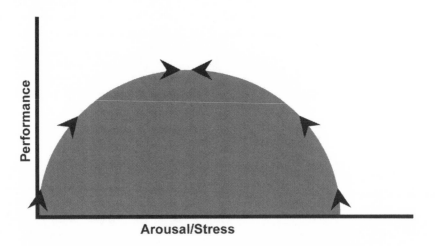

*Figure 4.2. Moving Toward Peak Performance on the Stress and Performance Curve*

The four steps of the 4 in 4 Framework directly address these two key components of resiliency so you can ascend both limbs of the curve to achieve your peak performance. Steps 1 and 2 of the framework will help you to not only reduce your sense of overwhelm or threat related to stress or self-doubt, but also effectively harness its energy and what each has to teach. Steps 3 and 4 will help you sustain your growth by leaning into your challenges and identifying, focusing on, and manifesting what's truly important in your life, regardless of the adversity you face.

Here's another way to think about it: as you leverage the foundation of mindfulness along with the four steps of the 4 in 4 Framework, you'll be expanding your inner resources to meet demands and direct your flow of energy up Maslow's Hierarchy of Needs. The skills you'll learn in Steps 1 and 2 will bring you a greater sense of internal safety and confidence. You'll discover when and how to reverse the flow of energy of stress and self-doubt from a *threat response* towards a *challenge* and/or *tend-and-befriend response,* so you can stem the tide of reactivity and burnout. Steps 3 and 4 enable you to further engage inspiration, creativity, and the behaviors that cultivate resiliency. These steps will help you to optimize your health, relationships, and productivity to experience more vitality, love, and a greater sense of significance in your life.

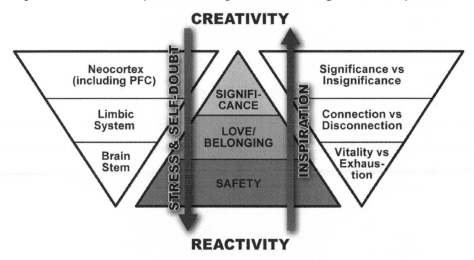

*Figure 4.3. Redirecting Your Flow of Energy Up Maslow's Hierarchy of Needs to Shift from Reactivity to Creativity and Transform Burnout into Resiliency*

As you learned in chapter 2, each of us has the capacity for reactivity and creativity, and we tend to flip between these states dynamically, often without even realizing it.

Again, think about what percentage of time you spend in reactivity (for example, responding in fear, frustration, irritation, or self-doubt) versus creativity (proactively engaging in wellness-enhancing activities, connecting meaningfully in your relationships, and feeling inspired, creative, productive, and effective at work). Consider again what it would mean if you could shift your reactivity-creativity equilibrium by just a few percentage points. What would it mean for your health, relationships, and sense of significance in your work? What would it mean for your capacity to lead more consciously both at work and at home?

The 4 in 4 Framework to Engage Conscious Leadership provides you with science-backed skills and mindfulness-based practices to become more aware and shift from the state of reactivity to creativity in the heat of the moment, as well as rewire your brain to shift your equilibrium so that you may also become less reactive and more creative over time.

Let's take a closer look at how each of the steps enables you to do so.

## An Overview of the Four Steps of the 4 in 4 Framework

The 4 in 4 Framework is so named because it has four steps, with four key components in each of its steps.

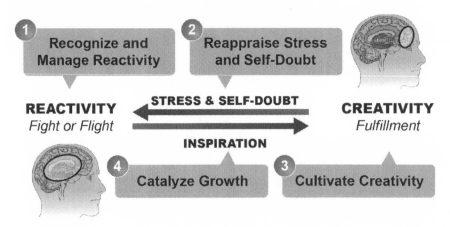

*Figure 4.4. The 4 in 4 Framework*

**Step 1: Recognizing and Managing Reactivity** helps you identify when you feel threatened by stress and self-doubt and take the edge off your reactions. You'll learn how to feel more in control and how to respond more wisely.

You cannot begin to effectively navigate stress, self-doubt, and reactivity unless you can recognize it first. Many of your reactive responses are inherently subconscious and are, therefore, blind spots in your behavior that can hijack your ability to act with wisdom and kindness. They can easily sweep you away, causing you to say or do things you later regret.

For example, think about the last fight you had with your partner or co-worker. You may have thought to yourself, *Where did that reaction come from? Why did I say that? I wish I could take that back.*

This step enables you to recognize your threat response, or your specific patterns of sensations, thoughts, feelings, and behaviors related to the way you fight and take flight in reaction to stress and self-doubt. It then helps you to further recognize when these reactions may be doing you and others more harm than good and prevent them from happening.

Imagine being able to recognize your anger, frustrations, and fears sooner and, within moments, being able to soothe these feelings before they ramp up and sweep you away. How much more confident would you feel if you knew how to calm yourself in moments and maintain your composure to communicate more effectively so you feel heard and the other person doesn't feel hurt?

Step 1 teaches you how to stay in control and take the edge off your reactivity with a powerful and simple skill that has been scientifically proven to calm your reactive response within seconds.[4] It also gives you a mindfulness practice to help you rewire your brain to turn this skill into a more helpful habit.

In a study conducted of novice mindfulness practitioners, eight weeks of practicing mindfulness was found to shrink the grey matter in their amygdalae, a finding that correlated with an overall reduction in their perception of stress.[5]

Thus, by mastering this step's skill and practice, you will know when your stress response is threatening to sweep you away, and you will be more capable of redirecting those thoughts, feelings, and emotions, so you can respond more calmly and effectively in the heat of the moment.

While taking the edge off of your threat response to stress and self-doubt is very helpful, often these same responses come up over and over again, or you may find yourself in the grip of an unyielding or highly maladaptive reaction.

For example, have you ever felt yourself lying awake at night, ruminating over some issue for hours, or stewing on something for days (or months or years)? Or maybe you've felt intensely hostile toward or deeply resentful of someone.

When this happens, it is an invitation to go to Step 2—to do the deeper work to extract the teeth out of the underlying threat and triggers of stress and self-doubt that are driving your reactive responses in the first place.

In **Step 2: Appraising and Reappraising Stress and Self-Doubt,** you'll explore how you can shift your perceptions about stress and self-doubt themselves, as well as neutralize their underlying triggers that may well have their hooks in you. You'll begin to appreciate how stress and self-doubt can also be assets and feel more secure and confident, even when facing the most challenging circumstances.

If I were to ask you what causes most of the stress in your life—the events that happen or your perceptions around the events—what would you say?

Most answer that their perceptions cause the stress. They're right—and it's great news. If it were the events, we'd be toast! While we may not have much control over many of the events in our lives and cannot change what has happened in the past, we have much more control over our perceptions and can choose to change them at any time.

Step 2 teaches you how to appraise (recognize) what is specifically triggering your stress and self-doubt and then how to reappraise these triggers (view them differently) so that you are less threatened or bothered by them.

To do this, you will be using four key questions that have been adapted from a powerful, proven cognitive behavioral approach to reframe the perceptions that cause much of your stress and self-doubt to begin with.[6]

Also, merely having stress or self-doubt may trigger more stress or self-doubt. So in addition to helping you reframe your triggers of stress and self-doubt, this step will also help you reframe the way you view stress and self-doubt themselves—which can transform your threat responses into challenge and tend-and-befriend responses. Once you do so, I promise you'll never look at stress and self-doubt quite the same way again (they may even put a little spring in your step).

The power of reappraisal comes from the shifts in mental activity it creates in your brain. In research where individuals reappraise a stressful perception (for example, by reframing their interpretation of an initially disturbing picture while their brains are being scanned with an MRI), researchers found that doing so activates their PFC and decreases their limbic reactivity.[7] Reappraisal is also associated with less negative emotion, better social functioning, and greater psychological well-being.[8]

In other words, when you learn to view events in a new way, you are less likely to be stressed by them.

Further, individuals who scored high on a test of mindfulness were the most skilled at reappraisal, in terms of activating their PFC and deactivating their amygdala.[9] Mindfulness provides you with the flexibility to step back and objectively view your thoughts, which provides you with the opportunity to shift your perspective in a way that serves you and others better. (If you are interested in reading more about how mindfulness facilitates reappraisal, see an extensive review sponsored by the National Institutes of Health.[10])

Given these benefits of mindfulness, Step 2 integrates two mindfulness practices: one that supports your reappraisal and another that cultivates a sense of resiliency and self-compassion around your experience of stress and self-doubt.

In sum, what you gain from Steps 1 and 2 are powerful skills and practices that increase your capacity to navigate through stress and self-doubt. Once you've shifted away from a reactive mindset, you have established the sense of safety and stability you need to begin shifting toward a creative mindset, which brings us to the next step.

How would your life change if you had a clear process to fully connect with your passion and purpose and create the life you want?

**Step 3: Cultivating Creativity** teaches you how to identify your core values and strengths, guided by a list of factors that overlap with the research revealing the keys to a "flourishing" life.[11]

You then learn how to incorporate your specific values and strengths into a step-by-step process that helps you further clarify your life vision, implement strategies, and manifest specific and measurable results in your health, relationships, and productivity.

Step 3 also teaches you mindfulness practices to enhance your wellness and vitality, connect more deeply with yourself and others, and become more creative and impactful while serving at home and at work.

As mentioned in the last chapter, eight weeks of mindfulness practice actually changes your brain, increasing your left prefrontal brain activity relative to your right. This correlates with a relative decrease in threat-related avoidant behavior and an increase in positive emotions, engaging behavior, and a challenge response to stressful situations.[12]

What you gain from this step is a powerful process to help you create a flourishing life, characterized by health and vitality, rich and meaningful relationships, and a greater sense of significance in what you do— expanding your resources to cope and become even more resilient in the demands you face.

There's a remaining challenge, however: while Steps 1 and 2 help you recover from stress and self-doubt and Step 3 helps you focus on what is truly important in your life, stress and self-doubt will still continually arise to throw you off track—which brings us to Step 4.

**Step 4: Catalyzing Growth** provides you with a life-changing practice that engages your deepest source of inspiration to stay aligned moment by moment with what's truly important in your life, especially when stress and self-doubt threaten to derail you. Rather than being frequently derailed by automatic negative thoughts (also known as ANTs),[13] you'll be able to more consciously construct positive thoughts. You'll experience a whole new way of thinking that will energize all aspects of your life.

Much of our experience and behavior relates to our internal dialogue that reinforces the way we perceive the world. Under stress, we tend to focus on questions like, "What's wrong with me?" or "What's wrong with other people?" This habit can hardwire in self-doubt or an attitude of cynicism, which can deplete your resources to deal with challenges. It can drive the flow of energy in your brain into your survival circuits, drain the joy out of your life, and act as kryptonite to your power as a leader.

Step 4 teaches you a powerful, four-step process to create a more inspired internal dialogue, which taps your inner resources by enabling you to mindfully ask better questions, find better answers, make wiser decisions, and take action that's more aligned with your core values and vision for your flourishing life.

Remember, what you give attention to grows. The habit of a more mindful and productive internal dialogue, as you stay aligned with your source of inspiration, drives the flow of energy into your brain circuits that cultivates your sense of significance and rewires your brain for greater resiliency. Consequently, the painful feelings of stress and self-doubt subside. This, coupled with a deeper sense of meaning, purpose, and well-being, facilitates a life of greater joy, impact, and fulfillment!

Therefore, Step 4 is the most important step of all. In addition to aligning yourself with your source of inspiration, the process of asking good questions and finding, evaluating, and applying your inspired answers helps you to not only catalyze your work and growth in Steps 1, 2, and 3, but inspire this process in those you lead, too.

## In Summary

The 4 in 4 Framework integrates brain science, cognitive behavioral therapy, positive psychology, and mindfulness to provide you with practical steps to leverage stress and self-doubt as positive fuel for your life and align yourself with what's truly important. It empowers you to optimize your health, relationships, and productivity; become more resilient; and achieve your peak performance.

But it also does something more. I mentioned earlier that if you stick with mindfulness practice for at least eight weeks, studies suggest you can *rewire and reshape your brain.* You can engage in *neuroplastic transformation.*

In other words, with the skills you learn in the 4 in 4 Framework, not only will you be able to achieve your peak performance, but you may also expand your inner resources to shift your performance versus stress curve up and to the right, so that you can achieve even higher levels of performance with a greater capacity to handle stress!

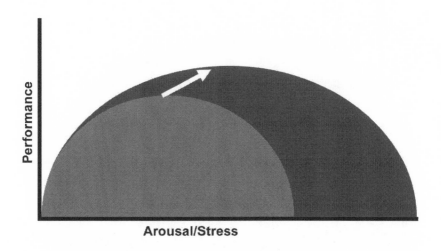

*Figure 4.5. How the 4 in 4 Framework Expands Your Capacity for Peak Performance*

So let's get to it. Next, in part 2, you'll discover how to gain greater mastery of each step of the 4 in 4 Framework and lead well from within. Then, in part 3, you'll learn how to apply this framework to lead well with others to make a bigger difference at work, at home, and in the world!

# Part 2

Applying the 4 in 4 Framework
to Lead Well from Within

# CHAPTER 5

# Step 1: Recognizing and Managing Reactivity

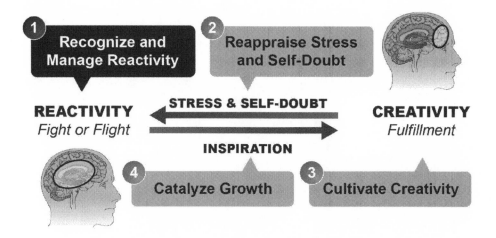

The 4 in 4 Framework is not only a program that I teach, but thankfully also practice daily. It has also saved me from imploding in a number of high-stakes situations and has enabled me to continually grow as a person and as a leader.

To introduce you to Step 1, and at the risk of being vulnerable again, I'd like to share a story illustrating how you can start working the framework into your daily life to turn overwhelming stress and anxiety into productive energy.

A few years ago, I was about to begin a ten-month journey of monthly meetings on the 4 in 4 Framework to Engage Conscious Leadership with a senior leadership team of one of the leading organizations in San Diego. In perfect irony, I was about to become the case study for the very topic I was about to teach.

My introductory session had been scheduled at the end of a workshop day with another speaker, and I'd been invited to attend her session so I could create a seamless transition into the work I'd be sharing.

The day had begun with anticipation. But as we approached three o'clock, the time I was scheduled to begin, I could see the group was tired and getting a bit restless. With my energy also flagging and my internal resources diminished, I grappled with how to best transition the group into a place of personal reflection in preparation for our work together. Unfortunately, apart from stirrings of unsettling self-doubt, the inspiration I was seeking was nowhere to be found.

At three o'clock sharp, I stood up and began my presentation. As I looked around to connect with my audience, the group seemed disengaged. This presentation was far more demanding than I'd imagined. A couple of leaders were typing on their phones, and the energy of the room felt completely flat. As my fears began to heighten, my initial enthusiasm shifted towards anxiety. I felt threatened. It was the beginning of a long journey together, and instead of establishing credibility and trust, I became afraid that I could lose the group at the outset.

Then, after more than fifteen hundred presentations and fifteen years of speaking—something that I just love doing—I began to experience sensations I had never before experienced.

I got cotton-mouth. My mouth became so dry I began to have difficulty speaking. All the moisture from my mouth seemed to have transferred itself to my forehead, armpits, and palms, which were now sweating profusely. My heart raced, and I felt sick to my stomach. Worst of all, my brain began to scramble. I struggled to remember which slides were coming next.

I knew I was failing and about to blow it. Forget about imagining the bad things that could happen. My worst-case scenario was happening right now. The wheels were coming off. Every fiber of my being wanted to bolt out of the room.

Fatigued and low on blood sugar, my trusty PFC, usually so helpful in regulating my limbic system, had been hijacked by my raging amygdala and was no match for it.

Again, what saved me from complete disaster was my years spent working the 4 in 4 Framework—and Step 1 in particular.

With the sliver of my PFC that remained online, I recognized I was feeling threatened and had "gone limbic." I began to tap into some of my internal resources. I paused and took three deep breaths. Silently, I mindfully repeated, "fear, fear," to myself. Simply naming my experience took some of the edge off my panic.

I could see how I needed to clear my head further, to regain more access to my PFC, further calm myself, and transform my stress into something useful. At fifteen minutes into the presentation, I announced to the group that I was having a difficult time and needed to take a ten-minute break to gather myself.

Where I had failed to grab their attention initially, my abrupt and unprecedented announcement succeeded in getting their attention, breaking the lull of energy in the room. In its place emerged an awkward silence, with leaders straightening up, looking befuddled, and gesturing to each other, "What's going on?"

As everyone got up to leave, one of the senior VPs approached me with empathy and compassion, saying, "I can see how you are struggling. Is there anything I can do to support you?"

I felt the pull of my pride and temptation to say, "It's OK. I'll be fine." But instead I found sufficient presence of mind to lean in to my tend-and-befriend stress response and received her gracious offering by saying, "Thanks—just give me a hug."

As we hugged heart to heart for a few seconds, I could feel my anxious sensations calm further as my body released oxytocin and my stress hormones continued to fall.

I grabbed a bottle of water and a snack and stepped outside to find further comfort under the blue sky. Meanwhile, I mindfully continued to observe and silently name some of my thoughts, feelings, and sensations, bringing a quality of kindness and self-compassion to my experience.

As I found a place of calm, I leaned in further to the challenge with a light touch of curiosity and silently asked for guidance about how I could best serve the group when I returned to the room. The answer arrived in a flash. I could offer myself up as a case study to teach the leaders about the stress response and how to recognize and take the edge off their reactivity.

Grateful and relieved for this clarity, I stepped back inside to reconnect with the group. I began by apologizing for how my stress had got the better of me and explained that I needed a few minutes to regain a sense of clarity so I could better serve them.

I then shared my next slide and how by "coincidence" I was about to teach them the relationship between stress and performance. Now I stood humbled before them as Exhibit A in this lesson.

I went over to the flipchart and redrew the stress versus performance curve that was now up on the slide, putting a big "X" on the curve to represent where I had been at the height of my anxiety (see figure 5.1 below).

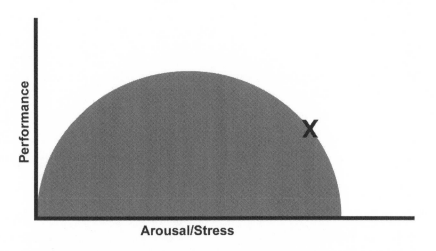

*Figure 5.1: Stress and Performance Curve with "X" at Height of Anxiety*

I explained how I'd felt threatened by overwhelming stress and self-doubt as I grappled for a way to open my presentation in a way that would best serve them and how my resulting anxiety had taken me over the peak of my curve and greatly impacted my teaching performance.

We discussed the key components and functions of the brain and how my amygdala had hijacked my PFC, which had scrambled my ability to think clearly and connect authentically with them. I then shared the sensations, thoughts, and feelings I had experienced and asked if they could remember a time when they, too, felt stressed and could relate. I invited them to reflect on their own experiences with reactivity and what they would most like to get out of the program. This "live demonstration" turned things around, as each person fully engaged in the conversation that followed.

After the session, one of the leaders, a soft-spoken woman, came up to me and shared how she had been crippled by stage fright. She expressed how knowing that she was not alone and could learn to not only better recognize her reactivity but also do something about it made her feel as if a big weight had been lifted off her shoulders.

Another leader then invited me to join the group to debrief in the bar, where I was pressed on whether I strategically staged my anxiety attack to set up our lesson in reactivity. I assured them this moment had not been planned and was very real.

As I drove home feeling raw, I reflected on what had happened in the session. I remembered praying at the outset for inspiration on how to best serve the group with something relevant to facilitate their self-reflection around reactivity. To this day, I still feel awe at what ultimately arrived.

I hope this story also serves you as we further explore how you can leverage this first step in the 4 in 4 Framework to recognize and take the edge off your reactivity whenever it arises.

## Recognizing Your Reactive Responses

As we discussed in part 1, we experience *stress* whenever something we care about is at stake (including our own self-worth, which we will talk more about in the next chapter). We can respond to stress in at least three different ways: with a *threat response* (where we fight or flee in response to a stressor we fear may overwhelm the resources we have to cope), a *challenge response* (where we feel we have sufficient resources to cope and can leverage our stress-related energy to meet the challenge at hand), or a *tend-and-befriend response* (where we reach out and connect to others around us for increased support and resources to handle the challenge).

When our threat response is activated and we are unaware of it, we can get lost in a spiral of reactivity—a dynamic interplay between our physiological responses, thoughts, feelings, and behaviors.

For example, imagine your threat response is triggered by an offer to speak in public. You feel stressed, doubt your ability, and think about how you could fail and embarrass yourself in front of the audience. The thought of it triggers a physiological response in which your heart beats faster and you sense a pit in your stomach. In this context, you are aware you are feeling afraid, and you take flight by turning down the offer to speak. While this escape provides you a feeling of relief, another part of you feels disappointed in yourself because you were unable to step up.

Or let's say one of your colleagues painfully criticizes you in a meeting. You feel betrayed and immediately sense tightness in your body; your fists clench beneath the table, and you can feel your blood boiling in anger. You think, "What an asshole!" To get even, you find yourself blurting out something sensitive your colleague shared with you in confidence a few days earlier. The moment you do so, you regret what you said and feel ashamed and embarrassed. You stay silent for the rest of the meeting, feeling anxious.

Each of these examples show how reactive sensations, thoughts, and feelings weave together to drive fight-or-flight-related behaviors that can further influence additional sensations, thoughts, and feelings.

Many of your reactive responses are reflexive and subconscious. They represent well-grooved patterns—your reactive signature—which may also indicate blind spots in your awareness. While your reactivity may at times be highly adaptive, such as when you or a loved one are physically or psychologically threatened, at other times this lack of awareness and your reflexive responses may cause you to overreact out of proportion to the situation at hand, which can lead you to say or do things that do more harm than good. In other words, you may find yourself falling down the right side of the stress and performance curve (see figure 5.1) into a place of high stress and low performance—just as I did during my presentation.

The benefit of doing the spadework to recognize your patterns of reactivity is that you can take the edge off your reactive responses earlier, right when they occur. Instead of your reactivity leading you to say or do things you may regret, becoming more aware and *recognizing* your reactivity enables you to lead well from within, so you can modify your behavior before you overstep your bounds and do harm to yourself or others. Or, if you have already exploded in a reactive outburst, you can quickly regain a sense of control and find clarity to change course and take your next best step forward.

The spirit of this spadework sits on the foundation of mindfulness, your ability to observe whatever you are experiencing with openness, curiosity, and kindness. Think of yourself as a social anthropologist or archeologist, compassionately unearthing your subconscious responses, approaching the dig with a fascination for what you'll find.

Every discovery you make is one less response that has the power to run you. As you expand your awareness of your reactivity, your influence over your threat response will grow, so you can leverage it more adaptively to serve you well. In fact, when you bring mindful awareness to your threat response, you can learn how to leverage your stress energy as a resource and slingshot it into the other two responses of challenge and tend-and-befriend, which we'll discuss further in the next chapter. You can also learn to use your stress as fuel for inspiration to shift from reactivity to creativity.

However, the first step is to recognize and manage your reactivity, before you can transform it. So let's get started by digging for your reactive patterns in your sensations, thoughts, feelings, and behaviors.

## Recognizing Your Reactive Sensations

As best you can, bring to mind as vividly as possible the most frightening scenario you possibly can, something that triggers tremendous stress or self-doubt in you and would drive you into a threat response—such as the example I shared at the beginning of the chapter. Now, close your eyes and notice the physical sensations you feel in your body.

What did you just sense?

The patterns of reactive sensations you feel are predictable; they simply represent your body moving from a physiological state of "rest and digest" to one of "fight-or-flight." You experience the same physical responses to perceived threats whether they're physical or psychological.

As we discussed in chapter 2, in your "rest and digest" state, your parasympathetic and sympathetic parts of your automatic nervous system (your brake and accelerator) are gently balanced. In "fight or flight," you step on the gas, rapidly shifting your system into hyperdrive and instantly shifting all available internal resources towards life-saving functions. What you most need in the moment to save your life is to efficiently pump well-oxygenated blood to your large muscles to fight your attacker or get out of harm's way.

In this moment, your digestive system is nonessential and shuts down. Consequently, you may feel a dry mouth (the cotton-mouth I felt at the beginning of my anxiety attack) or a pit in your stomach. Just as threatened animals are primed to drop their load to move faster, you may also feel an urge to go to the bathroom.

At the same time, you may feel your heart racing and notice your breathing is rapid and shallow. Your body is doing its job to provide an ample flow of well-oxygenated blood to your muscles, which may feel tighter as they become primed for action. You may notice the muscles of your back and neck tense up, your fists clench, and your jaw tightens (to instinctively protect you from a punch to the face that may cause a jaw fracture, which would have been catastrophic in prehistoric times).

On high alert, you may also notice that all of your senses feel heightened. You may be hyperfocused or experience "tunnel vision," or your brain may feel scrambled or even go completely blank. This is not a moment for abstract thinking. You are not counting tiger stripes or thinking about the difficult childhood your attacker may have had. Your instinctive reactions are solely focused on getting you out of there.

Can you relate to these reactive sensations? Can you think of others?

Be reassured that none of your reactive sensations are flaws. In fact, be thankful: they reflect your perfectly designed physiological response that evolved to protect you from harm. Did you also notice how quickly these responses were triggered when you thought about your stressor? You can be thankful for that, too. Our fight-or-flight responses evolved for speed. Any slower, and you could be done for when it really counts.

Keep familiarizing yourself with your reactive sensations. See if you can also identify the first inkling of your reactive sensations. It may be your earliest indication that something is threatening you, perhaps even before you consciously recognize what's happening. The earlier you can recognize your physical reactive sensations, the more control you will have in further assessing whether the situation at hand truly represents a threat and your ability to respond well to it.

## Recognizing Your Reactive Thoughts

Identifying your reactive thoughts can be a little tricky. Some of your thoughts are triggers for the stress response, and some represent the stress response itself. Our difficulty in differentiating which is which may result from the challenge we have in defining stress to begin with. As mentioned in chapter 2, Hans Selye defined stress as "the non-specific response of the body to any demand for change."[1] *Merriam-Webster* defines it as "a state of mental tension and worry."[2] In 1951, a physician elegantly expressed this confusion, writing in the *British Medical Journal* that "stress, in addition to being itself, was also the cause of itself, and the result of itself."[3]

Given that your reactive thoughts may both be a trigger and a manifestation of your stress response, we will simply refer to all these thoughts as stress-related thinking.

Further, as we've also mentioned, Kelly McGonigal defines stress as "what arises when something you care about is at stake."[4] This definition indicates that the thoughts and mindset you have about stress have a big impact on your response to it. When you think stress is the enemy, you are more likely to become stressed about being stressed and maintain an ongoing threat response. Alternatively, when you recognize that stress is also an asset that can mobilize your energy and internal resources to address what you most care about, you will more likely engage in a challenge or tend-and-befriend response. (We'll be exploring this further in the next chapter as part of Step 2: Reappraising Stress and Self-Doubt.) For now, it's important to simply learn how to recognize your reactive thoughts and discern whether they may reflect a threat response in the face of stress or self-doubt, or a challenge or tend-and-befriend response instead.

If you're thinking fight-or-flight-related thoughts, such as "I want to make that person suffer!" or "I'm not good enough; I can't do this; I'm not even going to try; I'm done with this," you're most likely experiencing a threat response and reactive thinking.

On the other hand, thoughts such as "This is hard, but let me see if I can figure out how to do it" or "Who can I best turn to for support?" indicate challenge and tend-and-befriend responses.

The thoughts you have can also predispose you to a cascade of threat-related thinking. Some thoughts are so big that they serve as meta-frames for the rest of your thinking, such as the way you contextualize your emotions and react to events. For example, Einstein captured one of the biggest thoughts we can have when he said, "The most important decision we make is whether we believe we live in a friendly or hostile universe."[5]

Imagine walking into a cocktail party alone, where you don't know anyone. You feel a bit amped up. Your heart is beating faster and your senses are heightened. If you think you live in a hostile universe, you will likely feel more threatened, interpret this "amped up" emotion as fear, be more likely to judge people negatively, grit your teeth and bear it, and nervously stand off to the side. On the outside, your demeanor (including the fearful microexpressions on your face) conveys to a stranger that you are not safe to approach, which keeps people away and reinforces the notion you are in an unfriendly environment. To overcome this and steady your nerves, you may head straight to the cash bar for a few stiff drinks.

Alternatively, if you think you live in a friendly universe, you will likely interpret your "amped up" emotion as excitement, think of others positively, have an open and inviting expression on your face and in your voice, and warmly approach people to introduce yourself.

Memories of past experiences can feed into your meta-frames, too. Neglect or abuse, or powerful rejection or loss, can lead you to decide that you indeed do live a hostile or threatening universe. Painful emotional memories, stored by the amygdala, can lead you to become hypervigilant in scanning for danger and lower your threshold for triggers of threat responses.

When stress and self-doubt do trigger a threat response, reactive thinking tends to fall into one of four buckets:

1. All the bad things that could happen
2. The regrets of your past
3. What's wrong with you
4. What's wrong with other people

As mentioned in chapter 2, these thoughts reflect the ruminative thinking of your default mode network, which continuously processes your social interactions. You may experience this as your inner critic of both yourself and others.

Each of these four buckets has many variations. See if you can relate to any of them.

For example, in thinking about *all the bad things that could happen,* you may find yourself fearing, "What if . . ." followed by the worst-case scenario. Or you may say, "This *always* happens," creating a myth of predictability that may give you an illusion of control. You may then find yourself taking flight from any possible loss of control, saying, "There's just no way I'm going to do this." Or you may say, "This always happens to me," leading you to feel like a victim and withdraw from others.

The *regrets of your past* tend to show up as a host of "if only" thoughts. "If only I hadn't made such a stupid investment, I'd be much more in control of my finances"; "If only I had not said that, we'd still be together"; "If only I hadn't made such a mess of things . . ." This kind of thinking often leads to painful self-judgment and feeling threatened as we beat up on ourselves. Sometimes our regrets can feel so threatening that we may take flight from them by denying or repressing them all together.

Thoughts about *"what's wrong with me"* are associated with a host of self-judgmental and self-critical thoughts: "I'm a failure"; "I'm an imposter"; "I'm no good"; "It's all my fault"; and "I'm worthless" are just a few. We may also fight to allay this threat and gain a sense of internal control with a litany of "shoulds" and "musts," as well as thoughts about how to prove self-worth. These may include thoughts like, "I should be further along by now," or "I must do as others say to fit in." The fight to prove self-worth is often also associated with fantasies about success, money, fame, and power.

Likewise, thoughts about *what's wrong with others* manifest as a stream of judgment and criticism of people around us. We fight for control or to prove self-worth by thinking about how to dominate or control others or how we are better than they are. We may blame others or fantasize how we can get back at them. Or we may take flight from our own self-doubt by projecting our inadequacies on others: "It's not my problem; it's theirs." If you find yourself thinking that *everyone* around you is a problem, it may be a good tip off that *you* are having a problem with reactivity. If you notice you seem to be focusing a lot on what's wrong with everyone else, also consider whether you are becoming more cynical. Cynicism may tip you off to an even bigger challenge at hand.

Recall that cynicism, along with emotional exhaustion and a reduced sense of accomplishment, is one of the three dimensions of burnout. If you notice your cynical thoughts about others are coupled with thoughts about how exhausted you are and self-doubt about being ineffective and not doing anything significant with your life, you may be experiencing the more advanced threat response to stress: burnout.

Note also that your reactive thoughts do not stand in isolation. They typically involve your physiological responses and give rise to or influence your emotions, which we'll discuss next.

## Recognizing Your Reactive Emotions and Feelings

The word *emotion* is derived from the French words *emouvoir* ("to stir up") and *esmovoir* ("to set in motion").[6] Among numerous theories about how emotions stir you up and set things in motion, the common thread is that emotions are a complex psychological state, triggered by a stimulus, that includes a physiological response, interpretations of the event, facial and vocal expressions, and a behavioral response. *Feelings* are your subjective experience of your emotions.[7]

According to Darwin, who in addition to his classic text on evolution also wrote *The Expression of the Emotions in Man and Animals,* the primary purpose of emotions is to ensure our survival and enhance nonverbal communication to bind us together for the benefit of our species.[8] For example, a look of disgust or fear from the members of your clan would have warned you not to eat something toxic or of impending danger.

In 1972, Paul Ekman, a psychologist and the leading authority on the facial expression of emotion, recognized a "big six" of basic emotions: fear, disgust, anger, surprise, happiness, and sadness. With flashcards of these emotions in hand and corresponding stories to match them, he traveled to meet Fore tribesmen, isolated from the outside world in a remote area of Papua New Guinea. Both adults and children of the tribe were able to recognize each of these emotions, even though the flashcard pictures were of Westerners they had never seen before.[9]

Within these "big six" categories and beyond, our emotions also have valence. They move us to act, typically driving us away from pain and towards pleasure. In 1980, James Russell, a professor of psychology at Boston College, created a helpful four-quadrant map of emotions, plotting the valence of displeasure versus pleasure against the level of arousal.[10] Likewise, we can plot a four-quadrant map of reactivity and creativity versus high and low levels of arousal that can help you more easily recognize your reactive and creative emotions. This can also help you to identify how your emotions are related to threat or challenge or tend-and-befriend responses.

Think for a moment how you typically feel when you experience the threat of stress or self-doubt. For example, when you have a high-energy reaction to the threat of stress or self-doubt, what are some of the emotions you feel? Conversely, when you have a low-energy reaction to these triggers, what emotions do you feel?

Now consider the emotions you tend to feel when you engage stress with a challenge or tend-and-befriend response or are in a creative frame of mind. How do you feel when your arousal is low and when your arousal is high?

Here's how some of the reactive and creative emotions map out, in figure 5.2 below.

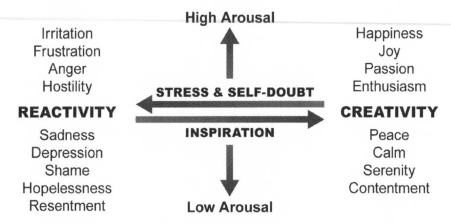

*Figure 5.2. Four-Quadrant Map of High-Arousal and Low-Arousal Reactive and Creative Emotions*

High-arousal reactive emotions tend to be our "fight" emotions, which may prompt us to strike out. These emotions include irritation, frustration, and anger. Anger comes in different shades and degrees of response, including the extremes of hostility and "whining." My dear friend Lee Lipsenthal, a leader in the world of physician well-being, used to say, "Whining is anger coming through a small hole!"

Low-arousal reactive emotions tend to be our "flight" emotions, which lead us to withdraw. Examples of these emotions include sadness, depression, shame, hopelessness, and resentment.

Low-arousal creative emotions, which at times may be associated with the tend-and-befriend response, include the soothing emotions of peace, calm, serenity, and contentment.

High-arousal creative emotions, which can also include the tend-and-befriend responses, may also be associated with the challenge response. Examples of these highly engaging emotions are happiness, joy, passion, and enthusiasm.

Can you think of other emotions that you can plot in each of these quadrants?

Because your reactive emotions are powerful drivers of what you do, more fully recognizing them as they occur can let you know when you are experiencing a threat response and perhaps keep you from doing or saying something you may regret—which brings us to reactive behaviors.

## Recognizing Your Reactive Behaviors

When we discussed the Leadership Circle Assessment in chapter 1, we learned that, based on Karen Horney's work, leaders may react in one of three ways when their threat response is triggered: they can become *controlling, protecting,* or overly *compliant.*[11]

In the *controlling* dimension, leaders "move against" people with "fight" behaviors. They fight for control, power, and/or to prove self-worth, which can show up as an autocratic style of leadership with a tendency to be domineering, aggressive, forceful, and invulnerable. Controlling leaders lead by ego and intimidation. They are driven to get ahead, primarily for personal gain. Instead of being in service to something larger than themselves, they primarily serve themselves. They fiercely protect the kingdom they have created. They micromanage and tend not to trust others. This fight for control also shows up as perfectionism, or the need to drive flawless and faultless outcomes and to meet standards beyond reproach in order to feel secure and worthy as an individual.

In the *complying* dimension, leaders display another form of "fight" behaviors. They "move toward" people, fighting for their approval to gain a sense of self-worth and security. Often, it is at the expense of what they really want (in this way, you could also say they are taking "flight" from the potential disapproval of others that may trigger their self-doubt). These leaders are driven to please others in order to be liked and accepted. They are reluctant to rock the boat, and they say things they think others want to hear. They can be wishy-washy, passive, and indecisive. At the same time, they can be rigid and conservative in following the rules so as to meet all expectations and not disappoint anyone.

In the *protecting* dimension, leaders take "flight" by "moving away" from others. These leaders can appear inaccessible, aloof, emotionally distant, and uncaring. At the same time, they can also fight to prove self-worth with arrogance, intellectual domination, cynicism, and being highly judgmental and critical of others.

Fight-or-flight behaviors can also show up in many other areas of our lives, such as the fight for money and material possessions or the fight for beauty through eating disorders or cosmetic surgery. In sports, we see it as the need to win at all costs, such as by using performance-enhancing drugs, fighting with opponents, or taking flight from the field of play as a sore loser. We may also take flight from stress and self-doubt with addictive behaviors, such as watching TV, surfing the Internet, viewing porn, eating comfort food, shopping, gambling, smoking cigarettes, taking drugs, and drinking alcohol. In religion, the fight for self-worth seeks to leverage a higher power as a source for control, revealing itself as a self-righteous, "holier-than-thou" attitude, fundamentalism, or at the extreme, holy war and ethnic cleansing.

Can you also think of other ways fight-or-flight behaviors show up in the world?

Now reflect on how fight-or-flight behaviors show up in *your* life. Can you relate to some of the behaviors mentioned above?

Since some may represent blind spots, identifying your reactive behaviors may require a bit of digging. Just a reminder: in the spirit of mindfulness, this is self-compassionate work. Many of our fight-or-flight behaviors were modeled by our parents. Some of these behaviors, such as addictions, may have a genetic component. Our behaviors have also been reinforced by other influential people, such as caregivers, grandparents, siblings, teachers, or friends.

In fact, some of our defenses (often our dominant ones) are subconscious because they have been "inherited" and then disavowed. Many years ago, a friend offered to take me through a guided imagery. I was both curious and completely naive about the process. She asked me to imagine myself traveling back to my home during my childhood. I closed my eyes and, drifting back in time, saw myself standing on our family's veranda in a golden glow with my proud parents looking on. Initially, I felt warmth at seeing this pure, wide-eyed child, but I was soon jarred when I noticed that I was standing in the center of the framing struts of a teepee. Most remarkably, the struts were sprayed with concrete.

At first, I couldn't fathom where this image originated. I began to consider its symbolism and was startled. I realized that I was looking at one of my defense mechanisms: a vulnerable child who walls himself off from life's threats by spraying concrete. It explained why in times of stress I tend to feel numb and disconnected.

This particular defense did not sit comfortably with me. I like to think of myself as a sensitive, intuitive, and passionate person who lives life to the fullest. I did not like to think of myself as walled off, numb, and disconnected.

I strained to think why I was so resistant to this type of defense, and I realized it was the defense my father employed. I remembered that when my father felt stressed out, he walled himself off by withdrawing emotionally. I also remembered how my mother shared with me the pain she felt when Dad withdrew from us, and I promised myself that I would never withdraw from the world and those I cared about.

However, as we grow up, we inevitably model our caregivers' behaviors, including their defenses. Thus, when I needed to employ defense mechanisms, I naturally employed those I had learned—even the ones I was determined not to use. And since I had promised myself that I would not wall myself off from others, I had no choice but to deny this behavior as a part of myself.

The medical literature provides support for the "inheritance" of defenses. For example, children of alcoholics are predisposed to this same addiction. Research suggests that genes are responsible for about half of the risk for alcoholism.[12] The other half relates to the environmental exposure, part of which may include how these defenses are passed on psychologically. For example, children of alcoholic parents may become determined not to repeat these behaviors, yet some unavoidably learn these behaviors and begin to drink heavily. Having promised themselves that they would never drink like their parents, they then deny this behavior as being a part of themselves, saying things like, "I don't drink that much. I'm certainly nothing like my parents."

The consequence of being unaware of our defenses is that we cannot exercise control over them or modify them. Thus, they trap us. Moreover, when we disavow the defenses we have learned from our parents and pass them on to our offspring, who likewise disavow them and pass them on to theirs, they can trap future generations as well.

Take a moment to reflect on how the most influential people in your life growing up reacted when they experienced stress and self-doubt. Perhaps take out a notepad and write down the name of each person, such as your mother, father, or other caregivers, and list their reactions below their names. Were they judgmental, perfectionistic, controlling, pleasing, or passive? Did they strive to keep up appearances, drink, use drugs, or shop or work compulsively?

Then, take a look at the list of their reactive behaviors and reflect on yours. Ask yourself, *In what ways do I fight and take flight in response to stress and self-doubt?* See if you can identify with any patterns of defensive behaviors that you have listed (especially the ones you may resist acknowledging). Also reflect on any other ways you tend to fight and take flight when you react to feeling stressed or insecure.

By shining the light of compassionate awareness on the reactive behaviors that previously lay in your blind spots, you have the opportunity to modify your behaviors and break the cycle of passing these disavowed behaviors from generation to generation.

Keep reflecting on the various ways you react. The more you are able to recognize your reactive sensations, thoughts, feelings, and behaviors, with openness, curiosity and kindness, the more influence you have over them. With awareness, instead of being led astray by your reactions, you are then well positioned to ask a key question to help you best respond to your reactions, rather than being led astray by them.

## The Key Question

Remember, the threat response and the reactivity it triggers is often highly adaptive. It's hard to argue with hundreds of thousands of years of evolution where it has effectively protected us from harm. Fighting or taking flight may well be what's most needed when someone truly threatens you or your loved ones. Further, many reactive emotions can serve us well. Anger and indignation can serve as a powerful force in standing up to injustice and oppression. Feelings of sadness over a loss speak to the importance of our heartfelt connections. Even self-doubt itself in our social interactions can protect us from social faux pas that could weaken our ties to our loved ones and communities.

The Leadership Circle also points out that Karen Horney's controlling, protecting, and complying behaviors have their benefits, too.

The controlling dimension can drive action and get results, especially in crisis situations such as medical emergencies or military combat. The quest to be perfect can also lead to setting high standards, performing with excellence, and seeking continuous improvement.

The protecting dimension, where one may be distant, rational, or aloof, offers the gift of remaining detached, being more discerning, and taking a wider view on difficult situations. This may be especially helpful when a team is becoming highly emotional and more balanced decisions based on facts and data are needed.

The complying dimension's strength is responsiveness to the needs of others, which engenders reliability, loyalty, and serving others well.

Of course, any of these dimensions can be damaging, too. Leaders who are controlling can become overly aggressive and drive themselves and others into burnout. Those who are protecting can be uncaring, arrogant, demeaning, and dismissive of others and drive the soul out of a culture. And leaders who are overly compliant may be unable to effectively redirect their team when things go off track, limiting their creative potential to make a meaningful contribution and becoming passive-aggressive instead.

Also note that some reactive responses are never adaptive. For example, hostility, which has been linked to both the initiation and progression of heart disease, not only hurts others but you as well.[13]

Likewise, resentment eats at you from the inside out. It's said that "resentment is like drinking poison hoping the other person will die!" In the community of Alcoholics Anonymous, resentment is considered the most dangerous emotion of all in predicting who will likely drink again.[14]

Also, remember that we have two other stress responses besides the threat response: the challenge and the tend-and-befriend responses. They are particularly adaptive in times of stress, as they help us to lean in to growth and learning and find social support.

The point is that none of our stress responses are bad in and of themselves. To lead well from within, your task is to determine whether your response is most adaptive in your current situation.

So when you find yourself experiencing stress or self-doubt, it's helpful to first reflect on whether your collective sensations, thoughts, feelings, and behaviors are manifesting as a threat (reactivity), as a challenge (creativity), or as a motivation to find helpful support (creativity).

Then, if you sense you are becoming reactive, the big question is, *In this moment, is my reactivity likely to do me and others more harm than good?*

If you sense your reactivity is likely to lead to more harm than good, consider an invitation to take the next steps to manage it.

## Four Steps to Manage Reactivity

To lead well from within, when your reactive responses may cause more harm than good, you want to slow things down by effectively tapping your brain's "brake" (your parasympathetic nervous system), so you can bring your PFC back online, soothe your reactivity, and be more proactive in your response.

The following four steps enable you to do so.

### Step 1: Pause.

Pausing gives you time for your PFC to catch up and come back online, especially if it's been hijacked by your amygdala. Because pausing inherently heightens your awareness, it begins to open a gap between stimulus and response, within which you can proactively choose your response.

So the first step is to simply pause, allowing yourself to mindfully be with whatever sensations, thoughts, and feelings you are experiencing. As best you can, release any resistance and relax into whatever you are experiencing with a sense of openness, curiosity, and kindness.

### Step 2: Take three heart-centered, soft-belly breaths.

Breathing with a soft belly helps activate your parasympathetic nervous system (PNS), the "brake" that regulates your revved-up sympathetic drive.

One of the largest PNS nerves in the body is the vagus nerve, which begins in your brain stem and branches off to stimulate major internal organs, such as your heart, gut, and lungs. It also stimulates contraction of the diaphragm. So when you breathe in and out with a full and relaxed excursion of the diaphragm (i.e., with a "soft belly"), you can increase activity in your PNS.

You can also intensify the calming effect of your soft-belly breathing by breathing out with a more prolonged exhalation, as if you were breathing out slowly through a straw. For example, you would breathe in for a five-second count and breathe out for an eight-second count.[15]

Additionally, imagining that you are breathing through the center of your heart can comingle a sense of self-compassion with your breathing. The organization HeartMath has shown that breathing through your heart center like this while thinking about someone you care about or a peaceful place decreases stress and improves cognitive performance, emotional balance, and mental clarity.[16]

Go ahead and experiment right now with taking three heart-centered, soft-belly breaths—five seconds in and eight seconds out—to see how you feel. As you're breathing, imagine you're also breathing in through your heart and breathing out kindness into areas of tension and tightness you may feel in your body.

Try it the next time you feel stressed and frazzled. When you begin to breathe this way, you'll likely notice your mind becoming clearer and sense a greater ability to be more proactive in what you do next.

### Step 3: "Name it to tame it!"

This phrase, coined by Dan Siegel, speaks to a powerful skill you can use to take the edge off your reactive feelings and thoughts in seconds. It's based on research by Matthew Lieberman from the University of California, Los Angeles, in which he and his team had research participants lie in a functional MRI scanner as they looked at pictures of people with angry or fearful faces. These pictures stimulated the participants' amygdala, activating their stress response, while the researchers observed their brain activity. They found that when they asked the participants to *name* their emotions, this activated their

PFC and deactivated their amygdala, shutting down their stress reaction almost instantly.[17]

If you also name your emotions, you'll be activating your PFC, effectively soothing your revved-up amygdala that's driving your reactivity.

So how do you best name your emotions? A second study by David Creswell in collaboration with Lieberman provides another important key to the solution. Together they looked more closely at the subjects who were the most successful at consciously activating their PFC and deactivating their amygdala when naming their emotion. They found that these subjects also scored highest on levels of mindfulness.[18]

So the best way to name your thoughts and emotions is to do it mindfully.

You might think, well, what's the alternative? The alternative is the reality most of us live daily. We often respond to our thoughts and emotions mindlessly. When we notice we are anxious, we get more freaked out about being anxious; or when we notice we're irritated, we get even more irritated.

Mindfulness engages your observing self. It puts you at the hub of your wheel of awareness, where you can simply observe your thoughts and emotions that lie on the rim of the wheel from a place of openness, nonjudgment, kindness, and compassion.

In this spirit, simply bring awareness to your reactive feelings and thoughts, and with a light touch of kindness, silently name in your mind whatever you notice. For example, you might say to yourself, "Ah, there goes anger," just as if you were greeting an old friend. Or you might simply repeat to yourself, "anger," "fear," "judging self," or "judging others."

When you name your thoughts and emotions, you no longer over-identify with them. Rather than experiencing, "I am angry!" you are now simply noticing, "I'm having an angry feeling." This shift further widens the gap between your stimulus and your response.

Now that you have activated your PFC and taken the edge off your reactivity, you can think more clearly about how to best respond next.

## *Step 4: Consider your best response.*

Much of reactivity stems from feeling our needs have been threatened or thwarted. Sometimes these needs are physical. So first, quickly do a scan of how you are doing at the bottom two levels of Maslow's Hierarchy of Needs to make sure you have taken care of your physical and safety needs. If you notice you are thirsty or hungry, drink some water or eat a nutritious snack as soon as you can to hydrate and get your blood sugar up. Further, if you are sleep deprived, exhausted, or fatigued, see if you can first get some rest before you come back and engage the individual(s) or issue at hand.

If you notice you are feeling emotionally unsafe in your environment and are unlikely to regain a sense of control with a few breaths or through positively influencing the situation at this particular moment, make a graceful exit. If you are dealing with someone difficult, you might say something like, "I feel like I am getting frustrated and am concerned I may say something I'll regret. I'm going to take a few minutes to settle, and then I would like to come back and talk with you further."

As you begin to think more clearly, ask yourself what you most want in the situation and how you can best act to achieve this outcome. When you are gripped by your threat response, every fiber of your being wants to either fight to be right and gain power over someone or take flight from the situation. Both can undercut what you really want, such as clearing the air to maintain an important relationship, securing a deal, or fulfilling your original intention to best serve others. Focusing on the desired outcome engages your PFC, which enables you to see things more clearly, keep your eye on the prize, and respond more effectively in stressful situations.

If after engaging these four steps you still feel reactive, your best response may well be to proceed to the next step of the 4 in 4 Framework (as we'll be doing in the next chapter) to learn from and work through the underlying issues that are continuing to drive your reactive response.

In the meantime, I hope you find these four steps helpful for taking the edge off your reactivity. Each were invaluable to me in averting complete disaster when I experienced my anxiety attack in front of the group, which I shared with you at the beginning of this chapter.

The moment I recognized my reactive sensations, thoughts, and feelings, I paused, took three deep breaths, and silently in my mind repeated "fear, fear," which took some of the edge off what would likely have evolved into full-fledged panic.

I recognized that I felt intensely vulnerable and could not continue to function in the room at the moment. I made as graceful an exit as I could in requesting a ten-minute break, during which I also replenished myself with some water and a snack.

I continued to mindfully observe and silently name some of my thoughts, feelings, and sensations and was aware of the kindness and self-compassion I was extending to myself in the moment.

As I found a place of calm, I then silently considered the way I could best respond when I returned to the room. While I wanted to save face, my highest purpose for this day was to serve the group, so I asked myself how I could best do so. The insight that arrived then enabled me to go back to the room and offer myself as Exhibit A in a case study of reactivity. It also compelled me to do the deeper work we'll be exploring together in the next chapter to understand what was so powerfully triggering my reactive response.

You'll notice that while I used all four steps, they were not in the exact order I presented above. These steps are a guide. Please use them in whichever order and way they will serve you best.

## Mindfulness Practice: Naming Your Experiences

Each step in the 4 in 4 Framework offers both a skill and a mindfulness practice to help you incorporate each step into your life. In addition to the skill of managing your reactivity using the four steps above, I'd like to share with you a formal mindfulness exercise that can help you mentally practice naming your experience. It will strengthen your capacity to take the edge off your reactivity in the heat of the moment and prepare you to more easily call upon this skill in difficult situations when you need it the most.

This practice builds upon the mindfulness breathing practice you learned in chapter 3, only instead of focusing your attention on your breathing, you are now focusing it on your sensations, thoughts, emotions, and feelings.

1. Allow yourself to get comfortable, either lying down or sitting up with an erect and alert posture. You may close your eyes or leave them open as you practice.

2. Bring to the meditation an intention to be open, curious, kind, and accepting of whatever sensations, thoughts, and emotions arise.

3. Bring your attention now to the center of your chest (or your heart center) and to the ebb and flow of your breathing. As you breathe, imagine your breath is flowing in and out through your heart center—or anywhere else you most notice your breathing, if this feels more natural for you.

4. Now, as you become aware of the sensations, thoughts, emotions, and feelings arising in your field of awareness, simply begin to label what you notice without judgment, such as whether what you are experiencing is good or bad or right or wrong. It may be helpful to imagine that you are meeting them as a friend, with a sense of openness and curiosity about meeting whoever is visiting.

5. Start by naming something familiar, like the ebb and flow of your breath. As you breathe in, observe and name this sensation by quietly saying in your mind, "in." As you breathe out, name this sensation in your mind as well: "out." Continue doing this for a few cycles: "in . . . out . . . in . . . out . . ."

6. If you notice anything that pulls at your attention more strongly than your breath, begin to name these sensations, thoughts, or feelings. Here are some examples and how you can name them:

   a. If you notice sensations, like tightness in your shoulders, simply in your mind or with a soft voice say, "tightness." Or if you are aware of an ache, say something like "ache" or "discomfort." Or you may notice an itch or a tingle. Name these as "itching" or "tingling." When you're ready, gently and intentionally return your awareness to your breath.

b. If you notice thoughts arising, name them in a nonjudgmental way. You can start by keeping it very simple, quietly noting, "thinking . . . thinking . . . thinking . . ."

c. You may notice that many of our thoughts focus on processing things in the past or anticipating or preparing for the future. If you notice thoughts processing the past, you can say something to yourself like, "Rehashing . . . rehashing . . ." If you notice thoughts anticipating or preparing you for the future, you can say something to yourself like, "rehearsing . . . rehearsing . . . rehearsing . . ."

d. Or you may notice how some of your thoughts focus on judging others or yourself. If you do, you can simply say, "Judging . . . judging . . ."

e. If you notice that you are doubting yourself or whether you are good enough, you can meet these thoughts by simply naming them, "self-doubt . . . self-doubt . . ."

f. Sometimes our thoughts can sweep us away with elaborate stories or beliefs we tend to tell ourselves over and over again. To keep it simple, you can just name it as "story . . . story . . ."

g. As you notice your thoughts, name them and repeat this name with a sense of kindness and nonjudgment as many times as it feels natural for you. Then, when you feel ready, return your awareness back to your breath.

h. Our thoughts are also usually associated with feelings. You can name these in a similar way. If you notice a sense of sadness or anxiousness, just say to yourself, "sadness . . . sadness . . ." or "anxious . . . anxious . . ."

i. If you notice that you are feeling angry, you can say, "anger . . . anger . . . " Sometimes, it can also be helpful to name these emotions with a touch of humor. If you feel edgy or irritated,

> explore what you experience as you name this, "going limbic
> . . . going limbic . . ."
>
> 7.  After you spend a few minutes naming your experiences,
>     when you feel ready, bring your attention back to your heart-
>     centered breathing for a couple more minutes.
>
> 8.  Finally, allow yourself to be aware of the points where your
>     body is making contact with your seat or what you are lying
>     upon. If your eyes are closed, now gently allow them to open.

This formal practice strengthens your sense of your observing self at the hub of your wheel of awareness. It is more about sensing the observing part of you that is noticing and naming than the specifics of what you are naming. As you identify more with your awareness, you are creating a stability of mind from which you can notice, name, and proactively choose your responses.

Formally practicing the labeling of your sensations, thoughts, emotions, and feelings enables you to bring the essence of this same practice to your everyday experience. Whenever you notice yourself becoming reactive, whether it feels like a pit in your stomach, more rapid breathing, nervousness, anger, or resentment, appreciate your awareness of it. Try to bring your attention to your heart-centered breathing and then, with kindness, compassion, and non-judgment, label your sensations, thoughts, emotions, and feelings.

As you do this, recognize that *you are not your sensations, thoughts, emotions, and feelings.* They are just experiences passing through your field of awareness.

Meeting and naming your experience with a spirit of openness and even hospitality takes the reactive edge off difficult experiences, offers the opportunity to further explore what these experiences have to teach you, and opens the door to other potentially transformative experiences.

I'd like to share with you a poem framed on the wall next to my desk in my office that inspires me each day to welcome whatever I am experiencing. It's by the thirteenth-century poet Rumi and is entitled "The Guest House":[19]

*This being human is a guest house.*
*Every morning a new arrival.*
*A joy, a depression, a meanness,*
*some momentary awareness comes*
*as an unexpected visitor.*
*Welcome and entertain them all!*
*Even if they're a crowd of sorrows,*
*who violently sweep your house*
*empty of its furniture.*
*Still, treat each guest honorably.*
*He may be clearing you out*
*for some new delight.*
*The dark thought, the shame, the malice,*
*meet them at the door laughing,*
*and invite them in.*
*Be grateful for whoever comes,*
*because each has been sent*
*as a guide from beyond.*

In the next chapter, you'll further discover what your reactive responses have to teach you as we explore the triggers of stress and self-doubt that drive your reactivity to begin with, as well as your overall mindset about stress and self-doubt. You'll then also learn a powerful skill to not only reappraise your triggers but transform your stress and self-doubt into your greatest source of fuel for a meaningful life.

# CHAPTER 6

# Step 2: Reappraising Stress and Self-Doubt

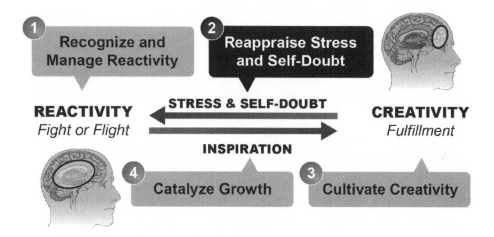

Step 2 moves beyond simply recognizing and taking the edge off your reactivity. Sometimes reactive responses are particularly damaging, or the same patterns occur over and over again. This perseveration lets you know that something has its hooks in you and that deeper work is needed to uncover the underlying stress and self-doubt that is driving your reactive responses to begin with.

On my first call with one of my coaching clients, Chris (whose name has been changed to protect confidentiality) shared with me a list of all the things triggering his overwhelming feelings of stress and self-doubt. This included difficult relationships with his wife and children, as well as family members he was in business with. All of this was causing anxiety, which he "medicated" with alcohol. He would come home each evening and end up drinking one or two bottles of wine. On weekends he'd also add a six pack or two of beer. But this "treatment" had side effects. After the alcohol wore off, it triggered more anxiety. He was ashamed of his drinking, which triggered doubts of self-worth. But it was the only way he knew how deal with his stress, causing a vicious cycle that triggered even more stress and self-doubt.

He said, "I don't know where to even begin!" I shared that we could begin by addressing his drinking or his relationships with his wife, children, or family members in his business that were triggering much of his stress. But I suggested that before we addressed his triggers, the very first relationship to begin with was his relationship to his stress and self-doubt. He had always viewed his stress as a bad thing, and he was doing everything he could to escape it.

After a couple of months of coaching on what you are about to learn in this chapter, all of his relationships, especially his relationship with stress and self-doubt, had dramatically improved, and he'd stopped drinking. He shared, "Stress is no longer an itch I have to scratch. And self-doubt does not stress me out like it used to. As a result, the things that use to bug me don't affect me as much anymore. I can now work with my challenges better, and I don't need to drink anymore. What's hugely exciting is I can now also see how stress is a power source that I can leverage to get me through any challenging situation."

What did Chris mean by all of this? Because he found a way to first change is relationship with stress and self-doubt, his underlying triggers of stress and self-doubt were easier to deal with, and he no longer needed to drink to cope with all of this discomfort. Moreover, he was excited that he'd discovered how he could use stress and self-doubt as an asset, an internal resource of energy that could help him be even more effective in dealing with demands at home and at work.

So then where do we begin in this chapter? Here in Step 2, you'll first discover the power of learning how to change your relationship with stress and self-doubt. Then you'll learn how to appraise and reappraise (i.e., evaluate and reframe) the underlying *triggers* that drive both.

Before we begin, however, let's again distinguish stress from self-doubt. As we saw in chapter 2, the threat-related version of stress asks the question, "Can I handle it?" while self-doubt asks, "How will I value myself in the process of doing so?" Although self-doubt is technically a subcategory of stress, it's a particularly powerful one that can threaten our ability to accept ourselves and trigger a highly stressful threat response.

So let's start with reappraising your mindset around stress before we dig deeper and do the same for self-doubt. Then we'll get to dealing with the triggers for both.

## Reappraising Your Stress Mindset

As mentioned earlier, it's not the events of your life that cause stress, but your perceptions about those events. Just as Carol Dweck's research showed us how your mindset (or perception) about failure determines whether failure will lead to further failure or further success,[1] it's our mindset about stress—whether we see it as debilitating or enhancing—that determines whether it depletes or energizes us.

If you approach stress, like Chris initially did, as something bad to be avoided, this perception can heighten your fear of stressful situations and cause you to miss out on some of the learning opportunities they offer. Conversely, if you approach stress as an asset, you can find the good in what it has to offer. You can learn, grow, and become even stronger and more resilient. You can leverage that stress into *energy* to fuel your transformation and a more meaningful life.

Before we get into the exercises to discover how you can reappraise stress, I want to give you an overview of the science that may have influenced your mindset around stress being harmful and some surprising newer science, which may shift your perception about the negative consequences of stress.

Since Hans Selye coined the term "stress" in 1936,[2] a large body of research has created concern about its debilitating dangers. Many well-intended healthcare providers, including myself, have warned about the harmful consequences of stress. But I'm not sure how well we've served in doing so.

Among the studies I've presented in my talks that warn of the dangers of stress, one of the most alarming is by Russ and colleagues, published in the well-renowned, evidence-based publication the *British Medical Journal.* This review aggregated data from ten studies of almost 70,000 individuals in England who were followed for a mean of about eight years. They found that individuals with low levels of "subclinical" stress had a 20 percent increased risk of death, those with more moderate levels of "symptomatic" stress had a more than 40 percent increased risk of death, and those with more severe levels of "highly symptomatic" stress had a more than 90 percent increased risk of death, largely attributed to cardiovascular disease, cancer, accidents, and injuries.[3]

If you've been feeling at all stressed lately, how does this research make you feel? There's a good chance you are now more stressed about being stressed! Ironically, knowing this research might be harmful to your health.

In *The Upside of Stress,* Kelly McGonigal highlights research that encourages us to rethink the way we view much of this data about the dangers of stress. One of the most compelling studies she references is by Abiola Keller, who has a PhD in population health sciences and a master's degree in public health.

In the study titled "Does the Perception That Stress Affects Health Matter?," Keller analyzed the data of almost 30,000 individuals, cross-linking data from the United States Census Bureau's National Health Information Survey to the National Death Index over a mean of about nine years.[4]

Keller found that individuals with a lot of stress, much like the data I shared above, had a 43 percent increased risk of death. But here's the kicker. She looked at a key question in the survey that related to whether the participants *thought* their stress was harmful. This increased risk in death was found in the group that thought it was. Individuals who reported the same high level of stress *but did not view their stress as being harmful* had a 17 percent decreased risk of death compared to individuals with low stress (although, unlike the increased risk, this latter finding was not statistically significant).

Keller concluded, "High amounts of stress and the perception that stress impacts health are each associated with poor health and mental health. Individuals who perceived that stress affects their health *and* reported a large amount of stress had an increased risk of premature death."

She went further to calculate that if the perception that stress was harmful was indeed responsible for an increased risk of premature death, it would have resulted in 182,079 deaths over the nine years of the study, or 20,231 deaths per year. In 2006, that would have ranked one's stress mindset at number fourteen on the list of leading killers in the United States, between hypertension and Parkinson's disease.[5]

So in other words, if you perceive stress is harmful to your health, it is likely it will be; on the other hand, if you perceive stress is not harmful to your health, it may not be. Rather, it can be leveraged as a source of positive energy.

Your mindset about stress not only affects your health, but your performance too. McGonigal also refers to the research of Alia Crum, who has a PhD in psychology from Yale and is currently a researcher with the Stanford Mind and Body Lab. In 2011 Crum published the results of a groundbreaking stress mindset intervention in a Fortune 500 company.[6] She randomized 229 employees to a two-hour stress mindset training or a wait-list control group.

Those receiving the training were taught a three-step process to reappraise their stress mindset, so they could see stress as an enhancing response rather than a debilitating one. First, they were taught to mindfully acknowledge when they were experiencing stress. Second, they were encouraged to welcome stress as a response to something they really cared about. And third, they were advised to utilize the energy of stress as a resource to move towards their goals, rather than expending it on managing their stress.

After following the employees for three weeks, Crum found that those who engaged this stress mindset intervention had significant improvements in physical symptoms and satisfaction with their health, as well as better performance at work with respect to generating new ideas, sustaining focus, being engaged, and collaborating well with others.

These findings were further maintained at a six-week follow up. Of note, these findings could not be explained by a reduction in stress. The employees did not reduce their stress; they had transformed their relationship and responses to it. They actually performed better because of it. This is the part of the power of reappraising your relationship with stress.

As mentioned in chapter 2, reappraising your relationship with stress not only transforms your mindset and performance. It transforms your physiology, too. In the threat response, your brain releases cortisol, which can damage your brain and health over the long term. Also, whereas the threat response causes your blood vessels to constrict, the challenge response causes your blood vessels to stay relaxed, which further optimizes your cardiac output and may ameliorate some of the adverse outcomes of the threat response on your health.[7]

Furthermore, while your brain releases cortisol in the challenge response, it also releases DHEA, a neurosteroid that promotes brain growth. So in the challenge response, your ratio of DHEA to cortisol, which constitutes a "growth index," is relatively higher than in the threat response. This index (and by extension the challenge response) has been correlated with academic performance in college students, greater focus and problem solving skills in military survival training, and greater resilience in recovering from trauma, even from painful early life experiences such as child abuse.[8]

In *The Upside of Stress,* McGonigal further collates numerous studies that reveal how the challenge response predicts better performance under stressful situations. For example, it's also been associated with more effective sharing of information and decision making in business negotiations, higher exam scores in students, better athletic performance, better focus and fine motor skills in surgeons, and even safer landings by pilots presented with the challenge of engine failure in in-flight simulations.[9]

Like the challenge response, the tend-and-befriend response is also physiologically distinct and helpful. We have already mentioned that this response activates the parasympathetic nervous system,[10] which can help regulate your fight-or-flight threat response. Furthermore, while it's well known that during stress we release hormones such as cortisol, it's not as well appreciated that we also release oxytocin, the love hormone. It's also been dubbed the "hug hormone" and "cuddle chemical."[11] This explains why, when you feel stressed, a part of you may want to reach out to your family and friends for support or protect those you care about. Simply being aware of these sensations can transform your tendency to take flight and isolate yourself in times of stress to connect with others instead. Further, oxytocin regulates the threat response and makes you feel more brave and trusting. It also protects and repairs your heart from the damaging effects of stress.[12]

McGonigal also refers to a number of studies that reveal the power of the tend-and-befriend response during stress. One study evaluated the association of stress with death in 846 people living in the Detroit area who were tracked over five years. The study also asked how much time the participants spent helping friends, neighbors, and extended family members. The study found that in those who did not routinely help others, every significant life event increased the risk of dying by 30 percent. But those who helped others appeared to be inoculated from the harmful effects of stress: they had no stress-related increase in their risk of death.[13]

So, based on all this research, can you begin to see how your perception, or mindset, about whether stress is negative or positive can influence your health, productivity, and physiology?

Like Chris, can you see how transforming your perception of stress as an asset can help you lean into your challenges or connect with others when this better serves you? If so, how do you do it?

Mindfulness, the practice of paying attention with a sense of *openness, curiosity,* and *kindness,* is the key. As we mentioned in chapter 3, curiosity engages your challenge response and cultivates growth and learning. Kindness both extends caring toward yourself and others and helps you find the courage to face your challenges.

See if you can imagine yourself reappraising your relationship to stress during a stressful experience (with the caveat being that your life is not in imminent danger) where a threat response may not be what serves you best.

For example, imagine that you're put on the spot and asked to give an impromptu talk in front of hundreds of people. You instantly feel your stress spike. With mindfulness, can you *open* yourself to this experience? Can you see yourself bringing a touch of *curiosity* as you explore your reaction and what matters most to you? Are you feeling threatened by thoughts of possible failure and humiliation, or can you feel an energy surge that compels you to give what matters a shot? Are you experiencing your stress as debilitating or enhancing? If you've initially experienced it as threatening, can you shift towards welcoming or embracing your stress? Can you instead see it as an asset that's mobilizing your energy to meet your challenge at hand? Can you appreciate and trust that much of your response serves to mobilize your internal resources to do the best you can? Can you be *kind* to yourself, as well as your audience, and think about how you can best serve them and make a difference in their lives?

In situations such as this, if you can learn to transform your mindset about stress from threat to challenge or tend and befriend, instead of needing to "name it to tame it" (as you learned to do in the last chapter), you may find yourself increasingly "naming it to savor it." Instead of naming your energy as "fear," you may name it as "excitement!" You may even feel grateful for being able to leverage it, saying, "OK, great! I'm amped. Let's do this. It's 'go' time!" In this case, rather than needing to shift to a parasympathetic state to take the edge off a threat response, you can enjoy the challenge and feel free to "go with the flow." In other words, you can "surf your sympathetics" and trust they will turn off when they are no longer needed.

Here's a great example of transforming or reappraising stress from threat into challenge. Pete Carroll, the much admired Seattle Seahawks football coach, acquired instant global notoriety and harsh criticism for calling a pass play from the one-yard line that got intercepted in the final seconds to lose the 2015 Super Bowl. Such judgmental comments can sometimes crush your morale and resilience. But surprisingly, a few months later, he told *Sports Illustrated,* "It's been thrilling to experience this. It really has!" He added, "You pour everything in your life into something and—it goes right, sometimes it goes wrong—it's in you. It becomes a part of you. I'm not going to ignore it. I'm going to face it. And when it bubbles up, I'm going to think about it and get on with it. And use it. *Use it!*"[14]

When you lean in and leverage your stress, you become more engaged in what Jon Kabat-Zinn calls "full catastrophe living," the title of his seminal book on mindfulness that he took from a line from Zorba the Greek, reflecting the passion with which Zorba embraced the full richness of his life.[15]

Here's the big reappraisal on stress: trust that the energy of stress can be a gift, whether it's helping to save your life or to meet your greatest challenges. When you begin to embrace this energy and use the most adaptive response to achieve what you most care about, you become more engaged and feel more alive in your life!

## Reappraising Your Self-Doubt Mindset

Now that you've reappraised your perception of stress, let's reappraise your perception of self-doubt, which can also drive a lot of internal stress. Before we get into how to do so, I'm happy to serve as your case study again. While I did not fully appreciate all of the research about the value of leaning in and directly embracing stress as an asset until relatively recently, it's something I've intuitively known for many years, especially as it relates to the power of learning how to embrace and transform your mindset about self-doubt.

When I fell apart during medical school, overwhelmed with self-doubt and spiraling into depression, I was terrified. Up until that point, I thought I'd managed to insulate myself from self-doubt, but in truth, it had simply retreated to my blind spot, continuing to subconsciously trigger my fight-or-flight threat responses.

In the introduction, I shared how as a young man growing up in South Africa, I truly believed that the pathway to success and confidence was to overcome self-doubt. I could not accept myself with these feelings. Consequently, I relentlessly fought to prove my self-worth through validation from friends and ambitiously striving to become the top student in college. I remember getting my grades back for the term, having received a 1st (the equivalent of an A), and actually feeling despondent that I had not received the class medal awarded to the top student. With a circle of friends who validated me, three class medals, and graduating in the top ten of my class, I was able to keep my self-doubt at bay. But it was all an arrogant delusion.

In retrospect, I can now see how self-doubt had run my life, not only in my striving, but in all the times I had taken flight from anything that might have triggered my self-doubt. For instance, there was just no way I would have approached any young woman I was attracted to. Sure, I could pretend I was just playing it cool and be aloof. But the deeper reason was that I was afraid of rejection and the self-doubt it may have triggered, which I was unable to accept.

When I arrived in the United States, without my validating support structures, cracks of vulnerability began to emerge. I patched them over with a dogged determination to get ahead. I held on to the belief that when I got into medical school, all would be OK. Then when I was accepted into a top medical school—the University of California, San Francisco—this initial success simply brought temporary relief rather than joy. I soon found myself feeling isolated and experiencing intense pressure among a group of achievers, where the threat of being average wasn't going to be enough to assuage my underlying self-doubt.

What kept me sane and feeling connected was the warmth, kindness, and support of a wonderful girlfriend, Cindy—up until I sabotaged the relationship. After my first year of medical school, believing that our being together was keeping me isolated from my classmates at medical school, I ended the relationship. In the weeks that followed, I realized I'd made a terrible mistake. Losing Cindy had only left me feeling more isolated and miserable. In growing despair, I called her to apologize, desperately hoping to get back together. I was shocked when she told me she had fallen in love with someone else. I then found out that he was financially successful and very good looking, which stoked my doubts about being good enough.

And then the wheels came off!

One evening, I went by Cindy's apartment to collect the remainder of my things. She was getting ready to go out with her new boyfriend. In a black leather miniskirt and white blouse, she had never looked more ravishing, all the more so because she was completely unavailable to me. I then did something I had never done before. I pleaded—no, *groveled*—for her to stay. All of a sudden, like a fly on the wall, I saw an image of this pathetic person falling apart, filled with insecurities. The image shattered my wall of denial and resistance that for so many years had shielded me from my underlying self-doubt. Unable to sustain my self-image of being a confident and secure person, which predicated my self-acceptance, something snapped. I experienced my first full-scale panic attack.

If you have never experienced one before, it feels like you are going to die. In my panic, and in front of Cindy, I called my parents to fly up from San Diego to San Francisco because I feared for my life.

The very next day, my parents visited me in my apartment and watched as I lay sobbing in pain on my bed. Then, watching them watching me fall apart, I had my second panic attack. Next thing I knew, they were escorting me to an emergency psychiatric evaluation at the very hospital where I was doing my medical training. I hit bottom and entered therapy, where I was initially treated with an anti-anxiety medication, which was later changed to an anti-depressant.

Looking back, I view this time as being one of the greatest gifts in my life. It humbled me and fried my ego. Then, six months into my counseling, when my therapist offered the insight that I flipped my lid, I was able to see clearly what I was most afraid of: my underlying doubts about my self-worth, that I was "good enough."

It was a profound relief to see this. In the light of awareness, I discovered I had a choice. I could continue to fight to overcome these feelings or learn how to lean in and embrace them. Intuitively (and without the benefit of knowing what we now know from the research on transforming your stress mindset), I recognized there was only one viable path forward—learning to embrace my feelings of self-doubt.

The moment I had this revelation, I told my therapist that I wanted to come off my anti-depressant "cold turkey." (Disclaimer: if you are on an anti-depressant, please know I am not at all suggesting you do this. Please work closely with your doctor on any decisions about your care.) My therapist warned me against it, saying that I would very likely rebound. I responded that I wanted to rebound. I wanted to feel the full intensity of my self-doubt and depression, so I could trust that I could lean in and embrace it.

Against his advice, I stopped my medications. Then two days later, as I was walking to medical school, I felt that painfully familiar feeling of depression braided with self-doubt arise as a heaviness and blackness inside of me. Only this time, I had a different response. I said to myself, "Bring it on. Here it is!" Instead of resisting these feelings, I welcomed them. I saw that I could hold them inside of me. These feelings that had felt so intensely threatening over so many years were more like a paper tiger. Here they were, and I was still alive, psychologically intact, and unscathed. In an instant, the doom transformed. I felt the energy and vitality of life stir in me once more; only now, free of needing to live a delusion, it did so on a more authentic foundation.

For the first time, I understood what true *confidence* was. It was not the absence of self-doubt, but rather the capacity and courage to embrace self-doubt, even learn from and leverage these feelings, as you follow through on whatever is most important to you.

I then became insatiably curious about self-doubt. Does everyone experience it? If so, why are we so freaked out and threatened by it? Does it hold any value? If it does, how can we best embrace and leverage it?

I began to ask my colleagues at medical school whether they experienced self-doubt. Everyone I spoke to said they had these feelings. Some seem baffled or thought I was a bit daft for asking about it, responding, "Doesn't everyone feel like this?"

This question lingered in my mind. I wondered if self-doubt was, indeed, normal, rather than some flaw or weakness, which all too often causes us to have self-doubt about having self-doubt.

After writing my book on evidence-based medicine, I decided to take a more scientific approach. I searched on PubMed to see if I could find any research on self-doubt. I was amazed by what I found.

While there were tens of thousands of articles published on self-esteem, there were less than two hundred articles published with the term "self-doubt" in their titles. There was no study exploring its prevalence, with which I was hoping to find an evidence-based answer.

Sensing a gap in the literature, I decided to conduct a study to explore whether self-doubt was normal, as well as learn why we seem to be so bothered by it.

In 2000, I had been working as a physician in a UCSF clinic at San Francisco International Airport and got permission to approach people at the airlines' gates to survey travelers about their experiences with self-doubt, which I more specifically defined as having doubts of self-worth. I called it the SFO Self-Doubt Study.

Let me just say I had a lot of self-doubt doing this study, going through security with my clipboards and summoning the courage to ask people to fill out this highly personal survey, answering questions they may not even share with their spouse. With my training in evidence-based medicine, I also had self-doubt about the fact that it was a convenience sample (where I had walked up to people as opposed to randomly selecting telephone numbers and calling people) and did not publish the results. I have some self-doubt sharing this unpublished data with you now.

Nonetheless, I hope you find these findings as helpful as I have.

Three hundred and fourteen people, about 80 percent of those I approached, agreed to complete the survey.

Let me ask you to guess. Of those 314, what number do you think shared that they experienced doubts of self-worth?

The answer was 311.

On further review, two of the three participants who denied having self-doubt were highly sarcastic with their answers on their survey, very possibly reflecting their underlying feelings of self-doubt. I approached the final person, a gray-haired man with a warm and kind presence, asking him to share more about why he said he didn't experience doubts of self-worth. He responded, "Make no mistake. As a young man, I was riddled with self-doubt." Then he shared how, once he found his way to his deep sense of faith and completely gave his life over in service of something larger than himself, his self-doubt disappeared. In doing so, he had liberated himself of the self-image with which he had previously felt compelled to prove himself worthy. In essence, with no "self," he had no self-doubt.

So essentially, with all participants in the survey acknowledging they experience or have experienced doubts of self-worth, we may conclude that self-doubt is indeed normal.

In my workshops and seminars, I ask everyone in the room to raise their hands if they know what it's like to experience self-doubt. Everyone always does. (This includes the leaders of some of the country's top organizations who attended my sessions at the Conscious Capitalism CEO Summit.)

With all hands raised, I then invite everyone in these sessions to look around the room and notice that it's self-doubt that unites us. It's only the struggle to overcome it that divides us.

Self-doubt is part of our common humanity. It links back to what we shared about your default mode network, which continuously processes our relationship to ourselves and others.

So if self-doubt is normal, for the purposes of our reappraisal, let's flip the question. Instead of asking how we can overcome it, let's ask, how is it useful?

Think about self-doubt in your own life. Can you think how it might serve you?

When I ask this question in my seminars, the types of answers that arise include:

*It keeps me from taking too much risk, which could harm my health.*

*It keeps me from saying regrettable things to others.*

*It keeps me from making impulsive or bad decisions at work or about my plans for my future.*

In short, self-doubt can keep you safe, socially appropriate, and on your path towards self-actualization. Essentially, it can help you meet your Maslowian needs for safety, love and belonging, and significance. All of this cultivates collaboration, creativity, and innovation, which has given us a survival advantage as a species.

So, if we all have the capacity for self-doubt, why is it that we so often feel threatened by it? If it can be helpful, why is it so often harmful? As much as self-doubt can keep us safe, connected, and on the path to significance, it can also make us feel very unsafe, reject ourselves, withdraw from others, derail us from pursuing what matters most in our lives, and lead to social fragmentation and conflict.

Wanting to learn more deeply why we tend to fear having self-doubt, I included three questions at the end of the SFO Self-Doubt Study. I asked the participants whether they strongly agreed, agreed, disagreed, or strongly disagreed with the following statements:

"When I grew up, my parents seemed more accepting of me when I succeeded than when I failed."

"I think people get more love and respect when they are successful in life."

Later in the survey, they were asked to choose which one of the following two statements they felt were most applicable to them:

"I am more accepting of myself when I feel I've proved myself worthy," or

"I accept myself unconditionally, doubts of self-worth and all."

With the help of a statistician, I found that individuals who felt their parents were more accepting of them when they succeeded rather than when they failed also agreed that people get more love and respect when they are successful in life, and they were statistically significantly more likely to choose the statement that they were more accepting of themselves when they proved themselves worthy.

Furthermore, the study also found a strong statistical correlation that these individuals were more bothered by feelings of self-doubt than those who accepted themselves unconditionally with it.

So, what does this all mean?

In short, the findings suggest that we are socially conditioned to fear self-doubt. They point toward an implicit contract that many of us internalized in our childhood:

*I will accept myself when I prove my self-worth.*

The corollary to this contract is painful and highly threatening:

*If I discover I'm not worthy, I cannot accept myself.*

In this contract, we move beyond the fear of being rejected by others to the deeper fear that we might reject and abandon ourselves.

I believe this contract drives our reactive fight to prove our self-worth and take flight from whatever triggers our self-doubt. It may also explain a host of "isms," such as workaholism, perfectionism, and alcoholism, as well as Type-A and safety-seeking behaviors that can put us at risk for burnout.

For some, this threat of self-abandonment may feel so intense that they take the ultimate flight from it, seeking the relative safety of physical death through suicide, rather than the pain and threat of the living death of self-invalidation.

While the contract points to the threat and discomfort behind our feelings of self-doubt, it also reveals the promise of a possible solution.

While as children we were unaware of what we internalized, as adults who are now aware of this contract, we can reappraise our mindset about self-doubt and rewrite our conditional contract, one that unconditionally affirms:

*I accept myself, doubts of self-worth and all.*

Here again, just as you did with stress, leaning in to your self-doubt with mindful self-compassion can free you from its fear-promoting tyranny. Mindfulness enables you to simply observe your thoughts and feelings of self-doubt from a place of openness, curiosity, kindness, and unconditional self-acceptance.

Rather than wasting unnecessary energy to overcome or avoid self-doubt at all costs, you can focus your energy and attention on caring for yourself and reflecting with curiosity on what your self-doubt has to teach and how it can best serve you. You may even be thankful for the insight it provides. Now you can leverage the best of what self-doubt has to offer and more fully focus on your health and vitality, forming heartfelt relationships and finding a greater sense of significance in your vocation, all of which cultivates growth, resiliency, and greater meaning in your life.

Reappraising your mindset about stress and self-doubt opens a doorway to even deeper learning and liberation. It enables you to more easily appraise and reappraise your underlying triggers of stress and self-doubt that drive much of these experiences and your reactive responses to begin with, which we'll cover in the next section.

## Appraising and Reappraising Your Triggers of Stress and Self-Doubt

Much of our experience with stress and self-doubt relates to external events, or what we call *triggers*. However, a large part of what triggers our experience is also internally generated—including our filters or beliefs about those events.[16]

For example, you may have beliefs about what *should* happen, what you expect of yourself and others, or how failure or rejection defines your sense of personal worth—all of which can trigger the experience of stress and self-doubt.

The good news is that just as you can appraise and reappraise your mindset about stress and self-doubt, you can also appraise and reappraise your beliefs about these triggers.

So let's begin by identifying the most common triggers of stress and self-doubt.

### *Appraising Your Triggers of Stress and Self-Doubt*

Triggers of stress and self-doubt often overlap. For example, when we feel stress and are unable to cope with it, we may doubt ourselves, and when we feel self-doubt, we feel stressed.

Triggers of *stress* may be both physical and psychological. Both may activate your limbic system and your fight-or-flight responses. Physical stressors include exposure to heat and cold, hunger, thirst, lack of sleep, or physical danger. A good many of our psychological stressors result from the fear-based simulations we continually run. As mentioned earlier, Dietrich has pointed out that our brain is designed to be a predictive machine.[17] In the last chapter, we discussed how, under stress, our thoughts tend to focus on "what if . . ." and all the bad things that could happen. In an attempt to run better simulations, we may also ruminate over "if only . . ." situations and the regrets of our past. These "movies in our mind" can feel very real and stressful.

David Rock, Director of the Institute for NeuroLeadership, identifies some of the most common stressors another way, with the memorable mnemonic SCARF.[18]

SCARF stands for:

- Threats to **Status**, which challenge our place in the social hierarchy and the deeper fears about resources we may have access to

- Threats to **Certainty**, which invoke the fear of "what if" and all the bad things that could happen

- Threats to **Autonomy**, which raise the fear of losing control

- Threats to **Relatedness**, which relate to the fear of being disconnected from the safety and security within our tribe

- Threats to **Fairness**. The importance of fairness goes back to prehistoric times when we would have needed to know who within our tribe was acting in ways that could do us in. Today we may be triggered when we or others are unjustly treated within our tribe or the global community.

When you fuse some of these triggers of stress together, you can create mega-triggers. One example is fusing the threats to relatedness and fairness, which gives you the mega-trigger of betrayal. When someone close to you treats you unfairly, such as a business partner embezzling from you or a spouse cheating on you, it can keep you up stewing all night or for days, months, or even years on end.

Reflect on some of the challenges you are currently facing at work or in your personal life. Can you identify people, organizations, or situations that are currently causing you stress by threatening your status, certainty, autonomy, relatedness, or sense of fairness?

In addition to triggers of stress, we are also susceptible to the following triggers of *self-doubt,* all of which can more deeply threaten your sense of self-worth as well as many of the SCARF factors.

Some of the most common triggers of self-doubt are:

- **Judgment and criticism,** not only of others, but often, more painfully, of ourselves

- **Rejection and abandonment,** such as feeling rejected by a loved one or even rejecting and abandoning ourselves

- **Neglect and abuse,** a far deeper pain that can lead to emotional scarring and prolonged feelings of self-doubt

- **Failure to live up to standards and expectations,** which is especially common in high achievers or Type-A personalities, including many business leaders, physicians, lawyers, and other hard-driving professionals. This trigger may show up as anxiety over the expectations others have for you or, even more powerful, the ones you have internalized for yourself.

- **Losing things that make us feel worthy,** which can happen if your personal self-worth is at all tied to external factors. For example, if your self-worth is linked to your financial self-worth, and you lose a lot of money, or you lose a job that gives you a sense of status, it can trigger a fair amount of self-doubt.

- **Transition,** which can be an ever-present source of self-doubt. For example, once we get used to our roles at work, we may develop a sense of mastery and self-worth as a result of feeling competent or accomplished. When we transition to a new role, or move to a new location where we do not have the same level of know-how or support, we can feel humbled in our new beginnings, which can trigger self-doubt.

Were you able to resonate with any of these triggers? The more you are aware of them, the more able you will be to proactively reappraise them.

### Reappraising Your Triggers of Stress and Self-Doubt

*Reappraisal* is a process where you reframe the way you see things. By reappraising your triggers, you can take the teeth out of their threat, broaden your view, and energize yourself to seize opportunities, learn, grow, and respond more effectively in challenging situations. Studies also show that individuals who use reappraisal report fewer negative emotions, better social functioning, and greater psychological well-being.[19]

The following table provides some alternative ways of viewing the triggers we've mentioned above. Please know this list of triggers is not exhaustive, and their reappraisals are not intended to be prescriptive, suggesting how you "should" look at them. Rather, these examples are intended to stimulate your thinking about how you could reappraise your own various beliefs or thoughts that trigger your stress and self-doubt.

| Trigger of Stress or Self-Doubt | Reappraisal |
|---|---|
| "What if . . . [and list all the bad things that could happen]" | "What if . . . [and consider all the good things that could happen]" <br><br> In other words, consider transforming your fear-based simulations to success-based simulations. |

| "If only . . . [and list your regrets about the past]" | "Yes, and . . . [explore all the learning and growth opportunities from potential "mistakes" or "failures"]"<br><br>In other words, "fail forward" with a growth mindset, using these learning opportunities from your past to enhance the present and future for yourself and others. |
|---|---|
| Judgment and criticism | Recognize that judgment and criticism are very different from caring and constructive feedback. People who put others down usually feel a need to enhance their sense of self-worth to compensate for their underlying feelings of insecurity and self-doubt. In other words, their judgments and criticism reflect more about them than about you. |
| Fear of rejection | Reflect on the number of times you have been rejected and compare it to the number of times you have had positive interactions with others in your life. The statistical likelihood you will be rejected is far lower than the likelihood you will have a positive interaction with others. |

| | |
|---|---|
| Fear of failure or not living up to standards and expectations | Change your definition of success so that you cannot fail. For example, consider the following definition: "Success is giving it my all and learning something from the experience." |
| Fear of transition and uncertainty | See the benefit of resting in uncertainty. It is the neutral gear shift to infinite possibility and growth. |

*Table 6.1. Reappraising the Triggers of Stress and Self-Doubt*

Now that we have learned how to appraise and reappraise the triggers of stress and self-doubt, let's pull it all together into one simple and powerful process.

## The Appraise-Reappraise Method™

To effectively reappraise your underlying stress or self-doubt, you first need to be able to appraise these experiences. I've created a process for you called The Appraise-Reappraise Method™, which I've adapted from Rational Emotive Behavioral Therapy, the pioneering cognitive behavioral therapy work of Albert Ellis.[20] In a 2003 survey conducted by the American Psychological Association, Ellis was named the second-most influential psychological thinker in history, behind Carl Rogers and ahead of Sigmund Freud and Carl Jung.[21]

The Appraise-Reappraise Method helps you reframe painful perceptions with two questions to help you appraise your current perception and two questions relating to reappraising stress and self-doubt.

### 1. Appraisal: What Happened? (Just the Facts)

While we cannot change events that have happened to us, we can change our perceptions. But we also need to be able to recognize the difference between *facts* and *perceptions,* so we can focus our energy where we have the greatest ability to influence change. Since it's all too easy to confuse the two, start your appraisal by making note of the facts of what happened or is happening.

One of my workshop participants, a well-respected national speaker, shared with me a painful experience that happened when she'd shown up to give a talk. She told me that she had been given sixty minutes to talk, but when she got there, the event chair said the conference was running behind schedule and asked her to give the talk in thirty minutes. She felt outraged and insulted. She couldn't let go of her anger and felt extremely stressed about condensing her talk on the spot. As a result, her talk was not one of her best, and she could not connect with the audience as well as she normally did. The intensity with which she shared her experience expressed how much hurt, frustration, and anger she felt about the incident.

I invited her to work the Appraise-Reappraise Method with me, starting with the question, "What happened?"

She began, "Can you believe it—she only gave me thirty minutes to speak after she had promised me sixty minutes!"

She was coloring the facts with her strong feelings, fusing her beliefs with the event. I worked with her to separate the event from her beliefs by just expressing the facts about what happened.

After a few minutes, she was able to acknowledge the plain fact that she had been promised sixty minutes to talk, and when she arrived, she was asked to speak for thirty minutes.

### 2. Appraisal: What Are My Beliefs About What Happened?

This question allows you to more clearly see your beliefs about the facts or events. For example, someone may say something to you (fact), and you may speculate on his intentions (belief).

Or, if your boss says she no longer wants you working on a specific project (fact) and you feel rejected, you may *believe* that you are not good enough or that your status at work is in jeopardy (belief).

Or, you may have a public speaking engagement scheduled (fact), and expecting yourself to live up to certain standards or expectations, you are filled with fear that if you fail you will feel humiliated and won't be able to accept yourself (belief).

While it is not pleasant to feel that people are talking negatively about us or rejecting us or to think of ourselves failing at a task, notice how it is mostly our *beliefs* about these actual or imagined events that add to our suffering about them.

For example, after my client was able to clearly state the facts about the situation, I invited her to fully express her beliefs about these facts. She began by saying that she did not feel respected and felt treated unfairly. She believed people should always follow through on the commitments they make. This experience had threatened her Status, Certainty, Autonomy, and sense of Relatedness and Fairness (i.e., the SCARF triggers mentioned above). Sensing something deeper behind the intensity of her response, I asked if there might also be something that was more deeply painful for her about this.

She paused and then shared that when the conference chair told her she only had thirty minutes, she felt discriminated against. She said, "As an African American woman, I felt like this woman was telling me to sit at the back of the bus!"

After acknowledging how painful this felt, I then invited her to dig deeper, asking what else this brought up for her. She responded that when she feels discriminated against, it causes her to doubt her self-worth. And when she doubts her self-worth, she has a hard time accepting herself.

So initially, when appraising what was beneath her response of anger, it became clear that she felt rejected. But at the core of her pain, more than the painful perception of feeling rejected by others, she felt the deeper pain of rejecting herself.

These beliefs were illuminated by separating her beliefs clearly and distinctly from the facts and digging deeper, layer by layer, to ask why these underlying beliefs were so painful, or what her deeper fear was.

Our deepest fears often lie in a cascading set of beliefs—a "fear tree" that you can map by sequentially asking, "If this fear were true, what would happen next?" Essentially, a fear tree allows you to run your ultimate fear-based simulation. Take heart to do so mindfully, with curiosity and kindness, as you explore these beliefs. When you ask this question until you can go no further, you may discover what lies at the root of your deepest fear.

In the last chapter, I shared that I had to take a break when I experienced cotton mouth and my brain scrambled during my presentation on navigating stress; I ended up using myself as Exhibit A in a case study on managing reactivity. Although I'd managed to take the edge off my own reactivity with Step 1 of the 4 in 4 Framework, later that evening, the event still had its hooks in me, and I had difficulty sleeping. So I turned to work with Step 2 and the fear tree in particular.

I began by asking myself what I believed might happen as a result of the event earlier that day.

My first thought was that I may have lost credibility and trust with the group.

If that were true, I then asked what I believed might happen next.

I feared I might lose my nine-month contract with the group.

And what then?

I feared it might erode my reputation.

And then?

I feared I might lose my livelihood.

And then?

I feared my wife would become stressed, and it could strain our marriage.

And then?

If it escalated, I could lose my family.

And then?

I would feel rattled by doubts of self-worth, and I might have a difficult time accepting myself, too.

But this was not my deepest fear. Looking back and making sense of my life journey, I now feel deeply connected to and guided by something larger than myself. At the height of my panic, for a painful moment, I'd felt completely untethered and lost. My deepest fear was that I might lose access to and feel disconnected from my deepest source of inspiration. And if that happened, life would have no meaning and would not be worth living at all.

As challenging as it is to keep digging, shedding a light on your deepest fears can be freeing. Seeing all of your beliefs and clearly distinguishing them from the facts about what happened enables you to move to the next two questions in the Appraise-Reappraise Method, to *reappraise* your beliefs to transform your pain and open new possibilities for moving forward.

Further, since most triggers may funnel into the depths of the same fear tree, if you can learn to embrace and work with your deepest fear with curiosity, kindness, and self-compassion, you can discover deep confidence to handle whatever challenges you may face.

### 3. Reappraisal: Am I Certain My Belief Is Really True?

Reappraising involves challenging your beliefs. Much of what we believe is distorted thinking or even pure fabrication. Albert Ellis calls this the "dispute," where you challenge your perceptions. So start with a reality check. Ask yourself, "Is how I'm seeing this really true?" Or, "What is the evidence that this should be so?"

Many of us hold on tightly to our beliefs, and giving them up is not easy. Sometimes shaking up your beliefs comes down to weighing the questions, "Do I want to be right?" or "Do I want to be happy?"

If you can shake up your limiting beliefs, you can make room for new growth in your life and open the door to viewing your triggers in more helpful ways.

Here's how we started the Reappraisal process with my client. With question 3, we began by exploring my client's belief that people should always treat others fairly and follow through on their commitments.

While it would certainly be ideal, we explored whether it was realistic to expect that others always act from a place of virtue and altruism (especially when under stress) or whether they more commonly acted from self-interest.

She acknowledged that most people tend to act out of self-interest. She realized while she could certainly hope colleagues would follow through on their commitments and be altruistic, having a fixed belief and expectation about how others should always act was causing her a lot of added stress.

Understanding that others tend to act out of self-interest also shook up her belief that she was being discriminated against. She acknowledged it was more likely that the conference organizer was looking to protect her own reputation than personally discriminating against her. Viewing the facts more broadly, she could see that if it was about discrimination, she likely would not have been invited to speak at the conference in the first place.

We then explored whether it made any sense that when others triggered her stress response that she would heap pain on her suffering by doubting herself and having difficulty accepting herself. She was surprised and disturbed to realize that she held an underlying belief that she could only accept herself if she felt worthy, and she wanted to work on changing this belief.

### 4. Reappraisal: How Can I View This Situation Differently?

After challenging and loosening the hold on your beliefs, you are then ready to ask the final key question of reappraisal: *"How can I view this situation differently so that it brings me less stress or self-doubt?"*

With the grip of her beliefs loosened and her desire to learn and grow strengthened, my client and I were ready to work on reappraising these beliefs and experiences.

She realized that the conference organizer most likely acted in self-interest and wanted to save face, rather than discriminate against her or attack her personal self-worth.

But the real growth opportunity for my client was her realization that in her difficulty accepting herself with her self-doubt, she was abandoning herself in her moment of greatest need. I asked her how she would have treated her best friend under the same circumstances, especially if this event had likewise rattled her friend with self-doubt.

She said she would unquestionably respond to her friend with unconditional, compassionate support. I invited her to "tend and befriend" herself with similar self-compassion by reframing the way she dealt with her own self-doubt. Essentially, this involved rewriting the internal contract we mentioned above: *"I accept myself, doubts of self-worth and all."*

As she reflected on this statement, the tone of her voice softened, and I could sense her energy being released. She shared how seeing things in a whole new light had relieved the stress she felt over the event.

With greater awareness about her underlying beliefs and the insight gained by reappraising them, she was able to release the grip these triggers had on her. But more importantly, appraising and reappraising her stress triggers gave her the opportunity to discover how she had been undermining herself, and she committed herself to a path of growth in learning to become more self-compassionate. While the incident may have initially weakened her, she found gold by working through this process and, most important, connecting more deeply with herself, which ultimately put her on the path to find greater strength and resilience.

Please note that reappraising things does not condone the behavior of others. It simply helps you to view situations in as healthy a way as possible, to free yourself from a reactive response that could do more harm than good. It also sets you up for wiser action so you can achieve the outcome you would most like to see.

Specifically, this reappraisal exercise activates your PFC and deactivates your limbic system, allowing you to time to pause and think more clearly, rather than reacting subconsciously from your emotional, fear-based brain.

For example, if my client had chosen to send a scathing, accusatory e-mail at the height of her anger when she was at her most limbic, she may well have burnt some bridges and damaged her reputation—doing her and the conference organizer more harm than good.

After reappraising her experience and taking a broader perspective, if she chose to have any subsequent communication with the conference chair, she would now have much greater clarity of mind to more effectively communicate whatever she would want to say.

Thankfully, I was also able to use questions 3 and 4 of the Appraise-Reappraise Method to shake up all my beliefs in my fear tree and view things differently, too. I realized that I may not have lost credibility with the group and that even if I ended up losing my contract, there would be others. I took solace in remembering that I'd always been resourceful in earning a livelihood. Further, even if I were to enter a difficult financial time, I trusted that my wife would stay with me. During our wedding vows, we used the metaphor of an arch bridge, pledging that the stressors of life would only make us stronger. With the SFO Self-Doubt Study, I'd already begun the work of learning how to accept myself with doubts of self-worth and trusting I can hold these feelings. And finally, when it came to the connection with my deepest source of inspiration, I had faith that while I could lose my way and turn away from my source, my source would always be available and never turn away from me. Faith can be a powerful inner resource to deal with life's most challenging demands.

I hope you find this method helpful to your learning and growth and that it brings you a greater level of freedom to refocus your energy on what matters most in your life.

Now, consider a challenging situation in your own life that is causing stress or self-doubt. Try working the Appraise-Reappraise Method by answering the following four questions:

1. What happened?

2. What are my beliefs about what happened?

3. Am I certain my belief is really true?

4. How can I view this situation differently?

If you'd like to take your ability to appraise and reappraise your stress and self-doubt to a whole new level, I encourage you to also practice this method mindfully.

## Mindfulness Practice: Working the Appraise-Reappraise Method Mindfully

Some exciting research reveals why mindfulness is so helpful in reappraising your triggers of stress and self-doubt.

As alluded to in chapter 4, in 2010, Gemma Modinos published a study which showed the power of mindfulness in facilitating reappraisal.[22] She had eighteen individuals lie in an MRI scanner and positively reappraise pictures of seemingly negative situations. For example, they could choose to foresee positive outcomes in challenging situations: if they saw a man lying in a hospital bed, they could imagine he would completely recover. They could transform the scene: if they saw a woman crying outside of a church, they imagined she was crying out of happiness at her daughter's wedding. Or they could objectify a picture of a disturbing scene, imagining it was only a movie.

Modinos's findings confirmed earlier research that reappraising stressful scenes activated the participant's PFC and deactivated his or her amygdala. But her research added something important. She also had her participants fill out a validated survey to evaluate their level of mindfulness. She found that the participants who scored highest on levels of mindfulness were the ones who were most skilled in activating their PFC and deactivating their amygdala as they reappraised the situations—just like Lieberman and Creswell discovered in their study about naming emotions (see chapter 5).

As you mindfully appreciate that you are not your thoughts, sensations, or emotions, you become less entangled with them and may experience greater space around the way you view your experiences. You gain greater flexibility to dig deeper and can more easily identify and reappraise the self-limiting beliefs causing much of your stress and self-doubt.

As we mentioned in chapter 3, mindfulness can also transform your threat response into challenge or tend-and-befriend responses. Reappraising stress and self-doubt (both your stress mindset and the triggers themselves) with openness, curiosity, and kindness helps to calm your troubled mind, improve your relationship with yourself and others, and support the learning and growth that comes from leaning in to your greatest challenges.

In this mindfulness practice, you allow yourself to settle and, with an attitude of openness, curiosity, and kindness, sequentially ask yourself each of the four questions of the Appraise-Reappraise Method, listening deeply for what answers arise.

After you complete your practice, if it's helpful, you can write down your answers to each of the four questions and note any insights you've had.

You can download the step-by-step instructions for this practice at SuperSmartHealth.com/BookBonus.

I invite you to use this practice whenever you feel challenged by a stressful or self-doubt-inducing event, so you can experience the additional benefits of mindfulness with this method. With a purely *cognitive* approach to the Appraise-Reappraise Method, we focus on reframing our patterns of thinking, which offers us two choices in the way we can view our story: we can believe our story, or we can rewrite it to cause us less stress or self-doubt.

However, when we add a *mindfulness* approach to the method, we discover a third choice in the way we view things. Not only can we choose to believe our story or rewrite it, we can observe and appreciate that either way, *these are just beliefs and stories to begin with.*

In addition to viewing the content of our story differently, we can also view the story from an entirely different perspective—from a place of tender, spacious awareness and a sense of our wholeness, from which we are able to hold all of our stories with greater equanimity or groundedness.

So when we ask ourselves the question, "How can I view this situation differently, so it causes me less stress and self-doubt?," from a mindful perspective, we have a built-in answer. We are able to view our stories from the spacious awareness of mindfulness itself, where our stories are less likely to get their hooks into us and cause us as much stress and self-doubt.

In the next section, you'll discover another mindfulness practice that further enhances your qualities of kindness and self-compassion to provide you with a deeper sense of safety, care, and comfort as you work with your stress and self-doubt.

## Mindfulness Practice: Loving-Kindness (Part One)

As we learned earlier in this chapter, childhood conditioning can cause fear and self-doubt. Fear arises if you believe you can only love and accept yourself when you are successful or when you prove your self-worth.

You also discovered how to rewrite this internal contract so you can accept yourself unconditionally. In other words, you can learn to embody a statement such as, *"I accept myself, doubts of self-worth and all."*

The loving-kindness practice you are about to learn embeds this new contract within you by rewiring your brain with a circuit of unconditional self-acceptance and a deep knowing that you love and accept yourself no matter what, including any self-doubt that may arise.

This loving-kindness mindfulness practice builds on the others you've learned by more explicitly expressing love, kindness, and compassion for yourself, with phrases that resonate with your deepest wishes and inherent capacity for creating an internal sense of safety, peace, health, love, and well-being. (You'll receive the second part of this practice in part 3 of this book.)

Here are the step-by-step instructions for this practice:

1. Allow yourself to get comfortable, either lying down or sitting up with an erect and alert posture. You may close your eyes or leave them open as you practice.

2. Bring to this meditation an intention to be open, kind, and accepting of whatever arises in this practice.

3. Now bring your attention to your heart center and to the ebb and flow of your breathing, feeling gratitude for your breath and this life you are blessed to live.

4. As you breathe, grateful for your breath, imagine your breath is flowing in and out through your heart center. As you do this, appreciate that this time you have set aside for yourself is an act of loving-kindness toward yourself.

5. As you continue breathing, notice any thoughts, sensations, or emotions that may arise, possibly including feelings of self-doubt, tension, self-criticism, and self-judgment. If they do, notice and appreciate your awareness of them. As best you can, simply observe whatever you are experiencing with a light touch of kindness and acceptance.

6. Now, gently shift your attention back to your heart-centered breathing. As you do, bring to mind someone who loves and accepts you unconditionally or whom you love unconditionally, someone who naturally brings a smile to your face. It could be a loved one, a special friend, mentor, or pet.

7. Notice what happens to the feeling in your heart center as you do.

8. As you feel your heart expand, breathe in through your heart, imagining you are amplifying your breath with loving-kindness. Then, as you breathe out, imagine you are breathing this love and kindness throughout your body.

9. As you continue to breathe in love and kindness though your heart center, allow yourself to breathe in any thoughts or feelings of suffering through your heart, absorbing them with a wish for you to be free of suffering. Then, as you breathe out, imagine yourself filling your entire body with love and kindness.

10. If it helps, you can gently place your hand over your heart as you breathe in any suffering and breathe out love and goodwill throughout your body.

11. As you rest in this field of kind and loving awareness, bring your focus of attention back to your breathing through your heart center. Now, in your mind, or whispering silently to yourself, express the following phrases as a benevolent wish:

    May I be safe.

    May I be strong.

    May I be filled with loving-kindness.

12. As you express these phrases, see if you can connect deeply with the meaning of these words. Let them sink in and be felt throughout your body:

    May I be safe.

    May I be strong.

    May I be filled with loving-kindness.

13. As you deepen your experience with these phrases, you may also find it helpful to integrate these phrases with your breathing.

14. Explore this integration by inhaling through your heart center and then, as you breathe out, whisper in your mind, "May I be safe." Imagine as you are breathing out that you are infusing every fiber of your being with what you are expressing.

15. Breathe in through your heart center and then, as you breathe out, say to yourself, "May I be strong," and let it sink in.

16. Breathe in through your heart center and then, as you breathe out, say to yourself, "May I be filled with loving-kindness," allowing yourself to feel deeply cared for by these words.

17. Breathe in through your heart center and then, as you breathe out, infuse every cell in your body, repeating these phrases as often as feels helpful to you.

18. Then when you are ready, gently open your eyes.

Once again, appreciate the time you have taken to deeply care for yourself. In this practice, the words "safety," "strength," and "loving-kindness" were chosen with the intention of helping you transform your threat response to a challenge and tend-and-befriend response. You may consider substituting any of these words with any others that feel more resonant to you.

Each time you express, resonate, and connect with these phrases or words, you are investing in yourself. From the hub of your wheel of awareness, observing whatever stress or self-doubt you may be experiencing with curiosity, kindness, and acceptance, you are internalizing your unconditional contract of accepting yourself, doubts of self-worth and all. By hardwiring a neural circuit of self-compassion around your experience of stress and self-doubt, you are building inner resources of resiliency to more easily handle your greatest challenges.

Further, you are stabilizing the base of your Maslowian Hierarchy of Needs, meeting your foundational safety and love and belonging needs.

In Steps 1 and 2 of the 4 in 4 Framework, with your new skills of managing your reactivity and reappraising your stress and self-doubt, you have learned to cultivate a deeper sense of safety and confidence within. Now that you have liberated significant energy from the base of the hierarchy, you can make the shift towards the state of creativity and experience a whole new world of possibility and growth.

In Step 3, you'll next learn how to more fully harness this energy to focus on what is truly important in your life—optimizing your health and vitality, deepening your most important relationships, and meeting your highest needs to find greater success and significance in your life at work and at home.

# CHAPTER 7

# Step 3: Cultivating Creativity

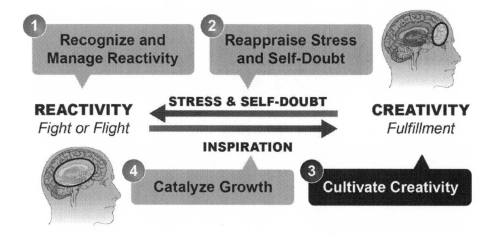

Now that you've learned how to defuse your reactivity, in Step 3 you'll be making the turn into creativity, where you'll feel inspired to optimize your health, relationships, and overall productivity. Here you will create an ideal life vision where you will clarify and manifest what matters most to you. Instead of running fear-based simulations about all that could go wrong, you'll be running success-based simulations to create the life you want to live—where you feel more energized, fulfilled, and resilient.

As exciting and energizing as this step is, it's not for the faint of heart. Some of my clients tell me they find this step challenging or even overwhelming.

Recall the Yerkes-Dodson stress and performance curve. As you approach levels of peak performance from the left side of the curve, your stress rises.[1]

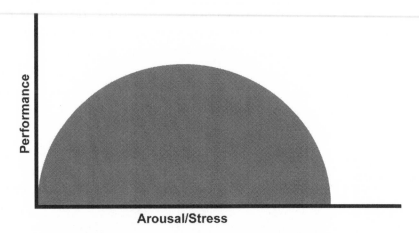

*Figure 7.1. Yerkes-Dodson Stress and Performance Curve*

As you engage with what matters most to you and challenge the limits of your capability, you can expect to experience *healthy* levels of stress (or "eustress"). This kind of stress is what fuels your best performance and allows you to experience that sense of flow and well-being at the peak of your performance curve.

In *The Upside of Stress,* Kelly McGonigal highlights a surprising finding from a study of the 2005-2006 Gallup World Poll.[2] The Gallup researchers asked over 125,000 people from 121 countries to indicate whether they had experienced a significant amount of stress in the previous day in order to calculate each nation's stress index. The study found that the higher the nation's stress index, the *higher* the nation's well-being. Further, individuals who were stressed but not depressed—i.e., aroused and positively activated by their stress—experienced higher life satisfaction. This study suggests that stress, when leveraged as an asset to engage with what you most care about, goes hand in hand with well-being, meaning, and fulfillment.

Still, the process of creating your ideal life design can feel daunting. You may feel overwhelmed, unsure where to begin. Or you may be experiencing a fear of failure (or even a fear of success), which can lead to avoidance and procrastination and ultimately cause you to slip down the right side of the stress and performance curve. If you do find yourself slipping down the right side of the curve into distress, try *reappraising* this entire process as the enlivening adventure of a lifetime and then break the process down into a framework with bite-sized, easy-to-implement steps.

This chapter will introduce you to a process that will help you do just that. Once again, the key is not to avoid stress, but to mindfully, with openness, curiosity, and kindness, find a way to best leverage it!

## The VSIR Process™

A few years ago, I attended an event called the Big Task Weekend. It brought together a diverse group of visionary leaders from top organizations to solve some of the world's biggest challenges. To structure our work together, a couple of senior executives from Cisco shared the framework behind how their company tackled all of their projects: they focused on *vision,* then *strategy,* and then *execution.*

I've adapted this approach to provide you with the VSIR Process™, which you can use to optimize your health, relationships, and productivity. Note: productivity refers not just to the way you work, but to all the ways you make money, take care of things at home, volunteer your time, and/or participate in any of your creative endeavors. You can also apply the VSIR Process to any other area of your life besides health, relationships, and productivity that's important to you.

*Figure 7.2. The VSIR Process*

VSIR is a circular process that stands for *Vision, Strategy, Implementation,* and *Results.* While this chapter will focus on how you can apply this process to your personal life, as you'll discover in chapter 12, you can apply it just as well to a business or organization.

The process includes:

- Creating your blueprint for your ideal life **vision**

- Formulating **strategies** outlining the specific components and sub-components of your overall vision

- Taking action to **implement** your strategies

- Clarifying and targeting the specific **results** you will achieve if your strategy is successfully implemented

Each of these components has its own vantage point and time frame. Your *vision* is your big, bold picture of your life well lived, viewed from 30,000 feet and projecting about five or ten years out. *Strategy* takes the 10,000-foot view and looks out about one, two, or three years. *Implementation* and *results* bring it down to ground level, focusing on the action you're taking today, tomorrow, next week, and/or next month.

Part of what makes this process so effective is that it is an iterative cycle, in which you are continually reflecting upon and refining each component. For example, if you don't achieve your results within your targeted time frame, you may reflect on whether you want to adjust your vision, whether your strategies are sufficiently comprehensive, or whether you or those to whom you delegated have been falling short on implementation. You may also consider whether your results are realistic to begin with.

All the components of VSIR draw extensively on the capacity of your PFC, which is involved in setting a vision, the executive functions of strategic planning and decision making, and your willpower to follow through with the actions you take. In the VSIR Process, you'll be using your PFC to run success-based simulations, where you are imagining a better future and forming your plan of action to get there. In fact, three of the four components—vision, strategy, and results—are all imaginary simulations. Implementation is the step when things really start to happen.

This leads me to another important point about the VSIR Process: because these are simulations, you don't have to do any of these steps perfectly. Often we get stuck because we think we have to have the perfect plan before we can act. Hence we may delay or wait for things to happen. What actually drives your VSIR cycle is implementation, or *taking action*. Taking action is what generates results and, if you iterate with a growth mindset, gets you closer to your vision (or, just as helpfully, gets you closer to realizing your vision may not be what you wanted after all!).

That said, the VSIR Process may end up appealing more to "chart the course" personality types rather than those with a more organic, "shoot from the hip" style. I give you full permission to adapt the process to fit your style and needs.

So don't spend too much time trying to get everything perfect at the outset. Explore, feel inspired, and have fun with the process. Most important, begin taking action to more fully engage in your flourishing life.

Now let's explore each of the components of VSIR in greater depth, starting with vision.

## Vision

Your vision is an image of your ideal future. It encapsulates your purpose and passion for being and generates the guiding force of inspiration in your life.

Creating the optimal conditions for inspiration is key to clarifying your vision. So before you begin, set aside some time and space where you can feel inspired, away from distractions and your daily frazzle. Unplug from your e-mails and phone in your office. Better yet, sit in your garden or visit your favorite park, beach, or trail. Get a journal to help you reflect on what's truly most important and design the life you want to create.

Now, begin to reflect on the following question: what is your vision for a meaningful life?

Set aside excuses or reasons why your vision won't work. Allow yourself to dream big! What is *your* moonshot? Let your passion soar and your motivationally rewarding dopamine circuitry hum.

While each person's vision may look different, some key elements are similar for everyone. When I invite my workshop participants to begin reflecting on their vision, I begin with the question, "What is your definition of optimal health?"

Why do I begin with this question? Because your answer reveals your currency for optimizing your life. In my workshops, I typically get a range of answers, but I'd like you to consider one in particular: optimal health is *energy optimized.*

Rather than simply defining health as the absence of disease, this concept of health invites you to consider what energizes or depletes you in all areas, not just physically. Specifically understanding what enriches or drains your *energetic* bank account is key to creating your life's vision.

I have found that the following seven elements greatly energize and enrich our lives with meaning:

- Learning
- Connecting
- Expressing potential
- Being of service
- Creating opportunity
- Experiencing significance
- Leaving a legacy

The way you love to learn, connect, express your potential, and be of service are key elements of your purpose-driven *vision.* Creating opportunity engages the *strategy* and *implementation* components of your VSIR Process, the *results* of which enable you to experience significance and leave your legacy.

These areas overlap significantly with Martin Seligman's recipe for a "flourishing" life. Seligman, the father of the Positive Psychology, uses the acronym PERMA:[3]

- Positive emotions
- Engagement

- Relationships
- Meaning
- Accomplishment

So, to begin formulating your vision, start by answering the following questions that align with the energizers for a meaningful life listed above. This spadework will help crystallize your vision of your ideal life.

1.  **What do I love *learning* about?** (Hint: think of the books you like to read, what fascinates you in museums, what documentaries interest you, what you search for on the Internet, etc.)
2.  **How do I like to *connect* with people?**
3.  **How do I like to *express myself* fully?**
4.  **What are my top character strengths?** Suggestion: you can identify your top strengths by completing the freely available VIA Survey of Character Strengths at http://www.viacharacter.org. Knowing your character strengths provides additional information for determining your highest service, below.
5.  Now that you've answered the questions above, bring it all together and answer this question: **What is my highest *service* and purpose?**

The result of living your highest service and purpose results in *living a life of significance,* your highest Maslowian need. And if you live a life of significance, when you look back upon your life, you'll know you are *leaving a powerful legacy* that extends beyond your life. As the iconic philosopher and psychologist William James said, "The great use of a life is to spend it for something that will outlast it."[4]

For example, to answer the questions above, I love *learning* by putting myself in very challenging situations that trigger stress and self-doubt, so I can learn how to more fully embrace them and grow from them. I find meaning in learning, so I can give. Most of the stories I've shared with you so far have been about the big stress-and-self-doubt-inducing challenges I've learned from in my own life, offered to hopefully contribute to your learning as well. I love *connecting* with people by learning about their dreams and frustrations, and

I love *expressing* myself in ways that can enrich their lives so they can make a bigger difference in the lives of others.

When my wife asked me why I volunteered to become the founding chair of AIHM—a very challenging and time-consuming role as we were running our business—I shared that I not only believed in the mission, but that I was also looking to "fry on purpose." I wanted to learn how to strengthen my *highest strengths,* which are related to teaching and leadership, so I can contribute more fully. My *highest service and purpose* is around helping leaders find and manifest their highest service and purpose.

After completing your spadework of reflecting on the values and strengths that energize you, you're now ready to describe your ideal life vision more specifically, integrating the dimensions of health, relationships, and productivity.

Pick a time horizon for your vision that feels right to you, giving you enough time to manifest your dreams, but not so far out that you feel disconnected from it. Many people find five or ten years out feels right to them.

Now paint a picture in your mind of your life well lived. Start writing whatever comes to mind, and write in the present tense to more fully engage with your vision, as if it is being manifested or has already been realized. Ensure your ideal life vision integrates how you like to learn, connect, and express yourself with what you've identified as your top character strengths and your highest purpose and service.

As you consider your vision, you might find it helpful to ask yourself the question, "When I think about my vision for my ideal life in *x* years, what does my life well lived look like to me in the areas of health, relationships, and productivity?" Even if you do not yet know your overall purpose, simply envisioning what your optimal health, relationships, and productivity would look like is purpose enough to begin with. Just start writing and allow your ideal life vision to crystallize for yourself as you do.

For example, you can write down your vision for health, relationships, and productivity like I've done below:

In five years, I see myself with a full heart, very active, having fun playing lacrosse and surfing with my sons, Zach and Dylan, and joyfully hiking the Torrey Pines beach trails with my wife, Sue. I'm deeply connected to Sue and my boys. Zach and Dylan talk freely to me about their personal lives and still ask for my advice. Sue and I are subsidizing their college education so they graduate debt free. Sue and I are deepening our love for each other, continually enriching the "spiritual home" that we designed together on our honeymoon. Together we are thriving in our work at SuperSmartHealth, free to work from anywhere in the world. I'm making a difference with this book, keynote addresses, workshops, online training programs, and group and one-on-one coaching. I'm living from my highest purpose and service, deeply connecting with and training leaders in business, healthcare, and government to lead well from within, from their highest selves. The leaders whose lives I touch are living from their higher purpose and making an even bigger difference in the lives of their families, employees, patients, clients, organizations, and communities they serve.

Of course, *your* vision is highly personal; there is no right or wrong. Write down whatever inspires and energizes you. Again, don't let perfection be the enemy of the good. Get something down on paper and trust you can come back again and again to refine it.

Also, as you flesh out your vision, you may also consider including other dimensions besides health, relationships, and productivity, depending on your personal beliefs or preferences. For example, you may consider adding areas such as your faith/spirituality, hobbies, and what you love to do for fun.

Your vision will likely be influenced by your current role or vocation. For example, if you are a healer, your vision may represent the blueprint for your ideal practice. It may include the patients or clients you want to serve, the healing practices you embrace, your optimal practice setting, the model with which you are making your reimbursement work, and more.

If you are leader in an organization, in addition to your personal vision, you may also incorporate your vision and mission for your organization, the culture you are creating, and the difference you are making in the lives of your clients with the value you bring. (We'll be discussing this further in chapter 12.)

In addition to writing down your vision, there are other fun and creative ways to further explore and connect with your vision and passion. For example, a vision board is a great way to bring your emotionally charged vision to life. Collect pictures, quotes, poems, or objects that feel inspiring and meaningful to you. Don't hold back; include whatever calls to you. Assemble the images into a collage. Then step back and reflect on what feels most important to you.

Also, one of the most powerful ways I enjoy working with participants in my workshops and coaching is with a vision drawing exercise. With colored pencils, markers, or crayons in hand, I invite them to take a few minutes to draw two pictures.

First, I invite them take a few minutes to draw their life as it is right now. Then, after completing the first picture, I have them set it aside, clear their mind for a few moments, and then draw a second picture: a vision of their life well lived.

If this approach appeals to you more than writing or creating a vision board, feel free to try it. First, draw a picture of your life as it is right now. Then set that picture aside, pause to clear your mind, and draw a picture of your life well lived. You can choose whatever time horizon you'd like for this second picture. Some imagine what they'd like to see their life as today, or five or ten years from now. Others imagine their picture as a eulogy, reflecting the legacy they'd like to leave.

Anything goes in these pictures: stick figures, quotes, realistic or abstract images. They may reflect your stress, self-doubt, fears, and frustrations, as well as your hopes, dreams, purpose, and themes of health, relationships, and productivity. Go with whatever emerges and allow yourself to be curious and surprised at the results.

The images that emerge are rich. Often they enable participants to see more deeply than through writing alone. In the first picture, many draw clouds covering the sun or fog; some use subdued colors in their life as it is, to reflect their yearning for clarity or vibrancy in their lives. I recall one participant who drew a matchbook, with each match representing a different option for his life. He realized this image represented his sense of overwhelm at needing to choose which match to strike first. It reflected his current difficulty in saying no to an abundance of tempting opportunities and focusing on and following through on any one thing. Another participant drew a high-performance sailboat with flaccid sails. The meaning of this image will become more apparent in just a moment.

In the second picture, representing a life well lived, themes of love, connection, freedom, and legacy frequently emerge. These pictures more typically represent deeper values than "stuff," like money or an impressive house or car. The reason is that when you begin to ask deeper questions about why money matters, you tend to realize money is not an end but a means to provide for what matters most: freedom, time spent with loved ones, the difference we want to make, and the legacy we want to leave.

In my workshops, to further explain the purpose of drawing these two pictures, I often refer to a TED talk by Nancy Duarte called the "The Secret Structure of Great Talks."[5] Here Duarte points out that the greatest speeches ever given have a similar architecture. As shown in the figure below, it's a repetitive pattern that oscillates between a state of "what is" and a vision of "what could be." Duarte uses the example of "I Have a Dream" by Martin Luther King Jr., where the gap is between the injustices of the time and a dream of a nation where "all men are created equal."[6]

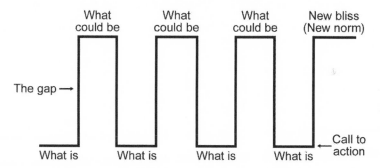

*Figure 7.3. The Architecture of Great Talks*

In the drawing exercise, the first drawing of your life as it is represents "what is," and the second drawing of your life well lived represents "what could be." The gap between these states creates structural tension, or cognitive dissonance, which is partly the reason why clarifying your vision can be an uncomfortable process. However, this tension is important and often what's needed to create change.

In your brain, this gap activates your anterior cingulate, which is your error detection unit. Your anterior cingulate then activates your PFC, engaging your executive functions of strategic planning and decision making, as well as the circuits that motivate you to take action to close the gap. Thus, even though they may feel uncomfortable or even daunting, this gap and its accompanying feeling of dissonance are important parts of what facilitates your transformation.[7]

Remember the participant who drew the high-performance sail boat with flaccid sails to represent his life as it currently is? I explained to him that identifying the gap between "what is" and "what could be" generates a low- and high-pressure system that creates the winds of change that drive transformation. This concept helped him to understand why he felt stuck in his life, even though he sensed his potential. He realized he had not yet sufficiently identified his gap, or sensed his dissonance, to fully engage the change needed.

As you clarify the gap between where you are and where you want to be, remember that the discomfort you may feel has value. Instead of being threatened or pulled off track by the harmful aspects of stress and self-doubt, I invite you to trust that you have the inner resources to harness the energy of that discomfort with your challenge response and growth mindset, mindfully engaging with curiosity and kindness, as you're drawn in to the next steps of VSIR Process.

In the architecture of great speeches in the figure above, you'll notice that leaders oscillate with reverie in the gap between the states of "what is" and "what could be" until they reach a climax—*the call to action*—leading to the "new bliss," or Martin Luther King Jr.'s "Free at last!" *Your* new norm of manifestation!

In the VSIR cycle, your strategies and implementation are your call to action, to manifest the results you want to see on your journey towards your vision.

So using whichever method resonates with you most—whether it's writing, creating a vision board, or drawing—go ahead and capture your vision.

Before we cross the street, we always look both ways. Here too you're going to "look left before you look right" in the VSIR cycle, and rather than proceed directly to the strategy for making your vision a reality, you next consider the *results* you want to aim for while your vision is fresh in your mind. Then we'll proceed clockwise in the cycle to consider your strategy and implementation to achieve these results and then again revisit your results to reflect on what you have achieved.

## Results

You may have heard of setting SMART goals, where SMART stands for Specific, Measurable, Attainable, Realistic, and Time framed. In this section, before we proceed to strategy and implementation, we're going to talk about aiming for SMART *results* instead.

When SMART goals are untethered from your larger vision, they can be ineffective or even distracting. You may feel like you're getting stuff done, but if you are not really thinking big enough or focusing on your deeper passion and purpose, you won't be on track to experience the significance or leave the legacy you want.

So with SMART results, "SMRT" stands for the same terms: Specific, Measurable, Realistic, and Time framed. However, the "A" is different. Instead of Attainable, it stands for *Aligned*. It reminds you to reflect on whether the results you are aiming towards are indeed congruent with your vision.

The benefit of setting SMART results is that it anchors your inspired vision on solid ground so you can more clearly identify the specific actions you'll need to take. What gets measured gets done.

As you set your SMART results, one helpful approach is to first clarify your baseline in key areas of your life right now and then establish where you would like them to be within a specific time frame.

One way to benchmark and track your performance or experience in the areas of health, relationships, and productivity (or any other domains you might want to add) is to use a Cantril Ladder, a tool used by Gallup to track well-being, among other things.[8]

The Cantril Ladder is an imaginary ladder with steps numbered from 0 at the bottom to 10 at the top, with 0 representing the worst possible life for you and 10 representing the best.

For example, when it comes to your health, 0 would represent the complete absence of any energy and vitality and 10 a sense of maximal physical, mental, emotional, and spiritual well-being. For your relationships, 0 would represent complete disconnection and 10 the most fulfilling and connected relationship you could imagine, whether it's your partner, children, colleague, friend, or any other person important in your life. And for your productivity, whether in work or any other vocation, 0 would represent complete disengagement and 10 maximal engagement and performance.

With the Cantril Ladder, you can quantify which rung of the ladder you are currently standing on and then which rung of the ladder you would realistically like to see yourself standing on at specific points in the future.

So if you feel your relationship with your spouse is currently a 6, in one week you might like to see it at a 7, in one month an 8, and in one year at a consistent 9.

In each of these areas, you can also assign more specific targets for each respective time frame. For example, in health, you could set a target weight or exercise level. In your relationships, it could be a special trip, renewing your vows, or funding your children's college tuition at a specific amount. In your productivity, it could be a revenue target, job title, completion of a major project, or the number of clients or patients you're serving.

An example of your SMART results in each of these key areas is shown in the table below (written as if they had already happened by a specified time frame):

|  | Health | Relationships | Productivity |
|---|---|---|---|
| **1 Week** | Weight: lost 2 lbs. to weigh 185 lbs.<br><br>Quit tobacco by Sunday<br><br>Started running 1 mile 3x/wk<br><br>Cantril Ladder (CL): daily energy and vitality level consistently 6/10 or above | CL: spouse and children 7/10<br><br>Apologized to spouse for . . . | CL: productivity 7/10<br><br>Completed book outline and began writing book |
| **1 Month** | Weight: 180 lbs.<br><br>Ran 2 miles 3x/wk<br><br>CL: daily energy and vitality level consistently 7/10 or above | CL: spouse and children 8/10 | CL: productivity 8/10<br><br>Income for month: $x |
| **1 Year** | Weight: 170 lbs.<br><br>Ran a half marathon<br><br>LDL cholesterol 130<br><br>CL: daily energy and vitality level consistently 8/10 | CL: spouse and children 9/10<br><br>Enjoyed surfing trip with children | CL: productivity 9/10<br><br>Income for year: $x<br><br>Book published |
| **5 Years** | Weight: 160 lbs.<br><br>Ran 10 miles/wk<br><br>CL: daily energy and vitality level consistently 9/10 | CL: Spouse and children 9/10<br><br>Renewed vows with spouse<br><br>Funded each child's college at $x | CL: productivity 9/10<br><br>Yearly income: $x<br><br>Savings: $x million<br><br>Bought beach house and renting current home |

Note that some of these targets, or key performance indicators (KPIs), are short term, while others are long term. You may continually reset your short-term targets, such as your weekly KPIs, to keep you on track for what you want to achieve each week as you move towards your desired longer-term results and vision. You can also calculate your short-term results based on your longer-term targets. For example, if you have a specific revenue or weight loss target at one year, you can calculate what you would need to achieve each week to be on track with that target and adjust accordingly.

Now reflect on the vision you created earlier and consider *your* SMART results for whatever time frames feel right to you as your key stepping stones toward your desired future.

If you drew your two pictures to create your vision and would like further inspiration, you may also take a look at each picture, and then on the Cantril Ladder scale of 0 to 10, rate the dimensions of your health, relationships, and productivity for each picture. See if you can also identify any other specific and measurable results in your life well lived that you'd like to include.

Allow yourself to be bold in declaring your specific results and don't worry too much about the "how" for now. Also recognize that the results you declare may have cross-linking synergies with the results in other areas of your life, so you may well be able to accomplish more than you think you can. For example, as you raise your level of energy and vitality, your productivity will likely increase, too. As you experience richer and deeper relationships with others or your highest sources of inspiration, your emotional and spiritual well-being will increase, further enhancing your sense of energy and vitality in all areas of your life as well.

At the same time, be mindful not to overload yourself with too many targets, especially if they involve new behaviors that require willpower to get started. Your willpower draws on the brain power of your PFC. Much as a muscle does, this part of your brain may fatigue and take some time to grow stronger.[9] If you take on too much, you may find your willpower spread too thin and yourself slipping in important areas or insufficiently engaging with or following through on the key changes you want to make. Start by reflecting on the one or two key changes you'd like to commit to first in each of these areas and then build around your success.

Go ahead and take a moment now to write down the most important and inspiring Specific, Measurable, Aligned, Realistic, and Time-framed results you want to see for yourself over the next week, month, year, and five-year period (or modify these time frames according to what works best for you).

Now that you have identified your SMART results in each of these areas of your vision, you are ready to create your action plan for doing so: your *strategy* and *implementation*.

## Strategy and Implementation

Your *strategies* are simply the key components (i.e., headings and subheadings) of your plan to achieve your vision and SMART results. Your *implementation* refers to the specific steps you're taking to execute your plan. Let's take a closer look how you can successfully create and implement your strategies in the areas of health, relationships, and productivity.

### *Health*

Let's return to our sample vision and SMART results for health. If you want to reach a certain weight, run a half-marathon at one year, or consistently enjoy a 9/10 sense of energy and vitality five years from now, take a moment to consider the overarching *strategy* that would frame your action plan to achieve these results.

Look for strategies that are both simple and powerful. One such strategy for health involves the simple approach of **take out the bad stuff** and **put in the good stuff.**

For the strategy **take out the bad stuff,** you might, for example, include the substrategies of *quitting tobacco* and/or *decreasing alcohol consumption*.

Under the strategy **put in the good stuff,** you might include the substrategies of *eating well, getting exercise, getting adequate sleep,* and *practicing mindfulness*—all major areas scientifically proven to contribute to your wellness, well-being, and performance.

You can then continue to refine strategies in each area. For example, beneath the substrategy of *eating well,* you can write down the elegantly simple strategy Michael Pollan presents in his book *In Defense of Food:* "Eat [real] food, not too much, mostly plants."[10]

In addition, to maintain or lose weight, you might employ a strategy to eat slowly and mindfully. With this approach, you'd listen to your body cues more closely, eat only when you are physically hungry, and stop when you feel full. This strategy may sound overly simplistic, but programs based on this principle of mindfulness-based eating have found reductions in body weight as well as a reversal of metabolic syndrome, a diabetes-related condition, which is a major risk for heart disease and incurs significant health claims for business.[11]

Now, take a look at your own vision and results for health and mindfully consider the strategic behaviors you might use to achieve them. Lean in to the challenge with curiosity and ask yourself, "What strategies would be most helpful to realize my vision of optimal physical health?" Allow yourself to be inspired, creative, and pragmatic in response to the answers that come. Go ahead and write them down in your journal, perhaps as headings and subheadings of your action plan; at the very least, begin framing your strategies in your mind.

Once again, the most important thing is to *take action* and *experience early success* with your efforts. So start by prioritizing just one, two, or three strategies that you feel you can realistically implement.

Let's now consider the *implementation* of your strategies. You can move into action by creating a to-do list of checkboxes, either below or beside each strategy. Your to-do list for implementation focuses on a very short time horizon: what you will do today, tomorrow, and over the next few weeks. It also gets very granular, getting into the specifics of the when, where, with whom, and/or how you will execute each of your strategies.

For example, if one of your health strategies is to *quit smoking tobacco,* you would write down your quit date, dispose of all your smoking paraphernalia, and write down who you are going to call for support.

To implement your strategy of *eating well,* you might create a to-do list that includes when you will dispose of all unhealthy foods in your pantry, your healthy-eating grocery list, and when and where you will shop. If you're ambitious, you might also include a specific meal plan for the week.

To implement your *exercise* strategy, you could write out a FITT plan, specifying the Frequency, Intensity, Time, and Type of exercise, selecting an activity that feels really fun, challenging, and energizing. You can find specific guidelines for fitness by searching online for the "National Institutes of Health Exercise Recommendations."[12]

To implement your *sleep* strategy, create a sleep routine with a set time to go to sleep each night and a set time arise in the morning and stick with it as best you can. While individual needs may vary, the National Sleep Foundation, whose guidelines are based on a review of over 300 studies, recommends 7 to 9 hours of sleep a day for adults ages 18 to 64, and 7 to 8 hours for adults 65 years and older.[13]

To implement your *mindfulness* strategy, a topic we've spoken extensively about throughout this book, block out a specific time of day for your mindfulness practices.

Now, based on the health strategies you've already listed or framed in your mind, clear a block of time to go ahead and create a similar implementation plan for yourself.

If you find it helpful to write down your strategy and implementation plan in the form of checklists, here's what this might look like.

| HEALTH | |
|---|---|
| **Take Out Bad Stuff!** | |
| **Quit Tobacco** | **Decrease Alcohol** |
| ☐ Quit tobacco, 1 January <br> ☐ Tell partner and best friend about plan tomorrow <br> ☐ Get quit line info tomorrow <br> ☐ See doctor for patches, 20 December <br> ☐ Get rid of cigs and ashtrays, 31 December | ☐ Starting tomorrow, no more than one glass of alcohol with dinner |

| Put In Good Stuff! | | | |
|---|---|---|---|
| **Eat Well** | **Exercise** | **Sleep Well** | **Mindfulness Meditation** |
| Real food, not too much, mostly plants, and only when hungry | ☐ Yoga on Monday, Wednesday, and Friday | ☐ 8 hours of sleep a night: in bed by 10:30 p.m., asleep by 11 p.m., awake at 7 a.m. | ☐ 15 minutes of mindfulness practice before falling asleep and just before getting out of bed in morning |
| ☐ Pantry raid, 2 Nov | ☐ Run 2 laps around park each morning | | |
| ☐ Create healthy shopping list every Sunday evening | ☐ Surf twice a week (waves willing ☺) | ☐ No looking at laptop computer or cell phone in bed before sleep | ☐ 3-day meditation retreat, 24 February |
| ☐ Drink 8 glasses of water per day | ☐ Bike ride with son on Sunday mornings | | |
| ☐ Drink a power vegetable protein shake each morning | | | |
| ☐ Eat fish twice a week | | | |
| ☐ Remember veggies 5 times per day | | | |

After you've outlined your strategies and to-dos for implementing your vision for optimal health, step back and congratulate yourself. You've just completed the framework of your own personal wellness program! If your program doesn't yet feel complete, put it aside and then come back to work on it further. You may also find it helpful to enhance it with the various wellness programs available through employers, insurance carriers, spas, or gyms to help you flesh out your personal program and/or provide you with further professional support and guidance as you implement it.

Once you've begun to implement your strategies for health, the most important thing is to enjoy the adventure of discovering how to further optimize your program. Keep engaging mindfully in your daily activities—with openness, curiosity, and kindness—allowing yourself to be guided by your energy levels throughout your day. For example, notice when you feel your energy expand and when you feel depleted. If you notice your energy crashing a few hours after meals, try adjusting what you eat earlier in the day. Experiment with adding or eliminating certain foods from your diet. If you feel sleepy during the day, see how you feel after adding thirty minutes to your nighttime sleep or a couple of strategic naps during the day. Notice how you feel after exercise and whether it would be helpful to dial your activity up or dial it back. Also notice when you simply need to rest, relax, rejuvenate, and reinvigorate yourself.

In addition to engaging your implementation plan mindfully, here are some additional implementation tips. First, if you use a calendar, it's vitally important that you schedule your key action steps in your calendar. If your action items aren't scheduled, they're unlikely to get done.

Also, research has shown that a key to successful implementation is to connect your new actions with specific cues or existing habits to make these new actions automatic.[14] This is especially important when you are initiating new healthy habits. For example, if you want to start a mindfulness meditation practice, think of a time of day when it would be easy and comfortable to do. I integrate my mindfulness meditation practice around my sleep habits. I meditate for a few minutes before I go to sleep and first thing in the morning.

Similarly, if you plan to start running in the morning, you could put your sneakers right below your bathroom sink to connect your new running habit to your already-existing toothbrushing habit. This timely and welcome reminder can be the difference between getting out the door to enjoy this new activity and "forgetting" yet again.

Another key to establishing your new behavior is to get social. Running with a friend or joining a socially supportive fitness class holds you accountable, provides extra motivation, and makes your activities even more fun! Examples of health programs with a strong social component are CrossFit and the Daniel Plan. The latter is an example of a lifestyle program, where small group and community support in a church-based setting have provided a model for success. To date, more than 15,000 people in the congregation from Saddleback Church have lost well over 250,000 pounds.[15]

One of the things I love to do more than anything else is surfing with my boys and good friends. It provides a potent combination of social interaction and engaging in an activity I thoroughly enjoy.

In addition to creating a clear cue for taking action, another major factor in establishing any new habit is focusing on the reward you gain from it.[16] With surfing, my cue is Surfline, an online forecast for waves coming in, and my rewards are spending time with loved ones, the beauty of the ocean, the thrill of dropping in on a great ride, and the afterglow of well-being I feel for hours after I'm out of the water. Hence, I'm hooked!

Keep looking for creative ways to tap into your cues and rewards to establish your health habits.

Research shows it takes, on average, 66 days or more to wire in your new behavior.[17] So while a new activity may feel a bit awkward or uncomfortable at first, take heart that it will become easier and more automatic, requiring far less willpower to sustain over time.

Also remember that growth always comes with some degree of stress and challenge. Just keep going! Once you get in the groove, your expanded capacity and mastery will make your activity even more enjoyable and rewarding as you begin to flow more gracefully with it. When I began salsa dancing, I was a complete klutz starting out. Finally, after sticking with it for a few of weeks, I found my rhythm. Then I met my wife, Sue, when she walked across the dance floor and asked me to dance. Habits do have their rewards!

Remember, as you continue to implement your health strategies, stay curious, be kind to yourself, and keep exploring. As you deepen your commitment to your health, know that you are deepening your relationship with yourself, which leads us to the next section: how to implement strategies to optimize your relationships.

## *Relationships*

Your relationships are vital to a life well lived. They affect your health and productivity and your well-being and resiliency. They are also crucial to your effectiveness as a leader. In addition to what we'll be covering on implementing strategies to optimize your relationships here, we'll be focusing extensively on relationships in part 3, which delves into how you can resolve conflicts, nurture your most important relationships, and cultivate actively engaged cultures so you can lead well in the world.

Enhancing your relationships involves deepening your connection with yourself, others, and whatever you identify as your highest sources of inspiration. A key to doing so is setting an intention to bring positive energy to all of your relationships and mindfully asking, with curiosity and kindness, key questions about how you can strengthen them.

The simple act of asking questions and listening quietly for answers deepens your connection with yourself, as well as your spiritual connection, whatever this may mean to you. (We'll be further discussing the power of asking and finding answers to questions in the next chapter.) These questions may include big questions, such as: What do I need physically, emotionally, mentally, and spiritually? How can I deepen my faith? How can I best connect with others?

There are a number of ways you can come up with *strategies* for optimizing your relationship with others. One strategy is to simply list the names of the people who are most important to you, both personally and at work, and then ask yourself how you can deepen these specific relationships. Under each name, just write down the specific ideas that come to mind. For example, "Take son to beach this Saturday"; "Help Dad with his taxes this Sunday"; and "Arrange surprise party for Jane next Friday."

Another way to further develop your strategies is to list the specific ways you could quantifiably improve your relationships, based on your SMART results using a measurement tool like the Cantril Ladder. So if you rated a specific relationship at a 6 out of 10 and you would like it to be a 9, you could ask yourself, "What would it take to achieve this result? What qualities would I need to bring? How would I need to pay attention? What would I need to do"?

For example, in response to the question, "What qualities would I need to bring?" you might sense that you need to **be more present, be more loving,** and **express yourself more fully,** which would become your broad strategies for improving this relationship.

Now you can consider more specific strategies you could directly implement with each. As you think about how you could **be more present,** you could consider the specific strategy of *protected block time.* This strategy is an antidote for the malady of our commonly divided attention. All too often, when we're at work we're thinking about our relationships at home, and when we're at home, we're thinking about what we should be doing at work. Or we're distracted by text messages and social media on our phones. We struggle to be fully present in the presence of others.

A simple way to implement this strategy is to schedule protected block time with your partner or friend, such as a special night each week or a trip away. You might use the abbreviation PBT in your calendar. As you schedule this time, remind yourself that your time with others is sacred and set a strong intention to be fully present with the person you are planning to be with.

Then, when you are with this person, be fully present—not just physically but mentally, too. This means switching off your cell phone or, at the very least, keeping it out of sight. In 2012, the term "phubbing" was coined to describe the all-too-familiar practice of snubbing someone in favor of your mobile phone. Even setting your phone down on the table at a meal or while having coffee causes your companions to doubt that you're fully present and to fear something more important is just a ringtone away. When you show up on your date, commit to doing so, all in!

**Being more loving** includes being aware of how your loved ones most like to receive love.

To this end, Gary Chapman's book *The 5 Love Languages* offers a helpful strategy.[19] It lists five different ways we receive love, including *quality time, words of affirmation, acts of service, thoughtful gifts,* and *physical touch.*

Partners are often mismatched based on these different "love languages." For example, you may enjoy expressing your love by doing things around the house such as making special meals, doing the laundry, or any of a number of things to help out (acts of service) and then be completely befuddled when your partner says, "You never show me that you love me." Your partner might respond, "You are always working or on your phone, and you don't make time for us to be together." (What's most meaningful to your partner is quality time.) Or your partner might say, "You never hold or caress me or initiate sex.

I wish you'd hug me more or give me a tender kiss once in a while." (What your partner is yearning for is physical touch.) Or, "It would mean a lot to me if you occasionally surprised me with flowers or a special card or a gift from your heart on my birthday or our anniversary." (In this case, thoughtful gifts are most meaningful.) Or, "I wish you'd tell me how much I mean to you or tell me that you love and appreciate me." (In this case, words of affirmation matter most.)

To be more loving with your loved ones, ask them how they feel most cared for. (You can also download a love languages assessment at http://www.5lovelanguages.com.) Then find creative ways to connect with them the way they prefer.

In addition to your broad strategy of being more loving, to optimize your relationships you may also consider how to **express yourself more fully.** One strategy to do so is to *set an intention* just before you enter your house, begin a meeting at work, see a patient or client, or make an important call to think consciously about how you can best make it a meaningful and memorable interaction. Your intention primes your subconscious circuits to find creative ways to make it so. (In chapter 10, you'll learn more about how to nurture your relationships in similar ways.)

Another strategy to express yourself more authentically is to find the courage to *resolve conflicts, heal damaged relationships,* and *let go of resentments,* all of which drain you of energy. Consider making a list of individuals you are in conflict with, have experienced built-up resentment, feel you owe an apology, or are open to forgiving. Then schedule a time and way you will reach out to communicate with them. While taking this kind of initiative can be challenging, it can also free up immense amounts of energy to rededicate to your key relationships and other creative endeavors. (You will also be learning more about resolving conflicts in chapter 10.)

Here's an example of how to *implement* these kinds of specific strategies to optimize your key relationships:

| RELATIONSHIPS | | |
|---|---|---|
| **Spouse** | **Father** | **Mother** |
| ☐ Do 5 Love Languages assessment together on 14 February<br><br>☐ Date night Thursdays (PBT)<br><br>☐ Kiss goodnight and 2 hugs per day<br><br>☐ Surprise anniversary trip<br><br>☐ Yoga on Friday together (PBT) | ☐ Visit each Sunday (PBT)<br><br>☐ Call every other day<br><br>☐ Help with taxes, 15 March<br><br>☐ Take to doctor on 16 April<br><br>☐ Plan birthday, 8 May | ☐ Visit Memorial Park and celebrate her birthday with Dad on 22 June |
| **Son** | **Daughter** | **Best Friend** |
| ☐ Heart-to-heart hug twice a day<br><br>☐ Walk to school (PBT)<br><br>☐ Surfing once a week (PBT)<br><br>☐ One trip away each year (PBT) | ☐ Heart-to-heart hug twice a day<br><br>☐ Read together each night (PBT)<br><br>☐ One trip away each year (PBT)<br><br>☐ Legoland, 25 September (PBT) | ☐ Call Tuesday to resolve misunderstanding<br><br>☐ Beach hike first Sunday each month (PBT) |

**PBT** = Protected Block Time

Now take a few minutes to begin outlining *your* strategies, along with a list of specific to-dos to implement them, to enhance your most important relationships. Remember to put your protected block time meetings in your calendar and let them trigger your intention to be fully present and bring your positive energy to these interactions.

## *Productivity*

As mentioned earlier, productivity includes the way you work, make money, take care of things at home, volunteer your time, and/or any other creative endeavors you are involved in. To optimize your productivity at work, at home, or in any of your creative pursuits, you can begin by asking yourself, "What strategies do I need to implement to achieve peak productivity in this area of my life?"

Of course, there are many ways of outlining *strategies,* and these will be influenced by the types of work or activities you are involved in. For example, if you're an entrepreneur or business leader wanting to be more productive at work, you could outline your **projects, business model, budget, capabilities, people, marketing,** and **work stream** as your broad strategic headings. These headings can also be adapted to healing professions and others as well.

So, under the heading of **projects,** you would list the main projects you are involved with (such as products, sales goals, services, or any other deliverable you are creating). For example, you may list developing an online program, preparing for a keynote speech, and your specific client work.

Then be sure to prioritize your time for your key projects so you can stay focused! Stephen Covey's urgent-important time management matrix from his book, *The 7 Habits of Highly Effective People,* is very helpful to adapt here.[20]

|  | **Urgent** | **Not Urgent** |
|---|---|---|
| **Important** | Crises<br>Time-sensitive opportunities<br>Any deadline related to your VSIR | Any task related to your VSIR |
| **Not Important** | Pressing e-mails, calls, and meetings related to other people's deadlines and unrelated to your VSIR | "Click bait" distraction on Internet<br>Irrelevant e-mails and calls<br>Mindless TV watching |

*Table 7.1. Urgent-Important Time Management Matrix*

Prioritize what's important, whether urgent or not. What's important is what gives your life greatest meaning and purpose, which should already be reflected in your vision and the SMART results you want to achieve through this VSIR Process. Pressing timelines, setbacks that need to be addressed, or timely opportunities dictate urgencies.

The big mistake is to prioritize what's not important and urgent (usually defined by other peoples' urgencies)—or worse yet, what's neither urgent or important—over what's important and not urgent. When we repeatedly do so, we risk derailing our longer-range vision.

It takes discipline to stay on track and to say no strategically. Part of learning how to say no is to deeply understand what you are saying yes to, specifically, your personal vision and your ability to make an even larger contribution in the world. (If you'd like to learn a powerful strategy for saying no, I highly recommend you read *The Power of a Positive No* by William Ury, who co-founded Harvard's program on negotiation.[21])

After you've identified your key projects, consider your **business model** and think through how your business makes money and can scale to a profitable enterprise. Without focusing on your business model up front, you may risk finding yourself stressed and burned out later on, with limited ability to fully expand your mission, vision, and purpose in the world.

Then think carefully through the **budget** for your projects, which will help you effectively make decisions about allocating resources to your strategic priorities.

Next consider how to best build your **capabilities**—that is, the skills or capacities you may need to develop to efficiently complete your projects and serve others with excellence. Examples include additional certifications, independent research to build your knowledge base, or learning how to best prototype and market your product. If you are a healer and electronic health records are driving you crazy, consider taking a course to become a "practice ninja" in this area. Also, you might think through what capabilities would be best to master yourself and which you can delegate or outsource.

Now consider the **people** related to your project or enterprise. List two groups: one is the team helping you deliver your project and the other includes your customers, clients, or markets to whom the project will be delivered. For your team, list the key roles needed for the success of each project and the names of the best people to fill them. For your customers/clients/markets, make notes about what they most need: What are their biggest frustrations or problems? What solutions are they looking for? How can you best enrich their lives?

Then plan your approach to **marketing** your projects or products. How can you best position your offering, your company, and yourself to those who need your products and services most? Based on your customers' and clients' needs and ideal solutions you listed under "people" above, reflect on how you can best serve them. The more you can orient and package what you have to offer to serve their deepest needs, the more value you can deliver. Then, to round out your marketing plan, you can outline your various specific strategies to reach out and promote your product or service to the groups of people whose lives you want to enrich.

Finally, to put this all into motion, you might consider how to optimize your **work stream** to fully plan for and implement each of the projects you have prioritized. Part of the challenge of productivity is that you have a constant stream of input—whether it's e-mail, phone calls, texts, social media posts, stuff you want to read, introductions to people, or bills to pay—all competing for the attention and time you've designated for your key projects each day. While a full treatment of this topic is beyond the scope of this chapter, there are a number of powerful systems for triaging all this input as well as managing your workflow around your key projects. These include David Allen's *Getting Things Done* [22] and a form of agile project management called "scrum," adapted from the process of software development. It's outlined in Jeff Sutherland's *Scrum: The Art of Doing Twice the Work in Half the Time.* [23]

Of course, an efficient work stream also depends on *leveraging the executive functioning of your PFC.* As we've discussed, your PFC is in charge of the all-important tasks of prioritizing, planning, linking concepts together, and making decisions—all important functions for optimal productivity. We've also mentioned how your PFC fatigues. So you need to make sure you are not squandering it on low-priority tasks, distraction, stress, or other people's agendas that may not be aligned with yours.

To maximize the efficiency and function of your PFC, schedule high-priority tasks during the peak performance times of your day. So, if you tend to be the most productive during the first part of the morning, this is your golden time to prioritize what you need to do, set aside protected block time to work on your most important projects, and engage in your highest priority tasks. Save your less important meetings, e-mails, and lower priority tasks for later in the morning or afternoon.

Also, to optimize performance, experiment with synchronizing your work stream with your body's natural activity-rest cycles of approximately 90 minutes of activity and 20 minutes of rest—also known as your *ultradian rhythm,* a concept popularized by productivity expert Tony Schwartz.[24]

Citing work by pioneering sleep researchers Nathan Kleitman[25] and Peretz Lavie[26] and performance researcher Anders Ericsson,[27] Schwartz suggests blocking out 60 to 90 minute uninterrupted chunks of time for your high-priority projects, with 15 to 20 minute breaks in between, to optimize your productivity. You can get a lot done in just two to three of these productivity blocks a day.

If you can set up your day so you get your most important projects or highest priority "to-dos" completed during the protected block time that coincides with the time of day you feel most alert, energetic, and creative, you will improve your productivity. Conversely, if you are responding to non-urgent e-mails or attending routine meetings that drain you during your high-performance time of day, you may feel too exhausted to start or make progress on that important project.

Further, to optimize your creativity during these blocks, you can also cultivate the ideal conditions for *divergent* and *convergent* thinking, concepts that you learned about about in the "Awareness, Inspiration, and Creativity" section of chapter 2.

For example, let's say you are at the beginning of a creative process, where you need to think outside the box to come up with highly original ideas. Or perhaps you have been working on something, and you are getting increasingly frustrated, feeling like you've hit a wall and realizing you need an entirely new approach. In these instances, *divergent* thinking is most helpful to generate relevant creative insights.

Research suggests a number of factors may facilitate divergent thinking: taking a break,[28] relaxation,[29] walking,[30] sleeping on it,[31] upbeat moods,[32] being playful,[33] and the color blue.[34]

So next time you feel stuck and are looking for ways to break through, rather than working harder, explore bringing some of these factors into your protected block time or taking a more extended break. Seed a helpful question and then let go of trying to find an answer. Go outside for a walk under the blue sky or by the blue ocean. Or try relaxing with a brief meditation, stepping into a warm shower, or having some playful fun. And then simply notice whatever answers may arrive. Also try seeding a question just before you go to sleep and see what answers may arise in your dreams or the dawn of your awakening.

On the other hand, if you are at the point in your process where you need to work in a very logical, linear way to solve your problems, or you are looking for ways to incrementally refine and practically implement your ideas, explore how you can create the optimal conditions for *convergent* thinking.

Here, a more serious mindset, and whatever creates more focused attention and concentration, may help facilitate this type of thinking.[35]

So step away from the foosball table and free yourself of all distractions so you can concentrate more fully in your protected block time. And while I'm not advocating the use of caffeine, if you already drink coffee or tea, you might explore whether pouring yourself a cup helps you to better focus on your most helpful answer or solution to your question or challenge at hand.

If you can determine your priorities, the people you need to connect with, and your most productive times of day, you can create a very specific implementation process for your work stream to optimize your creativity and peak performance.

For example, if you are a morning person, to leverage both your PFC and ultradian rhythm for peak performance, you might consider the following work stream:

| 8-8:30 a.m. | Planning and prioritization |
|---|---|
| 8:30-9:30 a.m. | Protected block time for projects |
| 9:30-9:45 a.m. | Break (get up, move, and replenish) |
| 9:45-11:15 a.m. | Protected block time for projects |
| 11:15-12 p.m. | Answer e-mails and calls |
| 12-1 p.m. | Lunch and exercise |
| 1-2 p.m. | Protected block time for projects |
| 2-5 p.m. | Less important meetings, in-basket, e-mails, planning for next day |

*Table 7.2. Example of a Productive Daily Work Stream*

Note that if you have a key decision to make or need to schedule a meeting with a client whose decision impacts your bottom line, use one of your high-priority blocks of time so your and your client's prefrontal cortices are optimally energized.

Finally, at the end of the day, remember what you learned in chapter 2 about the most treacherous time of the day: the transition between work and home. When your fatigued and undernourished PFC is likely to sap your powers of emotional regulation, remember to take a mini break before entering your home, so you can be more fully present and patient with those who you love.

In summary, if you find it helpful, I invite you to use or adapt the following template to outline your strategies and implementation plan for your optimal productivity, according to your vision.

| PRODUCTIVITY | |
|---|---|
| **Projects:** | List your highest priority projects with the key steps needed to implement each. |
| **Business Model:** | Describe the way you make money with your project(s). |

| | |
|---|---|
| **Budget:** | Clarify the budget you can allocate to your project(s). |
| **Capabilities:** | List the skills and capacities you want to expand. |
| **People**<br><br>Team:<br><br><br>Customers/<br>Clients/Patients: | <br><br>List the key roles needed for the success of each project and the names of the best people to fill them.<br><br>Describe your ideal client (including his or her needs and frustrations). |
| **Marketing:** | Outline your outreach and to-dos for your marketing plan. |
| **Work Stream:** | Outline the most productive schedule for your day, including protected block times for projects and scheduled breaks. |

Now, take a few minutes to outline the productivity strategies and implementation plan that would work best for your situation. Or, better yet, if you are feeling a bit fatigued now, schedule a protected block of time when you'll be fresh and productive to do so.

## Running Your VSIR Cycle

After implementing your strategies for health, relationships, and productivity, you again return to results in your VSIR cycle. In the previous "Results" section, where we "looked left before looking right," we were mainly defining results that were in alignment with your vision. As you return to results after implementing your strategies, you assess whether you achieved the results you were aiming for. Remember that your vision and strategic action plan are only starting points and, as such, are highly dynamic. As you're putting each component of your strategy into practice, think of your SMART results simply as the outcome of an experiment or test that you can continually iterate in your VSIR cycle.

You can maximize your likelihood of achieving your results by reminding yourself of them with motivating sticky notes on your bathroom mirror, or by tracking them in your journal or on a whiteboard. You can also track many of these targets, especially those related to health and productivity, with online or smart phone applications and portable or wearable devices. Explore which of these would be most helpful to you.

If, after taking action, you find you are not meeting your specific results in your intended time frame, you can reiterate the cycle by reflecting on ways you may want to refine your *vision*. Also, consider whether you were effective in your *strategy* or whether you need to change or add an approach in a key heading or subheading of your plan. Were you or others that you delegated to fully accountable on following through on *implementation,* and if not, how do you intend to step up or communicate or make changes with your team? To complete the cycle of assessment, consider whether your *results* you were aiming for were truly realistic within your specified time frame to begin with. And then take action to run the cycle again and again.

This cycle of continuous life quality improvement focuses and optimizes your energy in service of manifesting specific results in alignment with your purpose-driven vision. Be as honest as possible with yourself and make the changes that energize you and further catalyze your results on the journey of your life well lived. At the same time, also enjoy and appreciate your journey right now. Exploring your path of meaning and purpose is itself a life well lived!

Also, learn how to take things on in smaller chunks so you don't feel overwhelmed. As we've mentioned, willpower is a precious commodity that may fatigue. So if you are overly ambitious by establishing too many new positive habits, you may find yourself dropping the ball on others and feeling disappointed or frustrated.

Select one, two, or three new changes to begin with and anchor them to an existing habit or cue. Do the same thing over and over at the given time or context. Research shows that within about ten weeks, your new behaviors will wire themselves in to your powerful subconscious circuitry and will become more automatic and effortless. This will free up your willpower reserves so you can add new habits that further catalyze your vision without making you feel overwhelmed.

Look for creative ways of creating cross-linking synergies between your domains of health, relationships, and productivity (and any other domains you may have also included). Look for ways of weaving them together to design your days in an efficient, synergistic, and exciting whole.

For example, on a typical week day when I'm not traveling, I begin with a few minutes of mindfulness when I wake up in the morning, then enjoy protected block time with Sue and my boys in the kitchen, where I make the boys a vegetable protein and organic berry shake. Then after a heart-to-heart hug with Zach, who now drives himself to school, I walk Dylan to school, after which we share our goodbye hug. I then run up about 100 stairs above the park behind our house, take a mindful walk down the ramp, run around the park, do 20 minutes of resistance training on the kids' playground structures, and then make my way back in my office by half past eight. I then use the first thirty minutes to strategically plan my main objectives of my day, before moving into my protected blocks of time to get my key projects done. All of this activity integrates my health, relationships, and work. Think about how you can structure your day in a way that brings this all together to work best for you, too.

Further, getting exercise, such as going for a run (or for me, surfing), or engaging the input of colleagues and friends can also be immensely helpful when you feel stuck and are looking for a creative breakthrough with divergent, out-of-the box thinking at work or in any of your endeavors.

It's important to emphasize that the VSIR Process is designed to energize and support you in achieving what inspires you the most and to serve as a guide in which you set an *intention,* rather than an *expectation,* about what you should achieve. If you approach this process as a stern, judgmental taskmaster with unrealistic expectations, this process may devitalize you and trigger a threat response and reactivity.

Conversely, when you approach this VSIR Process with an accepting and enthusiastic spirit of exploration, while leaning into your challenge and tend-and-befriend responses to enhance your health, relationships, and productivity, you are shifting your reactivity-creativity equilibrium and promoting growth and resilience in your life.

For example, if you are eating Twinkies or you are smoking or you're sleep deprived or you're eating high-glycemic foods that spike and crash your blood sugar, guess what's going to happen? You're going to be kindling your limbic system. So, if your children come to you at a moment when you're sleep deprived and your energy reserves are low, they may push your buttons. You have the option of responding with love and wisdom or flipping your lid. What do you think you're going to do? Most likely, you will shift into a limbic response and its resulting reactivity.

On the other hand, if you are cultivating great health habits and relationships and are doing the work you love to do, this inoculates you from stressful threat responses and downstream burnout, helping you navigate the most challenging of circumstances with wisdom, discernment, and greater resilience.

Thus, your ability to continually run your VSIR cycle to create your vision and implement strategies that result in vibrant health, rich relationships, and a sense of meaning and fulfillment in the work you do sets a stable base that naturally shifts your equilibrium set point toward spending more time in creativity.

Again, the foundational practice for this process is mindfulness. The more you are able to engage in this process with conscious awareness, openness, curiosity, and kindness, the more successful you will be.

So before we conclude this chapter, I'd like to also introduce you to three mindfulness practices that can further deepen your ability to work the VSIR Process in service of the vital, loving, and fulfilling life you are creating.

## Mindfulness Practice: Working the VSIR Process Mindfully

Just as you can work the Appraise-Reappraise Method in Step 2 as a mindfulness practice, you can also mindfully work the VSIR Process to either initiate or refine whatever work you've already done. Engaging the process in a mindfulness practice may reveal new insights to deepen your experience.

In this mindfulness practice, you allow yourself to settle, and with an attitude of openness, curiosity, and kindness, you ask yourself sequential questions that help you to clarify the vision, strategies, implementation, and results that would be most congruent with the life you want to create.

If you'd also like step-by-step instructions for this practice, you can download them at SuperSmartHealth.com/BookBonus.

# Mindfulness Practice: The Energy Optimizing Body Scan

This next mindfulness practice is an adaption of the Body Scan, one of the three core practices offered in Jon Kabat-Zinn's Mindfulness-Based Stress Reduction Program. In the original practice, you bring an appreciative and affectionate awareness to each part of your body, starting from your toes, moving to the top of your head, and ending with your body as a whole.

This practice enables you to more fully appreciate and connect with the experience of being in your body, so you can become more "embodied." As you do, you may become more inclined and motivated to more fully care for your body, to nourish it with positive health habits and extend yourself a greater measure of tenderness, kindness, and compassion. And since this practice helps you become more acutely aware of the visceral sensations around your gut and heart space, it may also deepen your empathy and compassion for others.

Since we've been talking about optimizing your energy throughout this chapter (and throughout this book), I've adapted this process slightly to invite you to not only be aware of each part of your body, but also, as best you can, sense the energy in each part of your body to more fully appreciate and engage the vital life force within you.

For step-by-step instructions, visit SuperSmartHealth.com/BookBonus.

# Mindfulness Practice: Mindfully Engaging Your Energy within Your Hierarchy of Needs

In the last chapter, you learned a loving-kindness practice where you expressed a silent wish of safety and self-compassion: "May I be safe. May I be strong. May I be filled with loving-kindness." This practice was designed to contribute good energy to your lower-level needs in Maslow's Hierarchy, particularly those of safety and love and belonging.

This practice also builds on the Energy Optimizing Body Scan above to also help you feel energized, loving, and connected to purpose and significance in your life. Like the loving-kindness practice, it invites you to express a silent wish, one that moves your energy all the way up your hierarchy of needs.

It can be most powerful to do this practice after the Body Scan practice, when you have connected strongly with the energy abundantly available to you throughout your body.

Here are the step-by-step instructions for this practice:

1.  Allow yourself to get comfortable, either lying down or sitting up with an erect and alert posture. You may close your eyes or leave them open as you practice.

2.  Bring to this meditation an intention to be open, kind, and accepting of whatever arises.

3.  Now bring your attention to your heart center and to the ebb and flow of your breathing, feeling gratitude for your breath and this life you are blessed to live.

4.  As you breathe, grateful for your breath, imagine your breath is flowing in through your heart center and then, as you breathe out, imagine your breath is filling your entire body with energy and vitality.

5.  Rest for a few moments, continuing to breathe in through your heart and out into your whole body, sensing yourself filled with an abundance of energy.

6.  Then, when you feel ready, allow yourself to express the following phrases in your mind as a benevolent wish:

    May I be vital.

    May I be loving.

    May I serve well.

7.  If you are someone of faith who feels deeply connected to something bigger than yourself, consider modifying this wish as follows and notice if it feels any different:

> May I be vital.
>
> May I be loving.
>
> May I serve *you* well.
>
> 8. Allow yourself to repeat whichever phrase feels most meaningful as often as feels helpful to you.
>
> 9. Then when you are ready, gently open your eyes.

Allow yourself to connect deeply with the energy in your body and these phrases, imagining that you are connecting with your vital energy, transforming it into love and then into service and significance.

At the end of chapter 4, I shared one of Rumi's poems with you. Here's another:[36]

> *You were born with potential*
>
> *You were born with goodness and trust*
>
> *You were born with ideals and dreams*
>
> *You were born with greatness*
>
> *You were born with wings*
>
> *You are not meant for crawling, so don't.*
>
> *You have wings*
>
> *Learn to use them, and fly.*

May what you've learned in this chapter enable you to use your wings to manifest your vision of your life well lived.

In the next chapter, you'll learn how to soar to even greater heights with a process that further catalyzes your growth and transformation.

# CHAPTER 8

# Step 4: Catalyzing Growth

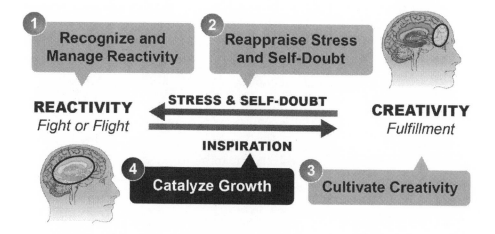

So far, in Steps 1 and 2 of the 4 in 4 Framework, you learned how to navigate and leverage stress and self-doubt, and in Step 3, you learned to harness this energy to cultivate creativity and focus on what's truly important in your life.

However, even with all of these skills and practices, ongoing stress and self-doubt can trigger reactivity at any moment to throw you off track. Further, the associated negative internal dialogue can take over and sabotage all you've learned. Even though you may aspire to cultivate optimal health, relationships, and productivity with the VSIR Process, your internal voice—one of the most intimate aspects of your being—may continue to chatter about "all the bad things that could happen"; "the regrets of your past"; "what's wrong with you"; and "what's wrong with others." Thus, your internal dialogue may create an undertow that keeps you susceptible to your threat response and ongoing reactivity and limits your ability to attain and sustain the vision of your life well lived.

Step 4 helps you catalyze your growth from the first three steps by transforming your internal dialogue, so you can continually make the turn from reactivity to creativity and stay aligned, moment by moment, with your flow of inspiration and what's truly most important in your life.

Before I explain Step 4, let me first share with you how I discovered it. In the introduction and in chapter 6, I shared how I'd found a deep sense of purpose after I fell apart during my second year in medical school. That experience caused me to appreciate just how overwhelming feelings of stress and self-doubt can be and led me to form the UCSF Medical Student Network, which provided my fellow medical students with emotional support to better navigate their stress and self-doubt and focus on what mattered most, to help them develop into more resilient and compassionate healers and leaders.

I also shared that after my medical residency, I was asked to become the first teaching fellow at UCSF, and that while I wanted to continue my work related to my passion for leadership and resiliency, I was advised to choose something "more academic." This led me to train UCSF faculty on evidence-based medicine (EBM) and then author one of the first textbooks on this topic, which has become the gold standard by which all healthcare decisions are now made.

What I haven't yet shared was the depth of despair I began to experience after ten years of training tens of thousands of healthcare providers in EBM across the United States.

I believed I'd made a terrible decision to become a leading expert on EBM, rather than pursuing what had inspired me most, and I felt like I had lost my way. I felt increasingly restless and disconnected from the heart of healing and my source of inspiration and sense of purpose.

Thankfully, this despair set me up for a life-changing discovery one fateful day in 2008, when everything came to a head. I'd awakened with the painfully familiar sense of depression, something that I had not experienced since medical school. I needed to get out the house, so I took my younger son Dylan, who was four years old at the time, for a walk that afternoon on the trail down to Torrey Pines Beach. As he walked in front of me, I choked back my tears, afraid he'd turn around and see me so sad. I also felt guilty that I was unable to enjoy this "idyllic" moment with my son amidst spectacular surroundings.

Later that evening, I put Dylan to bed. After he fell asleep, I lay next to him, restless and deeply troubled with thoughts and feelings of stress and self-doubt. I also felt ashamed that my despair had been keeping me from connecting with little Dyl all day, which further compounded my stress and self-doubt.

Then what I'd been ruminating over all day gave way to an overwhelming torrent of regret over the career decision I'd made. How could I have taken this path to become an expert in EBM when every fiber of my being had wanted to help others navigate stress to live a more meaningful life? And here I was, incomprehensively staring into a chasm of uncertainty, desperately searching for a way to do this myself. The question "What's wrong with me?" reverberated in my mind, tormenting me with self-judgment. I felt disoriented and sick to my stomach, and all my muscles felt tense, locked down in a painful contortion of despair.

As you know very well by now, I had gone limbic—I was overcome by a threat response, triggered by immense stress and self-doubt resulting from the belief that I was flawed and not good enough.

But as that question, "What's wrong with me?," reverberated within me, something miraculous happened. Another question popped into my mind, one that I had never asked before. I found myself asking, "How can I find my way home?"

As I became consciously aware of this question, I experienced a radical shift. The tension in my body instantly released. I felt a sense of clarity and stillness that I don't think I would ever have found with years of therapy or drugs.

I was in total awe of what had just happened. Something had suddenly flipped my mind to a new way of thinking and had entirely changed the way I was viewing my situation. I reflected with amazement at what had just happened, and then I realized: *All I did was ask a better question.* Instead of asking, "What's wrong with me?," I asked the question, "How can I find my way home?"

Another realization struck me. For the last decade, I had been teaching doctors the framework of EBM, which begins with helping healthcare providers to ask better questions too. As shown in figure 8.1 below, EBM is fundamentally a circular, four-step, scientific decision-making process enabling providers to:

1. *Ask* the right clinical questions.
2. *Find* the best available scientific research in computer databases to answer these questions.
3. *Evaluate* the research with a series of study assessment guides.
4. *Apply* the research to make the best possible healthcare decisions with their patients.[1]

The cycle then loops back to ask whether the actions you've taken are working.

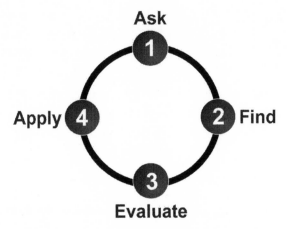

*Figure 8.1: The Framework of Evidence-Based Medicine*

I then saw the congruence and meaning in my journey. EBM was not the detour I had initially thought; it was, in fact, the path I was meant to travel.

I now see a beautiful resonance in how each step of the EBM framework helps us both navigate external uncertainty with science and our internal uncertainty with inspiration. It unifies science and spirituality on our journey to health and wholeness, which, for me, is the concept of "finding my way home."

In Step 4, I've adapted the EBM framework to incorporate what you've learned earlier about how your brain works and mindfulness to help you transform your inner dialogue and catalyze your growth mindset with this same four-step process that enables you to:

1. *Ask* better questions.
2. *Find* more inspiring answers.
3. *Evaluate* your answers to ensure they feel right.
4. *Apply* your answers by taking purposeful action in your life.

These four steps help you ask more inspiring questions, find more inspiring answers, and, therefore, take more inspired action, which is especially helpful in catalyzing your growth in the most challenging of circumstances.

More specifically, these steps cultivate your challenge response to stress, which helps you lean in to your circumstances mindfully, with openness and curiosity, and leverage your stress and self-doubt to learn, grow, and achieve the outcomes that matter most to you.

Let's now take a deeper look at each step in this Ask-Find-Evaluate-Apply cycle. We'll begin by exploring why *asking* better questions is so powerful and then discuss how you can best go about doing so.

## 1. Ask

In my workshops, I sometimes invite participants to engage in a brief exercise to experience the power of *asking better questions.* I ask if they would like to experience a similar shift to what I experienced that evening in 2008 when I shifted from asking, "What's wrong with me?" to "How can I find my way home?"

I then invite them to close their eyes and prepare to mindfully observe what they are about to experience in their body.

Next, I instruct them to say three firm "nos" silently in their mind, much like their parents may have told them as a child. I invite them to notice whatever physical sensations, feelings, or thoughts they experience as a result.

I then have them set this experience aside and clear their minds. Then I invite them to say three warm, affirming "yeses" and to notice what this feels like.

Before you read further, I invite you to put this book down and do this exercise so you can experience it for yourself, too.

Can you feel a difference between your no and your yes?

Most people say they can. For some, the difference is dramatic. Upon hearing no, they feel a tightness or constriction in their chest or their muscles, a sense of anxiety, or like the world is closing in on them.

In contrast, upon hearing yes, many feel a warmth and expansion around their heart, a sense of lightness or connectedness, or the world opening up to them with greater possibilities.

How can two simple words, within seconds, create such a different experience in your body, mind, and being?

I explain it with chaos theory. Chaos theory was popularized by the meteorologist Edward Lorenz in a famous talk he gave at the American Association for the Advancement of Science in 1972: "Does the Flap of a Butterfly's Wings in Brazil Set Off a Tornado in Texas?"[2]

Chaos theory explains how small changes in initial conditions (the flap of a butterfly's wings) can ripple through a complex system (the weather system) to create a cascade of exponential changes that result in a dramatic output (the tornado in Texas).

Well, the most complex system known to humankind is not the weather system. You could argue that it's the human brain, which has one hundred billion neurons, each of which can make between five and ten thousand connections. This means you have as many as one thousand trillion synaptic connections in countless neural networks in your brain, whose power would be equivalent to a computer with a one-trillion-bit-per-second processor.[3]

Much like chaos theory, where very small changes rippling through a complex system can lead to a massive change in output, think how your no and yes ripple through the complex system of your brain, recruiting neural networks associated with each of these words to create your profoundly different experiences.

And if this can happen for the single words of no and yes, think about how the way you ask your questions can profoundly influence the output of your brain.

For example, when I asked, "What's wrong with me?," my brain chewed on this question, priming and recruiting all its associated subconscious circuitry, which ultimately resulted in a painful threat response. In contrast, when I asked, "How can I find my way home?," my brain recruited a different set of neurons and circuits, resulting in both a challenge response and tend-and-befriend response, which was more inspiring and comforting. In other words, I was framing my question *creatively* rather than *reactively,* and it made all the difference in my experience.

The questions you ask set the direction of your life. In the last chapter, we discovered that cultivating creativity means focusing on what's truly important, including elements like learning, connecting, expressing potential, being of service, creating opportunity, experiencing significance, and leaving a legacy.

Reactive questions, like "Why me?" or "Who's to blame?," fuel a victim mentality or judgmental mentality, recruiting neurons and brain circuits that lead you away from cultivating creativity and your path toward manifesting a life well lived.

In contrast, questions like "How can I learn from this experience?"; "How can I connect to myself, others, or my source of inspiration?"; or "How can I best express myself and manifest my highest purpose and service?" engage your growth mindset, recruiting neurons and networks that lead you toward creativity and fulfillment. These types of questions lead you home.

Also, approaching these questions with an open-minded, curious, and accepting attitude is just as important as the content of the questions you ask. For example, asking "What can I do?" with a tone of resignation or resentment closes the doorway to opportunity and growth, while the same question asked with genuine curiosity opens it.

Also, thanks to neuroplasticity, your habit of asking inspiring questions establishes neural grooves that become your neural destiny. If you repeatedly ask, "What's wrong with other people?," you are likely to become a more cynical and reactive person. On the other hand, if you repeatedly ask, "What does this challenge have to teach me?," you will more deeply establish your growth mindset and become a more creative person.

So then, how can you begin to *ask* better questions?

Earlier I mentioned that Step 4 catalyzes the first three steps of the 4 in 4 Framework. If you look closely, our discussion of each of these steps included questions you may find helpful when working the steps themselves:

### Step 1: Recognize and Manage Reactivity

- What are the sensations in my body?
- What am I feeling?
- What am I thinking?
- How am I fighting or taking flight right now?
- In this moment, are my defenses likely to do me and others more harm than good?
- How can I best calm myself in this moment?
- How can I best respond to this situation?

### Step 2: Reappraise Stress and Self-Doubt

- What is triggering my stress (such as threats to Status, Certainty, Autonomy, Relatedness, and Fairness)?
- What is triggering my self-doubt (such as judgment and criticism, rejection and abandonment, neglect and abuse, failure to live up to standards and expectations, transition, and losing something that makes me feel worthy)?
- What happened (just the plain facts)?
- What are my beliefs about what happened?
- Can I be absolutely sure that the way I am seeing the situation is really true?
- How can I view the situation differently so that it causes me less stress or self-doubt?

### *Step 3: Cultivate Creativity*

- In this challenging situation, what is it that I'm here to learn?
- How can I better connect with this person?
- How can I better connect with myself?
- What would be the healthiest thing for me to do right now?
- What do I need physically?
- What do I need emotionally?
- What do I need intellectually?
- What do I need spiritually?
- How can I connect more fully with my deepest source of inspiration?
- How can I best express myself?
- How can I best serve?
- How can I best manifest my vision for my life well lived?

Can you think of any other inspiring questions to help you shift from reactivity to creativity?

Sometimes, when you are stressed, the best question you can ask is, "What is the best question I can ask right now?"

I invite you to write down any additional questions that you'd find helpful in the space below or in your journal.

Now let's talk about how you can create the optimal conditions to find inspiring answers to your questions.

## 2. Find

As we transition from the first to the second step in Step 4, a good question to ask is, "How can I best *find* the answers to my questions?"

As in evidence-based medicine, one approach is to search for your answers externally, whether online in trusted resources or from trusted experts, colleagues, family members, or friends. However, here we'll focus on how to create the optimal brain conditions so your answers can internally find *you*. (You can also integrate these internal answers with those you've found externally.)

Two factors are key for creating optimal conditions to find answers internally: first, regulate any stress-driven reactivity, and second, optimize your mental state to facilitate creative insights.

As you learned in chapter 2, whenever you feel fearful or threatened, your amygdala steps on your fight-or-flight accelerator, or your sympathetic nervous system (SNS). If your reaction is intense enough, it can cause "amygdala hijack," disrupting your higher cortical circuits (and your PFC in particular), which are essential for finding inspiring and creative answers to your questions.

For example, when an organization experiences a setback or hits an inflection point, many leaders commonly react with fear, resulting in well-grooved fight-or-flight behaviors. Unfortunately, that also means these leaders don't have access to the higher levels of innovative thinking and creativity they need most, not only to get through these turbulent times, but also to capitalize on the opportunities change brings. Further, as you'll learn in part 3, their reactivity may also cause their team to go limbic and shut down their creative thinking, too.

Fortunately, in chapter 5, you learned how to quickly manage your reactivity by first pausing and then taking a few soft-belly breaths, allowing your belly to expand as you breathe in and recede as you breathe out. This kind of breathing (also known as diaphragmatic breathing) activates the parasympathetic part of your nervous system (PNS), which taps the brake on your reactivity, helping you self-soothe, calm down, and focus more on your *pause and plan* functions.[4]

(Note: for optimal performance and engagement, I'm not suggesting you *shut down* your SNS with your PNS. Rather, this is more about learning to *balance* your SNS activity with your PNS more effectively, so you can experience a more relaxed state of alertness that can optimize your mental clarity and ability to find good answers to your questions.[5])

In addition, you also learned how breathing through your heart center while activating positive emotions like love or gratitude has been shown to decrease stress and improve cognitive performance, emotional balance, and mental clarity.[6] Experiment with ways to calm yourself and think more clearly to find the ones most effective for you. You can begin by asking the question, "What would most effectively help me find a greater sense of stillness and mental clarity right now?"

Continue your experiment by exploring some or all of the following mindfulness exercises, noticing what you are experiencing as you do:

- Simply become aware of your breathing. As various thoughts, feelings, and sensations arise, notice them come and go without judgment or trying to change them. Imagine your thoughts and sensations are simply clouds passing across the sky. Keep returning to your breath over and over again. How does this feel?

- Now, as you are aware of your breathing, explore lengthening your inhalation and exhalation. Try beginning with five seconds in and five seconds out. Play with different lengths of time for each. Explore lengthening the duration of your exhalation to eight seconds and pursing your lips as if you are breathing out through a straw (as prolonging your exhalation can further activate the PNS).[7] With an open and curious mind, consider which breathing pattern seems most natural and leaves your mind feeling most clear.

- Bring to mind someone or something that naturally evokes a feeling of love in you. Notice the sensation of love in your body. Where do you feel it? Now, imagine yourself breathing in through this part of your body. As you exhale, imagine you are infusing your entire body with love. How does this feel?

- Find a small object that is very special to you and easily fits in your pocket or purse. It might be a gift someone gave you or a small pebble or shell you found. Place this object in your hand and gently rub your thumb over it. As you do, activate a sense of gratitude. What do you notice?

You can use any of these practices as written, combine them, or create something else. The key is to experiment, mindfully observe, and discover what is most effective for you. You may also discover that the practice you cultivate may change over time. For a start, note the practices that most effectively bring you to a place of greater stillness and mental clarity. Then, freely use this practice at any time throughout your day to cultivate stillness, especially whenever you feel stressed.

The way the answers find us varies. For example, your answer may arrive as an "aha!" thought, a moment of insight, or through more effortful deliberation. Sometimes you may have the answer even before you've finished asking your question. It may present itself as a simultaneous thought or a knowing. Or sometimes you may find the answer a few days later, through something you stumbled upon while reading or what may seem like a chance encounter with someone—primed by the question you'd asked.

Where you sense your answers come from is also highly personal. You may take a mechanistic view, believing that your answers are retrieved from your stores of memory. Or you may embrace a scientific view, believing that the questions you've asked have engaged various neural networks that have formed new coalitions to give rise to new insights.[8] Alternatively, you may believe your answers are guided by your deepest values, such as love or compassion, or by your ethics or morality. Or you may feel your answers are connected to something larger than yourself, perhaps your sense of connection with God.

For me, asking questions in my mind is a humbling experience. It's my way of opening myself to a growth mindset, acknowledging what I don't know, and appreciating how much I have to learn. I then feel gratitude, and often awe, at the answers that arrive.

The night I asked myself the question, "How can I find my way home?," was the first time that I truly felt connected to something larger than myself.

In my stillness, I also found my answer, discovering that I'm not alone. In the process of asking questions and finding answers itself, I've found my sense of spiritual connection. It brings me a feeling of wholeness and being at home within myself.

## 3. Evaluate

Once the answers to your questions find you, the third step in Step 4 helps you to *evaluate* your answers. Here you'll reflect on whether the answers you receive are aligned with your deepest values—whether they feel right—or are more reflective of you simply wanting to feel relieved or feel good.

For example, ask yourself whether your answers represent your instinctive response to take flight from stress and self-doubt. Are you rationalizing something, so you can avoid facing your fears? Or is your answer to do the more challenging thing that needs to be done? For example, will you confront the co-worker who undermined your work, or will you grin and bear it to avoid the confrontation and the possibility you could become the subject of office politics?

If we only acted on what feels good or comfortable, we might not be able to confront someone, when we know that it is the right thing to do, or overcome addictions, lose weight, or engage in a challenging exercise regimen.

Your answers that bring relief or feel good can be very compelling. They connect with the powerful threat-and-reward circuitry in your limbic system and basal ganglia. On the other hand, your answers that feel *right* connect with your higher cortical circuits, including your PFC, which contributes to your wisdom and discernment and enables you to pursue your higher-level needs in Maslow's Hierarchy.

So, while you may feel the pull of your powerful subconscious circuitry, mindfully consider whether your answers are moving you up your hierarchy of needs, where you are not only meeting your physical and safety needs, but also your needs for love and belonging, and the sense of significance that comes from manifesting a life well lived.

Here are some "litmus test" questions you can use to evaluate your answers and gain confidence that your answers are indeed helping you meet your higher needs. Ask yourself the following:

- Does this answer feel right more than feel good?
- Does this answer get me to a place where I feel freer to receive and give love?
- Is this answer good for me and others?
- Does this answer get me closer to my vision of a life well lived?

You can use any or all of these to evaluate your answers, or you can come up with additional rules of thumb of your own.

Write down any other litmus test questions that might help you evaluate your answers:

Deciding to do what's right and following your inspiration can be stressful. After all, you are making hard decisions about what you most care about. Reflecting on what truly matters and what's truly at stake enables you to listen to what is calling to you, trust your inner knowing, and harness your stress energy to meet your challenges on your path of growth.

After you've evaluated your answers on this path, your next step is to apply them.

# 4. Apply

This vital, final step in Step 4 involves taking action in alignment with your inspiration and your knowing of what's right.

Taking action often requires a mix of courage and willpower, especially when your situation feels stressful. For example, when faced with the task of confronting or leaving someone, setting healthy boundaries, asking for forgiveness, or making amends, you may be afraid of upsetting others or being rejected by them. As we discussed previously, you also need willpower to initially engage in any new behaviors in order to establish healthy habits. Your willpower involves the activation of your PFC, which also serves to regulate your fear responses, and it's a precious asset that may fatigue.[9] So if you are afraid in anticipation of taking action, ensure you have optimized your courage and your willpower reserves to follow through in the face of your fear.

For example, if you are about to have a crucial conversation with your spouse, boss, or direct report, as best you can, make sure you are well rested, nourished, and hydrated so that your PFC is optimized and ready to go—especially if your amygdala, ever vigilant for threats, is likely to protest in fear.

For high-stakes actions, it can also help to mentally rehearse and run simulations of what might go wrong, so you can feel your stress and feel fully prepared to leverage this energy to meet your challenge in the heat of the moment.

Also, praying for strength or reaching out to someone you trust for support and accountability in following through can be immensely helpful, too. Remember, social support in the face of stress engages your tend-and-befriend response, which triggers the release of oxytocin. This hormone not only promotes intimacy and trust, but it also regulates your threat response. Known as the molecule of bravery, oxytocin gives you the courage to act in the most challenging circumstances.[10]

Know that your courage to act is not the absence of fear, but the capacity to take action in the face of your fear. While taking flight from acting may provide a brief respite of relief from fear, such as being criticized, rejected, failing, or making mistakes, avoidance has its consequences. Without action, inspiration can remain locked away as ideas and theories, limiting the expression of our full potential and power.

Further, procrastinating, as well as being thwarted from taking action, can leave you feeling intensely restless, with a sense of yearning for something unrequited. This type of restlessness is a type of *creative self-doubt*. It's the discomfort you feel from not following through on the stream of your inspiration and creativity. These questions of doubt involve your highest self, acting in service of something larger than yourself. An example might be, "How can I best act in alignment with my highest purpose and service?"

These questions are very different from those reflecting *reactive self-doubt.* With reactive self-doubt, we tend to agonize over questions like, "Am I worthy or good enough?" Unlike creative self-doubt, which tends to make us feel restless, reactive self-doubt tends to deplete us. Such questions typically trigger our threat response and ensuing fight-or-flight reactions.

The reason why it's important to distinguish between creative self-doubt and reactive self-doubt is that these two forms of self-doubt can braid themselves around each other and make us feel so intensely uncomfortable that we become completely immobilized from taking any action at all. For example, when we don't follow through on our dreams and the actions that we know are right, we may also feel shame and believe we're not good enough to do so. Together, they can feel so threatening that we give up on our dreams all together. On the other hand, if you try to avoid *all* forms of self-doubt, you can end up disconnecting yourself from your source of inspiration and creativity as well.

The wisdom of self-doubt lies in being able to distinguish between these two streams of self-doubt, so you can more clearly sense the currents of creativity and reactivity and then more consciously choose which stream to swim in.

With this wisdom, you can be guided to take action in the flow of your creativity and what's truly most important, without being swept away by the undertow of reactivity.

When you act from your true knowing, with your thoughts, words, and actions aligned, you live in integrity.

When you are guided by your inner wisdom and inspiration to act in love and service from your highest self, you have immense power.

So, I invite you to trust your knowing and yourself and act boldly. Just do it! Whatever actions you take will further catalyze your growth and learning. And your inspired actions will bring you back full cycle to again . . .

# 1. Ask

After you take action to apply your answers, you complete the cycle below by returning to the first step in Step 4 to *ask* your next question: "Is what I'm doing working?"

A powerful litmus test to help guide your response to this question can be your definition of optimal health you created in chapter 7. For example, if your definition of optimal health is "energy optimized," you would ask yourself the question, "Am I and others energized by my actions?"

For example, let's say you have asked yourself about whether you should make a change in your career track, and you trust your answer about taking your next step. But after you take action, you don't feel energized by the decision you have made. At that point, you can ask yourself questions to explore why you don't feel energized and consider additional changes, after which you can complete the cycle to again ask whether the changes you made are working. If they're not working, you continue to ask questions about how you can feel more energized and better thrive.

Note that the Ask, Find, Evaluate, and Apply cycle is not a closed loop but a spiral, with its trajectory representing the pathway of growth.

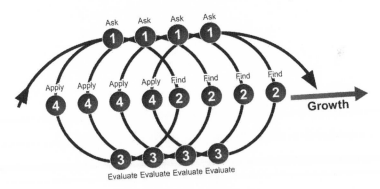

*Figure 8.2. Ask-Find-Evaluate-Apply Spiral of Growth*

In short, the four steps in Step 4 form a spiral of mindfulness-based inquiry and action that transforms your internal dialogue to catalyze your growth mindset. As you practice the Ask-Find-Evaluate-Apply spiral with mindful curiosity and kindness, you are continually driving energy up your Maslow's Hierarchy of Needs to find a sense of significance that comes from creating your life well lived.

## Mindfulness Practice: Working the Ask-Find-Evaluate-Apply Spiral of Growth

Step 4 is, in fact, a mindfulness practice you can use in your everyday life. Typically, this practice is preceded by an "invitation" or a "call." For example, you may first notice that you feel edgy, withdrawn, or in pain or that something is eating at you. Alternatively, you may feel restless, sensing something is off track, or you may feel inspired to express yourself in some way, but you are not yet sure how to go about it. Or you may be sensing a wide gap between your life as it is and your vision of your life well lived, and you feel motivated to close that gap.

These "invitations" may be related to any of the first three steps of the 4 in 4 Framework. For example:

- Your edginess or withdrawal may be related to fight-or-flight "limbic" reactivity (Step 1: Recognize Reactivity).

- Your pain or discomfort may be related to underlying triggers of stress and self-doubt (Step 2: Reappraise Stress and Self-Doubt).

- Your restlessness, creative tension, or desire to close the gap between your life now and your life well lived may reflect your intention to manifest what's truly important in your life (Step 3: Cultivate Creativity).

Be on the lookout for these invitations. Once you notice one, as best you can, allow yourself to receive it as a blessing. As challenging as it may be, it's an opportunity to grow. You might engage the challenge and any stress you might be feeling by saying to yourself, "OK, it's grow time!"

Then pause, take a few slow, deep breaths, and notice whatever thoughts, sensations, and feelings you may be experiencing with a sense of openness, curiosity, and kindness. You are now ready to mindfully engage in the four steps of Step 4 to catalyze your growth.

To summarize these steps as a mindfulness practice:

1. **Ask:** If you sense an invitation to practice Step 4 as described above or notice you're feeling stressed or recognize negative thoughts in your internal dialogue, choose to mindfully reseed better questions.

   Consider asking any of the questions relating to Steps 1, 2, or 3 of the 4 in 4 Framework we mentioned above or any others you find helpful.

   Questions that can be very helpful in times of stress and transform your threat response to a challenge or tend-and-befriend response include, "In this challenging moment, what is it that I'm here to learn?"; "How can I best connect with myself, others, and my deepest source of inspiration?"; "How can I best express myself right now?"; "How can I best serve?"

   If, in the heat of the moment, you cannot yet think of a helpful question, you can always start with the question, "What is the most helpful question I can ask right now?"

2. **Find:** Take a few seconds, or a few minutes, to mindfully create greater physiological stillness. Use the practice you identified in the "Find" section above to calm yourself, create mental clarity, become more receptive, and open up your higher brain circuits so the answers to your questions can more readily find you. For example, if you found it most helpful to take five slow, heart-centered breaths to calm yourself, do this here.

   If you are seeking new insight, instead of grappling or trying to think too hard, allow yourself to relax and let yourself go into your uncertainty and receive your answer whenever, wherever, and however it may present itself to you. For example, an answer may find you before you finish asking your question or a few days later. It may come at home or at work, while you are taking a shower or running, or even in your dreams. The answer may come to you as a thought or a knowing or through something you read or in a chance meeting or discussion with someone. Allow yourself to be patient, receptive, and in awe of what you may discover.

If you are feeling stressed, rather than first *asking* your questions and then creating stillness to *find* your answers, sometimes it can be most helpful to first *find* stillness before you *ask* your questions. You can then deepen your stillness so the answers can *find* you. Explore which sequence is most helpful to you.

3. **Evaluate:** When your answer arises, evaluate whether it feels right, is good for you and others, provides you greater freedom to give to and receive with others, or gets you closer to your vision of your life well lived. Or use any other litmus test questions you may have discovered in the "Evaluate" section above.

4. **Apply:** Then, once you fully trust the answer you receive, be sure to apply it with full awareness by taking mindful and purposeful action.

1. **Ask:** After you take action, complete the loop in your spiral by asking your next question: "Is what I'm doing working?" Consider whether the results align with your definition of optimal health. For example, if your definition is "energy optimized," ask whether you and others are energized by your actions.

If not, ask more questions.

If you and others are energized by your insights and actions and what you are doing is indeed working, take a moment to experience the wonder and appreciation of the source of inspiration that has provided you guidance.

# A Moment to Celebrate and Transition

At this point, I want to congratulate you for reading this far. We have come a long way together. Think of how much you have already learned!

In part 1, we set the foundation for leading well from within, specifically with the research supporting the effectiveness of Conscious Leadership, understanding how your brain works, understanding how to better work your brain with mindfulness, and an introduction to the 4 in 4 Framework.

In part 2, you learned how to apply the four steps of the framework to recognize and manage your reactivity, reappraise your stress and self-doubt, leverage this energy to cultivate creativity around what matters most in your life, and further catalyze your growth by transforming your internal dialogue with a powerful process of mindfulness-based inquiry.

You now have the knowledge, skills, and practices to *lead well from within*. Now you are ready for part 3, where you can harness all of your learning to further discover how you can apply this framework to *lead well in the world*.

# Part 3

Applying the 4 in 4 Framework
to Lead Well in the World

# CHAPTER 9

# Cycles of Reactivity and Creativity

In Step 3 of the 4 in 4 Framework, when you learned how to cultivate what's truly important in your life, you had the opportunity to consider how to enrich your relationships. In part 3, we'll be taking this idea further and discover how to apply all the steps of 4 in 4 Framework to your relationships, so you can *lead well in the world.*

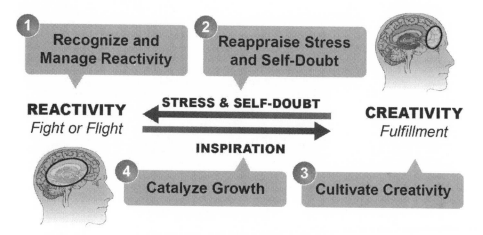

I invite you to reflect on the framework above. Consider how your relationships would improve if you could apply all four steps, not just to yourself but to your relationships, so you could 1) better recognize rather than react to the reactivity of others, 2) more fully understand what triggers others' stress and self-doubt, 3) appreciate what's truly important to them, and 4) re-establish your connection if your relationship goes off track. What would this mean for your relationships, both at work and at home?

In these next four chapters, we'll continue our journey from the inside out, first exploring how you are wired to connect in cycles of reactivity and creativity in your individual relationships. Then, in chapter 10, you'll learn how to apply this knowledge and the 4 in 4 Framework to resolve conflicts and further nurture your most important relationships. In chapter 11, we'll expand beyond individual relationships to explore *cultures* of reactivity and creativity. Finally, in chapter 12, you'll learn how to apply the 4 in 4 Framework to further expand your influence, transform your culture, and make an even bigger difference in the world.

So to set the foundation for transforming your relationships with others, let's begin with the brain science of connection.

## We Are Wired to Connect

Have you ever walked into a business meeting and, before anyone said a word, felt the tension in the room?

Are you able to sense what someone is about to do even before he or she does it?

Have you felt the pain of criticism or rejection at home or at work? How about the exhilaration of a productive collaboration or the pure joy and fulfillment of spending quality time with your loved one?

Have you ever spent time with someone who was depressed or angry and found yourself feeling the same way? How about someone with a naturally loving presence—did you find yourself feeling more calm, safe, and inspired?

Have you ever restrained yourself from blurting out something harmful—and felt relieved you did? Or experienced a great sense of joy and purpose in making a meaningful difference in someone's life?

These are intimately human experiences, built upon our capacity and need to connect with others. We anticipate how they will act, feel their feelings, know their thoughts, read the looks on their faces or their tone of voice, and consciously act in ways to effectively engage, influence, and inspire them.

In the next several sections, we'll explore how our brain is wired to socially connect through a number of overlapping neural networks and systems involving:

- Social pain and reward
- Mirror neurons
- Emotional empathy
- Cognitive empathy
- PFC regulation
- The autonomic nervous system

By the end of this section, you will more deeply understand how these systems that facilitate social connection are fundamental drivers of the human experience, why it's so devastating to feel rejection (and rewarding to feel connected), and how we regulate the emotions and impulses that can impair our social functioning. With this knowledge in hand, you will then discover a simple and profound way you can engage with others to enrich their lives and feel more deeply connected and fulfilled in all of your relationships.

## *Social Pain and Reward*

We all know that social rejection feels painful and meaningful social connection feels rewarding. But is that pain all "in your head," or is it real? Research reveals it's both—and the brain science behind these experiences.

In one study, participants played a video game that involved a virtual ball tossing game called "CyberBall." As they lay in an MRI scanner, they believed they were playing with two other partners. As the game progressed, the participant's two cyber partners were programmed to begin passing the ball only to each other, leaving the participant feeling left out and rejected. As the participants became excluded, their brain scans lit up in their anterior cingulate and insula—the very same brain regions activated when you experience physical pain.[1] This study proves social rejection is painful, and it truly hurts!

Remarkably, another study—a randomized placebo controlled trial—confirmed just how real this pain is. When participants who experienced this emotional pain were given the pain reliever acetominophen, their experience of emotional pain *and* the associated activity in their anterior cingulate and insula both decreased![2]

A *Science* commentary further points out that these areas are also activated by the pain of bereavement, being treated unfairly, and the envy you feel when you compare yourself to others who are more successful than you are.[3]

On the flip side, the research also shows that social rewards, such as cooperating, having a good reputation, being treated fairly, giving to charity, and even *schadenfreude* (the pleasure we feel from the downfall of people we envy) activates the very same reward circuitry with which we experience physical pleasure—the ventral striatum, activated by the feel-good neurotransmitter, dopamine.[4]

This explains why collaborating well with others at work, spending quality time with those you love, and donating your time and resources feel so good, as well as why the guilty pleasures of gossip or trashy celebrity magazines and reality television shows feel compelling to many. You're engaging the same circuits of pleasure that drive your basic survival needs and can even lead to the cravings of addiction.

At the core of our being, we are not just wired to connect; we are *driven* to connect. Our need for love and belonging is yoked to the very same pain-and-reward survival circuitry that ensures our physical survival—circuitry that underpins social cooperation and connection, which is further supported by other systems, such as mirror neurons.

### Mirror Neurons

Mirror neurons, a widespread system of nerve cells, are thought to play a key role in reading and anticipating the actions of others.

Mirror neurons were discovered serendipitously in the laboratory of Giacomo Rizzolatti at the University of Parma in Italy, as researchers were studying the relationship of brain activity to the body movements of maque monkeys.[5] By placing fine needle electrodes into single neurons, they could see exactly which neurons were firing when the monkey moved its hand to grasp, hold, or tear something or moved its mouth or lips, for example. All well and good and nothing particularly sensational.

Everything changed one day after lunch, when one of the researchers returned to the lab eating an ice cream cone. As the monkey watched the researcher lifting his hand to eat his ice cream, the other researchers noticed the neuron linked to the monkey's own hand movement was firing—*even though its hand was not moving.* To everyone's amazement, the monkey's brain seemed to be registering—or *mirroring*—what was going on in the researcher's brain.

Hence the term "mirror neurons" was coined,[6] setting in motion a flurry of further research on monkeys to confirm these findings, including numerous imaging studies and a neurosurgical study of an epilepsy patient that suggested mirror neuron activity occurred in humans, too.

Renowned neuroscientist V. S. Ramachadran suggested in his book *The Tell-Tale Brain* that mirror neurons not only enable the reading of intentions, but also enabled the empathy, language capabilities, and learning that catapulted human culture forward between 500 BCE and the present.[7]

However, the growing excitement for this research has also been met with pushback. In 2012, *Psychology Today* published an article titled "Mirror Neurons: The Most Hyped Concept in Neuroscience?"[8] In 2014, Gregory Hickok, a professor of cognitive science at University of California, Irvine, published the book, *The Myth of Mirror Neurons.* There he critiqued Rizzolati's research and its applicability to humans, including reference to studies that claimed mirror neurons were connected to political attitudes, music appreciation, contagious yawning, favoritism, love, and the degree of a male erection.[9]

While discounting the role of mirror neurons in empathy, language, and reading and understanding others' intentional actions, Hickok acknowledges scientific support for a more limited role for mirror neurons: "Others entertain an intermediate possibility, that mirror neurons can *augment* action understanding; or, to paraphrase a well-known tag line: mirror neurons don't *make* action understanding, they make action understanding *better.*"[10]

There is still much to learn about how mirror neurons connect us, particularly their role in cognition and communication. In the meantime, in a 2014 review celebrating the twentieth anniversary of his discovery, Rizzollati continues to stand by his research and assertion that mirror neurons are involved in understanding the actions and intentions of others.[11]

For example, when someone intentionally raises his hand at a meeting, your mirror neurons are likely to help you understand that he is raising his hand to ask a question, as opposed to simply stretching. To further understand why he is raising his hand, we need to discuss the concept of empathy. It involves at least two major subtypes and systems, which we'll explore further in the sections below.

### Emotional Empathy

Emotional empathy enables you to understand and share another person's emotional experience—to "feel" what another person feels, whether it be pain, joy, sadness, disgust, or any other feeling.[12]

One of the seminal studies on emotional empathy was conducted in 2004 by Tania Singer, now the director of the Department of Social Neuroscience at the Max Planck Institute for Human Cognitive and Brain Sciences.[13] She hooked up pain electrodes to the right hand of sixteen couples and had the female partner of each couple lie in an MRI scanner to see what happened in her brain as she was shocked, as well as what happened in her brain when her partner was shocked. Singer wanted to see if the scanned participants' response to the pain of being shocked themselves was similar to their empathic response to observing their partners being shocked.

Singer and her colleagues discovered that the same areas activated by physical pain and social rejection mentioned above—the anterior insular cortex and anterior cingulate cortex—were activated when the subjects experienced pain *and when they observed their loved one experiencing this pain as well.* Further, the degree to which these areas activated when their loved ones suffered correlated with the degree of empathy they felt for their partner. So we truly not only feel our own pain, but the pain of others, too.

What's also important about the anterior insular cortex and anterior cingulate cortex is that they have also been found to play a key role in our experience of emotions and emotional regulation. The insular cortex connects to a highway of nerves leading to and from your internal organs and viscera, including your heart and gut. This connectivity enables something called *interoception,* your body's visceral inner sense that contributes to your emotional awareness.[14] As mentioned in chapter 2, the insular cortex plays a role in intuition, compassion, and love.[15] It's also involved in your sense of fairness and trust and facilitates cooperation.[16]

Additional studies show that in addition to being activated by pain, our insula is also activated when we empathize with others' expressions of disgust[17] and distress or joy.[18] Here too our brain tends to be Velcro for negative experiences and Teflon for positive ones: our insular cortex tends to empathize more strongly with distress than joy.[19]

The good news is that the pain and distress felt in this part of the brain is also responsive to the comforting touch of a loved one. James Coan, the director of the Virginia Affective Neuroscience Laboratory at the University of Virginia, subjected sixteen married women to the threat of electric shock while holding their husband's hand, the hand of stranger, or no hand at all while they lay in an MRI scanner. While the touch of a stranger provided some reassurance, the scan showed that holding their husband's hand showed marked attenuation of activity in their insular cortex, which correlated with how good the wife felt about the marriage.[20]

The insula is also one of the parts of the brain affected by compassion meditation. In a study comparing sixteen long-term Buddhist meditators, with anywhere from 10,000 to 50,000 hours of meditation practice, with sixteen novice practitioners, activation of the insular cortex was found to be greater during presentation of sounds of suffering in expert meditators as compared to novice meditators. The degree of activation correlated with the expertise around compassion-based meditation, suggesting the insula is plastic and that empathy can be cultivated.[21]

In another study that compared highly experienced meditators with novice meditators as they completed a loving-kindness meditation, those who were more experienced had greater changes in their heart rate, which correlated with a stronger activation of their insula and their anterior cingulate cortex with compassion practice.[22] These experienced mindfulness practitioners were literally able to bring more "heart" into their connections with others.

In addition to its role in empathy, the anterior cingulate cortex also serves to detect errors and sense when things are amiss with people or situations. It's considered the linchpin between the thinking brain and feeling brain, situated between the PFC above and insula and amygdala below.[23]

Interestingly, the amygdala, which we have discussed in relation to threat, has also been found to be important in empathy, as it's keenly attuned to fear and distress in others as well. In fact, when the amygdala does not function well, evidence indicates psychopathic behavior can result. While evidence shows that enhanced amygdala activity can trigger fear, some research also shows that the amygdala can help us more deeply appreciate distress and suffering and encourage altruistic responses of concern.[24]

Thus all of these players—the input from your organs, including your gut and heart, your insula, your anterior cingulate, your amygdala,[25] and their connections to your PFC—comprise a powerful system of emotional empathy that enables you to deeply connect at an emotional level with the feelings of others.

Now let's take a look at another dimension of empathy, which helps us more fully understand each other at a cognitive level as well.

### Cognitive Empathy

Cognitive empathy relates to *thinking* about what the other person both thinks and feels. It involves the ability to stand in another's shoes and understand her perspective on the world.

Let's say your colleague is anxious about a presentation he needs to give to a major client. With emotional empathy you'd say, "I *feel* his distress." With cognitive empathy you'd say, "I *know* he is distressed, and he's thinking he could blow this deal."[26]

Cognitive empathy has also been referred to as a *theory of mind*, or *mentalizing:* "the ability to attribute mental states—beliefs, intents, desires, pretending, knowledge, etc.—to oneself and others and to understand that others have beliefs, desires, intentions, and perspectives that are different from one's own."[27]

Cognitive empathy involves the midline areas of PFC and other regions of the brain that overlap with the default mode network (DMN) we referenced in chapter 2.[28] This network is very much involved in our concept of self-identity, self-reflection, and thinking about the perspectives of others and our relationships with them. It's also what drives rumination and worry, especially as we process our social interactions with others (including those social faux pas we stew over).[29]

The fact that the DMN is a *default* network highlights just how important understanding ourselves, others, and social connections is to our survival. When other networks of the brain go quiet, this network is spontaneously "on," compelling us, for better or for worse, to continually think about our relationships with ourselves and others to ensure we stay socially appropriate and connected.

This network is even more influential than we may appreciate. In his book, *Social,* Matthew Lieberman states, "We may think that our beliefs and values are core parts of our identity, part of what makes *us.* But . . . these beliefs are often smuggled into our minds without realizing it." He then concludes, "The self is more of a super highway for social influence than it is the impenetrable personal fortress we believe it to be." This overlap in our cognitive empathy network, where we think both about our relationship with self and others, further serves as a "Trojan Horse" by which we are shaped by the personal values and beliefs of others and the culture we live in.[30]

Lieberman also points out that your cognitive empathy network acts in concert with your mirror neuron system (discussed above) to enable you to more deeply connect with and understand the actions of others. While the mirror neuron system helps you to understand *what* someone is doing, the cognitive empathy system enables you to conceive of *why* that person is doing it.[31]

For example, if we return to our example from the mirror neuron section above, your mirror neurons help you recognize that your business colleague is raising his hand during a meeting to ask a question, rather than merely stretching. Your capacity for cognitive empathy enables you to more fully understand and anticipate the reason he may be asking that question— whether he's genuinely curious to learn more and contribute to the solution, whether he's questioning the wisdom of what was suggested, or whether he's defiantly disagreeing with what was suggested. Recognizing a person's deeper intentions puts you in the best possible position to respond.

The wisdom with which you respond, and which enables you to create harmony and synergy in your relationships, involves the PFC, which we'll discuss next.

### Prefrontal Cortex Regulation

One of the most important accounts in medicine highlighting the crucial role of the PFC is the story of Phineas Gage—what happened on that fateful day of September 13, 1848, and how it affected his life thereafter.[32]

Phineas Gage, then twenty-five years old, was the foreman of a railway construction crew, preparing the way for the Rutland and Burlington Railroad in central Vermont. His crew was drilling and filling holes with gunpowder to blast through a rocky outcrop just south of the town of Cavendish. Gage was gently tamping down some gunpowder in one of the holes with a three-foot-seven-inch-long tamping iron, when he dropped it and caused a spark that ignited an explosion. This sent the thirteen-pound, three-and-a-half-foot tamping iron rocketing out of the hole and through his head, landing about twenty yards away. The rod entered under the left cheekbone and exited out of the top of his skull, destroying his PFC along the way.

Miraculously, he survived. Dr. John Harlow arrived about an hour later to stop the bleeding and tend to his wounds. He survived another eleven years, but the life he knew and how others knew him were forever changed.

In 1868, twenty years after the accident, Dr. Harlow shared a report of the accident and Gage's changes in the *Bulletin of the Massachusetts Medical Society*.[33] It's become part of medical lore, attesting to the important social function of the PFC.

Harlow described Gage before the accident as "a perfectly healthy, strong, and active young man . . . possessing an iron will as well as an iron frame." He further shared, "Previous to his injury, though untrained in the schools, he possessed a well-balanced mind and was looked upon by those who knew him as a shrewd, smart business man, very energetic in executing all his plans of operation."

Harlow describes just how life altering his changes from the accident were, stating, "His contractors, who regarded him as the most efficient and capable foreman in their employ previous to his injury, considered the change in his mind so marked that they could not give him his place again. He is fitful, irreverent, indulging at times in the grossest profanity (which was not previously his custom), manifesting but little deference for his fellows, impatient of restraint of advice when it conflicts with his desires, at times pertinaciously obstinate, yet capricious and vacillating, devising many plans of future operation, which are no sooner arranged than they are abandoned in turn for others appearing more feasible. A child in his intellectual capacity and manifestations, he has the animal passions of a strong man."

Harlow concludes, "His mind was radically changed, so decidedly that his friends and acquaintances said he was 'no longer Gage.'"

With the destruction of his PFC, Gage had lost his ability to regulate his basic impulses and desires, show socially appropriate restraint, extend respect to others, and identify and stay focused on what was really important in his interactions and his life—all crucial to effectively connecting well with others.

Let's return again to the example above about your colleague raising his hand during a business meeting, and let's say you interpreted his action as an act of defiance. Imagine that this interpretation caused you to feel threatened, irritated, and angry and that you feel compelled to react by saying something belittling to shut him down. Now imagine that you mindfully catch yourself, remember the main goal of the meeting, and consciously choose a path of restraint. Rather than reacting with a threatening demeanor, you decide to approach your colleague with openness and curiosity. Without any trace of malice, you begin by asking him to clarify what was most concerning to him.

As we learned from the story of Phineas Gage, your response of regulating your irritation, exercising restraint, initiating an expression of genuine interest and concern, and focusing on the outcomes that are most important draws significantly on the wisdom and willpower reserves of your PFC.

In her book *The Willpower Instinct,* Kelly McGonigal explains that there are three types of willpower based in different regions of your PFC that enable you to engage others with a more socially appropriate and collaborative response. The first is "will" power, which helps you to initiate and stick with healthy or productive tasks or positive interactions. The second is "won't" power, which inhibits or restrains you from saying or doing things you'll later regret. And the third is "want" power, which helps you keep your eye on the prize and align your actions with the important goals and outcomes you want to achieve.[34]

When you can fully leverage your PFC, you can more effectively regulate your more primitive drives, impulses, cravings, and reactions. In so doing, you are able to cooperate more fully with others, which is a major factor in your personal success at work and at home and our collective success as a species. Robert Sapolsky, a well-renowned neuroscientist and primate researcher from Stanford, succinctly stated that the main purpose of the PFC is "to bias an individual towards doing the harder, rather than the easier, thing."[35]

In other words, this part of your brain enables you to cooperate and engage with compassion and altruistic concern, aligned with your values, norms, ethics, and morality for the benefit of all, rather than only your baser instincts or "animal passions" focused on your self-interest and personal pleasures or concerns.

This capacity characterizes another type of empathy that Daniel Goleman has referred to as "compassionate empathy." It's also synonymous with "empathic concern," the term he used in his book *Social Intelligence.* "With this kind of empathy," Goleman states, "we not only understand a person's predicament and feel with them, but are spontaneously moved to help, if needed."[36]

While the PFC plays an important role in empathic concern and social intelligence, it's also important to point out it does not act in isolation. As we emphasized in chapter 2, the brain acts as a *highly networked multi-layered system,* with the PFC being an integral part of this network.

Here are just two of the many studies that support this idea.

In one study, participants could earn money if they chose to administer electric shocks to another or forego the money if they chose not to. For those showing empathic concern for others, an MRI scan revealed increased activity in the areas of the brain involved in pain, reward, pleasure, and emotional empathy, as well as in their PFC.[37]

The other study evaluated the MRI brain activity of individuals who had observed someone being rejected and were given the option of responding with a helpful or comforting e-mail. Both brain regions associated with emotional and cognitive empathy were activated in highly empathic individuals, with the anterior insula and midline PFC being more active with caring behavior toward the victim.[38]

So the PFC acts in concert with all of the other networks and systems mentioned above and regulates our emotions and baser instincts to socially connect us in helpful ways. Next, we'll discuss one more key player in this symphony that literally puts a face on our internal experiences. As you'll see, it dramatically affects how we communicate and relate to each other.

### The Autonomic Nervous System

In 2014, I was asked to give a keynote address at the Global Wellness Summit, a gathering of the leaders of the spa and wellness industry. I was slated to present just before they were about to launch their Global Wellness Institute. To help set this up and inspire the leaders in attendance who were shaping the future of this industry, I'd offered to talk on "The Brain Science of Engaging Conscious Leadership." The conference organizer enthusiastically agreed and arranged a follow-up Skype meeting for me and the chair and co-chair of the conference to go over what I'd be sharing in my presentation.

During the Skype meeting, which took place about six weeks before the conference, I shared with the chair what I'd be covering about Conscious Leadership and leading well from within (much of which was based on the material in this book). With our agreement about what I'd be sharing, it was a warm, easy flowing, and engaging call, and I was feeling excited to present. Just as we were about to wrap up the call, the co-chair joined us, and I quickly brought her up to speed on our discussion. Then, just before we were about to say our final goodbyes, the conference chair asked the co-chair if she had any final thoughts. The co-chair responded, "I'd really like you to speak on the topic of beauty." At this point, my stress level spiked off the chart!

My stress unavoidably leached into the clipped tone of my response: "But I'm not an expert on beauty!" Yet she was insistent, saying it was a topic they really wanted to include. The chair then agreed. With a short few weeks before the conference and relatively little time to develop experitse on something I did not know much about, I feared I would not be able to do this, and my anxiety escalated. While I was trying my best to stay composed, my stress unavoidably revealed itself all over my face. I tried to talk them out of it but to no avail. In the end, we agreed on the topic, "The Impact of Brain Science on Leadership, Beauty, and Spa." As I got off the call, my mind was reeling. What had I done? In less than six weeks I'd be standing in front of four hundred industry leaders, trying to sound coherent about a topic I was completely unsure about. I felt anxious and was tempted to take flight and call back to decline the invitation. And then, as I imagined the fallout of withdrawing at this late stage, I became more anxious. For a moment, I felt overwhelmed and immobilized. In a daze and lightheaded, I had moved from fight-or-flight to freeze, completely uncertain about what to do.

In the spirit of Step 1 of the 4 in 4 Framework, and to convert my threat response into a challenge response, I paused, took a few heart-centered breaths, named my feelings, and then went for a surf to further calm down and clear my mind. When I came back home, I was ready to begin researching and sat down to see what I could find online at my computer. Miraculously, I was saved by the science.

In my research, I was awestruck by the elegant beauty of what I found. I discovered a common thread in the scientific evidence. The very same brain region activates when we appreciate the beauty of someone's physical apprearance,[39] art and music,[40] or mathematical equations;[41] or experience the allure of sex and money; or the perception of a fine bottle of wine;[42] or even the good deeds of another.[43] It's the *PFC*!

More specifically, it was the orbito-PFC, a part of the PFC located behind the eyes that funtionally overlaps with the ventromedial (lower middle) PFC.[44]

This region of the brain plays a key role, not only in decision making[45] (protecting what we find beautiful), but also in processing your relationships and regulating your emotions and stress response[46] (as mentioned in the section above).

Drilling down further, this region of the PFC also plays an important role in activating the parasympathetic nervous system (PNS).[47] Remember, this part of your autonomic nervous system taps the brake on your sympathetic nervous system (SNS), which can be helpful when you are feeling revved up by your fight-or-flight threat response.

Now, here's where things get even more interesting.

It turns out the autonomic nervous system plays a major role in how we read each other's expressions and relate to each other. To describe the autonomic nervous system's role in social engagement, Stephen Porges, a research professor in psychiatry at the University of North Carolina, Chapel Hill, developed a concept called polyvagal theory.[48]

According to polyvagal theory, your autonomic nervous system works in a hierarchical fashion that aligns with the evolutionary development reflected in the concept of the triune brain, as described in chapter 2.

Like the triune brain, your autonomic nervous system also has three levels: the part of your PNS that includes your *myelinated* vagus nerve, your SNS, and the part of your PNS that includes your *unmyelinated* vagus nerve.

Here's how it works. The most recently evolved region of your brain—the PFC—regulates the most recently evolved level of your PNS, which includes the cranial nerves controlling the muscles of your face and the *myelinated vagus nerve* that regulates your voice box, heart, lungs, gut, and other organs of your body. The fatty insulating sheath (i.e., the myelin) around this nerve increases conduction speed, which allows everything to function more quickly and smoothly.

When you feel safe, your higher cortical circuits and PFC function at their best, and this part of your PNS is your default setting. Things are humming along. You are gently tapping the brake on your SNS, keeping it in balance, so you feel a relaxed state of alertness. With an optimal capacity to engage your higher cortical circuits, you are able to feel more love and empathy, think more clearly, make better decisions, and engage in whatever you are doing with greater creativity. All your internal organs are running smoothly: you're breathing easily, and your heart rate is ticking along at its relatively low baseline rate. In short, you're happily cruising along in a growth-promoting state, resting and digesting, feeding and breeding, and staying and playing.

Moreover (and this is what got me really excited about how we are wired to connect), *you express this internal state on your face and in the tone of your voice.*

According to Porges, in its evolution, the PNS became physiologically linked to the cranial nerves that connect to your muscles of facial expression, your voice box, and the stapedius muscle in your middle ear.

So when you feel safe and parasympathetically engaged, you naturally express a non-threatening and warm, welcoming appearance, and you have a pleasant prosody in the tone of your voice. With the small muscle in your ear stabilizing your ear bones to decrease low frequency sounds, you can more easily pick up the sound of a human voice amidst distracting background noise. Essentially, in this state, you have softer facial features, a more pleasing tone of voice, and can listen more fully to others, even in a noisy, distracting environment. You embody the tend-and-befriend response. You are naturally more socially engaged, with a physiology that connects you more fully in your relationships. People read your facial expression and respond to the tone of your voice, instinctively perceiving you as being safe, kind, wise, and approachable.

However, when you feel unsafe and threatened and then react with a threat response, everything shifts in an instant, as your lower, survival-oriented regions of your brain progressively take over. Here your limbic system (and your amygdala in particular) triggers your SNS to step on the gas and drive your fight-or-flight response to protect you from harm.

As you learned in chapter 2, when you gear up to fight or take flight, your PNS-related, growth-promoting functions shut down. For example, you shift resources away from digestion, so you may feel a pit in your stomach and a dry mouth. At the same time, your heart rate and breathing speeds up, and all your muscles go tense. Your fists clench and your jaw tightens.

With the parasympathetic influence withdrawn from your cranial nerves, your previously inviting demeanor and appearance disappear, too. The softness in your facial expression may be replaced by a stony stare and heavyset jaw. Your speech may lose its prosody and become clipped. This sends others a signal that you are stressed, potentially dangerous, and not to be trifled with.

Also, when you feel threatened, your brain may scramble, scattering your clear thinking and creativity. You may actually lose IQ (and EQ) points. You may also lose access to your circuits of empathy and compassion and experience tunnel vision, to focus on your safety in that situation.

According to Porges, if danger continues to escalate and you cannot effectively fight or take flight to find safety, then the most primitive part of your brain—your brain stem—kicks in, activating the most primitive part of your autonomic nervous system, the part of your PNS that includes your *unmyelinated* vagus nerve. This may dangerously slow your heart rate and drop your blood pressure, causing you to faint. In effect, when you feel very unsafe and trapped, you move beyond fight or flight to freeze and feign death as your last salvo to save your life.

You may already recognize that I had transitioned between all three levels of my triune brain and autonomic nervous system during my call with the chair and co-chair. When the call began, I was relaxed, with a higher cortical, parasympathetically mediated, warm, engaging demeanor. I felt totally engaged in conversation with the chair.

Then when the adamant request came for me to speak on beauty, I felt threatened. My limbic system sympathetics kicked in, and I went into fight-or-flight. While I tried my best to appear composed, my facial expression and tone of voice betrayed the stress I felt. It was not pretty. In fact, when I saw the co-chair at the conference and we spoke about our Skype interaction, she half-joked, "I thought you were going to murder me!"

Then, after the call, I moved from fight-or-flight to freeze, when I felt really overwhelmed.

Thankfully, with the help of Step 1 of the framework, I was able to reconnect with my higher-level parasympathetics to calm myself, regain perspective, and stay the course—eventually able to reconnect with the chair and co-chair and laugh about what happened.

It also made for a great story in the presentation itself. After sharing the same science I shared with you above, I showed a picture of the Mona Lisa with her famous smile. In the context of all we had discussed, we reflected on why she was so beautiful. A large part of that beauty had to do with the softness around her eyes, her warm gaze, and her engaging smile, which expressed that she was calm, safe, and approachable. Hence, she was *attractive*.

You could say that leading well from within—by learning how to hack your autonomic system to better engage your stress and express yourself with greater clarity, equanimity, and compassion—will not only enable you to become a more effective and creative leader, but likely a more attractive and even more beautiful leader, too!

So let's take a moment to summarize all of the above: we are wired to connect through multiple neural systems and networks, including our social pain and reward systems, mirror neurons, emotional and cognitive empathy, our PFC regulation, and the three components of our autonomic nervous system. The activity of these networks manifests, not just in our internal experience, but in our facial expressions and the tone of our voice, meaning that we don't experience our reactivity and creativity in isolation. As a species, we are intimately linked with each other in ways that are socially contagious. Whether we like it or not, our reactivity or creativity is usually obvious to others, and they respond accordingly, triggering cycles of reactivity and creativity within relationships.

## Cycles of Reactivity and Creativity in Relationships

Think about the last time you had a fight with someone who was highly stressed. Perhaps that person was fighting for power and control, fighting to prove self-worth, or taking flight and stonewalling. Did his or her "vibe," demeanor, or words trigger your own stress or self-doubt? Did you go limbic? With your facial expression, tone of your voice, or words, did you react in ways that further triggered that individual's stress and self-doubt—causing that person to further react? Did it feel like you were just going around and around in a painful exchange, leaving you feeling angry and drained?

Now think of a time when you were in the presence of someone warm and loving, where you felt safe, and he or she brought out the best in you. Did you, in turn, respond with warmth, appreciation, and enthusiasm that brought out the best in that person, resulting in an effortless, energizing, and joyful interchange?

With what we've discussed above, now you understand why. Since we are wired to connect, we don't just experience reactivity and creativity personally, but in cycles of reactivity and creativity with others as well. In the *cycle of reactivity*, one person's limbic, fight-or-flight response triggers stress, self-doubt, and the fight-or-flight response in the other person. This reactivity in the second person then triggers more stress, self-doubt, and fight or flight in the first person, and so on, as shown in the figure below.

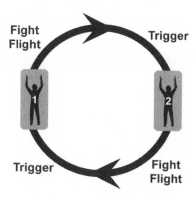

*Figure 9.1. The Cycle of Reactivity*

This cycle is a struggle for power and control, where both individuals feel threatened. Neither party takes responsibility for the interchange, and each can switch between being the persecutor and victim. While each may experience brief surges of energy from self-righteous indignation, feeling right, or getting his or her digs in, ultimately this form of energy (or pseudoenergy, as I call it) depletes each individual and both parties end up feeling drained, exhausted, and disconnected.

So if the cycle of reactivity is fight/flight–trigger, fight/flight–trigger, what then does the *cycle of creativity* look like? I'd been reflecting on this question for some time and then learned the answer from my mother.

All her life, Mom had rarely been sick. At seventy years of age, she was vibrant and exceptionally fit, an avid walker and tennis player who awoke at dawn four times a week to work out at the gym.

So, when she started to experience abdominal pain, feel fatigued, and lose weight, I was very concerned and called her physician to evaluate her. Since he was about to leave the country for a few weeks and could not see her, I facilitated her evaluation and ordered a CAT scan of her abdomen. I will never forget the moment the radiologist called me with the result. It was like a kick to my stomach, and I cried out, "No! No!" I knew at that moment I was about to lose my mother.

The next telephone call I would make would be the hardest of my life.

When my mother picked up the phone, she enthusiastically told me how she had had the test and thought everything went well. With a very shaky voice, I told her, "Mom, I am so sorry . . . you have pancreatic cancer, and it's spread to your liver."

She responded, "Oh, my God, that's the silent killer, isn't it?" She knew she was going to die. I said, "Mom, hold on—I'll be there with you soon."

Within five hours of telling her, I flew down from Berkeley to San Diego to hold her in my arms.

I promised her that the time she had left would be the most fulfilling of her life. A year later, just before she died, she told me that that the past few months had been the most meaningful and fulfilling she had ever experienced. It all came down to one thing. Over those few months, Mom experienced her relationships in a completely different way.

Up until her diagnosis, my mother had always struggled with doubts of self-worth. As beautiful and as radiant as she was, she frequently craved approval and validation. Many times she got very angry and reactive with us when we didn't acknowledge how beautiful she looked or how tasty her cooking was. And there were times when she came back from parties with Dad, screaming at him about not paying her enough attention. She frequently criticized the way he expressed affection and called him a "cold fish." We often reacted to her reactivity too, causing her more pain and self-doubt. My siblings and I would get angry and frustrated. Dad would frequently withdraw or, worse yet, tell Mom to "be reasonable." Mom would then feel persecuted and victimized. Everyone else was to blame and was treating her badly. She would then lash out in anger, and we, in turn, would also feel persecuted. All too often we failed to meet her pain with compassion, and we were all complicit in fueling these painful cycles of reactivity. It was grooved into our family dynamic. Memories of painful events would be frequently dredged up and scripts of unhealthy conversations replayed over and over, leaving us all feeling drained of energy.

Things changed dramatically after her diagnosis. She no longer craved attention. My dad, who was eighty-two at the time, dedicated himself to caring for her. He took her to her oncology visits and frequent blood tests. He meticulously recorded each test result and scheduled every appointment. With tenderness, their love blossomed. He prepared her food, and when he walked with her, he put his arm around her or held her hand. At the same time, my siblings and I made frequent trips to San Diego, and her sister flew out from South Africa to be with her. Her friends came around constantly with food and then gave her a celebration of life party.

One might think she no longer craved validation, because all the love and attention she received satisfied her craving. But that wasn't it. She never pitied herself and at first did not want me to tell any of her friends that she had cancer. She didn't want any special attention. If anything, she was humbled by the attention she received. She was in awe of the "fuss" her family and friends made over her and said she didn't feel like she deserved it.

In large part, the reason she no longer sought validation was that she knew time was running out and doubts of self-worth no longer seemed important. What really mattered in her relationships was not receiving validation, but rather receiving the warmth and love in the connection itself. She wanted to reach out and feel close to all of us, like the way you tightly embrace those closest to you before leaving on a long trip. She treasured love and intimacy and wanted to drink it up the way those condemned savor their last meal.

At one point in her illness, while we were waiting to see her oncologist in the patient room, Mom felt scared about the thoughts of leaving us and asked, "Where will I go when I die?" My dad responded, "No matter where you go, you will never be alone. Our souls will be forever intertwined." This touched Mom to her core.

In her last few months, something else changed about Mom. Even as her face grew gaunt, it softened as her heart fully opened. Not only did she appreciate the love she received, but also she exuded love. It was so nourishing that we were drawn to her. We wanted to be with her, to feel connected to her and experience the warmth and caring she radiated.

One morning while lying in bed reading, she came across a poem that moved her and called Dad to share it with him.

The poem, written anonymously, is "The Time Is Now."

*If you are ever going to love me,*

*Love me now,*

*While I can know*

*The sweet and tender feelings,*

*Which from true affection flow.*

*Love me now*

*While I am living.*

*Do not wait until I'm gone*

*And then have it chiseled in marble,*

*Sweet words on ice-cold stone.*

*If you have tender thoughts of me,*

*Please tell me now.*

*If you wait until I'm sleeping,*

*Never to awaken,*

*There will be death between us,*

*And I won't hear you then.*

*So, if you love me, even a little bit,*

*Let me know it while I am living*

*So I can treasure it.*

Mom told Dad that the poem made her appreciate how lucky she was to feel so much love before she died. At the same time, the poem saddened her. She saw how tragic it was that people withhold expressing love for each other until it's too late. Before she died, she took the time to tell each one of us how much she loved us and would miss us.

Two days before she died, when she began to slip away and no longer seemed conscious, the rabbi came to visit her. He also had cancer and had a special empathy for Mom. He spoke to her quietly, and we weren't sure that she could hear him. He then reached out to clasp her hands in his and leaned forward to ask, "Yvonne, after all these years, what have you learned is the meaning of your life?"

We stood at the bedside in silence, hoping for her to answer. We didn't think she could. And if she could answer, I thought she would say, "To get love." It was something she had yearned for all of her life. Then to our surprise, Mom opened her eyes for a few seconds and responded, "To give love." As she closed her eyes, her words trailed off, "To give love, to give love, to give . . ." These were among the last few words she ever spoke.

Mom's words filled my heart, where they remain. After reflecting on her words and the shift she had made, I shared with a dear friend that in the last year of her life Mom had shifted from seeking to *get* love to *give* love. My wise friend listened and then said, "But what if your mom had also learned how to *receive* love in her lifetime?" I then realized she had been receiving and savoring our love in the last year of her life as well as giving it back in abundance.

And then, in a flash of insight and with deep appreciation for the final lesson my mother taught me, I clearly saw the cycle of creativity. It's simply a cycle within which we give and receive love with each other.

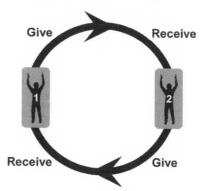

*Figure 9.2. The Cycle of Creativity*

In this cycle we give and receive, mindfully engaged with heart and mind, expressing ourselves with authenticity and care, and listening with empathy and understanding.

Mom ultimately taught me that the way we show up in our relationships changes everything, whether it's with our family, friends, colleagues, clients, patients, or anyone else whose life we touch.

Take a moment to reflect on the times you've been in the presence of someone who unconditionally gives and receives love with you and you've been able to freely give and receive love with that person. How did you feel? How did that person feel?

If the word *love* feels a bit too strong for interactions at work, think about when you've been able to give and receive from your highest self, with presence, wisdom, and kindness. What do you notice about how others respond? How does their physiology, presence, and sense of being shift, and how energizing is that for you and the person you are connecting with?

As you expand your awareness of how we are wired to connect and your ability to lead well from within by shifting your physiology from a reactive threat response to a more creative challenge response or tend-and-befriend response, it inevitably changes how others experience you. They are likely to be more present, relaxed, energized, and engaged around you, too.

Dr. Mike, a pediatrician who completed my eight-week online program on Leading Well from Within as well as a series of group coaching sessions, e-mailed me a revelation he had about how this cycle of creativity affected his daily interactions with his patients and their parents.

He shared, "I have noticed that at the end of the day I am seeing parents who are much more tolerant of me being late. Also, they are happier with the advice I give. Patients seem more likely to follow advice given. It came to me suddenly during a session that it is not the patients that are changing, but me. I am coming off as less stressful, and that is being reflected back to me by my patients and family."

Dr. Mike knew that as he became more present, relaxed, and energized, his patients and their families became so too, and this contributed to their healing.

I also know all too well—not only as a physician, but as an advocate for my mother—what this shift to a cycle of creativity feels like, as well as how it amplifies the healing presence of healthcare providers (although it applies just as well to the healing presence of anyone).

The first doctor I took mom to after her diagnosis seemed to be stressed out (if not burnt out). When we were brought into his office, he did not stand

and motioned for us to take a seat on the other side of his desk. His presence was absent of empathy, warmth, or care, which immediately put Mom in a state of dis-ease. He never acknowledged how difficult Mom's cancer must have been for her. Then, within about ten minutes of a brusque conversation, he turned to my mom with a clipped tone and said, "So, tell me. Do you want chemo or not?" My mom, shaking in fear, stammered, "I don't know . . . I don't want to lose my hair?" Her vacillation seemed to irritate him, which further unnerved us all.

As we left the appointment, Mom appeared shell-shocked. All this doctor had succeeded in doing was to amplify Mom's feeling of fear. On the way to the car, I promised my mother she would never see this doctor again. She had just experienced a painful cycle of reactivity that I knew was toxic to her immune system and state of being.

Thankfully, we found her another oncologist, Dr. Laurie Frakes. As Mom was brought back to her office, Dr. Frakes was there to meet her in the transition area on the way to the room. She exuded care and kindness. She immediately sensed how tense Mom was feeling and opened her arms, saying, "Welcome! Would it be OK if I gave you a hug?" Mom's tension instantly released.

The visit with Dr. Frakes energized her. On our way out of her office, Mom turned to me with mix of relief, appreciation, and hope, exclaiming, "That woman is a pill!" She intuitively knew that, regardless of the therapy, Dr. Frakes, with her empathy and compassion, was the healing treatment itself. Mom had experienced a healing cycle of creativity with a clinician who truly listened with empathy and understanding and gave with authenticity and care. In the end, while the research suggested Mom might only have had three to six months to live after her diagnosis, she lived fourteen months, enjoying the richest time of her life, pain free, and surrounded by love until her very last breath.

Not that we need data to support the value of connecting more deeply with each other, but research confirms the powerful effect of giving and receiving with empathy in the healthcare industry.

A couple of studies actually randomized patients with colds to receive "enhanced" *empathetic* care versus the "standard" healthcare delivery. Just before the doctors went into the patient's room, they received a packet with the type of care they were assigned to give. The "standard" packet included the basic ingredients of a clinical encounter, including taking a history and focusing on the physical exam and diagnosis. The "enhanced" packet included the above with additional instructions to take the time to strongly empathize and connect with patients, communicate a positive prognosis, and educate and empower them to take care of themselves. Individuals who perceived their care to be "perfectly empathetic" had colds of both a shorter duration and lesser intensity.[49] One study showed that this care altered the patients' immune response. (They had congruently greater changes in Interleukin-8 and neutrophil counts, which are physical markers of inflammation.)[50]

What this study suggests is that the empathic presence of a caregiver has the power to transform the immune system and heal patients, which may well have contributed to why Mom lived longer than was expected.

A number of studies also show that relationship-centered care and empathy affect a variety of other patient outcomes, including patient satisfaction,[51] reduction in physical pain,[52] a positive response to psychotherapy,[53] adherence to clinical advice, and even "business" outcomes, such as patient retention, loyalty, and reduced malpractice risk.[54]

This cycle of creativity improves outcomes in business settings, too. I had the pleasure of meeting New York City restaurateur and Chairman of the Shake Shack, Danny Meyer, at the Conscious Capitalism CEO Summit and subsequently at his office in New York, where he expressed this idea beautifully. He explained that while waiters and other staff are trained to be of service, they are not necessarily trained to listen and respond very well, something his restaurants pride themselves on doing. While Meyer noted that "*service* is a monologue," where you are just trained to rotely serve the client, he emphasized that "*hospitality* is a dialogue," where you more fully connect with the client.

Hospitality is a cycle of receiving and giving with your clients: first, you receive by deeply listening to and anticipating their needs, and then you give in authentic and truly caring ways that exceed their expectations. It's a cycle of creativity that applies to any business.

In chapter 11, we'll be taking a closer look at how the cycle of creativity can help leaders actively engage and inspire their employees to provide outstanding customer hospitality that not only drives high levels of customer satisfaction, but a healthy bottom line. But for now, you can simply reflect on the relationships with your own organization. How might learning to transform cycles of reactivity into cycles of creativity apply to your relationships with the customers or clients you serve? With your employees? Or even your most important relationships at home?

You have learned in chapter 2 and part 2 that reactivity and creativity exist in a dynamic equilibrium. What this chapter adds, and figure 9.4 below shows, is that just as you oscillate between the states of reactivity and creativity within yourself, you oscillate between cycles of reactivity and creativity as you interact with others too.

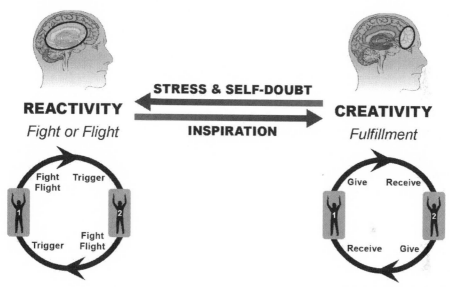

*Figure 9.3. The Dynamic Equilibrium of Cycles of Reactivity and Creativity*

The good news is that the same skills and practices you learned in part 2 to shift yourself from a state of reactivity to a state of creativity—even in the heat of the moment—can be applied to your relationships, too. With awareness, skill, and ongoing practice, you can also rewire your brain and shift your equilibrium so you spend more time overall engaged in cycles of creativity. In the next chapter, you'll learn how to more easily make this shift within your relationships at work and at home—by applying the 4 in 4 Framework.

# CHAPTER 10

# Resolving Conflicts and Nurturing Your Relationships

In the last chapter, you learned how we are wired to connect with others and how our relationships are characterized by cycles of reactivity and creativity. In this chapter, we're going to discuss how you can use the 4 in 4 Framework to shift between these cycles to feel less reactive and conflicted and more creatively engaged, energized, and fulfilled in your relationships.

Relationship conflicts, whether at work or at home, are very common. They also make up a significant part of the coaching work I do. One of my clients, Eric, a successful business owner from Chicago, shared with me near the beginning of our engagement that one of the biggest things he wanted to work on was reconnecting with his son, Tony. (Again, names have been changed to protect confidentiality.)

After Eric's first wife left when Tony was eleven years old, Tony felt abandoned. He became angry, irritable, and depressed. Eric, who struggled with his own doubts of self-worth, found it difficult to empathize with Tony as a teenager and deal with his emotional swings. He was especially frustrated with Tony's defiance, not doing his homework for school and his habitual lying. In exasperation, Eric would say things like, "I don't know what the fuck is wrong with you. You better get your shit together. The only person you are hurting is yourself!"

And he did. Tony started cutting himself and at age fifteen attempted suicide. He was institutionalized for two weeks and refused to see Eric, which was a painful low point in their relationship.

Tony moved out of Eric's house when he was seventeen, and for the next four years, their relationship was tenuous at best. Then something happened that Eric says took their relationship "from awful to horrendous."

Eric reached out to Tony, then an angry young man of twenty-one years, to let him know that he was getting married. He wanted Tony to be his best man. However, with his trust being low in Tony, Eric first wanted Tony to meet with him and his future wife, Jennifer, to discuss this further. They met at a restaurant, where Tony "unloaded" on Jennifer, saying, "I've never liked you. My dad could have done better!" Eric felt blindsided by the attack, which destroyed any remnant of trust between them. He told Tony that what he said was the most painful thing he had ever witnessed one person saying to another, and he disinvited Tony from attending their wedding.

The next two years, Eric and Tony were estranged. They did not see each other and only spoke infrequently on the phone. Eric tried to maintain contact with text messages, the majority of which were not returned, further triggering Eric's anger and resentment. Still, Eric loved his son, and their ongoing cycle of reactivity, which led to their estrangement, was causing him deep pain. When Eric's mother died, he saw Tony again, which opened the door for them to connect, but their relationship remained strained. Tony also moved from Chicago to New York City to live with Eric's brother. It was soon thereafter that Eric reached out to me to explore how he could reconnect with his son.

A year later, Eric had the opportunity to tell his son how much he loved him and that he was proud of the young man he had become. Eric shared with me how his son teared up in response and said that he had waited so long to hear those words and told him how much it meant to him. Eric now feels fully reconnected with Tony, free of much of the painful residue of their earlier years. They are able to more freely give and receive with each other in a cycle of creativity, and they feel a new lightness and joy in each other's company.

So what happened to create such a dramatic shift? And how might these lessons help you with any conflict you may be experiencing?

Part of what Eric learned early in coaching about his relationship with his son was how he was contributing to the cycle of reactivity. He told me, "I now understand how I was taking Tony's behaviors at face value, rather than seeing his underlying suffering." He further acknowledged how his reactive responses of anger, self-righteous indignation, and exasperation, along with the tone of voice he was using in their infrequent phone calls, was triggering Tony and causing him to further withdraw. He saw how Tony's stonewalling then triggered more frustration in him and how he was trying to break down this impenetrable fortress with pointed attacks, but to no avail.

Once Eric could more clearly see the triggers and fight-or-flight behaviors, which were causing problems, and the cycle of reactivity in their relationship, we shifted to focus on his deeper intention for the outcome he wanted to create, which was a closer relationship with his son. Using what you are about to learn in this chapter, we spoke about how Eric could begin to mindfully engage in asking questions within himself about how he could more fully receive Tony with a greater measure of empathy and understanding, as well as give of himself to Tony with greater care and compassion.

Eric and I also began to do some work around his own suffering and self-doubt with the Appraise-Reappraise Method and self-compassion practices that you learned in chapter 6, as well as the compassion practice you will learn at the end of this chapter. The more self-compassion Eric experienced, the more compassion he felt for Tony.

Bit by bit, over the subsequent weeks in his discussions, as Eric's heart softened, he looked for small opportunities to simply ask Tony how he was doing and how he could be of support. He became more curious about what Tony was sharing and less judgmental. He also became more patient and expressed a more caring tone during their calls. They began to speak more frequently, and Tony started returning more of his texts.

His son then shared with him that he had begun therapy to address his depression and asked Eric to fly to New York to join him at one of his therapy sessions. Eric asked me what I thought he should do. I strongly encouraged him to go and to continue listening with a loving ear and expressing himself with an open heart. This would mean continuing to practice self-compassion and compassion. I also suggested that if the moment felt appropriate, he could let his son know he was not alone with stress and self-doubt by sharing some of his own vulnerability around his struggles too.

Eric flew to New York for the therapy session and shared that he felt well prepared for one of the most profound experiences he had ever had with Tony.

He said, "It was there that I truly understood just how sad and broken Tony was, and this just melted the final, icy layer of resentment that covered my deeper care for him." Eric listened deeply to what Tony was sharing and then took the opportunity to reassure Tony that he was not alone and that they were more similar than different. He shared with Tony that he too struggled with self-doubt and a harsh inner critic and had suffered from depression.

This sharing shifted something in the relationship. It created a new foundation of trust. Over the next few weeks, they had a number of heartfelt conversations by phone, where they were able to more effortlessly give and receive with each other. Eric said, "We just began to share with and support each other, not as a father watching over his son, but as people with similar pain and hopes and dreams." At this same time, Tony began to thrive at school and at work and to take better care of his health.

When Tony then asked his father to join in another therapy session six months after the first, this time by Skype, Eric then shared how much he loved him and was proud of the man he had become.

Eric has arrived at a whole new place with Tony. Whereas, before, he was locked in a cycle of power and control, now all he wishes is for Tony to have a satisfying life. He says, "I want him to have the best life he chooses for himself. Not the life that he thinks I would choose for him or what I think he should choose. I want him to become all he can become as a husband, father, and man in a way that would make him most fulfilled."

Eric and Tony managed to profoundly shift their cycle of reactivity, in which they triggered each other's fight-or-flight behaviors, to a cycle of creativity, in which they found a way to more freely give and receive with each other. This shift, and especially the moment when Eric shared his vulnerability, established greater safety and trust in their relationship. This then opened the door for them to more freely express and experience love for each other and ultimately to support what was most significant in each other's lives.

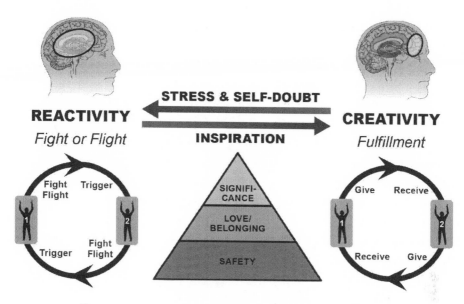

*Figure 10.1. How Cycles of Reactivity and Creativity Align with Maslow's Hierarchy of Needs*

Essentially, shifting from cycles of reactivity to creativity in your relationships enables you to more fully meet your combined Maslowian Hierarchy of Needs (as shown in figure 10.1 above), both at home and at work.

Part of making the shift is to not only meet the needs of safety within yourself, but to create greater safety in your relationships, too. When you mindfully give and receive with kindness, empathy, and authenticity, it diffuses the threat response and sets a foundation of trust upon which you can more freely give and receive with a tend-and-befriend response to more fully engage your *love and belonging* needs. This then enables you to further support or collaborate with others and, if you choose, to synergize on opportunities, harnessing your challenge response to achieve meaningful results for whatever you deem to be mutually *significant*. We do not climb this Maslowian pyramid alone, but together. Learning how to better receive and give with each other enables us to do so.

In this next section, you will learn how you can use the 4 in 4 Framework to better receive and give to transform your cycles of reactivity into cycles of creativity with others.

## Applying the 4 in 4 Framework to Your Relationships

The 4 in 4 Framework helps to facilitate the shift from reactivity to creativity anywhere along the relational spectrum—from resolving conflicts and finding agreement with the most difficult people in your life to nurturing all of your relationships, including those that bring you greatest joy.

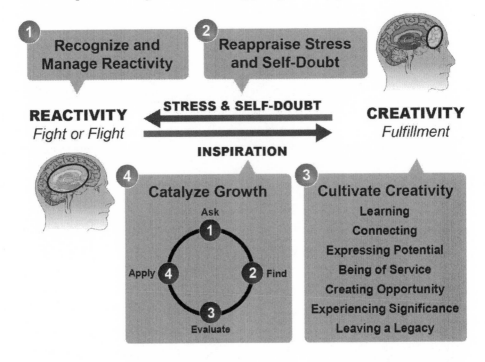

In chapter 8 (Step 4 of the 4 in 4 Framework), you learned how to use the Ask-Find-Evaluate-Apply cycle, shown above, to mindfully ask better questions; find, evaluate, and apply better answers; and therefore take more effective action. This process can help you make the shift from reactivity to creativity in your interactions with others as well and will be the key step in helping you resolve conflict and nurture relationships.

As Eric discovered, whether you're trying to resolve active conflict or you want to nurture already strong relationships, the two most important categories of questions you can ask yourself are:

How can I best receive in this relationship?

How can I best give in this relationship?

Notice that we've begun with receiving rather than giving. In his perennial bestseller *The Seven Habits of Highly Effective People,* Stephen R. Covey encourages us to "seek first to understand, then to be understood."[1] In receiving, we seek to understand both our own perspective and underlying beliefs *and* those of the person we are relating to.

Using Step 4 of the framework, we *ask* questions silently within our minds that enable us to gain deeper insight into ourselves, and we ask questions of the other person so we can more deeply understand, connect, and empathize with that person. The resulting insights, in turn, free up energy to allow us to give more effectively. Once you've asked yourself and the other person the right questions, you listen carefully to *find, evaluate,* and *apply* the answers that feel right for your relationship.

The other steps of the 4 in 4 Framework help you to frame the specific questions you ask using Step 4. If you are in conflict, you will also incorporate Steps 1, 2, and 3 of the framework to navigate resolution. If you are looking to nurture your relationships, you'll mostly incorporate Step 3.

Also remember, mindfulness is an essential foundation for this framework. It is vitally important to approach the questions you ask of yourself and others with openness, curiosity, and kindness to cultivate cycles of creativity.

Since it's challenging to nurture your relationships when you are in conflict, let's begin with defusing any active conflict. Then we'll discuss how to use the 4 in 4 Framework to further nurture your relationships.

## Resolving Conflict

Conflict typically arises because one or both parties are not getting their needs met. When we are in conflict, we may feel unsafe, uncared for, or unheard regarding what is truly important to us. The art of resolving this type of conflict is to learn about the other person's issues and needs and identify and communicate your needs so you can best hear and respond to each other's needs, in a way that does not continue to trigger each other.

I'd like to invite you to bring to mind an unsettling conflict you've had with someone, where he or she is also aware of the conflict and the two of you are clearly embroiled in a cycle of reactivity. Bring it to mind as vividly as possible. How are you and the other person feeling? Are you both feeling threatened? How are you each reacting? How are you fighting or taking flight? How are your reactions further triggering each other?

As you bring this conflict to mind, you may feel any number of emotions, including anger, anxiety, or even regret that you lost your composure. You can take heart in knowing much of your cycle of reactivity can be explained by how the brain naturally reacts under stress. Remember, if you are feeling threatened, it can lead to amygdala hijack. Your threat response may draw resources away from your higher cortical circuits that enable you to experience empathy and compassion, regulate your emotional responses, and make good decisions aligned with your interests and what you both truly want. Thus, when you both feel threatened, it can become very difficult for you to step into each other's shoes, understand each other's perspectives, and problem solve about what's good for both of you.

Instead, when you "go limbic," you tend to get drawn into a power struggle with each other. You may find yourselves sidetracked in an alleyway of distraction, where the endgame is *being right* rather than *what's right,* based on mutual interests. The triggers that cause each of you to go limbic and become reactive are powerful. Your triggers may be feeling unsafe or uncared for or that you're not being heard or understood regarding what's most important to you. You may feel judged, labeled, rejected, or dismissed by another. Or you may feel threatened in relation to the SCARF factors we discussed in chapter 6: Status, Certainty, Autonomy, Relatedness, or sense of Fairness.

When you feel threatened, you instinctively respond, often fighting or taking flight with the low-performance leadership qualities we discussed in chapter 1. You may both dig in your heels and fight to regain your power, becoming more controlling and autocratic or arrogant and critical. Alternatively, you may take flight by becoming withdrawn or distant or overly compliant and accommodating. When you do so and suffer in silence, it can lead to internal resentment and frustration, which can tip you back into anger and seeking power and control.

All of this can leave each of you feeling even more threatened and unsafe and locked in a struggle to find safety. This struggle sucks all your energy into the base of Maslow's Hierarchy, leaving you feeling drained and emotionally exhausted. When you feel this way, you may further withdraw and choose to avoid each other all together.

Whether you are a leader of an organization, healer, parent, or leader who interacts with others in any other capacity, the good news is that you can break this cycle of reactivity and shift to a cycle of creativity with each other. You can renew and refocus your energy and move it up Maslow's Hierarchy to establish safety, trust, and a greater sense of connection; you can find agreement about your mutually significant interests. Your ability to do so draws significantly on your qualities of high-performance leadership we discussed in chapter 1. As you may recall, these qualities include leaders being consistently self-aware, relational, authentic, and able to achieve meaningful results.

What this takes is to prime yourself for action with a deep intention and commitment to resolve your conflict. Without this intent, it's unlikely that Eric would have been successful in resolving his connection with Tony. He might have waited, hoping that something would change, rather than being proactive and finding the courage to move through his discomfort to create this change.

So start with feeling your intent to resolve your conflict. Think about why it's important to you. Then mindfully proceed with openness, curiosity, and kindness, both for yourself and, as best you can, for the person you are in conflict with. That person may be suffering just like you.

Now you are ready to use the four steps in Step 4 to make the shift from reactivity to creativity by asking questions and finding, evaluating, and applying your answers to resolve the conflict and find agreement in the way best suited to your particular relationship.

### *Ask the Right Questions (Step 1 of Step 4)*

The first step to resolving your conflict is to ask the right questions. These questions can help you better understand yourself and the other person. As mentioned above, you may ask these questions silently in your mind to better understand yourself, as well as use them to guide you in asking the other person questions so you can more fully understand that person's perspective. These questions can help you prepare for a conversation with someone you are in conflict with, or you may reach for some of them in the heat of the moment if you sense you may be sliding into conflict with someone and want to avert it.

The first three steps of the 4 in 4 Framework, as referenced below, can be used to help you frame many of your key questions to more clearly identify your conflict, identify the underlying triggers that may be driving it, and resolve your conflict.

I invite you to consider the following lists of questions as an overarching "study guide." Of course, not all of these questions will apply to every situation. Feel free to skip any that don't seem to apply and to make up your own that serve you more specifically.

This first list of questions relates to the way you receive—that is, listen with empathy to understand the source of the other's reactivity and that person's creative needs, as well as your own. By also compassionately recognizing your own reactivity and creative needs, you may discover what is blocking your ability to receive so you can get out of your own way and be clear about what you are asking for, so you can better connect to resolve the conflict.

- Is the other person limbic? (Step 1: Recognizing Reactivity)
- Am I limbic? What are my sensations, thoughts, and feelings? (Step 1: Recognizing Reactivity)
- What are the underlying triggers of stress and self-doubt that are causing me to be reactive? (Step 2: Reappraise Stress and Self-Doubt)
- What are the underlying triggers of stress and self-doubt that are causing the other person to be reactive? (Step 2: Reappraise Stress and Self-Doubt)
- How can I most objectively see what happened? (Step 2: Appraise-Reappraise Method, question 1)
- What are my beliefs about what happened? (Step 2: Appraise-Reappraise Method, question 2)
- What are the other person's beliefs around what happened? (Step 2: Appraise-Reappraise Method, question 2)

- Is my belief really true? (Step 2: Appraise-Reappraise Method, question 3)

- How could I view things differently to help resolve the conflict? (Step 2: Appraise-Reappraise Method, question 4)

- How can I demonstrate an openness and willingness to listen with empathy so the other person can feel safe with me? (Step 3: Cultivate Creativity)

- How can I avoid interrupting the other person so that person feels heard and feels received by me? (Step 3: Cultivate Creativity)

- What is truly important to me in this situation? (Step 3: Cultivate Creativity)

- What is truly important to the other person in this situation? (Step 3: Cultivate Creativity)

This list of questions relates to the way you *give*—that is, compassionately and authentically express yourself—to resolve the conflict:

- Are my reactive responses causing me and the other person more harm than good? (Step 1: Recognizing Reactivity)

- Is the way I am expressing myself triggering the other person's stress and self-doubt? (Step 2: Reappraise Stress and Self-Doubt)

- How can I better express myself with my tone and body language that allows the other person to feel safe and heard and minimizes triggering that person's stress and self-doubt? (Step 2: Reappraise Stress and Self-Doubt)

- How can I better express myself, addressing facts and behaviors in ways that the other person does not feel blamed, labeled, judged, or criticized? (Step 2: Reappraise Stress and Self-Doubt)

- How can I best express myself with authenticity and honesty so that all my concerns are most likely to be heard? (Step 3: Cultivate Creativity)

- How can I best express what's important to me so that I can get my needs met? (Step 3: Cultivate Creativity)

- How can I best acknowledge what's important to the other person? (Step 3: Cultivate Creativity)

- What can I do to meet the specific needs of the other person? (Step 3: Cultivate Creativity)

- How can I best request that my specific needs be met? (Step 3: Cultivate Creativity)

- What are my alternatives if my specific needs or interests cannot be met? (Step 3: Cultivate Creativity)

- How can I best ask for forgiveness, if this is warranted? (Step 3: Cultivate Creativity)

- How can I best acknowledge my forgiveness, if this is warranted? (Step 3: Cultivate Creativity)

Again, whether you use these questions or discover your own, the purpose of these questions is to help you become more aware of the reactivity needing to be defused in yourself and the other person, using the 4 in 4 Framework, and to prepare yourself for a natural, authentic, openhearted interaction.

You may find it most helpful to reflect on these questions in advance of meeting with someone to resolve your conflict, or in the moment to guide your discussion. However, when you are speaking with the other person, also be mindful not to let your thinking about these questions clutter your mind and prevent you from being fully present to giving and receiving in the moment. Sometimes internally asking one simple question—how can I best give and receive in this moment?—is what's most helpful during the interaction itself.

### Find Your Answers (Step 2 of Step 4)

Once you've asked the "right" questions to frame your situation, you can now move toward creating stillness for yourself so the answers can find you.

Whether you are preparing for your interaction or are in conversation, keep pausing and breathing through your heart center. This helps you regulate your amygdala and limbic reactivity and keep your PFC and higher cortical circuits engaged, so that you can think more clearly, be more receptive to insights, and connect with your deepest wisdom.

Even before you engage in your discussion, allow yourself to settle and breathe in through your heart center and breathe out this loving-kindness into your body and wherever you may feel tense. Then, as best you can, imagine the suffering of the person you are in conflict with and breathe in that suffering through your heart center, while amplifying a sense of loving-kindness to absorb that person's pain, and imagine breathing out goodwill to that person. You can then bring this practice and sense of loving-kindness into your interaction.[2]

From this place of greater stillness and clarity, really listen to your answers and intuition. Be mindful of any answers that feel like judgment or criticism of the other person and may make you feel more self-righteous, thus short-circuiting your intention to resolve your conflict. Also be aware of answers that bring you a feeling of relief so you can avoid what feels uncomfortable. Acting on these answers may lead you to become overly accommodating, not saying what you really feel to be "nice." Find answers that feel genuine and then further assess them with the next step.

### Evaluate Your Answers (Step 3 of Step 4)

To evaluate your answers, ask yourself questions such as, *Does this answer feel right more than feel good? Is this answer good for myself and others? Does this answer ultimately get me to a place where I am more likely to give and receive love?*

Remember, answers that feel good may simply bring you relief from your limbic threat response, while those that feel right are more aligned with your higher cortical values and thoughtful interests.

Sometimes your "right" answers may feel straightforward and lead to an easy resolution. But they may also not initially feel comfortable. Sometimes your answers may guide you to hold a boundary or express something you feel uncomfortable saying (and the other person may feel uncomfortable hearing). While in the short term your answer may not feel good, you will know if it is right and what's needed. Surgery serves as a good analogy here. Just as a surgeon needs to cut unhealthy tissue so good healing can take place, sometimes you need to compassionately communicate things that may be difficult for others to hear, in order to clear unhealthy energetic blocks and more freely give and receive again in a healthier relationship.

Once you trust your answers, it is time to implement them with the next step, Step 4.

### Apply Your Answers to Take Action (Step 4 of Step 4)

When you have determined the answers that feel right, it's time to apply these answers and take action to resolve the conflict and find agreement. These actions may include courageously expressing yourself, following through on what's important to the other person and you, or living up to your end of an agreement. It may also involve saying you are sorry, making amends, and asking for forgiveness. Or it may involve accepting an apology and extending forgiveness.

If your are preparing to engage in a conversation to resolve your conflict, you may also find it helpful to set up the following rules of engagement with the other person to give you the greatest likelihood of success.

These rules are focused on the way you each pledge to give and receive with each other. They are designed to keep you grounded in the cycle of creativity and avoid the communication triggers that can ensnare you in the cycle of reactivity. They maintain a fundamental sense of safety so you can begin to work through your issues, build trust, feel heard and understood, and have a chance of mutually meeting your higher Maslowian needs around what truly matters most to each of you.

1. First, **agree that one person gives while the other receives.** This helps to ensure you both get a chance to talk and feel heard and understood; you also avoid the pitfalls of trying to continuously talk over each other.

2. Next, **agree on the specific rules for the giver and receiver** as outlined below.

   a) The *giver* agrees to state the facts and take full responsibility for his or her experience without blaming, judging, labeling, or criticizing the receiver. The giver agrees to use "I" statements instead of "you" statements. For example, instead of saying, "*You* acted like such a jerk and made me mad!," you'd say, "When *I* saw you doing/saying [just the simple observable facts], *I* felt hurt and angry."

The giver also agrees to be mindful of his or her own nonverbal communication and to refrain from talking with a patronizing, accusatory, or sarcastic tone, or using aggressive gestures such as finger pointing, all of which can feel threatening and activate the survival brain of the other. Finally, the giver agrees to avoid ascribing motives or intentions to the receiver.

As the conversation proceeds, the giver may ask questions to clarify the intentions of the receiver. The receiver may then answer briefly, without taking over the giving role, allowing the giver to complete everything he or she wants to express.

b) The main rule for the *receiver* is to simply listen, which is easier said than done. Often, when we are listening, what we are really hearing is our own thought stream in response to what is being said, rather than what is actually said. Then, all too often, the receiver feels compelled to respond by justifying his or her actions or explaining why what the giver said is not true. To avoid this temptation, the receiver agrees to listen without comment, protest, or justification.

The receiver not only agrees to refrain from defensive verbal responses, but also gestural ones too, such as rolling the eyes to dismiss something or crossing the arms to shut the giver out. Once the receiver senses the giver has fully expressed himself or herself, the receiver may thank the giver for sharing and then paraphrase what was heard by saying something like, "I just want to make sure I've heard you well. What I've heard you share is . . . Am I understanding it correctly, or is there anything else you'd like to add?"

3. Then, **agree on who will give first.** Once the giver has fully given and the receiver has fully received, the roles switch, and the receiver becomes the giver. These roles may continue to switch until resolution and agreement is found.

Remember, while these rules are helpful, they are insufficient without a true commitment and intention to work towards resolution together. The more you can both bring a sense of openness, kindness, and curiosity about understanding each other's perspective and finding resolution, the more successful you'll be.

### Asking Questions Again

After you have taken action, you then loop back to the first step in the Ask-Find-Evaluate-Apply spiral to ask, "Are we now resolved?" or "Are we now in agreement?"

When the answer is yes and you've successfully taken action, you may experience an energy release, where the energy begins to flow in your relationship again.

If the answer is no and you feel the conflict is still unresolved, or you are still holding on to energetic residue from your interaction, return to your checklist of questions about receiving and giving from Step 1 and consider what other questions you can ask and actions you can take.

Occasionally, if you have taken 100 percent responsibility for your part in the conflict and truly believe you have done all you can to resolve it, or if you cannot come to an agreement with the person, it may be best to forgive that person, agree to disagree, and/or consider alternative paths of action. This may include seeking professional help or the possibility of no longer engaging in the relationship.

Note that this approach to resolving conflicts and finding agreement applies to your relationships at work (such as your colleagues, your customers, and those you lead), *and* your relationships at home (such as your partner, children, and friends). Also, remember that your relationships are highly interrelated. If you are having difficulty at home—say, fighting continuously with your children or going through a divorce—this conflict would kindle your limbic system, likely making you more edgy with your colleagues, customers, or employees at work. On the other hand, if you experience deeply connected, supportive, and nourishing relationships at home, you would likely have more resilience to deal with stress in any context and experience more satisfying work relationships as a result. That's why it's so important to cultivate cycles of creativity both at work *and* at home.

The benefit of this process also goes beyond simply resolving your conflict and finding agreement in this particular interaction. When you intentionally work through your issues, you establish a precedent for working through difficult times together. This memory, or knowing, builds further strength and resiliency into your relationship.

I tell my boys that the most important thing in our relationship is not being "perfect" with each other but being "real" and trusting that if we get into conflict, we have these skills to "make the turn" from reactivity to creativity to make up. In fact, we use this terminology intentionally. When we get into conflict, we say to each other, "We need to find a way to make the turn." This immediately engages our intention and commitment and the trust that we'll be able to do so together. When we do, we take the time to acknowledge and celebrate how we "made the turn!"

Now, with your conflicts resolved and greater *safety* established (or if you are already feeling connected in your relationship), your questions can now focus more on how to further nurture your relationships to deepen your experience of *love and belonging* and the meaning and *significance* you can create together.

## Nurturing Relationships at Home and at Work

In the cycle of creativity, the way we receive and give to nurture our relationships is similar to the way we receive and give to resolve our conflicts. Success in both rests on mindfully *receiving* from others by listening with heartfelt empathy and *giving* to them by expressing yourself with authenticity and compassion, following the four steps of Step 4 in the 4 in 4 Framework.

### *Ask the Right Questions (Step 1 of Step 4)*

Since the principles of nurturing relationships are the same whether at home or work, the questions you ask (and answers you receive) will likely overlap for your various relationships. But different contexts have their own conventions, dynamics, and rules that may yield different insights in each area, too. So we'll address these specific types of relationships separately:

- Family and friends
- Colleagues at work
- Clients or customers
- Patients (if you are a healthcare provider)
- People you lead

Remember, I offer these lists of questions as a guide to inspire and equip you for empathic and authentic interaction. Before asking yourself these questions, set your intention to ask good questions to enrich the lives of others and yourself. Use the ones that feel relevant to your specific relationship and, better yet, let them inspire you to find other questions of your own.

Look for opportunities to reflect upon and routinely activate your questions. Create a habit by identifying "cues" that will trigger your intention to ask your key inspiring questions.

For example, you can set your intention to ask how you can best give and receive each time your reach for the door handle to enter your house, board room, patient room, or open your computer to send an e-mail. Or you can think through your questions any time you are making plans to go out on a special date or as part of your routine in preparing for a meeting with a colleague, client, or employee. You can also think about setting this intention as you step up to interact with people you don't know too well, but whose day you'd like to brighten, such as individuals who are helping you at the bank, post office, laundry, or grocery checkout.

Can you also think of other cues or when it would be most helpful for you to ask these questions to more fully connect with the different people in your life?

Remember, what you give your attention to grows. The more you can routinely trigger your questions and heartfelt intention, the more you will find answers that will enrich your relationships and your life.

Now let's further explore the questions you could ask in some of your important relationships. Again, these questions, which you initially ask quietly in your mind, not only prime your intent to nurture your relationship. They also serve to inspire the questions you may ask the person you are with so you can learn from his or her answers and deepen your connection together.

## Questions to Nurture Relationships with Family and Friends

Many of us feel the most deeply connected and fulfilled in our relationships with family and friends. These connections are relatively unconstrained by the rules and conventions we feel in the workplace, which gives us freer rein to share what's in our heart and most fully receive and give love in cycles of creativity.

Bring to mind a family member or friend who is close to your heart and reflect on the following questions. At the same time, feel free to think of other questions that would help you more deeply receive and give in your relationship with this person.

*Receive:*

- How can I better understand [insert name]?

- How does _____ typically fight and take flight when he or she feels threatened?

- What causes _____ pain or triggers his or her stress and self-doubt?

- What brings _____ joy?

- What is truly most important to _____?

- How does _____ most like to receive my love?[3]

- How can I better listen to _____?

- How can I open my heart more fully to _____?

*Give:*

- How can I be more present with _____?

- How can I best express my love to _____?

- How could I express myself better so that _____ feels truly appreciated and valued?

- What could I do to have some fun with _____?
- What could I do that would be of help to _____?
- What could I do to surprise _____?

Did any of these questions resonate with you? Can you think of any other questions you could ask yourself and your family members or friends to enrich your relationships with them?

## Questions to Nurture Relationships with Colleagues at Work

To nurture your relationships with colleagues at work, some key questions focus on understanding what's most important and inspiring to them. Other questions may explore how you can most effectively collaborate together to ensure you can meet your visions of what's truly important to both of you in the context of your work together.

As we've mentioned, relationships are relationships, whether they are at home or at work. So as you think about the questions you could ask yourself about your colleagues, first consider if any of the questions in the section above might be relevant and helpful to your relationships at work. Then consider the following questions that address the work environment more specifically.

*Receive:*
- What is [insert name]'s highest priority today?
- What is _____'s longer-term goals?
- What are our collective priorities and goals?
- How can we best collaborate to achieve these goals together?
- What are _____'s biggest frustrations?
- What are _____'s personal aspirations?
- What gives _____'s the greatest sense of meaning and fulfillment in what he or she does at work?
- What gives _____'s the greatest sense of meaning and fulfillment in what he or she does at home?

*Give:*

- How can I best collaborate with _____?

- How can _____ and I work most creatively together?

- How can I build trust with _____?

- How can I support _____ to overcome his or her biggest frustration or obstacles?

- How can I support _____ around his or her objectives?

- What can I do to inspire _____ in what he or she is doing?

- How can I most productively facilitate and/or contribute to a collective Vision, Strategy, Implementation, and Results (VSIR) Process with _____?

Were any of these questions helpful to you? Can you think of any others that would inspire an even deeper connection and productive collaboration with your colleague?

## Questions to Nurture Relationships with Clients or Customers

Whether it's through sales, marketing, and/or customer service, most businesses involve creating, communicating, and sharing something of value with clients or customers.

The big questions for nurturing your relationships with clients or customers focus on how to understand what your customers most want and how to provide something of value to meet their needs or desires and make a meaningful difference in their lives.

Once again, as you prepare to engage with your clients or customers, reflect on which questions in the two sections above may also be relevant. Here are a few additional questions for you to consider:

*Receive:*

- What is my client's biggest frustration?

- How can I uncover any concerns that my client may have?

- What is my client's biggest need?
- What are the factors that most drive my client's decision?
- What outcomes or results would be most important to my client?

*Give:*
- How can I best create rapport with my client?
- How can I best express the value of what I have to offer to my client?
- How can I best serve his or her needs?
- How can I best demonstrate and deliver value for my client?
- As I wrap up my interaction, how can I close to be remembered as a valued resource for my client?

Which of these questions were most helpful? Can you think of any others that would be inspiring to building goodwill and enhancing the value you are providing for your client?

## Questions to Nurture Relationships with Patients

If you are a healthcare provider, it's all the more important to provide outstanding "customer service." The health and lives of those you care for is at stake.

The big questions for nurturing patient relationships focus on understanding your patients' aspirations and concerns that inspire and impact their health, wellness, and well-being, as well as how to best support and engage them to achieve their vision for optimal health.

Again, as you mentally prepare for your patient interactions, reflect on any of the questions in the sections above (particularly those for nurturing relationships with clients), as well as the questions below, allowing them to further inspire questions of your own:

*Receive:*
- What is my patient's definition of optimal health?
- What are the underlying stressors that most affect my patient's health?

- What is my patient's perception of what is going on with him or her?
- What are the barriers that limit my patient from fully engaging in his or her care?
- What are the factors that most drive my patient's healthcare decisions?
- What are the most important healthcare outcomes to my patient?
- Is my patient clear on his or her diagnosis and recommendations?
- How can I more effectively listen so my patient feels fully heard?

*Give:*
- How can I best express my care and compassion to my patient?
- How can I reduce my stress and be more present with my patient?
- How can I ensure my patient feels fully engaged by me, even as I make notes in the chart or electronic health record?
- How can I best communicate difficult diagnoses with my patient?
- How can I most clearly explain things in ways that would be easiest for my patient to understand?
- How can I best partner with my patient so that he or she feels inspired and empowered to take action and achieve his or her vision for optimal health?

Can you think of any other questions you can ask to cultivate your patient's health, healing, and well-being?

## Questions to Nurture Relationships with Those You Lead

In many ways, all of the questions above are about leadership (i.e., leading well from within so you can lead well in the world)—whether you are a parent, friend, colleague, healer, or a leader of an organization—which is what this section will focus on.

High-performance leaders have a special gift that brings out the very best in those they lead. They make everyone around them feel like a genius. Jennie Jerome, Winston Churchill's mother, captured this perfectly in her memoirs when she shared her experience with two prominent British politicians of the 1800s: William Gladstone and Benjamin Disraeli. After sitting next to Gladstone, she wrote, "I thought he was the cleverest man in England. But when I sat next to Disraeli, I thought I was the cleverest woman."[4]

Thus, if you are a leader of an organization, as you prepare for your interactions with those you lead, you may reflect on all of the questions above, as well as those below, to think about how you can bring out the genius in those you lead.

*Receive:*

- How can I best identify my employee's full talents?
- How can I best listen to what my employee can contribute?
- Where does my employee find his or her greatest sense of passion and purpose?
- What's our greatest collective strength and highest purpose?
- How can I best receive input at all levels about when we are off track, as well as how to get back on track?

*Give:*

- How can I create the conditions for my employee to achieve his or her peak performance?
- How can I best inspire our collective vision and mission statement?
- How can I inspire creativity in others without triggering their reactivity?
- How can I support those I lead to take ownership of their projects?
- How can I cultivate a culture of active engagement?
- How can I best challenge those I lead to innovate and stretch?
- How can I inspire those I lead to ask good questions and find, evaluate, and take action in their own Ask-Find-Evaluate-Apply Spiral of Growth?

As you may sense, some of these questions about leading an organization relate not only to leading individuals within it, but also to transforming the culture where everyone in the enterprise thrives. We'll be delving more deeply into this topic in chapters 11 and 12.

Now that you've asked good questions, you're ready to move on to the second step of Step 4 and allow the answers to those questions find you.

### Find Your Answers (Step 2 of Step 4)

Take some time to still yourself and allow the answers to your questions to find you. As mentioned previously, one way to do this is to imagine yourself breathing in and out through your heart center. First, allow yourself to receive and breathe in the goodwill of others into your heart. Then you can imagine yourself amplifying this feeling of goodwill by wishing them well and breathing out that goodwill into them. You can do this as you prepare to engage with others as well as in your interactions with them.

As you engage in this heartfelt practice, you are activating your parasympathetic nervous system, so that you can think more clearly, be more receptive to insights, and connect with your deepest wisdom to allow the answers to your inspired questions to find you.

### Evaluate Your Answers (Step 3 of Step 4)

Now evaluate your answers by asking yourself, "Does this answer feel right more than feel good?"; "Is this answer good for myself and others?"; and ultimately, "Does this answer get me to a place where I am more likely to give and receive love?"

### Apply Your Answers to Take Action (Step 4 of Step 4)

If the answers do feel right, bring these answers to life in your relationships by taking action on what feels "right."

In chapter 7, we also spoke about a strategy to nurture your relationships that includes being more loving, expressive, and present. You can take action with even greater presence by applying what you've learned so far in mindfulness practice. What you've learned are practices to observe your sensations, thoughts, feelings, and behaviors with openness, curiosity, and kindness and to then repeatedly shift your focus of attention onto something specific within your field of awareness, such as your breath, your thoughts, a silent wish, or energy in your body.

All too often, when we are with others, we are distracted. We may be thinking of work, something else we think we should be doing, ruminating over an interaction, managing uncomfortable emotions, "zoning out," or daydreaming. Or we may be looking over their shoulder for the next thing to grab our attention or thinking about how we can extricate ourselves from our interaction.

To be more present, much like you can choose to focus on your breath during mindfulness practice, you can simply bring this same focus of attention to the person you are with, so you can more easily be fully and mindfully present in your interaction. In other words, *let the person you are with become the intentional focus of your attention.* When your mind inevitably wanders, repeatedly take action to shift your attention back to that person to increase your presence and more fully nurture your relationship.

As you mindfully engage in the habit of taking action with Step 4 of the 4 in 4 Framework, you are transforming your brain to create a new neural destiny. By regularly shifting from cycles of reactivity to creativity in your relationships, you are creating the neural pathways to more easily resolve conflicts, find agreement, and deepen your ability to connect from the inside out.

In part 2, you learned how to develop self-compassion to resolve inner conflicts and nurture your relationship with yourself. In this chapter, you learned how to resolve conflicts and nurture your relationship with others. In this next section, you will learn about another mindfulness practice that can help you to further cultivate your compassion for others.

## Mindfulness Practice: Loving-Kindness (Part Two)

At the end of chapter 6, you learned part one of a loving-kindness practice where you silently expressed a wish for yourself to be safe, strong, and filled with loving-kindness. This is part two of that practice, where you extend similar wishes to yourself and then to others in a widening circle of compassion, starting with those you care about, then to those you may not know very well, and then even to the most difficult people in your life.

1. Allow yourself to get comfortable, either lying down or sitting up with an erect and alert posture. You may close your eyes or leave them open as you practice.

2. Bring to this meditation an intention to be kind, open, compassionate, and accepting of whatever arises.

3. Now bring your attention to your heart center and to the ebb and flow of your breathing. As you breathe, imagine your breath is flowing in and out through your heart center. Appreciate that the time you are setting aside for yourself is an act of love and kindness toward yourself and others.

4. Now explore bringing to mind someone who loves and accepts you unconditionally, someone who naturally brings a smile to your face. It could be a loved one, special friend, mentor, or pet. Notice what happens to the feeling in your heart space as you do.

5. Observe how you are not only the recipient of this loving feeling, but the source of it, too.

6. Notice how this feeling may be infusing your awareness and how this affectionate awareness provides a sense of spaciousness and tenderness—a reservoir of kindness that you can extend to yourself and others.

7. As you rest in this field of kind and loving awareness, bring your focus of attention back to your breathing through your heart center. Now, in your mind, or whispering silently to yourself, begin to express the following phrases:

   May I be safe.

   May I be peaceful.

   May I be filled with loving-kindness.

8. Allow yourself to repeat these phrases as much as is helpful to you.

9. If it's helpful, you can also integrate these phrases with your breathing, breathing in through your heart center and then

silently expressing a phrase as you breathe out, imagining that you are infusing every fiber of your being with the essence of the phrase as you do so.

> Breathe in and then, as you breathe out, express,
> "May I be safe."
>
> Breathe in and then, as you breathe out, express,
> "May I be peaceful."
>
> Breathe in and then, as you breathe out, express,
> "May I be filled with loving-kindness."

10. Now, with this reservoir of goodwill you've cultivated within your heart for yourself, allow yourself to shift your attention to others by expressing these wishes in widening circles of compassion for others.

11. Start thinking of someone you deeply care about. Then, each time you breathe out, imagine you are infusing him or her with your goodwill and kindness, while expressing these thoughts:

> May you be safe.
>
> May you be peaceful.
>
> May you be filled with loving-kindness.

12. Repeat these phrases.

13. When you feel you've connected with these wishes for this person, shift next to think about someone you feel neutral about. Perhaps it's someone who delivers your mail or launders your clothes. Breathe in through your heart center and on each successive breath out, express:

> May you be safe.
>
> May you be peaceful.
>
> May you be filled with loving-kindness.

14. Repeat these phrases.

15. When you feel you've connected with these wishes for this person, shift next to think about someone who is problematic for you. See if you can express this goodwill to this person, too. Note that you do not have to condone his or her actions to express goodwill.

16. See if you can appreciate how this person is much like you in the way he or she suffers, too.

17. Breathe in through your heart center and, on each successive breath out, express:

    May you be safe.

    May you be peaceful.

    May you be filled with loving-kindness.

18. Repeat these phrases.

19. When you feel you've connected with these wishes for this person, move next to returning this wish to yourself. Breathe in through your heart center and, on each successive breath out, express:

    May I be safe.

    May I be peaceful.

    May I be filled with loving-kindness.

20. Repeat these phrases, and when you feel you've connected with these thoughts, allow yourself to gently open your eyes.

21. Appreciate that you have just taken the time to deeply care for yourself and for others.

Now that you have the tools and practices to shift from cycles of reactivity to cycles of creativity in your relationships, chapter 11 will extend this concept further, helping you to leverage these cycles of creativity into thriving *cultures* of creativity that can transform families, organizations, communities, and the world!

# CHAPTER 11

# Cultures of Reactivity and Creativity

Back in chapter 1, I invited you to bring to mind the most inspiring leader you could think of—a high-performance leader—and reflect on the qualities that person possesses that so inspire you. I then asked you to bring to mind a low-performance leader and to contrast the qualities of both.

I'd like you to bring these leaders to mind once more. Now reflect on the *culture* that surrounds them—that social fabric of shared values, norms, and behaviors[1] driving the way things get done—whether it's within the families, organizations, communities, or nations they lead.

How would you describe the culture that surrounds the high-performance leader? The low-performance leader? How are they different?

It's been estimated that leaders determine 80 percent of the culture that surrounds them.[2] For better or for worse, leaders either cultivate or deplete the cultures in which they are immersed.

Let me explain what I mean by that. The word *culture* comes from the Latin *cultus,* which means "care," and from the French *colere,* which means "to till," as in to till the ground.[3] While the reactive mindset of low-performance leaders depletes the cultural soil of nourishment, causing people and their endeavors to wither, the creative mindset of high-performance (or conscious) leaders *cultivates* this soil, empowering people and allowing their endeavors to flourish. The same is true for the culture in families, communities, nations, and even the world as a whole.

In the previous two chapters, we discussed how leading well from within enables you to shift from reactivity to creativity in your own life, which enables you to transform your relationships from cycles of reactivity to cycles of creativity. These relational cycles of heartfelt receiving and giving lie at the heart of what nurtures culture.

In this chapter, we'll explore how a creative leadership mindset has the capacity to ripple through relationships with social contagion to transform cultures of reactivity into cultures of creativity, cultivating a rich soil where you, your people, and your enterprise thrive.

In the next chapter, you'll learn how to apply the 4 in 4 Framework to make this a reality in the cultures you lead, cultivating a high-performance culture of creativity and further expanding your capacity to lead well in the world.

Although this chapter will primarily focus on how cultures of reactivity and creativity operate within businesses, the principles are the same for any culture, whether that group measures "profit" in terms of impact by number of lives significantly improved (such as a non-profit organization), patient satisfaction scores or health outcomes (as in healthcare organizations), player improvement or number of games won (such as a sports team), or the overall thriving of its members (such as a family). We'll talk more about this later in the chapter.

## Connecting the Dots between Leadership, Culture, and Profit

Figure 11.1 shows how low-performance leaders with a reactive mindset trigger cycles of reactivity that generally result in a low-performing, disengaged culture. In contrast, high-performance leaders, inspired by a creative mindset, cultivate cycles of creativity that facilitate a high-performing, engaged culture. Both have implications for the customer experience and the financial bottom line.

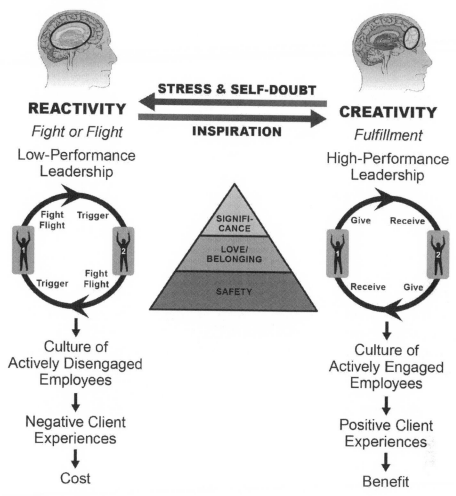

*Figure 11.1. How Leadership Performance Affects the Reactivity and Creativity of Culture*

Recall from the Leadership Circle study in chapter 2 that low-performance leaders, with a reactive leadership style, tend to be either overly *complying* (conservative, pleasing, passive), *protective* (arrogant, critical, distant), or *controlling* (perfectionistic, driven, ambitious, autocratic).

Low-performance leaders more often feel threatened by their underlying stress and self-doubt and adopt a reactive mindset in response. They tend to go limbic, losing access to their circuits of empathy and compassion, triggering socially contagious fight-or-flight cycles of reactivity that spread through the culture, causing others to feel threatened and go limbic, too. Because they now feel unsafe, employees protect themselves by manifesting many of the same behaviors of low-performance leaders. As this threat of stress becomes pervasive, it unavoidably shows up on the faces and in the voices of employees and creates a tone of fear or cynicism in the culture, eroding morale, customer service, and the bottom line.

The culture of threat and fear becomes a self-perpetuating cycle that continues to transform relationship dynamics within that culture. To describe these dynamics, Stephen Karpman introduced a concept in 1968 known as the Drama Triangle.[4] The Drama Triangle consists of the three roles people tend to take when they feel threatened—Persecutor, Victim, or Rescuer—to deal with their underlying feelings of stress or self-doubt.

The Persecutor, whether a bad boss or domineering parent, gets his power by fighting to control or dominate the Victim. The Victim feels disempowered and threatened and may take flight in self-pity, fighting back, blaming others, abdicating his responsibility, or perhaps appealing to a Rescuer for comfort and validation. The Rescuer then gets her sense of self-worth by helping the Victim, with the implicit exchange being, "I need you to be broken so I can fix you." In doing so, the Rescuer may enable unhealthy behavior and prevent the Victim from finding the power to stand up to the Persecutor.

These prototypical dynamics perpetuate and further ingrain the cycles of fight-or-flight reactivity, which can spawn unhealthy factions and generate a *culture* of reactivity, which then leads to employee disengagement. These dynamics drain an immense amount of energy from relationships, making it very difficult to get anything done productively at work or at home.

Further, when employees feel unsafe, the culture's collective energy gets trapped at the base of Maslow's Hierarchy of Needs. In his book *The Five Dysfunctions of a Team,* Patrick Lencioni describes how low-performing teams struggle with issues of trust (which shows up as invulnerability), fear conflict (which manifests as artificial harmony), fail to commit (which creates ambiguity), avoid accountability (which causes low standards), and are more interested in personal, ego-driven results than the overall results of the organization.[5] Essentially, these teams are trapped in survival mode at the base of Maslow's Hierarchy. They are unable to cultivate a true sense of safety, trust, love, and belonging, drastically limiting the capacity of its members and the organization as a whole to serve its customers well or self-actualize the purpose and significance of their enterprise.

Now let's contrast this scenario with a culture of creativity, starting with high-performance leaders. According to the Leadership Circle study in chapter 2, high-performance leaders, with their creative leadership style, are *relational* (having interpersonal intelligence; caring; and the ability to foster team play, collaborate well, and mentor well), *self-aware* (having a learner mindset, composure, balance, and selflessness), *authentic* (having integrity and courage) and *achievement oriented* (being purposeful and visionary, strategically focused, decisive, and results driven). In addition, and especially important to cultivating culture, they have *systems awareness* (demonstrating systems thinking and community concerns, as well an ability to create sustainable productivity). All of these characteristics enable them to create cycles of creativity—of giving and receiving—in their individual relationships, which are key to developing a creative culture.

These characteristics are also socially contagious, spreading into the culture where employees likewise begin to display these same characteristics to collectively express the heart and soul of the organization, creating cycles of giving and receiving within their relationships as well. When employees feel inspired by their leader as a person and by that leader's vision and thus experience the sense of safety and belonging that leader creates, they become more engaged and connect more fully with their colleagues and customers.

As we discussed in chapter 9, when people feel safe, they tend to have a well-balanced parasympathetic and sympathetic nervous system, giving them full access to their circuits of empathy, compassion, executive decision making, and creative thinking. They naturally express a warm demeanor, displaying a friendly facial expression and tone of voice that naturally attracts and engages others. As they are fully engaged in mind, heart, and soul, they become able to deliver exceptional hospitality and customer satisfaction, creating ever-expanding cycles of giving and receiving, which lead to profitable results.

In contrast to the relationship dynamics of the Drama Triangle, a creative culture tends to create what David Emerald calls The Empowerment Dynamic.

In this transformed version of the Drama Triangle, rather than focusing on minimizing the problem of stress, all individuals focus on achieving a productive outcome instead. Here the Victim becomes the Creator, taking full responsibility for the situation and what he wants to accomplish. The Persecutor becomes the Challenger, and the Rescuer becomes the Coach. The Challenger and the Coach serve as high-performance leaders to bring out the best in the Creator.[6]

The Empowerment Dynamic also transforms our experience of stress. Unlike the Drama Triangle, where the struggle for power and control triggers a threat response, The Empowerment Dynamic enables a tend-and-befriend response to provide genuine support, as well as a challenge response that inspires learning and growth. These proactive stress responses further cultivate a culture of creativity.

As a result, the dynamics of a creative culture are highly energizing. The energy freely moves all the way up Maslow's Hierarchy to satisfy the needs for safety, love, and belonging and the sense of significance that comes from manifesting purpose-driven results.

And those results are impressive. A confluence of data shows that high-performance leadership, engaged cultures, and conscious companies outperform others on numerous important business outcomes.

According to the Leadership Circle data we discussed in chapter 1, leaders with a creative mindset achieve higher levels of business performance as assessed by sales and revenue growth, market share, profitability, return on assets, quality of products and services, new product development, and overall performance.[7]

As we broaden our focus from leaders to cultures, one of the most widely used tools for evaluating culture is the Organizational Culture Inventory (OCI), which aligns beautifully with the Leadership Circle's creative and reactive leadership profiles. It describes the qualities of creative and reactive cultures, using the terms *Constructive* or *Defensive* (and if the culture is defensive, whether it is either *passively* or *aggressively* so). Research regarding the OCI reportedly shows a positive relationship between the Constructive culture styles and numerous outcomes, including those of safety and reliability, successful merger integration, creativity, adaptability, customer satisfaction, and employee engagement.[8]

In 2012, Gallup published the results of a large meta-analysis directly evaluating the outcomes of employee engagement. It incorporated 263 research studies across 192 organizations in 49 industries and 34 countries. Within each study, the researchers labored to calculate the relationship between employee engagement and performance outcomes by studying 49,928 business work units that included 1,390,941 employees in total.[9]

When comparing the top-quartile and the bottom-quartile of employee engagement, they found a median decrease of 48 percent in safety incidents, 37 percent in absenteeism, 41 percent in patient safety incidents, 41 percent in quality defects, and a 25 percent and 65 percent reduction in turnover in high- and low-turnover organizations, respectively. They further found an increase of 10 percent in customer ratings, 21 percent in productivity, and 22 percent in profitability.[10]

Another study by Gallup found that organizations with an average of 2.6 engaged employees for every actively disengaged employee in 2010 through 2011 experienced 2 percent lower earnings per share (EPS) compared with their competition from 2011 through 2012. In contrast, companies with 9.3 engaged employees for every actively disengaged employee experienced a 147 percent higher EPS compared with their competition during this same period.[11]

So what do cultures of creativity look like in practice? Let's take a look at a few examples of some inspiring organizations that highlight this connection between high-performance leadership, a culture of creativity, and a thriving enterprise.

## Examples of Cultures of Creativity

"Tell me about some companies you love. Not just like, but love."

This is what Raj Sisodia, the co-founder and co-chairman of Conscious Capitalism, asked thousands of people all over the world, including business professionals, marketing professors, MBA students, and about 1,000 consumers. He then probed more deeply with questions such as, "Would most people say that the world is a better place because this company exists? How extensive a track record have they built? Do they have intensely loyal customers? How well do they treat their part-time employees? How high is their employee turnover? Do they have a reputation for squeezing their suppliers? Do communities welcome them or oppose them when they try to enter or expand? Do they have a record of environmental violations? Do they follow uniformly high standards of conduct worldwide? How have they responded to industry downturns or crises of confidence?"[12]

Hundreds of companies bubbled up. After a two-year period of intensive research and investigation, twenty-eight companies, eighteen of which were publicly traded, qualified as companies that were truly loved by their stakeholders. Sisodia called them "firms of endearment," which is also the name of the bestselling book he coauthored about how these "World-Class Companies Profit from Passion and Purpose."[13]

Sisodia tracked the cumulative performance of these companies over a fifteen-year period from 1998 through 2013. While the cumulative stock market return of the S&P was 118 percent during this time frame, the cumulative returns of companies were 1,681 percent. Collectively, these high-performing organizations have outperformed the S&P by a factor of 14 to 1![14]

Think about your experience with the companies referenced in this book: Amazon, BMW, CarMax, Commerce Bank, Container Store, Costco, eBay, Google, Harley-Davidson, Honda, IDEO, IKEA, JetBlue, Johnson & Johnson, Jordan's Furniture, LL Bean, New Balance, Patagonia, REI, Southwest Airlines, Starbucks, Timberland, Toyota, Trader Joe's, UPS, Wegmans, and Whole Foods. Or think about other companies that are also part of the Conscious Capitalism family, like Panera Bread, The Motley Fool, Tom's, and Zappos.

If you're familiar with any of these businesses, you know that these beloved companies are palpably different. I've had the privilege of taking a deeper look into two companies in particular that embody the essence of a creative culture: Zappos and Gwinganna Lifestyle Retreat.

## *Zappos*

I had the pleasure of presenting at the Conscious Capitalism CEO Summit with the leaders of several conscious businesses, one of whom was Tony Hsieh, CEO of the online retailer Zappos. Hsieh shared how the simple purpose of Zappos is "delivering happiness," which is also the name of his bestselling book.[15] He also adapted *Delivering Happiness* into a fun-to-read comic book that he gave to each person at the summit.

In the book, he shares his personal journey, which explains how much of the Zappos culture came to be. Before he became CEO at Zappos, he founded LinkExchange, an innovative Internet marketing company, during the early days of the dot-com revolution. There he learned the importance of company culture. At first the company seemed like a family; he felt happy working with people who wanted to be part of something fun and exciting. However, after they received venture capital funding and rapidly expanded, it felt strange to walk the floor and see people he did not recognize. When he found himself hitting the snooze button six times before getting out of bed one morning, he realized he was no longer happy. He'd lost his passion for what he was doing. Looking back, he realized it was a sign that he had not paid close enough attention to his company culture.

After selling LinkExchange to Microsoft for $265 million, which required him to stay at his company another twelve months, he found himself even more unhappy, feeling uninspired, unmotivated, and apathetic. He began to make a list of the happiest periods in his life and realized none of them involved money. He said he realized what made him most happy was creating, building, and doing things he cared about.

He also found great happiness being with his tribe and attending rave parties with them, where he felt an overwhelming sense of spirituality and connection. This came as a surprise to Hsieh, who was usually known as the most logical and rational person in the group. The culture of these raves were guided by values expressed in the acronym PLUR, which stands for Peace, Love, Unity, and Respect. He writes, "It was a mantra for how people were meant to carry themselves and behave both in business and in life. To me, it was really more a philosophy of meeting people, no matter how they looked and what their backgrounds were. We are all human to the core, and it can be easy to lose sight of that in a world ruled by business, politics, and social status."[16]

After finally leaving LinkExchange, he carried this awakening into Zappos, a company that he first invested in and then stepped into as CEO. Zappos, which takes its name from the Spanish word for "shoes," initially began as an online shoe retailer. According to Hsieh, Zappos almost went under during the dot-com and stock market crash. Remarkably, everyone stepped up, working as a unified team, finding a sense of passion from working closely and creatively together. These difficult days served to further unify their tribe and galvanize their culture.

They also learned what was not working at Zappos. They had been outsourcing their warehousing, fulfillment, and customer service, all of which was underperforming and leaving many customers frustrated. They realized that to be successful they needed to bring it all in house and become the very best at customer service. While customer service had always been important, they made a conscious decision to make it the entire focus of their brand—which required considerable restructuring. They flipped the switch and stopped all remaining drop shipments, which at the time represented 25 percent of their revenue. Realizing that to keep their culture strong they would all need to be under one roof, in 2004 they decided to move their headquarters from San Francisco to Las Vegas. To his pleasant surprise, and underscoring the strength of the Zappos culture, seventy of the ninety employees were willing to uproot themselves and make this move.

Under Hsieh's leadership, Zappos evolved into an intensely customer-focused company (below their logo, the tagline proudly reads, "Powered by Service"). The core ingredients to their success are the very elements of a creative culture: Hsieh's high-performance leadership results in creating a happy environment for employees so that they can deliver happiness to their customers (or "happiness in a box," as one customer reported she felt upon receiving her shoe order[17]). With this shift to focusing on being the very best at customer service, the success of the company exploded, and in November 2009, it was bought by Amazon in a stock agreement that was worth $1.2 billion at closing. It continues to run as a "wholly-owned subsidiary" of Amazon under the Conscious Leadership and cultural stewardship of Hsieh.[18]

At the end of his presentation at the Conscious Capitalism Summit, Hsieh invited everyone in the audience to come to Las Vegas to get a sense of Zappos' culture (as well as the development in downtown Las Vegas, where their new offices were to be housed). He even offered to put us up in his apartment building during our stay. After the conference, I e-mailed him to take him up on his offer. He replied within ten minutes and set everything up for my family and me.

When we arrived for the guided tour to the smell of fresh popcorn at their Henderson location, you could immediately sense something different about the energy of their company. The place had a buzz! People were alive with excitement. You could feel their passion and enthusiasm. The tour guide was loose, cracking jokes and happy to playfully tease us.

Before the tour began, I read their ten values of how they deliver happiness, which were playfully painted on the walls (in other words, these values were not a plaque on the wall):

1. Deliver WOW Through Service
2. Embrace and Drive Change
3. Create Fun and a Little Weirdness
4. Be Adventurous, Creative, and Open-Minded
5. Pursue Growth and Learning
6. Build Open and Honest Relationships with Communication
7. Build a Positive Team and Family Spirit
8. Do More with Less
9. Be Passionate and Determined
10. Be Humble

Many of these values align with the qualities of high-performance leadership. They also serve a major role in the hiring process to ensure the employee is a cultural fit for the organization.

As we toured the various open-area cubicle work spaces, employees turned around to greet us with warm, welcoming smiles and the clatter of kazoos, rattles, and cheers. It was wonderfully weird. Hsieh himself did not have some walled-off corner office. His cubicle was smack-dab in the middle of the other cubicles, embodying his humility. We were shown one of the few private offices, a room with a throne and a poster above it that read, "I am royalty and part of the Zappos family!" This was where employees received coaching if they wanted it. Clearly displayed on many of the walls were whiteboards with call response times, their proudest and most celebrated achievements. As we walked down the stairwell, those walls were filled with big, blue letters that read, "To Culture." Surrounding those words was joyful, positive, and motivating graffiti expressing what that meant: "Zappos rocks my socks off!"; "It's about the family!"; "I'm on my way to be Better, Faster, Stronger!"; "Zappos wows me every day!"

As we left the Zappos building, inspired by what we had just experienced on our tour, our then thirteen-year-old son, Zach, turned to me and said, "Dad, I want to work there one day." I asked him why. He answered, "That place just makes me happy!" The word "happiness" had not been explicitly mentioned on the tour. Zach just felt the happiness that the culture delivered.

### Gwinganna Lifestyle Retreat

During my 2014 presentation at the Global Wellness Summit to the leaders in the spa and wellness industry, I asked them what they thought distinguished the very best wellness retreats or spas—or any business or organization in healthcare, for that matter—from others around the world. The factor that resonated most strongly was whether the place had a *soul.*

I then shared my experience of visiting Gwinganna, a destination wellness retreat situated on a plateau in the mountains on over five hundred acres in a hidden region of the Tallebudgera Valley on Australia's Gold Coast. Its name means "lookout," given its position offering spectacular views of the ocean and valley below. It's been recognized with numerous awards, including the 2015 World Travel Award as Australia's leading spa.

As soon as you step onto the property, you not only sense its immense beauty, but something more. You feel the "soul" of the place. You feel it in the love with which the place is tended, in the food, in the uniquely restorative and energizing "yin and yang" activities, and in the remarkable staff, who clearly find joy in their work and offer the genuine, heartfelt hospitality that restaurateur Danny Meyer would be proud of.

Like Zappos and other conscious businesses, the soul of a business is a reflection of its leaders. Gwinganna's owner, Tony de Leede, and General Manager and Wellness Director, Sharon Kolkka, are the epitome of Conscious Leaders. I feel blessed to know them as friends.

One of the leading business people in Australia, Tony helped develop Fitness First, the largest privately owned health club group in the world. He credits the inspiration of developing Gwinganna as a wellness retreat to his mother, Yvonne Marie de Leede.

"My parents migrated to Australia in 1950," shared Tony. "My father was Dutch, and my mother was half Dutch, half French. Typical of Europeans at that time, they drank, smoked, ate rich foods, and did not really exercise."

His father had his first heart attack at age forty-two. "He followed the medical advice given to heart attack victims at the time: slow down, don't exert, stay calm, don't move too much. Sadly, my father died at age forty-nine of heart disease—we did not know then what we know now. I had just turned sixteen.

"After my father died, my mother changed her lifestyle. She gave up smoking, curbed her drinking, and embraced a healthy lifestyle. She changed her eating regime, started daily vigorous walks, and started swimming all year round at Cronulla beach (south of Sydney). She started practicing t'ai chi (then, many people thought this was some kind of Chinese food), and she started meditating. She also discovered and started going to what I believe was Australia's first health retreat two or three times a year (then called a fat farm). I was always impressed by how recharged, rejuvenated, and relaxed she was after her 'health retreat' visits.

"My mother was very strong and disciplined in the way she embraced health. She became very active, she ate well, and as a result, she improved her quality of life. I recognized early on that I did not have my mother's discipline. But, I also accepted that in order to live a long and healthy life, I should live like my mother. Being a realist, I decided that the best chance for me was to develop my own health and lifestyle retreat and spend a lot of time there."

When he discovered Gwinganna in 2002, he knew it was the place he had been looking for. "The first time I stayed at Gwinganna, I found that the serenity and soul of this hidden mountain retreat captured my desire to live a better life." He bought Gwinganna and over four years developed the retreat with Sharon Kolkka, a partnership that was destined to bring the soul of Gwinganna alive.

I first met Sharon at the Global Wellness Summit in Bali in 2011, where we sat next to each other at an evening event. We instantly sensed we were kindred spirits and spoke all evening about our common passion for helping people navigate stress and cultivate a deep sense of meaning and well-being in their lives.

With Sharon's permission, I'd like to share with you her remarkable story that explains much of the soul of one's experience at Gwinganna. Like Tony Hsieh and Tony DeLeede, her story also reflects how Conscious Leaders often first make meaning in their own lives and then give back in service to make a meaningful difference in the lives of others.

Sharon shared with me that in her thirties she had a painful breakup with a partner that crushed her spirit. She went into a deep and dark depression where she repeatedly thought about suicide. The only thing that stopped her was her then six-year-old daughter, Sarah. It was 1992, and Sharon had just been awarded the Fitness Leader of the Year award. On the outside, she looked like the picture of health. "Everyone thought I was the model of health, happiness, and vitality," she said. "But inside I felt like a barren desert. I'd felt like I had lost my soul."

She connected some of this deep pain to her upbringing with her mother, which she described as "mentally and emotionally brutal." She said, "The message I got was, 'You better behave and look a certain way, or people will not accept or love you. You'd better keep your emotions in check, or you will look weak and people will not love you or approve of you. If you fail at either of these, people will leave you—you can't trust love alone.'"

While she initially resented her mother, years later after her breakup, when Sharon asked her mother about her earliest memories, she began to understand that her mother's reactivity came from her deep pain of abandonment. Sharon's grandmother found herself unmarried and pregnant at fifteen years old. The family initially tried to keep mother and baby together; however, due to the ensuing social stigma and cultural pressure in 1918 Edwardian England, Sharon's great-grandfather forced his sixteen-year-old daughter to give up her eighteen-month-old child (Sharon's mother) for adoption. He then moved the whole family to America, thus abandoning the helpless young child, which set up deep emotional wounds in Sharon's mother that played out in her adult life and affected her ability to be a good mother. When Sharon heard this story, she came to fully understand her mother's suffering, appreciate her resiliency, and find it in her heart to forgive her completely.

Nevertheless, Sharon's fear of abandonment had played out in her own life, leaving her feeling abandoned, worthless, lost, and alone after her breakup with her partner. Knowing that she could not abandon her daughter in suicide, she said, "I had to find a way to live."

She began to reach out for support, found a therapist, studied Buddhism and mindfulness, and gravitated toward people who seemed to have a "soulful and spiritual presence." She also began to appreciate that no one externally was responsible for her experience—not her partner or her mother—but that it was her reactive mind and internal experience that were causing her suffering. This insight provided a major release that opened the space for a life-altering experience.

One summer night in 1994, she had a dream that changed everything. She dreamed that she had woken up and was lying on her bed, facing the ceiling. The curtains were blowing in the breeze. All of a sudden, she became aware of a figure filled with white light standing beside her. She said, "I just screamed in absolute terror!" Then, all of a sudden, the apparition of white light rose up to the ceiling and then streamed right down into her body, where it entered her heart. At that exact moment, she woke up and realized she was in exactly the same position on the bed, in her room, with the curtains blowing, as she had seen in her dream. However, she was tingling all over and was filled with a sudden sense of deep love and extreme peace, unlike anything she had previously known.

"With a background in anatomy and physiology and years of deep appreciation of the fact-finding nature of science," she said, "I would not have believed it had I not experienced it myself. I felt like, in that moment, I reunited with my soul. It's my foundation of faith and trust."

According to Sharon, from that moment on, everything in her life has flowed. Since that time, she has never set goals, only intentions—all of which have manifested.

For example, she set an intention to find a way to help people find the deeper sense of well-being she was experiencing in her life. In 1995, she found her way to becoming a personal trainer on a wellness retreat. After working in a fitness club, which she said focused on "muscles, cardiac fitness, and the self-esteem that comes from looking good," the retreat was a revelation. She saw how it provided a more holistic approach to wellness and well-being, focusing not only on all the organ systems, but also on healing the entire person, mind, body, and spirit. She learned about how to help people navigate stress and optimize their energy. In particular, she discovered Qigong, the ancient Chinese healthcare practice that integrates physical postures, breathing techniques, and focused intention to cultivate and optimize Qi, the life force or vital energy that flows through all things in the universe.[19]

After becoming the program manager at the retreat, she received a phone call from Tony de Leede. She had met Tony standing in line at a fitness conference in 1989. One of the great characteristics of great leaders is their ability to spot talent. She said they instantly connected, and soon she felt like Tony was interviewing her for a job. Another of Tony's characteristics is his interest in people, according to Sharon. "He always seems to keep a file in his head of people he has met and knows how to access that file for potential employees when an opportunity arises," she said. Over the next few years, they only connected occasionally at fitness conferences.

In 2002, after he bought Gwinganna, Tony made a big push to recruit Sharon as the general manager. She thought long and hard for eighteen months before she took the leap of faith to accept his offer. Her three conditions were that she would only ever answer to him (and not a board), she would choose and manage her own team, and Gwinganna would forever sustain an environmentally conscious footprint.

Together with Tony, Sharon met with the architects and builders to design the retreat from the ground up. Sharon wrote a three-page document outlining the philosophy for Gwinganna, which is fully manifested today. The purpose statement from the very beginning has been "to inspire optimal well-being in all who visit Gwinganna." Sharon makes it clear this purpose statement applies to both guests *and* staff. And it's not some generic statement or slogan. When you meet Sharon, you genuinely feel it to your core and sense how her philosophy lives in the spirit of the place.

Sharon began to assemble her team based on the philosophy that all its members would share the common goal of inspiring well-being for the common good of humanity. She turned down people who came just for a job and hired the best she could find who shared this sense of purpose.

She invests herself in working closely with her employees and takes a personal interest in the well-being of each and every one. She keeps a close eye out for signs of stress and burnout, saying it's not good for her colleagues or for the guests, many of whom arrive at the retreat feeling stressed and burned out themselves.

Every employee, as part of their induction, stays as a guest at least one night to more deeply understand the guest experience and the support Gwinganna offers. The benefit is that each employee at Gwinganna commits to more than providing service. They commit to fully supporting their guests, loved ones, and themselves with care and compassion to optimize well-being.

Also, just as at Zappos, all employees at Gwinganna are encouraged to just be themselves. You feel the authenticity of each employee. Nothing feels scripted. Interactions feel real, with a free-flowing dialogue of receiving and giving. All employees are also encouraged to express their unique talents and creativity. For example, the therapists creating the massage treatments have the leeway to create one-of-a-kind customer experiences. One of the treatments I received blended the therapist's passion for music and massage to create an immersive experience called the "Spirit of Sound." I can still feel how the music vibrated off the table, interspersed with physical and musical percussion, resonating with the joy with which she worked.

The results of this culture of creativity, with its deep commitment to inspiring well-being, are rich and rewarding guest experiences that make Gwinganna a highly profitable enterprise. Tony shared with me that he never purchased Gwinganna to make a profit. He just wanted to create one of the best retreat centers in the world. Yet the product of their endeavor has far exceeded their financial expectations. Forty percent of guests return, and Gwinganna has experienced a steady 7 to 15 percent compounding growth year after year, even through the economic downturn.

This brings us back to the answer to our initial question about what distinguishes the very best health and wellness retreats. They have a soul. Gwinganna has seamlessly integrated what Tony saw in the soul of the land with the soul of their inspired leadership and culture, to nourish the souls of all their employees and guests. This place has a soul that inspires optimal well-being in all who visit! It may serve as an example for any organization, especially those looking for inspiration to cultivate greater well-being in the health and wellness industry.

## Creating Cultures of Creativity in Organizations, Families, Communities, and the World

At the Global Wellness Summit, I showed the following slide (figure 11.2), using pictures of Sharon Kolkka and employees and guests at Gwinganna to help illustrate the connections that make companies successful.

### Connecting the Dots

*Figure 11.2. Connecting the Dots between Leadership and Profit*

High-performance leaders appreciate the importance of deeply caring for their employees, which results in engaged employees operating in a culture of creativity, which results in rich and rewarding customer experiences, which keeps customers coming back, making it highly likely they will recommend the product or service to others—which results in profit (and happy shareholders).

Or, in the language of Conscious Capitalism, you could say that conscious, purpose-driven leadership cultivates a conscious culture that creates exceptional value for all its stakeholders, resulting in a thriving enterprise.

Note that this sequence operates not just in organizations, but in families, communities, and nations as well. Can you see how this four-stage process might apply to the other cultures you may lead, such as your family, your child's sports team, a healthcare organization, a volunteer organization, a charity or religious group, or your town or city? What would be the equivalent of high-performance leadership, employee engagement, exceptional customer experiences, and profit in each of these cultures you're a part of?

Or think about nations with exceptional leaders who have created a thriving national culture. You might wonder what the analogy of profit is in this situation. What might come to mind is a nation's GDP (Gross Domestic Product). This outcome is now being accompanied by new measures that evaluate how well a nation is thriving. One of these measures was introduced in the country of Bhutan by its fourth king, Jigme Singye Wangchuck: the Gross National Happiness Index. This index includes nine domains: good living standards, psychological well-being, health, time use, education, good governance, community vitality, cultural and ecological diversity, and resilience.[20] Under the king's Conscious Leadership, the index was designed to create policy incentives for the government, NGOs, and businesses to create a culture that would increase what he viewed as the most "profitable" output for his country—the happiness of his people.[21] The United Nations has further recognized the profound societal value of this index and emphasized that in order to attain global happiness, the outcomes of economic development must also be accompanied by social and environmental well-being.[22]

So, now that we have connected the dots between high-performance Conscious Leadership, cultures of creativity and engagement, and the bottom line, let's further explore how you can put this into practice and apply the 4 in 4 Framework to the cultures *you* lead.

## CHAPTER 12

# Transforming Families, Organizations, Communities, and the World

In the last chapter, we discussed how low-performance leadership and high-performance leadership largely determine whether a culture is reactive or creative. Now recall from chapter 4 the Yerkes-Dodson stress and performance curve, which shows how either too little or too much stress can cause low performance.[1]

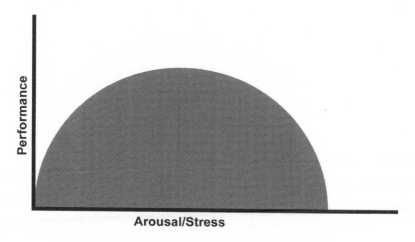

*Figure 12.1. Yerkes-Dodson Stress and Performance Curve*

On one hand, when individuals feel overwhelmed by a high level of stress (when their perceived demands exceed their perceived resources), they "go limbic" and lose full access to their higher cortical circuits—and PFC in particular. As a result, they have trouble connecting with empathy in their

313

relationships, thinking clearly, making decisions, and producing creative and innovation solutions. On the other hand, when they experience a low stress and energy state, where they don't have a clear vision, or they feel bored or apathetic, individuals aren't engaging their internal resources and, therefore, don't perform very well either. There is a sweet spot—a specific level of stress— where individuals tend to feel optimally energized, focused, and engaged to function at their best. They are confident their resources either equal or exceed the demands before them and are motivated to fully engage.

Since individuals make up organizations, this curve also reflects how organizations as a whole perform under stress—and, based on what you learned in the last chapter, how your influence as a leader can affect that performance.

For example, consider what typically happens at an inflection point where the performance of an organization faces a crisis or growth stalls or recedes. Many leaders get intensely stressed. They react and "go limbic," resulting in a low-performance leadership state. Experiencing the situation as a threat, they may become more intense, micromanage, and lead by threat and intimidation: "You better perform, or you're gone!" (Some leaders operate this way even in the absence of inflection points.)

Remember, the state of a leader is socially contagious within a culture. So the leader's experience of threat spreads as fear in cycles of reactivity throughout the organization. People hunker down in survival mode, and the culture as a whole becomes reactive. Without as much access to their higher cortical circuits, employees' empathy erodes, morale plummets, energy is depleted, creativity and innovation are shut down, and customer service suffers. As a result of this collective threat response, organizational resources as a whole are diminished, and performance plummets down the right side of the curve— and this is where, with low-performance, reactive leadership, a company becomes at risk of going out of business.

At the other extreme, if leaders ignore a brewing crisis and pretend that everything is OK or if they have created an organizational culture that is too "laissez faire," without sufficient vision, strategy, decision making, oversight, accountability, and boundaries for bad behavior, the organization as a whole will not fully engage their collective resources and, therefore, will not operate at a high level either, also putting it at risk of going out of business.

Leaders need to know how to sense and modulate the stress level of the culture to optimize the organization's energy and performance. In other words, they need to help increase and fully engage their company's resources to meet the demands they face.

High-performance Conscious Leaders have the awareness and skills to cultivate a high-performance culture, operating at the peak of its performance curve. They not only have the self-awareness to do so, but as the Leadership Circle study points out, they also have systems awareness, which you can think of as mindfulness (or situational awareness) at an organizational level.

In this chapter, you'll learn how you can mindfully apply the 4 in 4 Framework to navigate stress at an organizational level and cultivate a high-performance culture of creativity and growth, whether it's at work, at home, or in your community.

## Applying the 4 in 4 Framework to Cultivate a Culture of Creativity

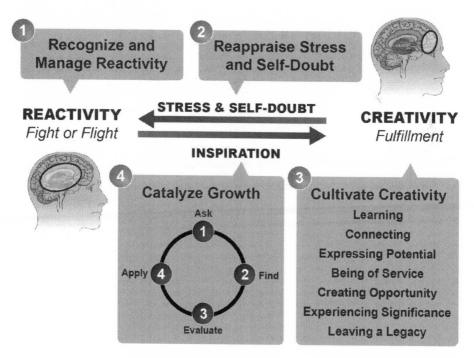

Let's take a closer look how each of the four steps of the 4 in 4 Framework empowers you to facilitate the shift from a reactive to a creative culture.

### Step 1: Recognizing and Managing Reactivity

Just as you have learned to recognize reactivity in yourself and your relationships, you can also more fully *recognize* reactivity in your culture by noting specific reactive behaviors in your culture and where they tend to occur.

One way to do this is to pay attention to the ways individuals treat or avoid each other in your environment. How prevalent is blame, gossip, judgment, bullying, and/or destructive conflict? Or, just as concerning, does your culture tend to avoid conflict with superficial politeness or, as Lencioni puts it, with "artificial harmony"?

Also, look at the roles people are playing. Are the dynamics of the Drama Triangle, with its Victims, Persecutors, and Rescuers, prevalent within your company, organization, family, or community?

If you sense unhealthy reactivity in the culture of your organization, you can also more formally assess it using culture survey tools such as the Leadership Circle's Leadership Culture Survey.[2] Like their Leadership Circle Profile for individuals, their culture survey assesses whether the culture as a whole is more compliant, protective, or controlling than is desired.

You can also use the Organizational Culture Inventory (OCI) mentioned in the previous chapter to identify reactivity by assessing the Passive Defensive or Aggressive Defensive tendencies in your culture.[3] For a culture's Passive Defensive tendencies, this inventory assesses behaviors, such as whether members of the culture are superficially pleasant to seek approval, feel pressure to conform, are reluctant to take the initiative, or play it safe to avoid being punished for making mistakes. For a culture's Aggressive Defensive tendencies, the inventory assesses behaviors such as whether the culture encourages members to gain status by confronting and criticizing others and opposing their ideas, vie for positions of power to control subordinates, compete to get a leg up on each other, or strive for perfection to avoid mistakes at all costs.

When you sense that reactivity may be doing more harm than good in your culture, you can adapt the four steps you learned in chapter 5 to *manage* your culture's reactivity:

1. Pause.
2. Take three heart-centered, soft-belly breaths.
3. Name it to tame it.
4. Consider your best response.

As an organization, it may be helpful to first *pause* and then take a collective *breath* to reflect on what is going on. While I mean this in part metaphorically, it can be very helpful to do this literally, too.

At one of my AIHM board meetings, where multiple members of the board went limbic over a high-stakes issue that was threatening to derail a major collaboration, I put both my hands up and said, "OK, everybody stop! Let's all take three heart-centered breaths and come back to address this one person at a time." We did so, and it brought the temperature of the room down instantly. Having regained access to our higher cortical circuits, we were able to continue the conversation more calmly, see all sides of the issue more empathetically, and come to a good decision about our next steps.

I know these steps to manage reactivity have also taken root in our culture at home. Just the other day, I was talking to my wife, Sue, in the kitchen at breakfast. My younger son, Dylan, who is eleven years old, sensed the heat rising in our conversation. He interjected. "Guys, stop! Now, each of you take three deep breaths." That not only caused us to pause and breathe, but also to laugh in awe at how he reminded us to do so.

In addition to pausing and breathing, the third step of managing reactivity is to *name it to tame it*. Just nonjudgmentally naming what is going on as a leader, with openness, curiosity, and kindness, can keep the reactive dynamic from festering below the surface of the organization and begin healing it.

In the introduction, I shared how, after my conflict with a fellow leader during a joint board meeting, we paused for a break to take a collective breath. Then, when we reconvened, I addressed the group and said, "We have been outside talking about a darkness that has descended into the room. Sometimes when we face darkness, the best thing is to just call it out. For my part, I am sorry that my fear got the best of me and for inviting this darkness into the room. Yesterday we spoke about the importance of constructively engaging each other, speaking our truth, and avoiding the pitfalls of destructive conflict or, worse yet, artificial harmony. Well, here we are in this moment of conflict. More important than any of the issues we face is how we will constructively engage each other right now to find healing and trust in the face of our conflict."

Looking back, this was my way of naming what was happening to tame it, without any personal judgment or blame. It was an important reset that helped us to manage the reactivity, build a healthier culture, and ultimately formalize our collaboration.

In addition to naming your culture's reactivity in the moment, you could more formally name its reactivity through a culture assessment and then gather with your group to reflect on the findings. This too can defuse reactivity and create a supportive environment for change.

Once you've identified and taken the edge off the reactivity in your culture with the first three steps, the fourth step is to consider *how to best respond.* Often this entails considering next steps for managing anything systemic that may be causing reactivity, including looking more deeply at the underlying stress and self-doubt that is driving the culture of reactivity to begin with. This brings us to Step 2 of the framework.

### Step 2: Reappraising Stress and Self-Doubt

Just as we can reappraise our view of stress and self-doubt in our own lives, it can be helpful to appraise how our culture views stress and self-doubt. Do members of the culture, whether within your organization, family, or community, view stress as a threat to be avoided or as an asset that can be productively engaged? How about self-doubt?

If members view stress and self-doubt as predominantly negative, leaders helping to reappraise this relationship by adopting or integrating the new science of stress can have powerful results at work, home, and in the community.

For example, in the late 1980s, the state of California set up a task force to study the effects of the California school system's noble commitment to raising the self-esteem of its students. The premise was that raising self-esteem would act to decrease the underlying troubling feelings of self-doubt and thereby offer a "social vaccine" to many social problems, including welfare dependency, drug addiction, or crime and violence.[4] A watchdog group reflected, "Twenty years later, observers are hard pressed to find any evidence that the self-esteem task force solved any problem."[5]

An extensive review by Dr. Nicholas Emler, a professor of social psychology at the University of Surrey in England, revealed that relatively low self-esteem is not a risk factor for delinquency, domestic violence, drug and alcohol abuse, doing poorly academically, or being a racist. Conversely, the review found that some individuals with very high self-esteem are more likely to hold racist attitudes, reject social pressures to conform, and engage in risky pursuits like drinking and driving.[6]

In the late 1990s, reporter John Stossel picked up on the backlash against the self-esteem movement and, in his segment on the television program *20/20*, questioned why the movement had lost steam. This segment showed how children who were placated in school with easy tests, high grades, and constant affirmation seemed to deal poorly with failure later in life. They became more frustrated and angry, and some committed crime.[7]

The unfortunate irony in the California schools experiment of trying to raise children's self-esteem by overprotecting them from challenges that might trigger their stress or self-doubt was that many children seemed to grow up becoming *less* resilient and *more* reactive, rather than the reverse. It was looking like less stress was *not* the answer to creating more resilient kids.

What if, the answer to enhancing resilience was to leverage stress and self-doubt, rather than eliminate it? I discovered an interesting finding in the SFO Self-Doubt Study I conducted in 2000 that addresses this question. In the study I evaluated the relationship between self-doubt and self-esteem by asking the 314 participants how much self-doubt bothered them and having them fill out the widely used and well-validated Rosenberg Self-Esteem Scale.[8]

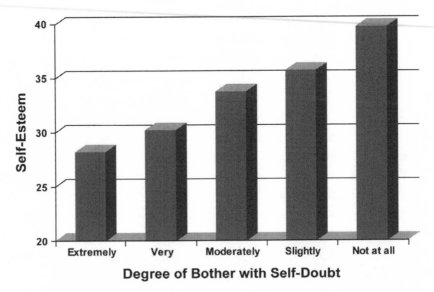

*Figure 12.2. Relationship between Self-Doubt and Self-Esteem*

As a result, this study found the following highly statistically significant correlation between self-esteem and how much one is bothered by feelings of self-doubt.[9] In other words, the more self-esteem people had, the less they were bothered by self-doubt.

At first glance, this data might seem to support the hypothesis that raising self-esteem decreases bother with self-doubt, which could lead to less reactivity and better social outcomes. But as we have mentioned, the research has not seemed to pan out.

The alternate hypothesis, and what seems to be more plausible from this significant relationship, is that learning to lean in and embrace self-doubt, so that you are less bothered by it and hence more comfortable with it, enables you to more fully take on your challenges and experience higher self-esteem as a product of your courage and success.

What if, instead of a curriculum on self-esteem, teachers in the 1980s had taught children that stress and self-doubt are not only normal, but that with mindful curiosity and kindness, they can be leveraged as assets to engage more fully with what they most care about (as you learned to do in chapter 6)? How might this alternate approach have helped them to become more resilient, treat themselves and others with greater compassion, and more fearlessly engage in meaningful challenges? How might this approach have inspired their creativity and performance and transformed the social outcomes in their community?

The research I shared with you in chapter 6 on reappraising the stress response (including how it improves outcomes in business settings) suggests this approach would have had a more beneficial effect. Further, research by Kristin Neff, the thought leader on self-compassion referenced in this same chapter, finds that self-compassion was associated with more stable, enduring feelings of self-worth than self-esteem was, as well as lower levels of social comparison, public self-consciousness, self-rumination, and anger. Also, while self-esteem had a robust association with narcissism, self-compassion did not. Further, self-compassionate individuals tend to experience less anxiety and depression, more empathy and emotional intelligence, and demonstrate greater motivation, initiative, and desire to reach their full potential.[10]

To cultivate a greater sense of safety and more creative culture at home and at work, consider how you might talk with your children or colleagues about mindfully and self-compassionately reappraising their relationship to stress and self-doubt. For example, I share with my boys that stress and self-doubt are normal, that everyone experiences these feelings (including me), and that we typically have them because we deeply care about something important in our lives. Whenever they experience these feelings, I tell them they have nothing to prove and to be kind to themselves as well as curious about the source of their discomfort. I explain that stress and self-doubt are just like friends or teachers, giving us energy and understanding to take action on what matters most to us and others.

Within AIHM, I often speak about how the flow channel of growth runs between the banks of destructive conflict and artificial harmony. Just like a river that carves its way through the terrain, this flow channel is a place of creative abrasion. We acknowledge that the stress and doubt in healthy dissent is an important part of creativity, and we commit to treat each other with kindness and compassion, so we can create enough safety and trust to feel challenged, rather than threatened, during periods of stressful growth and change.

In fact, at our annual AIHM board meeting in March 2015, we began crafting the following resolution that we later unanimously approved to embed in our culture.

In times of conflict and times of ease, we, the AIHM Board, pledge to each other kindness, compassion, and direct, honest communication in all matters. We will celebrate and acknowledge each other's efforts and, as best we are able, extend our trust in the good intentions of each other, especially in times of conflict and creative abrasion. May we be quick to forgive and slow to anger. May we listen closely to complaints and be courageous and kind in our vulnerability, knowing that it is not ours to resist conflict, but to navigate resolution.

This is our way of reappraising the threat of stress in our rapidly growing organization and cultivating tend-and-befriend and challenge responses instead. When we experience "problems," I typically respond, "This is a fascinating challenge!" Now, when some of my board members call me with issues, they lead off with, "What we have here is another fascinating challenge!"

While reappraising stress and self-doubt at work and at home is extremely powerful, it does not mean we simply allow unnecessary triggers of stress or self-doubt to continue to create an undue burden of threat on the culture.

In one of my workshops for a medical group, a physician shared her appreciation for the resiliency program being offered and then added, "While this is all well and good, I feel like someone is beating my shin with a hammer. And while I'm all for learning how to better deal with this pain, I'd also like this beating to stop!"

As important as it is to provide skills for personal resiliency in an organization, it's just as important, wherever possible, for leaders to look for ways to eliminate burdensome triggers of stress and build a systemic capacity for organizational resilience.

The common stress and self-doubt triggers we spoke about in chapter 6 apply here too, such as the SCARF factors (threats to Status, Certainty, Autonomy, Relatedness, and Fairness), as well as judgment, criticism, and unrealistic expectations.

For example, this clinician and many other healthcare providers and business people are experiencing increasing regulations, growing uncertainty, declining autonomy and reimbursement, and a growing workload that feels increasingly unrealistic and at times unfair—all of which can constantly trigger stress and self-doubt.

Many triggers can also be woven into the culture as values, norms, hidden beliefs, symbols, and habitual behaviors, all within systematic processes and expectations.

For example, the value of hard work, while noble, may also become woven in as an unhealthy norm if employees are expected to continually work late nights and weekends. The implicit belief is often that work is more important than family and personal well-being. When the organization views this sacrifice as a badge of honor that elevates one's status, everyone feels the pressure. If you don't toe the line, you are looked down upon, judged, and criticized—and your status falls. Ultimately it can lead to burnout or attrition in the organization. This especially affects women professionals, who, after having a baby, may either choose to or feel pressured to level down or drop out of their professions in which they've worked so hard to succeed.

To identify and counter these systematic triggers of stress and self-doubt, as a leader, you can adapt the four questions from the Appraise-Reappraise method in chapter 6 to appraise and reappraise reactivity in your culture at work, at home, and in your community organizations:

1. What happened?
2. What are my beliefs about what happened?
3. Am I certain my belief is really true?
4. How could I view this situation differently?

As you ask the first question, "What happened?," start by looking as objectively as possible at the behaviors, norms, symbols, and narratives in the culture.

Then, with the second question, explore the underlying beliefs driving these behaviors, norms, and narratives. In other words, try to get beyond, "This is just how we do things around here." Answering this question also involves understanding where the pockets of resistance and reactivity lie within the culture. What are the possible threats to the SCARF factors? Who is driving the narrative, and what are his or her underlying beliefs and intentions? While some of the concerns and resistance may be helpful for creating healthy change, individuals may also gossip and fearmonger to create instability or position themselves as the savior, in order to gain personal power and control.

With the third question, a Conscious Leader challenges the underlying beliefs beneath "this is how we do things." In service of the organization, this leader is also willing to step in courageously to assume greater "frame control"—to speak to a higher truth and challenge the underlying narrative—especially if other individuals are coming from a place of reactivity, power, and control.

With the fourth question, the Conscious Leader helps reframe the narrative, shapes the collective perspective, and takes action, wherever possible, to remove reactive triggers from the culture and the system, creating greater safety and trust in the organization. It involves taking action on the SCARF factors, being mindful to respect the Status of employees, to communicate with great transparency to reduce Uncertainty, and to look for specific ways to promote Autonomy, Relatedness (i.e., a sense of belonging), and Fairness in the culture. The Conscious Leader may also need to hold the boundary on destructive behavior, taking action to communicate directly with disruptive individuals as well as reframing and elevating the underlying narrative to reinforce a more creative frame that is aligned with the mission and purpose of the organization.

The Conscious Leader may also reflect on how organizational or governance structures can constrain and systematically trigger reactivity within a culture. Leaders may consider how their structure reflects and maintains the underlying values that drive it, challenge whether the values and structure are helpful, and consider possible changes that could systematically reappraise the experience of stress and self-doubt throughout the organization so it can better serve its mission and vision.

In his book *Reinventing Organizations,* Fredric Laloux describes how organizational structures evolve along a spectrum, from highly reactive to highly creative cultures.[11]

According to Laloux's evolutionary framework, our earliest organizations, existing about 100,000 years to 50,000 years ago, reflect a *Reactive-Infrared* paradigm. These were foraging bands of family kinships of typically less than a dozen people (some of which still exist in remote parts of the world). These groups had no elder, chief, or leader and were extremely reactive, with very high rates of violence.[12]

Around 10,000 years ago, *Impulsive-Red* organizations represent a breakthrough. Here Laloux uses the metaphor of "wolf pack," and examples include the Mafia, street gangs, tribal militias, and terrorist groups with a chief, foot soldiers, and division of labor. These groups have leaders, but the leadership style is "predatory," where the chief must constantly use his power to keep group members in line. Fear holds the group together, so they have a highly reactive, short-term focus.[13] This organizational structure includes leaders with a reactive mindset that typify low-performance leaders in the Leadership Circle profile.

Starting at around 4,000 BCE in Mesopotamia, the *Conformist-Amber* paradigm emerges, where groups are better able to exercise self-discipline and control through stable hierarchies and a clear definition of right and wrong. Here Laloux's metaphor is "army," and his examples include the military, the Catholic Church, most government agencies, and public school systems. Its leadership style is "paternalistic-authoritative," with "highly formal roles within a hierarchical pyramid and top-down command and control." These organizations value stability and status quo above all, and creativity is relatively constrained.[14]

The next evolutionary leap occurs during the Renaissance and then gains accelerating momentum through the Age of Enlightenment, the Industrial Revolution, and the Second World War. Represented by the metaphor of "machine," the *Achievement Oriented-Orange* paradigm opened up possibilities for greater creativity, and examples include the majority of corporations and many organizations today. One of its revolutionary breakthroughs was its meritocracy: anyone can move up the ladder to lead. Leaders are decisive and goal and task oriented. Innovation and performance accountability are the keys to success, which primarily consists of beating competition and achieving profit and growth.[15]

Based on its widespread prevalence, you may find yourself working in one of these "orange machines." While this structural paradigm can facilitate creativity, it is still a multilayered hierarchy of top-down leadership, within which low-performance leaders can easily abuse power and trigger reactivity in their employees. At best, these organizations are highly productive and creative. At worst, with micromanagement and stringent layers of oversight, people feel like cogs in a machine, which crushes the spirit of autonomy and creativity. In the wrong hands, leaders can squeeze every ounce of energy out of employees, cause them to burn out, and ultimately destroy the company.

So while employees may engage in their own inward transformation to more easily flow from reactivity to creativity, if the governance structure itself promotes reactivity in the culture, they'll be constantly swimming against the current. For transformation to be optimized, personal *and* organizational development need to be aligned.

Reflect on whether your organization resembles any of the above-mentioned structural paradigms and whether it is creating an undue burden of reactivity and draining energy from your organization. If so, the good news is that organizations have continued to evolve. In the next step, we'll discuss these other organizational structures Laloux has identified, which may liberate more energy and better cultivate and sustain a culture of creativity in your organization.

### Step 3: Cultivate Creativity

In chapter 7, we discussed how, by cultivating a foundational sense of safety, Steps 1 and 2 of the framework help free up more of your energy to focus on your love and belonging needs and achieve a greater sense of significance. You then learned how to cultivate creativity more specifically in the areas of health, relationships, and productivity by creating a *vision* with *strategies* that you *implement* to drive the *results* you want to see, in a process called VSIR.

As you've applied Steps 1 and 2 to your organization, family, or community organization, you've also established a foundational sense of safety by identifying and defusing the reactivity present in your culture. Now you can shift to optimizing energy and cultivating creativity in your culture with the same VSIR Process.

The VSIR Process is especially powerful for engaging productivity in an organization. First of all, as we saw in chapter 11, part of what makes Tony Hsieh, Tony de Leede, and Sharon Kolkka such inspiring leaders is their ability to clarify their purpose-driven values and *vision* for their organizations and inspire everyone in that organization to engage with that vision.

In addition to clarifying vision, high-performance leaders also effectively facilitate the implementation of *strategy* to achieve that vision.

Tom Curren, founder and president of Hawthorne Group, is a leading expert on strategy who has also served as a consultant to AIHM. As Marriott's former Senior Vice President of Corporate Planning and Business Development, he created and introduced Courtyard by Marriott, currently a $500 million business and the most preferred brand in the mid-market lodging segment. He defines strategy as "a dynamic process that's an interlocking set of decisions, collectively owned by the organization, about how the company will achieve its mission, the organization's unique reason for being." In short, he says, "Strategy is an integrated set of decisions about what an organization will do *and not do* to get there."

While the late business management guru Peter Drucker famously stated that "culture eats strategy for breakfast,"[16] he also recognized the great value of strategy. In *Management: Tasks, Responsibilities, Practices,* he defined strategic planning as "the continuous process of making present entrepreneurial (risk-taking) decisions systematically and with the greatest knowledge of their futurity; organizing systematically the efforts needed to carry out these decisions; and measuring the results of these decisions against the expectations through organized, systematic feedback."[17]

Together with vision, Drucker's definition of strategic planning includes strategy, implementation, and measuring and iterating around intended results, which comprise all of the elements of the VSIR Process.

*Figure 12.3. The VSIR Process*

You can follow the same sequence for your culture that you followed for your personal life in chapter 7. After clarifying the vision and mission of your organization, you next "look left before you turn right" and determine your SMART results and key performance indicators to track them. Then you put your strategic plan in place, implement that strategy, and measure your results. If you miss your intended results, you then reiterate the cycle, reflecting on any changes in your vision, whether your strategy was comprehensive enough or if it was missing key components, where people fell short on implementation, or whether your results were realistic to begin with. You then make ongoing changes as needed to get to where you want to go. (In other words, VSIR is a cycle of continuous quality improvement.) If you achieve your intended results, you and your team can then work toward your next set of intended results in your timeline or set new ones and work the next cycle of the VSIR Process.

Many businesses and organizations have more than one strategic business unit. The overarching strategic plan not only tracks the key performance indicators to optimize performance for each business unit, but also involves understanding how to unlock the synergies between business units.

Within AIHM, Tom Curren helped us identify that our core strategic business units include membership and education, comprising conferences, online education and our fellowship program. We are working to understand how each business unit cross-pollinates and creates opportunities for all of the other units, as well as integrates with our platform elements of information technology, financial planning and control, and marketing and communications to synergistically optimize our productivity and performance.

Conscious, high-performance leaders know how to synergize the diverse skillsets of the individuals within these business units as well. For example, when your team has been tasked with creating a new offering, you as the leader will want to identify your gifted divergent and convergent thinkers and orchestrate their collaboration. For example, when you want to consider all of the options and search for innovative, breakthrough ideas, you may first turn to your divergent thinkers and task them with generating as many ideas as they can. You might also facilitate optimal conditions for their work, perhaps by encouraging them to go for a walk, take regular breaks, or be more playful.

When it's time to shift to refining and practically implementing an idea, you may then turn to your convergent thinkers and task them with analyzing the divergent thinkers' ideas, focusing on the best one, and making that idea a reality. You might also support their work by helping them eliminate all distractions, focus their attention with a more serious mindset, and use logical thinking to identify the single best option. In this way, you can capitalize on your team's synergies and effectively remove the chaos from creative endeavors.

In addition to productivity, the categories of health and relationships are just as applicable for your organization, family, or community as they are for you personally—and they have a similar synergistic relationship. So integrating your VSIR for health, relationships, *and* productivity in your organization further enables you to optimize the system as a whole. In fact, this is the rationale for investing in comprehensive wellness and well-being programs. They not only reduce health costs, but they provide the baseline energy that fuels productivity and performance. These programs, if designed well, also connect people and build relationships.

Further, high-performance organizations implement strategies to systemically cultivate relationships through a sense of belonging in the culture. For example, Southwest Airlines (another Conscious Business) holds monthly lunch meetings to build a sense of togetherness. These meetings provide opportunities to share best practices and stories about how the company has made a difference in employee and customer lives, to celebrate successes and acknowledge individuals for their specific contributions and important life events. *48 Hours* aired an interview with a Southwest Airlines employee who had shared at one of these company lunches that her father had been diagnosed with terminal cancer. As a result, she says, "When I come in here and see people, they'll stop and ask, 'How's your dad? How are you doing? Let us know if there is something we can do for you.'" She then chokes up and tearfully exclaims, "That means more to me than getting a check from Southwest. That means more to me than anything in the world!" She later referred to Southwest as her "family."[18] Sharing regularly in this way not only galvanizes a sense of belonging and family, but also a sense of significance in the work being done. All of this brings energy into the system to facilitate greater levels of creative engagement and optimize performance.

Further, as we mentioned in Step 2 above, Laloux's evolutionary spectrum of organizational structures can help you reflect on your ideal governance structure, which can help you optimize workflow, liberate energy, and cultivate your culture of creativity.

The next organizational structure to evolve after the "orange machine" is the *Pluralistic-Green* paradigm. According to Laloux, it arose during the eighteenth and nineteenth centuries in relatively small circles of people in industrial countries who began to champion socially conscious ideals, such as the abolition of slavery, woman's liberation, separation of church and state, freedom of religion, and democracy. This thinking steadily grew throughout the twentieth century and then accelerated within the counterculture of the 1960s and 1970s.[19] Examples of these companies are many of those "firms of endearment" described earlier by Sisodia, as well as those who are part of the Conscious Capitalism movement, such as Ben & Jerry's and Southwest Airlines referenced above.

The metaphor for these companies is "family." As we've mentioned before in the context of Conscious Capitalism, while these companies value profits, they are primarily driven by higher purpose. In these companies, purpose-driven and Conscious Leadership drives conscious culture, which is consensus oriented, participative, and highly service oriented and customer centric. As the subtitle of John Mackey (Co-CEO of Whole Foods) and Raj Sisodia's book *Conscious Capitalism* states, this movement is "Liberating the Heroic Spirit of Business." The focus is on doing well by doing good. Social purpose and empowerment drive employee motivation. And as we saw in the previous chapter, these organizations generally outperform on business outcomes.

While a major breakthrough, this Pluralistic-Green paradigm—the "family"—still may engage a similar, multilayered hierarchy to orange organizations. It is often led by a high-performance Conscious Leader, a wise and benevolent matriarch or patriarch of the family. And as with many families, which can facilitate a sense of love and belonging, Laloux notes that this structure can, at times, still be "mildly or wildly dysfunctional."

This brings us to the most recent stage that Laloux presents in his book: the *Evolutionary-Teal* paradigm. (In the appendix of his book, he also acknowledges organizational stages beyond Evolutionary-Teal will likely emerge.)[20]

The metaphor often used for teal organizations is a "living organism" or a "living system" that is constantly evolving towards its own evolutionary purpose.[21] In this system, self-management with distributed leadership largely replaces the top-down hierarchical leadership of previous organizational structures.

Laloux shares how the cultures of these organizations view life as a journey, unfolding toward a deeper calling instead of pre-planned goals and routes. A premium is placed on a growth mindset, where mistakes are only opportunities to learn and the focus is on strengths rather than failures or "what's wrong." Its values involve being true to yourself and mindfully integrating mind, body, and soul in all aspects of life, both at work and at home.[22]

According to Laloux, the three major breakthroughs in the culture of teal organizations are wholeness, self-management, and evolutionary purpose.[23]

Remember from chapter 1 that *wholeness* is related to the root of the word *health*.[24] Thus, this breakthrough is a major step toward creating healthier organizations. In teal organizations, wholeness is cultivated by encouraging employees to be their authentic selves and bring all of who they are to work, instead of just their narrow, "professional" selves, which can make them feel like cogs in a machine. Mindfulness is valued and quiet rooms are often provided to facilitate rest, rejuvenation, and meditation practices. Working spaces are mindfully designed, often paying attention to light and bringing in nature. Personal spaces are warmly self-decorated without status markers. Roles in which people serve for the good of the whole are valued above job titles. Conversations center around values, which are translated into explicit ground rules. Storytelling practices are often used to support self-disclosure and facilitate a greater sense of trust and connection. And specific meeting practices are engaged to resolve conflicts and keep the ego in check to prevent reactivity from fragmenting the culture.[25]

A central theme of this book has been how to optimize energy—specifically, how to reclaim, renew, and refocus your energy on what matters most within your own life. This theme applies to optimizing energy within organizations, too.

Laloux credits much of the success of teal organizations to "liberating previously unavailable energies" and "harnessing and directing energy with more clarity and wisdom."[26] For example, in this self-governing model, energy is boosted when individuals are connected to a purpose greater than themselves, when individuals can manage themselves according to their own standards, rather than a boss's, and when individuals can take on roles that match their talents, rather than predefined job descriptions that are rarely a perfect fit. Less energy is wasted by the hallmarks of orange organizations: defending ego and turf, reporting requirements for unnecessary policies, and meetings required simply to inform the chain of command.

Finally, energy is harnessed and directed, with clarity and wisdom, in a variety of ways. Individuals are empowered to make decisions as needed, rather than losing information through the chain of command in order to reach the decision maker. Such decisions can now fully take the context into account, able to draw upon emotional, aesthetic, and intuitive wisdom. Decision making becomes more efficient, as it can happen instantly, spreading throughout the organization, rather than getting stuck waiting for management. Laloux references the saying, "When a fisherman senses a fish in a particular spot, by the time his boss gives his approval to cast the fly, the fish has long moved on." Perhaps best of all, as individuals align with the organization's evolutionary purpose, their work will feel effortless and supported, rather than fighting against prevailing winds.

You might think these innovative ideas to liberate energy in an organization would be difficult to scale, but examples of success stories include AES Corporation, a Fortune 200 global power company with seventeen billion dollars in revenue that employs 18,500 people and provides sustainable energy to seventeen countries. On its website, it describes its culture as follows: "The energy our people bring to what they do is what powers AES. At its essence, our culture is how we channel that energy through the ways in which we work together." The tagline under their logo is "We are the energy."[27]

If you want to learn more about the specific practices and case studies of teal organizations, I encourage you to read Laloux's *Reinventing Organizations*.

Now think about your business, family, or community organization. What "color" is its governance structure? If you are leading an organization, take a moment to reflect on this governance structure and what might better serve to cultivate your culture of creativity.

Within the AIHM, after reading Laloux's work, it became apparent to me that we were an organization with green and teal values stuck in an orange machine governance structure. Part of shifting to Academy 2.0 involves reflecting on how our governance structure needs to evolve to manifest our ambitious vision. Laloux points out that evolution does not necessarily require jettisoning earlier structures completely. Higher levels may also incorporate earlier levels, much like Russian nesting dolls (or your triune brain).

Shifting from earlier structures toward a teal structure represents a considerable shift toward an organization's creative mindset and culture.

Laloux quotes Richard Barrett, an internationally recognized thought leader on the evolution of human values: "Companies either operate from the fears of the ego or the love of the soul."[28] Laloux then notes how the movement toward teal shifts from "external to internal yardsticks." He says, "When we are fused with our ego, we are driven to make decisions informed by external factors—what others will think or what can be achieved. In the Impulsive-Red perspective, a good decision is the one that *gets me what I want.* In Conformist-Amber, we hold decisions up to the light of *conformity to social norms* . . . In Achievement-Orange, *effectiveness* and *success* are the yardsticks . . . In Pluralistic-Green, matters are judged by the criteria of belonging and *harmony.*"[29]

However, the Evolutionary-Teal paradigm shifts toward an internal yardstick, where "we are now concerned with the question of inner rightness: does this decision seem right? Am I being true to myself? Is this in line with who I sense I'm called to become? Am I being of service to the world?"[30]

This shift towards acting from a sense of inner rightness by asking more inspiring questions is a perfect segue to the fourth step of the 4 in 4 Framework.

### Step 4: Catalyzing Growth

In chapter 8, you learned how Step 4 helps transform your internal dialogue to further cultivate creativity and catalyze your growth. It activates your curiosity and capacity to transform threat into challenge with the following four steps:

1. *Ask* better questions.

2. *Find* more inspiring answers.

3. *Evaluate* your answers to ensure they feel right.

4. *Apply* your answers by taking purposeful action in your life, as shown in the cycle in the figure below.

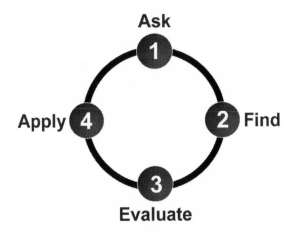

*Figure 12.4. The Ask-Find-Evaluate-Apply Cycle*

These same steps can be used to facilitate a more inspired external dialogue in order to cultivate cycles and cultures of creativity in families, organizations, communities, and even nations (especially during political campaigns). You can think of culture as being the sum of all conversations going on in each of these domains.

A leader's internal dialogue can ripple into the external dialogue and influence the culture in socially contagious ways. For example, at the beginning of this chapter we mentioned how leaders may "go limbic" at inflection points when they feel that their company's success is being threatened. Chapter 5 discussed how, when we feel threatened, our internal dialogue tends toward fear-based, judgmental thoughts or questions, like: "What if . . ." (followed by all the bad things that could happen); "If only . . ." (followed by regrets from the past); "What's wrong with me?" (associated with thoughts and feelings of shame and self-doubt); and "What's wrong with others?" (seeking who is to blame).

The inner critic then becomes expressed as an external critic, where judgment and criticism often leak out into the conversation, putting employees on the defensive. This ripple effect can lead to gossip, blame, and persecution, further leading to a reactive culture of fear and mistrust, which erodes morale. When people protect themselves and become reluctant to take risks, creativity is stifled. Then, as the organization becomes mired in dealing with problems under pressure and experiencing stress as a constant threat, the joy of work is lost and customer service suffers.

However, with Step 4, leaders can adopt an alternative mindset and inspire a different conversation, leading to different actions and outcomes for their organization. What if, at the inflection point, leaders became more mindful and engaged in a more inspiring internal dialogue that reflected a challenge or tend-and-befriend response more than a threat response? For example, what if instead of reflecting on what may be wrong with them and others, they asked questions more in alignment with the recipe for a flourishing life we discussed in chapter 7: "In this difficult moment, what is it I am here to learn? How can I best connect with my colleagues, clients, or vendors? How can I best connect with myself and my deepest source of inspiration? How can I best express myself? What is my best service at this time?"

The leader can then inspire individuals and teams to ask similar questions or find other helpful questions and encourage all to listen deeply to their answers and act accordingly.

In the book *A More Beautiful Question* (a title inspired by the E.E. Cummings quote, "Always the beautiful answer who asks a more beautiful question"), Warren Berger offers three types of questions that can be especially helpful to inspire creativity at work or at home.[31] These questions involve "why, what if, and how."

"Why" opens up the field of creative possibilities. Berger shares a story about how the founder of Polaroid, Edwin Land, was inspired to invent the instant camera after he took a picture of his four-year-old daughter on vacation. When she asked to see the results, he explained that he had to send the film out. She then asked, "Why do we have to wait for the picture?" This "why" question had the power to inspire an invention and rise of an iconic company.

According to Berger, "why" questions are best asked at the initial stages of creation to help you understand the challenge. "Why is something happening? Why hasn't someone solved it before? Why would it be worth doing?"

Next you move into "what if" questions, where you begin to imagine an alternative future and the world of possibility and opportunity. It's also where you can let your imagination run free with wild and crazy ideas.

Then you begin to move into pragmatic action with "how" questions. "How are we actually going to get this done? How would we pay for it? How would we test out the idea initially to see if it works? How can we prototype it?" Your "how" questions move you from ideas into action to manifest your creativity.

In addition to these "why, what if, and how" questions, some of the most powerful questions we can ask to cultivate a culture of creativity have to do with our connection with others, specifically how we receive and give with each other. In chapter 10, you learned that cycles of creativity involve asking how you can receive from others with empathy and understanding and give with authenticity and care. When you ask how you can better give and receive, these questions automatically put you in a state of service (or better yet, hospitality). When leaders inspire everyone in an organization to develop the habit of asking these questions, it can lead to a deeper sense of love and belonging in the culture, along with extraordinary client service, such as that delivered by the high-performing companies we've referenced. If you are a healer, these questions about how to best give and receive serve the heart of healing in your interaction with patients. When these questions are collectively asked within a healthcare system, it leads to a healing culture.

Framing good questions in the Ask-Find-Evaluate-Apply process is also a powerful technique for leaders to facilitate problem solving or to provide feedback to their employees.

David Rock, who coined the acronym SCARF, believes the commonly used technique of constructive positive feedback—saying something positive at the beginning and at the end, with the meat of the concern in between— may act as "an arsenic sandwich." He says, "The bread might make the meal appear more palatable, but it's still going to kill you."[32] Even when positively couched, feedback can still feel lethal if it triggers threats to Status, Certainty, Autonomy, Relatedness, and Fairness.

The Ask-Find-Evaluate-Apply process provides another option to constructive positive feedback, or even the temptation to offer solutions that may inadvertently diminish the recipient's status and autonomy. Instead, leaders can invite their colleagues to identify key questions that would be most helpful in the situation.

For example, when faced with a particular challenge, a leader might say, "While I don't have the solution at this moment, let's see if we can come up with the best questions we could ask here." The leader could then add something like, "I trust that with your skill and wisdom, the answer to these questions will find you and lead to the right action." In leveraging the Ask-Find-Evaluate-Apply process in this way, leaders can effectively raise their colleagues' status, autonomy, and sense of control, and as we mentioned in chapter 10, help them discover their own genius.

Reflect on how you can best introduce the Ask-Find-Evaluate-Apply process within your organization or practice or with your family. Then reflect on the specific questions that would catalyze creativity and growth, not only during times of stress, but also as a matter of routine to inspire a culture of creativity and growth at work and at home.

When you inspire and empower people around you to ask questions, listen deeply to connect with their "inner rightness," and take congruent action, you provide them the opportunity to self-actualize their full potential and allow the culture you are serving to evolve towards its highest purpose.

## Optimizing a Culture's Energy and Performance

As mentioned in chapter 4, the ability to mindfully engage each of the steps in the 4 in 4 Framework enables individuals to do more than just achieve peak performance. It creates neuroplastic brain change. As you'll recall from the figure below, it shifts the performance curve up and to the right so that individuals experience an even greater capacity for performance at higher levels of stress.

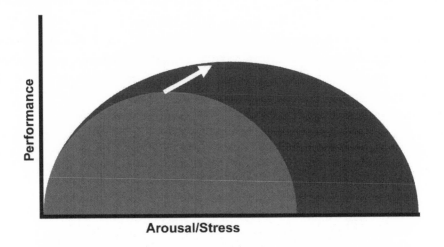

*Figure 12.5. Expanding the Stress and Performance Curve*

Since living, breathing individuals, with their developing brains, make up living, breathing organizations (or a "living system," as teal organizations are), this peak performance curve also represents the collective performance capacity of organizations themselves.

Thus, when an organization applies the mindfulness and neuroscience-based steps of the 4 in 4 Framework to cultivate a conscious culture of creativity, it may do more than achieve peak performance. The habits that lead to new ways of thinking, beliefs, norms, and behaviors may create a collective neuroplastic transformation that shifts the curve up and to the right for the entire organization. This provides a neuroscience-based explanation of how companies can move from good to great!

The mindfulness-based steps of the 4 in 4 Framework empower individuals and cultures to cultivate safety and trust, experience love and belonging, and self-actualize their greatness and sense of significance, facilitating the flow of energy all the way up Maslow's Hierarchy of Needs.

As a mindful or Conscious Leader, who is open, curious, and kind, you may find it helpful to ask yourself where your organization or family currently lies in relation to its capacity for peak performance, where your organization or family may be experiencing energy blocks along Maslow's Hierarchy of Needs, and in what creative ways can you liberate and optimize the energy and performance in your culture.

In October 2015, a week before AIHM's annual conference that would bring together about a thousand attendees, I sensed that our organization was in a state of turbulence. We were facing some challenges as a result of our rapid growth, and under this stress, some of our internal communication had become edgy, and certain relationships had become strained. I reflected upon how we could restore our sense of safety and trust, reconnect with our sense of love and belonging, and experience joy and fulfillment from the significant difference we'd be making at the conference and beyond. In light of all this, I asked myself how I could best structure our board meeting before the event to align our energy so that we could best serve all who would be attending the conference.

What came to me was to begin the board meeting by reading the resolution we had passed at our March board meeting, in which we pledged our kindness, compassion, and direct, honest communication to each other in times of conflict and times of ease. I initially thought about next addressing some of the challenges head on, but upon deeper reflection, I sensed it would be better to welcome, boost, and liberate our energies by next reflecting upon and appreciating all we achieved the previous year, to bring an energy of awe into the room. Then we would address our challenges by focusing on our high-level strategic plan to provide a sense of clarity and direction for our collective energy to flow.

As I was preparing for this meeting, it also came to me that ending with a mindfulness practice could powerfully help us to combine our collective heartfelt energy to serve all those at the conference and embody one of the most treasured core values of AIHM: "love is the greatest healer of all."

I was uncertain about what mindfulness practice might serve to help us galvanize our core value of love in service of others and reflected on this all week. Finally, the night before the board meeting, I woke up at four in the morning and, in a flow of inspiration, wrote out the following practice. Here is what I shared with my board at the end of our meeting later that day. (Please feel free to adapt this practice for yourself and your team in whichever way helps you to serve best.)

## Mindfulness Practice: May We Serve Well Together

1. Assume a state of relaxed alertness in whatever way feels most natural to you and close your eyes.

2. Allow yourself to settle, noticing whatever thoughts, sensations, or feelings you are experiencing, just being with whatever you are noticing without any resistance.

3. Bring your attention to your breath—following it, receiving it with gratitude for this life we are blessed to live.

4. Now bring to mind someone who you feel loves you unconditionally and whom you love unconditionally, someone who brings a natural smile to your face, someone who fills your heart with love and kindness. It could be a loved one in your family, a dear friend or pet, or anyone else who evokes a loving feeling in your heart.

5. As you bring this person to mind, see if you can feel your heart expand with love and kindness.

6. With this feeling of love and kindness in your heart, imagine breathing in through your heart and that you are amplifying your breath with love and kindness.

7. Now, with each breath in through your heart, as you breathe out, imagine you are breathing the energy of love and kindness sequentially with each breath into your feet, legs, thighs, pelvis, abdomen, chest, hand, arms, shoulders, neck, and then your face, to fill your entire body with loving-kindness.

8. As you may be sensing your entire body filled with loving-kindness, allow your love to further expand and breathe out your loving-kindness as a wish for each person in the room: "May you be filled with loving-kindness." Continue breathing in through your heart and breathing out this sense of goodwill for each person here.

9. Now, sensing the room filled with loving-kindness, allow yourself to receive this loving-kindness, breathing it in through your heart, further amplifying this loving-kindness in your heart, and breathing it out into the room, together sensing the ocean of loving-kindness we are breathing into.

10. Let us sense together the power of this ocean of loving-kindness, how it has the capacity to absorb and neutralize any harmful fear, anxiety, or conflict, whether it be around any personal suffering or concerns within our organization.

11. Breathing in this loving-kindness and breathing out into our ocean, let us envision how this pool of loving-kindness will nourish us throughout the conference and how we can draw on the love and kindness from each other in this ocean when we are at the podium or in our conversations, speaking with each other or our attendees.

12. As we meet our clinicians, who have gathered to search for a sense of community, let us remember to breathe in from this ocean of loving-kindness and breathe out loving-kindness and goodwill to each person we interact with.

13. As we meet new people, let us breathe in the goodwill or any suffering they may be experiencing, connecting with our heart and this ocean of loving-kindness, and breathe out love and kindness for them, inviting them into this ocean of loving-kindness, too.

14. Let us think of our message of unity: "*we together* transforming healthcare." This ocean of love and kindness is an ocean of unification; it connects us all together.

15. Let us imagine all healers leaving this conference filled and connected to this ocean of loving-kindness and now spreading as a gentle wave through their families, their patients, their colleagues, and the communities they serve, further expanding this ocean of loving-kindness as a spreading wave of health and healing that is manifesting our vision and transforming healthcare for all of humanity and our planet.

16. Now, let's come back to the ocean of love and kindness, feel the power of its energy, and deeply feel our intention: "May we be filled with loving-kindness. May we feel forever connected to this ocean of loving-kindness."

17. And feeling this energy, let us deeply connect with our intention for this week and beyond: *may we all serve well together!*

After we shared this experience together, there was a palpable shift. A greater sense of cohesion and trust emerged. Love replaced fear. The next night our board convened, as is our custom, to take an evening to personally check with each other. We noticed that we shared at a depth and vulnerability we had never before shared with each other. Further, the sense of community we were able to collectively create throughout the week was deeply felt and appreciated by conference attendees. Participants repeatedly shared that while they initially came for their professional development, they were deeply moved at how they had found a loving and compassionate community dedicated to healing and the creation of health. They shared how they had "found their tribe" and their "way back home"!

While it's important to acknowledge that no one moment forever changes a culture and that leaders must continually nurture it, at that moment in time our board came together and collectively embodied the answer to the question, "Who do we need to become to manifest the vision for the change we want to see in the world?"

## Be the Change You Want to See in the World

On September 11, 2001, two months before Mom died, we watched in horror as terrorists killed thousands at World Trade Center, the Pentagon, and on three airplanes. Over the remaining few weeks of her life, we witnessed the power of love and creative relationships to transform and heal the nation.

It was a profound experience to share with Mom. In many ways, the terrorist attacks transformed America and her allies much like Mom's cancer diagnosis transformed her. Just as issues of stress and self-doubt no longer seemed important to Mom in the face of her imminent death, for a period a time in American society, our collective issues of stress and self-doubt were subsumed by the enormity of tragedy.

Likewise, just as Mom's reactive need to overcome her insecure feelings by seeking acknowledgment gave way to feelings of love and connection, the reactive drive to get ahead and prove self-worth in society gave way to an overwhelming outpouring of love and support—a collective tend-and-befriend response—for everyone affected by the tragedy.

Gone was worship of celebrity, wealth, and power. If anything, it was sacrilegious. Gone was the irony so often used to depreciate others. Now it was in bad taste. Early television coverage of the tragedy even suspended advertising. Gone was homage to material possessions, which now seemed banal.

Instead, people reached out to others. All wanted to feel connected, express themselves, and be of help.

An article in a special commemorative issue of *Newsweek* tells the story of Andrea Popovich, who stopped to help a pregnant woman at the aftermath of ground zero. Later, when she heard the woman had given birth to a healthy baby and made a donation in Popovich's name to the United Way, she broke down in tears saying, "This was such a small act. But I feel so connected to this woman now, and her baby." Popovich then captured what everyone felt: "That is something that comes out of emergencies like this. You see that you are related to everybody."[33]

In the few days after the tragedy, it was not uncommon for people in New York to ask complete strangers if they were OK and then sit down and talk with them. Everywhere people felt a greater respect and concern for each other. We reached out to commiserate with others, trying to make sense of the tragedy. Many discussions ended by telling someone you cared about, "I love you." People made way for others in traffic. Thousands lined up and waited for hours to give blood, and millions donated to relief funds set up by the Red Cross and other charities. In California, prisoners experienced such a wave of empathy and compassion that they asked to raise funds for firefighters and police officers.

Like Mom's cancer diagnosis, the tragedy of the September 11th attack transformed lives. These events eclipsed the predisposition towards self-absorption and brought us all closer together.

As time distances us from tragic events, life slowly returns to normal, and the familiar feelings of stress and self-doubt again become more prominent. Inevitably, along with these feelings come the reactive responses that erode our sense of closeness and pull us apart.

We need not await another tragedy to draw closer together. Each of us has the power right now to transform our relationships and make a bigger difference in the world. Most important, Conscious Leaders have the capacity to create this sense of community and galvanize others to positive change.

Think of the great Conscious Leaders of our time, like Nelson Mandela, Martin Luther King Jr., and Gandhi, who have been able to bring people together in service of the highest good to affect positive change in the world. Think of the leaders at every level in families, organizations, communities, and the world who have had the capacity to sustain great transformation and change. Think of those leaders I invited you to bring to mind in chapter 1 who best embody high-performance Conscious Leadership for you. Let them inspire you again now. You too have this power to affect change. As Gandhi said, all it takes is to "be the change you want to see in the world."

With the 4 in 4 Framework, you now have the tools and practices to do so. May you learn to lead well from within so you can lead well in the world to benefit the families, organizations, communities, and the global humanity you serve. In the conclusion that follows, you'll receive a summary of all you've learned in this book and practical suggestions to lead well in *your* world, starting now.

# Lifelong Practice and Ongoing Transformation

Congratulations on becoming a more Conscious Leader!

You've come a long way. You've learned that conscious organizations with creative leaders perform better than others. The science proves it. And you've learned that if you want to create a more conscious organization or family or community, change has to start with you.

You've learned how that change happens: by shifting your mindset from a state of reactivity to creativity. Specifically, you've learned how the threat of unmanaged stress (and your unconscious reactions to it) can flip you into low-performance leadership and how being more conscious, curious, and compassionate—with yourself and others—can flip you back into high-performance leadership.

You've also learned how to make this change—with the skills and mindfulness-based practices of the 4 in 4 Framework. You can recognize when you're going into a threat reaction, take a moment to reframe what's really going on, more fully engage your higher brain regions to make a more conscious decision in alignment with your deepest values, and shift your mindset and internal dialogue to continually wire in a pattern of more inspired thinking and catalytic growth.

In essence, you've learned the secret formula to thriving under stress. When demands exceed resources, you experience threat and low performance. But if resources exceed demands, you will experience challenge or tend-and-befriend responses to stress, rather than a threat response, and be capable of thriving, even in the most stressful circumstances. You now understand how to tap more fully into the inner resources and power *you already have* to meet whatever demands you face, so you can experience the increased energy and state of "flow" that optimizes performance and allows you to not only flourish in all areas of your life, but help others do so as well.

But if you want to lead well from within and lead well in the world, understanding isn't enough.

The next step is to *practice* what you've learned on an ongoing basis and incorporate it into your daily life. It takes about eight weeks to break old habits and create new ones,[1] but if you set an intention and act on it, using the processes outlined in this book, *you can do it.*

As you take action, you will find that it will become easier to leverage your stress and self-doubt into positive, productive energy and shift from a reactive, low-performance leadership state to a creative, high-performance leadership state in the heat of the moment. Over time, you'll also experience:

- Greater resilience
- More vibrant health
- Deeper relationships
- Greater impact and significance at work and at home

In short, you will become increasingly more resourceful in meeting your Maslowian needs in the areas of life that matter most to you, so you can expand your positive influence in the world.

So how do you take action to build on what you've learned to sustain ongoing change in your life and affect positive change around you?

The remainder of this chapter will further summarize and simplify all you have learned from the 4 in 4 Framework so you can easily incorporate it in your life. And if you'd like additional support to do so, we will explore that too.

## Summarizing the Benefits, Skills, and Practices of the 4 in 4 Framework

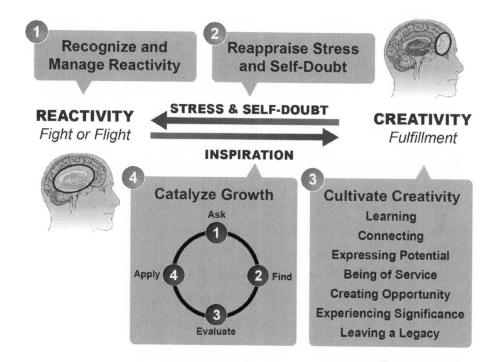

As you have learned throughout this book, each of the four steps of the 4 in 4 Framework includes skills and practices designed to both help you shift in the moment as well as rewire your brain for more enduring change. The table below summarizes the benefits, skills, and mindfulness-based practices of each step.

| Step | Benefit | Skills | Mindfulness Practices* |
|---|---|---|---|
| **1**<br><br>**Recognize and Manage Reactivity** | Helps you to identify and take the edge off your reactivity and consider your best response | Recognizing Your Reactive Sensations, Feelings, Thoughts, and Behaviors (pg. 113)<br><br>Four Steps to Manage Your Reactivity (pg. 128) | Naming Your Experiences (pg. 132) |
| **2**<br><br>**Reappraise Stress and Self-Doubt** | Enables you to leverage stress and self-doubt as an asset, as well as extract the teeth out of the triggers of stress and self-doubt that drive your reactivity | The Appraise-Reappraise Method (pg. 157) | Working the Appraise-Reappraise Method Mindfully (pg. 164)<br><br>Loving-Kindness, Part One (pg. 166) |

| 3 Cultivate Creativity | Helps you reflect and express what's truly important in your life | The VSIR Process (pg. 173) | Working the VSIR Process Mindfully (pg. 206) The Energy Optimizing Body Scan (pg. 207) Mindfully Engaging Your Energy within Your Hierarchy of Needs (pg. 207) |
| --- | --- | --- | --- |
| 4 Catalyze Growth | Empowers you to change your internal dialogue to catalyze Steps 1, 2, and 3 and continually realign with what's truly important | The Ask-Find-Evaluate-Apply Spiral of Growth (pg. 215) | Working the Ask-Find-Evaluate-Apply Spiral of Growth (pg. 228) |

*All of these mindfulness practices build on the foundational mindfulness breathing practice you learned in chapter 3 (pg. 83).

Also, in part 3, you learned additional skills and practices to apply the 4 in 4 Framework to lead well in the world. You learned the skills to cultivate cycles of creativity to resolve conflicts (pg. 269), nurture your most important relationships at home and at work (pg. 279), and cultivate more creative cultures in your families, organizations, communities, and the world (pg. 315). You also learned the accompanying mindfulness practices of Loving-Kindness, Part Two (pg. 288), and May We Serve Well Together (pg. 340).

All of these skills and practices allow you to lead more consciously and be the change you want to see in the world, as well as inspire and equip others to do the same.

## Suggestions for Lifelong Practice and Ongoing Transformation

Now, how do you work these skills and practices into your daily life? Here are some suggestions:

- As a baseline, commit to any of the formal mindfulness practices mentioned above for at least ten minutes a day—and more, as you choose. Allow yourself to also be curious with these practices and feel free to explore how you might modify them to make them your own. Plan your mindfulness practice into your day so it becomes a new habit. For example, consider practicing for five or ten minutes when you wake up in the morning and then five or ten minutes before going to sleep in the evening.

- Commit to informally practicing mindfulness by being more present in the moment, bringing mindful awareness to whatever you are doing. One way to do so is to use a cue to trigger mindful awareness, such as setting an alarm on your phone a few times a day. Or you can use daily habits as mindfulness cues, such as each time you pass through a doorway at the office, reach for the door handle when you come home from work, or brush your teeth. Pause with openness, curiosity, and kindness, take a few heart-centered breaths, and become more consciously aware of your sensations, thoughts, feelings, and behaviors; notice what you intend to do next.

- Whenever you feel overwhelmed and reactive as a result of being threatened by stress or self-doubt, apply **Step 1: Recognize and Manage Reactivity.** See if you can recognize your reactive sensations, feelings, and thoughts, and identify what you are likely to do next. If you sense you are about to do more harm than good, remember to pause, take a few heart-centered breaths, and with compassion, "name it to tame it" and consider your best response.

- If you find yourself continuing to be bothered by underlying stress and self-doubt, use **Step 2: Reappraise Stress and Self-Doubt** to transform your mindset. For example, instead of being stressed about being stressed, see if you can leverage this energy of stress as an asset to achieve the outcomes that matter most. When it's "go time" and you feel amped up, explore being grateful for this energy and "naming it to savor it." Then go ahead and "surf your sympathetics" to take care of business. Alternatively, if you feel the oxytocin pull to reach out and connect with others under stress, instead of taking flight and withdrawing, explore "tending and befriending" and reaching out for social support. If you continue to be triggered with stress and self-doubt, remember that you can also use the Appraise-Reappraise Method to evaluate and reframe the way you view your triggers to extract the teeth out of them.

- Once you have transformed your stress into an energy source, you are ready for **Step 3: Cultivating Creativity.** Here you focus on manifesting your vision of a life well lived in alignment with your deepest values and purpose. Keep engaging your VSIR Process to do so. Continue to refine your *vision* and explore how you can best *implement strategies* to manifest specific, measurable, realistic, and time-framed *results* in the most important areas of your life. See if you can execute one thing each day to enhance your health, relationships, and productivity. For example, go for an hour-long walk after work; have that talk with your partner you've been putting off; or close all your browsers, shut down your e-mail, and set your alarm for ninety minutes of undisturbed block time to finally get that project done. The sum of the actions you take equals a flourishing life, characterized by health and vitality, rich and meaningful relationships, and a greater sense of significance in what you do.

- Most importantly, as a matter of routine in times of both stress and ease, apply **Step 4: Catalyze Growth** and engage the Ask-Find-Evaluate-Apply Spiral of Growth. This step transforms your internal dialogue to help you establish the habit of asking good questions to find good answers and take good action in your life. As mentioned in chapter 8, Step 4 also catalyzes the first three steps of the 4 in 4 Framework, which provides the architecture for asking good questions. You can review the questions relating to each step of the framework beginning on page 218.

Essentially, the 4 in 4 Framework is a system of mindfulness-based inquiry that helps you reflect and take inspired action in a continual spiral of growth. If you were to boil down the entire framework into the one simple step that engages and drives all the others, it would be to enter this spiral of growth with the first step of Step 4: *to mindfully ask inspiring questions in your life.*

For example, when you experience challenging situations, instead of defaulting to automatic questions, such as "What's wrong with me?" or "What's wrong with others?," it can be helpful to ask more inspiring questions that are in alignment with the key elements of your flourishing life, such as:

- In this difficult moment, what am I here to learn?
- How can I more fully connect with myself or others?
- How can I best express myself?
- How can I best be of service?
- Is what I plan to do next in alignment with my values and life vision?

To nurture your relationships and the cultures you influence, continue to cultivate cycles of creativity by asking questions about giving and receiving, such as:

- How can I best give and receive with my family and friends?
- How can I best give and receive with my colleagues at work?
- How can I best give and receive with my clients, patients, or customers?
- How can I best give and receive with the people I lead?
- How can I inspire employees to give and receive with their colleagues and with our clients/patients/customers to further cultivate a culture of creativity?

Also remember, if you are ever stuck about which questions to ask, often the best question is "What are the best questions I could ask right now?"

In the end, it's your questions—asked mindfully with openness, curiosity, and kindness—and the actions they lead to that are the key to leveraging stress and self-doubt, thriving in your life, and expanding your influence to transform your family, organization, community, and even the world!

## Further Support for Your Ongoing Growth and Transformation

You now have everything you need to develop into an even higher-performing conscious leader. You have the theory, the scientific evidence, the framework, and the skills and practices to enhance your leadership capacity.

But you may want even more support. If so, I would be honored to help you further develop and solidify your skills as a conscious leader.

For individuals, SuperSmartHealth offers one-on-one coaching to deepen your learning and provide you with support to clarify and achieve the specific results you want for your life. We also offer online training and group coaching.

For organizations, we offer keynote speaking, live workshops, and executive coaching.

Just go to SuperSmartHealth.com to learn more.

So now, I encourage you take what you've learned here to become a more resilient, compassionate, productive, inspiring, and conscious leader—whether it's in business, healthcare, your organization, your family, or your community. A leader who can inspire and engage others to make a meaningful difference together. A leader who leads well from within to lead well in the world!

In service, with heartfelt appreciation,

Daniel

# Daniel Friedland, MD

Dr. Daniel Friedland is an expert on neuroscience- and mindfulness-based high-performance leadership.

He helps leaders and their organizations:

- Transform stress and burnout into resilience
- Make smarter health, business, and life decisions
- Optimize health, relationships, and productivity
- Thrive with greater meaning and purpose

Dr. Friedland wrote one of the first textbooks on Evidence-Based Medicine, which is the way healthcare providers are now trained to make science-based decisions. He is also the author of *The Big Decision,* which he wrote with his then 14-year-old son Zach, to inspire and empower better life decisions at home and at work.

An in-demand international expert in applying the framework of Evidence-Based Medicine to enhance decision-making, leadership, and resiliency, Dr. Friedland has worked with Fortune 500 companies; healthcare systems and medical groups; the US Army, Navy, and Air Force; Vistage; Young Presidents' Organization (YPO); Entrepreneurs' Organization (EO); The Global Wellness Summit; Conscious Capitalism; and leaders in the Texas and Australian governments—having delivered over 1500 programs and reaching more than 75,000 healthcare and business professionals around the world.

Dr. Friedland is the founding chair of the Academy of Integrative Health and Medicine and the president and CEO of SuperSmartHealth, where he provides keynote addresses, live workshops, online programs, and executive coaching to cultivate Conscious Leadership.

"Dr. Danny" feels blessed to live in San Diego with his wife and two sons, where he gets to "surf his sympathetics" in the waves of California!

For more information about Dr. Danny and the programs, resources, and services he offers, please visit SuperSmartHealth.com.

# Acknowledgments

This book has been a journey of growth and learning and an adventure of a lifetime, which continues to unfold. I am deeply grateful to all who have shared in this journey and enriched this work.

I feel truly blessed to have worked with Amanda Rooker, Executive Editor of SplitSeed, for her genius in editing my manuscript. The philosophy of SplitSeed is to help nurture "an idea that can no longer be contained by a single individual and is ready to grow and bear fruit in the lives of others." Her deep care and skillful nurturing of *Leading Well from Within* at every stage of its development was transformative not only for the manuscript, but for my own professional journey as well.

Thanks to Colin Webber for the numerous iterations that led to capturing the heart of the message in the cover design, Julie Felton for her great eye in designing all the interior graphics, Jay Polmar, Liliana Gonzalez Garcia and the good people from iPublicidades for the layout design, and Janina Kwilos for her meticulous attention in indexing the book.

In many ways, this book is an integration of the work of all of the researchers, authors, and pioneers it references. I am deeply grateful to all who have been cited, including Jon Kabat-Zinn, Raj Sisodia, John Mackey, Frederic Laloux, Daniel Siegel, Daniel Goleman, Stephen Covey, Kelly McGonigal, Kristin Neff, Srinivasan Pillay, Carol Dweck, Arne Dietrich, Jim Blascovich, Shelley Taylor, Paul MacLean, Mihaly Csikszentmihalyi, Richard Davidson, Matthew Lieberman, David Rock, Giocomo Rizzolatti, Paul Ekman, Robert Yerkes, John Dodson, Albert Ellis, Abraham Maslow, Christina Maslach, Tait Shanenfelt, Stephen Karpman, David Emerald, Gary Chapman, Stephen Porges, Abiola Keller, Alia Crum, Warren Berger, Rollin McCraty, Martin Seligman, Tony Schwartz, the Evidence-Based Medicine Working Group, Robert Anderson, and The Leadership Circle.

Also many thanks to Tony Hsieh, Tony De Leede, and Sharon Kolkka for the honor of sharing their inspiring stories in chapter 11, which illustrate how Conscious Leadership cultivates cultures of creativity.

A significant part of my story has included my growth as a leader with the Academy of Integrative Health and Medicine. I am deeply appreciative for the opportunity to have served over the years with its many great board and staff leaders, including Mimi Guarneri, Dan Asimus, Bradly Jacobs, Scott Shannon, Jennifer Blair, Russell Faust, Sanford Levy, Rauni Prittiken King, David Riley, Molly Roberts, Pamela Snider, Ellen Stiefler, Lucia Thornton, John Weeks, Leonard Wisneski, Rob Wyse, Nicholas Jacobs, William Meeker, Carol Bowman, Daphne Goldberg, Patrick Hanaway, Wendy Warner, David Rakel, Victor Sierpina, Jeffrey Sollins, Allan Warshowsky, Edward Linkner, Robert Anderson, Nancy Sudak, Steve Caldwell, Andy Mikulak, Tieraona Low Dog, Tabatha Parker, Seroya Crouch, Stephanie Romanoff, and my mentor, Lee Lipsenthal. When I first shared the early iteration of this work with Lee and that I was waking up at four a.m. feeling compelled to write, he cautioned that if I didn't listen my inspiration at this time of the morning, I'd "be toast!"

I am also indebted to Tom Curren from Hawthorne Consultants, whom we brought in to help develop AIHM 2.0—which included my development into Chair 2.0. Thanks, Tom, for helping me to become a better leader.

Wherever you are now, please know how grateful I am to you, Mom, for teaching me about receiving and giving love; and to you, Dad, for showing me the power of neuroplasticity. Dad, I watched you distill your life into pure goodness, and I hope to honor your memory in my aspiration to always be kind, too.

Zach and Dyl, words cannot convey just how much I love you. Thanks for teaching me how to become a good dad. I am in awe of the remarkable young men you are becoming. I hope this book inspires your ongoing growth. May you continue to lead good lives and learn to lead others well.

Sue, from the moment you crossed the dance floor and invited me to salsa dance with you, I knew my life would be forever changed. I feel so blessed to create our spiritual home and raise our boys together. I love and so appreciate you. You are an extraordinary mother, wife, and partner in SuperSmartHealth. I am so grateful for your sage input on the book and all you do to run our company and create our online presence—all enabling me to share this purposeful work.

And finally, my humble appreciation to the Source of inspiration that continues to inspire my life and this work, and has blessed me with my family and a purpose to share.

# References

## Introduction: The Case for Conscious Leadership

1   Dictionary.com, s.v. "mindset," accessed May 12, 2016, http://www.dictionary.com/browse/mindset; Merriam-Webster, s.v. "mindset," accessed May 12, 2016, http://www.merriam-webster.com/dictionary/mind–set.

2   Simon Sinek, *Start with Why: How Great Leaders Inspire Everyone to Take Action* (New York: Penguin Portfolio, 2011).

## Chapter 1: Evidence and Inspiration for Engaging Conscious Leadership

1   IBM, "IBM 2010 Global CEO Study: Creativity Selected as Most Crucial Factor for Future Success," (press release), accessed May 12, 2016, https://www-03.ibm.com/press/us/en/pressrelease/31670.wss; IBM Institute for Business Value, *Capitalizing on Complexity: Insights from the Global Chief Executive Officer Study,* (full report), accessed July 8, 2016, https://public.dhe.ibm.com/common/ssi/ecm/gb/en/gbe03297usen/GBE03297USEN.PDF.

2   Viktor E. Frankl, *Man's Search for Meaning* (Boston: Beacon Press, 1959; repr., New York: Simon & Schuster, 1984).

3   The Leadership Circle, accessed July 8, 2016, https://leadershipcircle.com.

4   For those unfamiliar with these kinds of assessments, a 360-degree assessment is a common type of leadership survey in businesses and corporations, where surveys are not just completed by the leaders themselves, but may include bosses, subordinates, and family members as well.

5   Leadership Circle representative, personal communication with author, May 18, 2016 (63,000 leaders have been evaluated with the Leadership Circle Profile).

6   The Leadership Circle, "Leadership Circle Profile," accessed May 12, 2016, https://leadershipcircle.com/assessment-tools/profile/.

7   Robert Anderson, "The Leadership Circle and Organizational Performance," (paper summarizing results of the study conducted by the Leadership Circle, accessed July 8, 2016, http://ourleadershipmatters.com/wp-content/uploads/2016/02/The-Leadership-Circle-and-Organizational-Performance.pdf.

8   Carol Dweck, Mindset: *The New Psychology of Success* (New York: Ballantine Books, 2007).

9   Ibid., 4.

10  Ibid., 4.

11  Judith Hicks Stiehm and Nicholas W. Townsend, *The U.S. Army War College: Military Education in a Democracy* (Philadelphia: Temple University Press, 2002), 6.

12  Leslie Kwoh, "When the CEO Burns Out," *Wall Street Journal* online, May 7, 2013, accessed May 12, 2016, http://www.wsj.com/articles/SB10001424127887323368760457846912400 8524696.

13  Christina Maslach and Susan E. Jackson, "The Measurement of Experienced Burnout," *Journal of Organizational Behavior* 2, no. 2 (1981): 99–113. doi: http://dx.doi.org/10.1002/job.4030020205.

14  T. D. Shanafelt, O. Hasan, L. N. Dyrbye, C. Sinsky, D. Satele, J. Sloan, and C. P. West, "Changes in Burnout and Satisfaction with Work-Life Balance in Physicians and the General US Working Population between 2011 and 2014," *Mayo Clinic Proceedings* 90, no. 12 (December 2015): 1600-13. doi: http://dx.doi.org/10.1016/j.mayocp.2015.08.023.

15  Liselotte N. Dyrbye and Tait D. Shanafelt, "Physician Burnout: A Potential Threat to Successful Health Care Reform," *JAMA* 305, no. 19 (May 18, 2011): 2009–10. doi: http://dx.doi.org/10.1001/jama.2011.652.

16  J. S. Haas, E. F. Cook, A. L. Puopolo, H. R. Burstin, P. D. Cleary, and T. A. Brennan, "Is the Professional Satisfaction of General Internists Associated with Patient Satisfaction?" *Journal of General Internal Medicine* 15, no. 2 (Feb. 16, 2000): 122-8. doi: http://dx.doi.org/10.1046/j.1525-1497.2000.02219.x; H. T. Stelfox, T. K. Gandhi, E. J. Orav, and M. L. Gustafson, "The Relation of Patient Satisfaction with Complaints against Physicians and Malpractice Lawsuits," *American Journal of Medicine* 118, no.10 (Oct. 2005): 1126-33. doi: http://dx.doi.org/10.1016/j.amjmed.2005.01.060.

17  J. L. Boone and J. P. Anthony, "Evaluating the Impact of Stress on Systemic Disease: the MOST Protocol in Primary Care," *Journal of American Osteopath Association* 103, no. 5 (May 2003): 239-46.

18  T. C. Russ, E. Stamatakis, M. Hamer, J. M. Starr, M. Kivimäki, and G. D. Batty, "Association between Psychological Distress and Mortality: Individual Participant Pooled Analysis of 10 Prospective Cohort Studies," *BMJ* 345 (July 31, 2012): e4933. doi: http://dx.doi.org/10.1136/bmj.e4933.

19  R. M. Poses, L. Baier-Manwell, M. Mundt, and M. Linzer, "Perceived Leadership Integrity and Physicians' Stress, Burnout, and Intention to Leave Practice," abstract, *Journal of General Internal Medicine* 20 (2005): S182. (This was an abstract presented at the 28th Annual Society of General Internal Medicine Meeting in 2005. Also of note: A p-value of <05 is considered statistically significant, indicating that the findings discussed are unlikely due to chance.)

20  T. D. Shanafelt, G. Gorringe, R. Menaker, K. A. Storz, D. Reeves, S. J. Buskirk, J. A. Sloan, and S. J. Swensen, "Impact of Organizational Leadership on Physician Burnout and Satisfaction," *Mayo Clinic Proceedings* 90, no. 4 (April 2015): 432-40. doi: http://dx.doi.org/10.1016/j.mayocp.2015.01.012.

21  American Psychological Association, "Stress in America," report released Feb. 7, 2013, accessed May 12, 2016, https://www.apa.org/news/press/releases/stress/2012/full-report.pdf.

22  Conscious Capitalism, "The Four Principles of Conscious Capitalism," accessed June 30, 2016, http://www.consciouscapitalism.org/aboutus.

23  Academy of Integrative Health and Medicine (AIHM), "What Is Integrative Medicine?," accessed May 18, 2016, https://www.aihm.org/about/what-is-integrative-medicine/.

24  Academy of Integrative Health and Medicine (AIHM), "Vision, Mission, Values," accessed May 12, 2016, http://aihm.org/about/mission-values-and-goals/.

25   Online Etymology Dictionary, s.v. "health," accessed May 12, 2016, http://www.etymonline.com/index.php?term=health.

26   J. Neuberger, "Do We Need a New Word for Patients? Let's Do away with 'Patients,'" *BMJ* 318 (June 26, 1999): 1756. doi: http://dx.doi.org/10.1136/bmj.318.7200.1756.

27   Academy of Integrative Health and Medicine (AIHM), "Vision, Mission, Values," accessed May 12, 2016, http://www.aihm.org/about/academy-values/. To learn more about AIHM, visit http://aihm.org.

## Chapter 2: Learn How Your Brain Works to Better Work Your Brain

1   The Leadership Circle, "Leadership Circle Profile."

2   Project on the Decade of the Brain, accessed May 12, 2016, http://www.loc.gov/loc/brain/.

3   Quote Investigator, quote attributed to Emerson M. Pugh, accessed May 12, 2016, http://quoteinvestigator.com/2016/03/05/brain/.

4   P. D. MacLean, *The Triune Brain in Evolution: Role in Paleocerebral Functions* (New York: Plenum Press, 1990); *The Evolutionary Neuroethology of Paul MacLean: Convergences and Frontiers,* Gerald A. Cory and Russell Gardner, eds. (Westport, CT: Greenwood Publishing Group, 2002). *The Evolutionary Neuroethology of Paul MacLean* addresses some of the controversies around McLean's model and also offers a rebuttal.

5   Daniel J. Siegel, *The Mindful Brain: Reflection and Attunement in the Cultivation of Well-Being* (New York: W. W. Norton, 2007), 34.

6   C. A. Seger and B. J. Spiering, "A Critical Review of Habit Learning and the Basal Ganglia," *Frontiers in Systems Neuroscience* 5 (August 30, 2011): 66. doi: http://dx.doi.org/10.3389/fnsys.2011.00066.

7   N. D. Volkow, G. J. Wang, J. S. Fowler, D. Tomasi, F. Telang, and R. Baler, "Addiction: Decreased Reward Sensitivity and Increased Expectation Sensitivity Conspire to Overwhelm the Brain's Control Circuit," *BioEssays* 32, no. 9 (September 2010): 748-55. doi: http://dx.doi.org/10.1002/bies.201000042.

8   MacLean, *The Triune Brain.* This point is also supported by the following research evidence: L. R. Baxter Jr., R. F. Ackermann, E. C. Clark, and J. E. Baxter, "Brain Mediation of Anolis Social Dominance Displays. I. Differential Basal Ganglia Activation," *Brain, Behavior and Evolution* 57, no. 4 (April 2001): 169-83. doi: http://dx.doi.org/10.1159/000047235; L. R. Baxter Jr., "Basal Ganglia Systems in Ritualistic Social Displays: Reptiles and Humans; Function and Illness," *Physiology & Behavior* 79, no. 3 (Aug 2003): 451-60. doi: http://dx.doi.org/10.1016/S0031-9384(03)00164-1; N. Greenberg, "Sociality, Stress, and the Corpus Striatum of the Green Anolis Lizard," *Physiology & Behavior* 79, no. 3 (August 2003): 429-40. doi: http://dx.doi.org/10.1016/S0031-9384(03)00162-8.

9   Siegel, *The Mindful Brain,* 34-35.

10   A. Viard, P. Piolino, B. Desgranges, G. Chételat, K. Lebreton, B. Landeau, A. Young, V. De La Sayette, and F. Eustache, "Hippocampal Activation for Autobiographical Memories over the Entire Lifetime in Healthy Aged Subjects: An fMRI Study," *Cerebral Cortex* 17, no. 10 (October 2007): 2453-67. doi: http://dx.doi.org/10.1093/cercor/bhl153.

11    E. A. Phelps, "Human Emotion and Memory: Interactions of the Amygdala and Hippocampal Complex," *Current Opinion in Neurobiology* 14, no. 2 (April 2004): 198-202. doi: http://dx.doi.org/10.1016/j.conb.2004.03.015.

12    Rick Hanson, *Hardwiring Happiness: The New Brain Science of Contentment, Calm, and Confidence* (New York: Crown Publishing, 2013), xxvi.

13    T. Steimer, "The Biology of Fear- and Anxiety-Related Behaviors," *Dialogues in Clinical Neuroscience* 4, no. 3 (2002): 231-249.

14    Siegel, *The Mindful Brain,* 35-40; also see BrainFacts.org, "Neuroanatomy," created April 1, 2012, accessed July 8, 2016, http://www.brainfacts.org/brain-basics/ neuroanatomy/articles/2012/mapping-the-brain/.

15    X. Gu, P. R. Hof, K. J. Friston, and J. Fan, "Anterior Insular Cortex and Emotional Awareness," *Journal of Comparative Neurology* 521, no. 15 (October 2013): 3371-3388. doi: http://dx.doi.org/10.1002/cne.23368; S. Cacioppo, F. Bianchi-Demicheli, C. Frum, J. G. Pfaus, and J. W. Lewis, "The Common Neural Bases between Sexual Desire and Love: A Multilevel Kernel Density fMRI Analysis," *The Journal of Sexual Medicine* 9, no. 4 (April 2012): 1048-54. doi: http://dx.doi.org/10.1111/j.1743-6109.2012.02651.x.

16    Siegel, *The Mindful Brain,* 40-44; 152; 337-345.

17    Kelly McGonigal, *The Willpower Instinct: How Self-control Works, Why It Matters, and What You Can Do to Get More of It* (New York: Avery, 2012), 12-14; 36-37.

18    S.M. Fleming and R. J. Dolan, "The Neural Basis of Metacognitive Ability," *Philosophical Transactions of the Royal Society B: Biological Sciences* 367, no. 1594 (May 19, 2012): 1338-49. doi: http://dx.doi.org/10.1098/rstb.2011.0417; T. Jankowski and P. Holas, "Metacognitive Model of Mindfulness," *Consciousness and Cognition* 28 (August 2014): 64-80. doi: http://dx.doi.org/10.1016/j.concog.2014.06.005.

19    Brain Rules by John Medina, "Rule #4: We Don't Pay Attention to Boring Things," accessed May 12, 2016, http://www.brainrules.net/attention.

20    Joseph E. LeDoux, *The Emotional Brain: the Mysterious Underpinnings of Emotional Life* (New York: Simon & Schuster, 1996).

21    A. H. Maslow, "A Theory of Human Motivation," *Psychological Review* 50, no. 4 (July 7, 1943): 370-396.

22    Maslach and Jackson, "The Measurement of Experienced Burnout."

23    R. L. Buckner, J. R. Andrews-Hanna, and D. L. Schacter, "The Brain's Default Network: Anatomy, Function, and Relevance to Disease," *Annals of the New York Academy of Sciences* 1124 (March 2008): 1-38. doi: http://dx.doi.org/10.1196/annals.1440.011; C. L. Philippi and M. Koenigs, "The Neuropsychology of Self-Reflection in Psychiatric Illness," *Journal of Psychiatric Research* 54 (July 2014): 55-63. doi: http://dx.doi.org /10.1016/j.jpsychires.2014.03.004.

24    M. D. Fox, A. Z. Snyder, J. L. Vincent, M. Corbetta, D. C. Van Essen, and M. E. Raichle, "The Human Brain Is Intrinsically Organized into Dynamic, Anticorrelated Functional Networks," *Proceedings of the National Academy of Sciences USA* 102, no. 27 (July 5, 2005): 9673-8. doi: http://dx.doi.org/10.1073/pnas.0504136102.

[25] X. Di and B. B. Biswal, "Modulatory Interactions between the Default Mode Network and Task Positive Networks in Resting-State," *PeerJ* 2, no. 367 (May 1, 2014): e367. doi: http://dx.doi.org/10.7717/peerj.367.

[26] Daniel J. Siegel, *The Developing Mind: How Relationships and the Brain Interact to Shape Who We Are*, 2nd ed. (New York: The Guilford Press, 2015), 2-3.

[27] Siegel, *The Mindful Brain*, 48-50.

[28] Arne Dietrich, *How Creativity Happens in the Brain* (New York: Palgrave Macmillan, 2015), 48-49.

[29] The American Institute of Stress, "What Is Stress?," accessed May 1, 2016, http://www.stress.org/what-is-stress/.

[30] J. Blascovich and W. B. Mendes, "Social Psychophysiology and Embodiment," in *The Handbook of Social Psychology*, 5th ed., eds. S. T. Fiske, D. T. Gilbert, and G. Lindzey (New York: John Wiley & Sons, Inc., 2010), 207.

[31] Dietrich, *How Creativity Happens in the Brain*, 116-126.

[32] Daniel Goleman, *Emotional Intelligence: Why It Can Matter More Than IQ*, 10th Anniversary Edition (New York: Bantam Books, 2005), 17.

[33] Kelly McGonigal, *The Upside of Stress: Why Stress Is Good for You, and How to Get Good at It*, 2nd edition (New York: Avery, 2015), xxi.

[34] J. Blascovich and I. Tomaka, "The Biopsychosocial Model of Arousal Regulation," *Advances in Experimental Social Psychology* 28 (1996): 1-5; J. Blascovich, W. B. Mendes, S. B. Hunter, and K. Salomon, "Social 'Facilitation' as Challenge and Threat," *Journal of Personality and Social Psychology* 77, no. 1 (July 1999): 68-77. doi: http://dx.doi.org/10.1037/0022-3514.77.1.68; J. Blascovich, W. B. Mendes, J. Tomaka, K. Salomon, and M. Seery, "The Robust Nature of the Biopsychosocial Model Challenge and Threat: A Reply to Wright and Kirby," *Personality and Social Psychology Review* 7, no. 3 (2003): 234-43. doi: http://dx.doi.org/10.1207/S15327957PSPR0703_03; Blascovich and Mendes, "Social Psychophysiology and Embodiment," 203-210.

[35] S. E. Taylor, L. C. Klein, B. P. Lewis, T. L. Gruenewald, R. A. R. Gurung, and J. A. Updegraff, "Biobehavioral Responses to Stress in Females: Tend-and-Befriend, not Fight-or-Flight," *Psychological Review* 107 (2000): 411-429. doi: http://dx.doi.org/10.1037/0033-295X.107.3.411.

[36] Blascovich and Tomaka, "The Biopsychosocial Model of Arousal Regulation"; Blascovich et al., "Social 'Facilitation' as Challenge and Threat"; Blascovich et al., "The Robust Nature of the Biopsychosocial Model Challenge and Threat"; Blascovich and Mendes, "Social Psychophysiology and Embodiment," 203-210.

[37] R. A. Dienstbier, "Arousal and Physiological Toughness: Implications for Mental and Physical Health," *Psychological Review* 96 (1989): 84–100. doi: http://dx.doi.org/10.1037/0033-295X.96.1.84.

[38] Jim Blascovich, personal communication with author, May 19, 2016.

[39] Blascovich and Mendes, "Social Psychophysiology and Embodiment," 208.

[40] A. Hänsel and R. von Känel, "The Ventro-Medial Prefrontal Cortex: A Major Link between the Autonomic Nervous System, Regulation of Emotion, and Stress Reactivity?," *BioPsychoSocial Medicine* 2 (November 5, 2008): 21. doi: http://dx.doi.org/10.1186/1751-0759-2-21.

41   Committee on Women's Health Research, Board on Population Health, and Public Health Practice, *Women's Health Research: Progress, Pitfalls, and Promise* (Washington, DC: National Academies Press, 2010), 59.

42   A. Martens, J. Greenberg, and J. J. Allen, "Self-Esteem and Autonomic Physiology: Parallels between Self-Esteem and Cardiac Vagal Tone as Buffers of Threat," *Personality and Social Psychology Review* 12, no. 4 (November 2008): 370-89. doi: http://dx.doi.org /10.1177/1088868308323224.

43   K. Koslov, W. B. Mendes, P. E. Pajtas, and D. A. Pizzagalli, "Asymmetry in Resting Intracortical Activity as a Buffer to Social Threat," *Psychological Science* 22 (2011): 641-49. doi: http://dx.doi.org/10.1177/0956797611403156.

44   M. D. Mumford, "Where Have We Been, Where Are We Going? Taking Stock in Creativity Research," *Creativity Research Journal* 15 (2003): 107–120. doi: http://dx.doi.org/10.1080/10400419.2003.9651403; Robert J. Sternberg, "Creativity," in *Cognitive Psychology*, 6th ed. (Belmont, CA: Wadsworth, Cengage Learning, 2012), 479.

45   These theories of creativity include Arne Dietrich's Darwinian theory of creativity, which proposes creativity involves a process that generates a variability of ideas and our brain selects between them (Dietrich, *How Creativity Happens in the Brain,* 67); the works of Donald Campbell and Dean Keith Simonton on blind variation and selective retention (D. T. Campbell, "Blind Variation and Selective Retention in Creative Thought as in Other Knowledge Processes," *Psychological Review* 67 [November 1960]: 380-400; D. K. Simonton, "Creativity and Discovery as Blind Variation: Campbell's (1960) BVSR Model After the Half-Century Mark," *Review of General Psychology* 15 [2011}: 158–174. doi: http://dx.doi.org/10.1037/a0022912); and the process of divergent and convergent thinking put forward by Joy Paul Guilford in J. P. Guilford, *The Nature of Human Intelligence* (New York: McGraw-Hill, 1967).

46   Guilford, *The Nature of Human Intelligence.*

47   R. E. Jung, B. S. Mead, J. Carrasco, and R. A. Flores, "The Structure of Creative Cognition in the Human Brain," *Frontiers in Human Neuroscience* 7 (July 8, 2013): 330. doi: http://dx.doi.org/10.3389/fnhum.2013.00330.

48   A. Dietrich, "Functional Neuroanatomy of Altered States of Consciousness: The Transient Hypofrontality Hypothesis," *Consciousness and Cognition* 12, no. 2 (June 2003): 231-56. doi: http://dx.doi.org/10.1016/S1053-8100(02)00046-6.

49   *Wikipedia, The Free Encyclopedia,* s.v. "Yesterday (Beatles Song)," accessed July 9, 2016, https://en.wikipedia.org/wiki/Yesterday_(Beatles_song).

50   Brilliant Dreams, "Twelve Famous Dreams: Creativity and Famous Discoveries from Dreams," accessed May 12, 2016, http://www.brilliantdreams.com/product/famous-dreams.htm.

51   A. Dietrich, "The Cognitive Neuroscience of Creativity," *Psychonomic Bulletin and Review* 11, no. 6 (December 2004): 1011-26. doi: http://dx.doi.org/10.3758/BF03196731.

52   *Wikipedia, The Free Encyclopedia,* s.v. "Yesterday (Beatles Song)."

53   C. J. Limb and A. R. Braun, "Neural Substrates of Spontaneous Musical Performance: An fMRI Study of Jazz Improvisation," *PLOS ONE* 3, no. 2 (2008): e1679. doi: http://dx.doi.org/10.1371/journal.pone.0001679. (A similar finding also occurred in a study with improvisation on freestyle rap: S. Liu, H. M. Chow, Y. Xu, M. G. Erkkinen, K. E.

Swett, M. W. Eagle, D. A. Rizik-Baer, and A. R. Braun, "Neural Correlates of Lyrical Improvisation: An FMRI Study of Freestyle Rap," *Scientific Reports* 2 (2012): 834. doi: http://dx.doi.org/10.1038/srep00834.)

54    Johns Hopkins Medicine, "This is Your Brain on Jazz: Researchers Use MRI to Study Spontaneity, Creativity," February 26, 2008, accessed May 12, 2016, http://www.hopkinsmedicine.org/news/media/releases/this_is_your_brain_on_jazz_researchers_use_mri_to_study_spontaneity_creativity.

55    Mihaly Csikszentmihalyi, *Flow: The Psychology of Optimal Experience* (New York: Harper Perennial Modern Classics, 2008).

56    A. Dietrich, "Neurocognitive Mechanisms Underlying the Experience of Flow," *Consciousness and Cognition* 13, no. 4 (December 2004): 746-61. doi: http://dx.doi.org/10.1016/j.concog.2004.07.002.

57    Ibid.

58    Committee on Women's Health Research, *Women's Health Research,* 59.

59    M. D. Lieberman, N. I. Eisenberger, M. J. Crockett, S. M. Tom, J. H. Pfeifer, and B. M. Way, "Putting Feelings into Words: Affect Labeling Disrupts Amygdala Activity in Response to Affective Stimuli," *Psychological Science* 18, no. 5 (May 2007): 421-8. doi: http://dx.doi.org/10.1111/j.1467-9280.2007.01916.x.

60    Norman Doidge, *The Brain That Changes Itself: Stories of Personal Triumph from the Frontiers of Brain Science* (New York: Penguin, 2007).

61    Jeffrey M. Schwartz and Sharon Begley, *The Mind and the Brain: Neuroplasticity and the Power of Mental Force* (New York: HarperCollins, 2002).

## Chapter 3: How to Better Work Your Brain with Mindfulness

1    Maslach and Jackson, "The Measurement of Experienced Burnout."

2    Luis Felipe Morales Knight, "Mindfulness: History, Technologies, Research, Applications," (paper, Pepperdine University, Malibu, CA, 2009) accessed May 13, 2016, https://allansousa.files.wordpress.com/2009/11/mindfulnessarticleluis.pdf.

3    Anderson Cooper, "Mindfulness," CBS News, *60 Minutes*, December 24, 2014, accessed May 13, 2016, http://www.cbsnews.com/news/mindfulness-anderson-cooper-60-minutes/.

4    Warren Rojas, "A Meditation on the Quiet Time Caucus," Roll Call, January 8, 2014, accessed May 13, 2016, http://hoh.rollcall.com/a-meditation-on-the-quiet-time-caucus/.

5    Otto Scharmer, "Davos: Mindfulness, Hotspots, and Sleepwalkers," *Huffington Post,* March 28, 2014, accessed May 13, 2016, http://www.huffingtonpost.com/otto-scharmer/davos-mindfulness-hotspot_b_4671062.html.

6    "The Mindful Revolution," *Time*, February 3, 2014, accessed May 13, 2016, http://content.time.com/time/covers/0,16641,20140203,00.html.

7    Cooper, "Mindfulness."

8    M. Goyal, S. Singh, E. M. Sibinga, N. F. Gould, A. Rowland-Seymour, R. Sharma, Z. Berger, D. Sleicher, D. D. Maron, H. M. Shihab, P. D. Ranasinghe, S. Linn, S. Saha, E. B. Bass, and J.A. Haythornthwaite, "Meditation Programs for Psychological Stress and Well-Being: A Systematic Review and Meta-Analysis," *JAMA Internal Medicine* 174, no. 3 (March 2014): 357-68. doi: http://dx.doi.org/10.1001/jamainternmed.2013.13018.

9   L. Zylowska, D. L. Ackerman, M. H. Yang, J. L. Futrell, N. L. Horton, T. S. Hale, C. Pataki, and S. L. Smalley, "Mindfulness Meditation Training in Adults and Adolescents with ADHD: A Feasibility Study," *Journal of Attention Disorders* 11, no. 6 (May 2008): 737-46. doi: http://dx.doi.org/10.1177/1087054707308502.

10  H. J. Alberts, R. Thewissen, and L. Raes, "Dealing with Problematic Eating Behaviour: The Effects of a Mindfulness-Based Intervention on Eating Behaviour, Food Cravings, Dichotomous Thinking and Body Image Concern," *Appetite* 58, no. 3 (June 2012): 847-51. doi: http://dx.doi.org/10.1016/j.appet.2012.01.009; C. M. Courbasson, Y. Nishikawa, and L. B. Shapira, "Mindfulness-Action Based Cognitive Behavioral Therapy for Concurrent Binge Eating Disorder and Substance Use Disorders," *Eating Disorders* 19, no. 1 (January-February 2011): 17-33. doi: http://dx.doi.org/10.1080/106 40266.2011.533603.

11  Courbasson, Nishikawa, and Shapira, "Mindfulness-Action Based Cognitive Behavioral Therapy"; K. Hoppes, "The Application of Mindfulness-Based Cognitive Interventions in the Treatment of Co-Occurring Addictive and Mood Disorders," *CNS Spectrums* 11, no. 11 (2006): 829-51.

12  E. L. Garland, S. A. Gaylord, O. Palsson, K. Faurot, Mann J. Douglas, and W. E. Whitehead, "Therapeutic Mechanisms of a Mindfulness-Based Treatment for IBS: Effects on Visceral Sensitivity, Catastrophizing, and Affective Processing of Pain Sensations," *Journal of Behavioral Medicine* 35, no. 6 (December 2012): 591-602. doi: http://dx.doi. org/10.1007/s10865-011-9391-z; B. Ljótsson, L. Falk, A. W. Vesterlund, E. Hedman, P. Lindfors, C. Rück, T. Hursti, S. Andréewitch, L. Jansson, N. Lindefors, and G. Andersson, "Internet-Delivered Exposure and Mindfulness Based Therapy for Irritable Bowel Syndrome—a Randomized Controlled Trial," *Behaviour Research and Therapy* 48, no. 6 (June 2010): 531-9. doi: http://dx.doi.org/10.1016/j.brat.2010.03.003.

13  J. Kabat-Zinn, E. Wheeler, T. Light, A. Skillings, M. J. Scharf, T. G. Cropley, D. Hosmer, and J. D. Bernhard, "Influence of a Mindfulness Meditation-Based Stress Reduction Intervention on Rates of Skin Clearing in Patients with Moderate to Severe Psoriasis Undergoing Phototherapy (UVB) and Photochemotherapy (PUVA)," *Psychosomatic Medicine* 60, no. 5 (September-October 1998): 625-32.

14  P. Grossman, U. Tiefenthaler-Gilmer, A. Raysz, and U. Kesper, "Mindfulness Training as an Intervention for Fibromyalgia: Evidence of Postintervention and 3-Year Follow-Up Benefits in Well-Being," *Psychotherapy Psychosomatics* 76, no. 4 (2007): 226-33. doi: http://dx.doi.org/10.1159/000101501; S. Schmidt, P. Grossman, B. Schwarzer, S. Jena, J. Naumann, and H. Walach, "Treating Fibromyalgia with Mindfulness-Based Stress Reduction: Results from a 3-Armed Randomized Controlled Trial," *Pain* 152, no. 2 (February 2011): 361-9. doi: http://dx.doi.org/10.1016/j.pain.2010.10.043; S. E. Sephton, P. Salmon, I. Weissbecker, C. Ulmer, A. Floyd, K. Hoover, and J. L. Studts, "Mindfulness Meditation Alleviates Depressive Symptoms in Women with Fibromyalgia: Results of a Randomized Clinical Trial," *Arthritis & Rheumatology* 57, no. 1 (February 15, 2007): 77-85. doi: http://dx.doi.org/10.1002/art.22478.

15  J. Dalen, B. W. Smith, B. M. Shelley, A. L. Sloan, L. Leahigh, and D. Begay, "Pilot Study: Mindful Eating and Living (MEAL): Weight, Eating Behavior, and Psychological

Outcomes Associated with a Mindfulness-Based Intervention for People with Obesity," *Complementary Therapies in Medicine* 18, no. 6 (December 2010): 260-4. doi: http://dx.doi.org/10.1016/j.ctim.2010.09.008; J. Daubenmier, J. Kristeller, F. M. Hecht, N. Maninger, M. Kuwata, K. Jhaveri, R. H. Lustig, M. Kemeny, L. Karan, and E. Epel, "Mindfulness Intervention for Stress Eating to Reduce Cortisol and Abdominal Fat among Overweight and Obese Women: An Exploratory Randomized Controlled Study," *Journal of Obesity* (2011): Article ID 651936. doi: http://dx.doi.org/10.1155/2011/651936; E. B. Loucks, W. B. Britton, C. J. Howe, R. Gutman, S. E. Gilman, J. Brewer, C. B. Eaton, and S. L. Buka, "Associations of Dispositional Mindfulness with Obesity and Central Adiposity: the New England Family Study," *International Journal of Behavioral Medicine* 23, no. 2 (April 2016): 224-33. doi: http://dx.doi.org/10.1007/s12529-015-9513-z.

[16] E. B. Loucks, W. B. Britton, C. J. Howe, C. B. Eaton, and S. L. Buka, "Positive Associations of Dispositional Mindfulness with Cardiovascular Health: The New England Family Study," *International Journal of Behavioral Medicine* 22, no. 4 (August 2015): 540-50. doi: http://dx.doi.org/10.1007/s12529-014-9448-9.

[17] M. D. Mrazek, M. S. Franklin, D. T. Phillips, B. Baird, and J. W. Schooler, "Mindfulness Training Improves Working Memory Capacity and GRE Performance while Reducing Mind Wandering," *Psychological Science* 24, no. 5 (May 2013): 224-33. doi: http://dx.doi.org/10.1177/0956797612459659.

[18] T. L. Jacobs, P.R. Shaver, E. S. Epel, A. P. Zanesco, S. R. Aichele, D. A. Bridwell, E. L. Rosenberg, B. G. King, K. A. MacLean, B. K. Sahdra, M. E. Kemeny, E. Ferrer, B. A. Wallace, and C. D. Saron, "Self-Reported Mindfulness and Cortisol during a Shamatha Meditation Retreat," *Health Psychology* 32, no. 10 (October 2013): 1104-9. doi: http://dx.doi.org/10.1037/a0031362.

[19] T. L. Jacobs, E. S. Epel, J. Lin, E. H. Blackburn, O. M. Wolkowitz, D. A. Bridwell, A. P. Zanesco, S. R. Aichele, B. K. Sahdra, K. A. MacLean, B. G King, P. R. Shaver, E. L. Rosenberg, E. Ferrer, B. A. Wallace, C. D. Saron, "Intensive Meditation Training, Immune Cell Telomerase Activity, and Psychological Mediators," *Psychoneuroendocrinology* 36, no. 5 (June 2011): 664-81. doi: http://dx.doi.org/10.1016/j.psyneuen.2010.09.010.

[20] C. P. West, L. N. Dyrbye, J. T. Rabatin, T. G. Call, J. H. Davidson, A. Multari, S. A. Romanski, J. M. Hellyer, J. A. Sloan, and T. D. Shanafelt, "Intervention to Promote Physician Well-Being, Job Satisfaction, and Professionalism: A Randomized Clinical Trial," *JAMA Internal Medicine* 174, no. 4 (April 2014): 527-33. doi: http://dx.doi.org/10.1001/jamainternmed.2013.14387.

[21] J. E. Stahl, M. L. Dossett, A. S. LaJoie, J. W. Denninger, D. H. Mehta, R. Goldman, G. L. Fricchione, and H. Benson, "Relaxation Response and Resiliency Training and Its Effect on Healthcare Resource Utilization," *PLOS One* 10, no. 10 (October 13, 2015): e0140212. doi: http://dx.doi.org/10.1371/journal.pone.0140212.

[22] Joe Pinsker, "Corporations' Newest Productivity Hack: Meditation," *The Atlantic,* March 10, 2015, accessed May 13, 2016, http://www.theatlantic.com/business/archive/2015/03/corporations-newest-productivity-hack-meditation/387286/.

23  B. K. Hölzel, J. Carmody, K. C. Evans, E. A. Hoge, J. A. Dusek, L. Morgan, R. K. Pitman, and S. W. Lazar, "Stress Reduction Correlates with Structural Changes in the Amygdala," *Social Cognitive & Affective Neuroscience* 5, no. 1 (March 2010): 11-7. doi: http://dx.doi.org/10.1093/scan/nsp034.

24  A. Lutz, L. L. Greischar, N. B. Rawlings, M. Ricard, and R. J. Davidson, "Long-Term Meditators Self-Induce High-Amplitude Gamma Synchrony during Mental Practice," *Proceedings of the National Academy of Sciences USA* 101, no. 46 (November 16, 2004): 16369-73. doi: http://dx.doi.org/10.1073/pnas.0407401101; J. A. Brefczynski-Lewis, A. Lutz, H. S. Schaefer, D. B. Levinson, and R. J. Davidson, "Neural Correlates of Attentional Expertise in Long-Term Meditation Practitioners," *Proceedings of the National Academy of Sciences USA* 104, no. 27 (July 3, 2007): 11483-8. doi: http://dx.doi.org/10.1073/pnas.0606552104; A. Lutz, J. Brefczynski-Lewis, T. Johnstone, and R. J. Davidson, "Regulation of the Neural Circuitry of Emotion by Compassion Meditation: Effects of Meditative Expertise," *PLOS One* 3, no. 3 (March 26, 2008): e1897. doi: http://dx.doi.org/10.1371/journal.pone.0001897.

25  Mat Smith, "Life Lessons from the World's Happiest Man," *Esquire,* December 15, 2015, accessed May 13, 2016, http://www.esquire.co.uk/culture/news/a4915/matthieu-ricard-what-ive-learned/.

26  R. J. Davidson, J. Kabat-Zinn, J. Schumacher, M. Rosenkranz, D. Muller, S. F. Santorelli, F. Urbanowski, A. Harrington, K. Bonus, and J. F. Sheridan, "Alterations in Brain and Immune Function Produced by Mindfulness Meditation," *Psychosomatic Medicine* 65, no. 4 (July-August 2003): 564-70. doi: http://dx.doi.org/10.1097/01. PSY.0000077505.67574.E3.

27  Jon Kabat-Zinn, *Wherever You Go There You Are: Mindfulness Meditation in Everyday Life* (New York: Hyperion, 1994), 4.

28  S. L. Shapiro, L. E. Carlson, J. A. Astin, and B. Freedman, "Mechanisms of Mindfulness," *Journal of Clinical Psychology* 62, no. 3 (March 2006): 373-86. doi: http://dx.doi.org/10.1002/jclp.20237.

29  D. H. Shapiro, "A Preliminary Study of Long Term Meditators: Goals, Effects, Religious Orientation, Cognitions," *Journal of Transpersonal Psychology* 24, no. 1 (1992), 23–39.

30  First People, "Native American Legends: Two Wolves, A Cherokee Legend," accessed May 13, 2016, http://www.firstpeople.us/FP-Html-Legends/TwoWolves-Cherokee.html.

31  R. A. Emmons and M. E. McCullough, "Counting Blessings Versus Burdens: An Experimental Investigation of Gratitude and Subjective Well-Being in Daily Life," *Journal of Personality and Social Psychology* 84, no. 2 (February 2003): 377-89. doi: http://dx.doi.org/10.1037/0022-3514.84.2.377; R. A. Sansone and L. A. Sansone, "Gratitude and Well Being: the Benefits of Appreciation," Psychiatry (Edgmont) 7, no. 11 (November 2010): 18-22.

32  Full of Mindfulness, "Mindfulness–Japanese Kanji," August 22, 2015, accessed May 13, 2016, https://fullofmindfulness.wordpress.com/2014/08/22/mindfulness-japanese-kanji/.

33  Dr. Dan Siegel, "Wheel of Awareness," Inspire to Rewire, accessed May 13, 2016, http://www.drdansiegel.com/resources/wheel_of_awareness/.

34    BrainyQuote.com, "Viktor E. Frankl Quotes," accessed August 1, 2016, http://www.brainyquote.com/quotes/quotes/v/viktorefr160380.html.

35    W. Hasenkamp, C. D. Wilson-Mendenhall, E. Duncan, and L. W. Barsalou, "Mind Wandering and Attention during Focused Meditation: A Fine-Grained Temporal Analysis of Fluctuating Cognitive States," *Neuroimage* 59, no. 1 (January 2, 2012): 750-60. doi: http://dx.doi.org/10.1016/j.neuroimage.2011.07.008.

36    The Leadership Circle, "Leadership Circle Profile."

## Chapter 4: Introducing the 4 in 4 Framework to Engage Conscious Leadership

1    Alex J. Zautra, John Stuart Hall, and Kate E. Murray, "Resilience: A New Definition of Health for People and Communities," in *Handbook of Adult Resilience,* reprint edition, John W. Reich, Alex J. Zautra, and John Stuart Hall, eds. (New York: The Guilford Press, 2012), 4.

2    R. Yerkes and J. Dodson, "The Relation of Strength of Stimulus to Rapidity of Habit Formation," *Journal of Comparative Neurology and Psychology* 18 (1908): 459–482.

3    Csikszentmihalyi, *Flow.*

4    Lieberman et al., "Putting Feelings into Words."

5    Hölzel et al., "Stress Reduction Correlates with Structural Changes in the Amygdala."

6    Albert Ellis and Debbie Joffe Ellis, *Rational Emotive Behavior Therapy* (American Psychological Association, 3 ed., 2011).

7    K. N. Ochsner, S. A. Bunge, J. J. Gross, and J. D. Gabrieli, "Rethinking Feelings: An FMRI Study of the Cognitive Regulation of Emotion," *Journal of Cognitive Neuroscience* 14, no. 8 (November 15, 2002): 1215-29. doi: http://dx.doi.org/10.1162/089892902760807212.

8    J. J. Gross and O. P. John, "Individual Differences in Two Emotion Regulation Processes: Implications for Affect, Relationships, and Well-Being," *Journal of Personality and Social Psychology* 85, no. 2 (August 2003): 348-62. doi: http://dx.doi.org/10.1037/0022-3514.85.2.348.

9    G. Modinos, J. Ormel, and A. Aleman, "Individual Differences in Dispositional Mindfulness and Brain Activity Involved in Reappraisal of Emotion," *Social Cognitive & Affective Neuroscience* 5, no. 4 (December 2010): 369-377. doi: http://dx.doi.org/10.1093/scan/nsq006.

10    E. Garland, S. Gaylord, and J. Park, "The Role of Mindfulness in Positive Reappraisal," *Explore (NY)* 5, no. 1 (January-February 2009): 37-44. doi: http://dx.doi.org/10.1016/j.explore.2008.10.001.

11    Martin Seligman, *Flourish: A Visionary New Understanding of Happiness and Well-Being* (New York: Free Press, 2011).

12    Davidson et al., "Alterations in Brain and Immune Function Produced by Mindfulness Meditation"; Koslov et al., "Asymmetry in Resting Intracortical Activity as a Buffer to Social Threat."

13    Daniel G. Amen, *Change Your Brain, Change Your Life* (New York: Harmony Books, 1998), 56.

## Chapter 5: Step 1: Recognizing and Managing Reactivity

[1]   The American Institute of Stress, "What Is Stress?"

[2]   Merriam-Webster, s.v. "stress," accessed May 13, 2016, http://www.merriam-webster.com /dictionary/stress.

[3]   James H. Humphrey, ed. *Anthology of Stress Revisited* (Hauppauge, NY: Nova Science Publishers, 2005), viii.

[4]   McGonigal, *The Upside of Stress,* xxi.

[5]   Goodreads, "Albert Einstein Quote," accessed May 1, 2016, http://www.goodreads.com/ quotes/429690-the-most-important-decision-we-make-is-whether-we-believe.

[6]   Merriam-Webster, s.v. "emotion," accessed May 13, 2016, http://www.merriam-webster.com /dictionary/emotion; Dictionary.com, s.v. "emotion," accessed May 13, 2016, http://www.dictionary.com/browse/emotion.

[7]   K. R. Scherer, "What Are Emotions? And How Can They Be Measured?" *Social Science Information* 44 (2005): 693–727. doi: http://dx.doi.org/10.1177/0539018405058216; L. F. Barrett, B. Mesquita, K. N. Ochsner, and J. J. Gross, "The Experience of Emotion," *Annual Review of Psychology* 58 (2007): 373-403. doi: http://dx.doi.org/10.1146/annurev.psych. 58.110405.085709.

[8]   C. Darwin, *The Expression of the Emotions in Man and Animals* (London: John Murray, 1872); U. Hess and P. Thibault, "Darwin and Emotion Expression," American Psychology 64, no. 2 (February-March 2009): 120-8. doi: http://dx.doi.org/10.1037/ a0013386.

[9]   P. Ekman and W. V. Friesen, "Constants across Cultures in the Face and Emotion," *Journal of Personality and Social Psychology* 17 (1971): 124–129. doi: http://dx.doi.org/10.1037/ h0030377.

[10]   James Russell, "A Circumplex Model of Affect," *Journal of Personality and Social Psychology* 39 (1980): 1161–1178. doi: http://dx.doi.org/10.1037/h0077714.

[11]   The Leadership Circle, "Leadership Circle Profile."

[12]   National Institutes of Health, "Genetics of Alcohol Use Disorder," National Institute on Alcohol Abuse and Alcoholism, accessed May 1, 2016, http://www.niaaa.nih.gov/ alcohol-health/overview-alcohol-consumption/alcohol-use-disorders/genetics-alcohol-use-disorders.

[13]   J. Suls, "Anger and the Heart: Perspectives on Cardiac Risk, Mechanisms and Interventions," *Progress in Cardiovascular Diseases* 55, no. 6 (May-June 2013): 538-47. doi: http://dx.doi.org/10.1016/j.pcad.2013.03.002.

[14]   *Alcoholics Anonymous,* 4th ed. (New York: A.A. World Services, 2001), 64, 66.

[15]   G. S. Everly Jr. and J. M. Lating, *A Clinical Guide to the Treatment of the Human Stress Response* (New York: Springer, 2002), 225-226.

[16]   R. McCraty, M. Atkinson, and D. Tomasino, "Impact of a Workplace Stress Reduction Program on Blood Pressure and Emotional Health in Hypertensive Employees," *Journal of Alternative and Complementary Medicine* 9, no. 3 (2003): 355-69. doi: http://dx.doi.org /10.1089/107555303765551589; R. McCraty, M. Atkinson, D. Tomasino, J. Goelitz, and H. N. Mayrovitz, "The Impact of an Emotional Self-Management Skills Course on Psychosocial Functioning and Autonomic Recovery to Stress in Middle School

Children," *Integrative Physiological and Behavioral Science* 34, no. 4 (1999): 246-68. doi: http://dx.doi.org/10.1007/BF02688693; R. McCraty, B. Barrios-Choplin, D. Rozman, M. Atkinson, and A. D. Watkins, "The Impact of a New Emotional Self-Management Program on Stress, Emotions, Heart Rate Variability, DHEA and Cortisol," *Integrative Physiological and Behavioral Science* 33, no. 2 (1998): 151-70. doi: http://dx.doi.org /10.1007/BF02688660.

[17] Lieberman et al., "Putting Feelings into Words."

[18] J. D. Creswell, B. M. Way, N. I. Eisenberger, and M. D. Lieberman, "Neural Correlates of Dispositional Mindfulness during Affect Labeling," *Psychosomatic Medicine* 69, no. 6 (July-August 2007): 560-5. doi: http://dx.doi.org/10.1097/PSY.0b013e3180f6171f.

[19] Jalal al-Din Rumi, "The Guest House," in *The Essential Rumi*, trans. Coleman Barks and John Moyne (1995; repr., New York: HarperOne, 2004). Reprinted with permission.

## Chapter 6: Step 2: Reappraising Stress and Self-Doubt

[1] Dweck, *Mindset*, 4.

[2] The American Institute of Stress, "What Is Stress?"

[3] Russ et al., "Association between Psychological Distress and Mortality."

[4] A. Keller, K. Litzelman, L. E. Wisk, T. Maddox, E. R. Cheng, P. D. Creswell, and W. P. Witt, "Does the Perception that Stress Affects Health Matter? The Association with Health and Mortality," *Health Psychology* 31, no. 5 (September 2012): 677-84. doi: http://dx.doi.org/10.1037/a0026743; McGonigal, *The Upside of Stress*, xii-xiii.

[5] M. Heron, D. L. Hoyert, S. L. Murphy, J. Xu, K. D. Kochanek, and B. Tejada-Vera, "Deaths: Final Data for 2006," *National Vital Statistics Report* 57, no. 14 (April 17, 2009): 1-134.

[6] A. Crum, "Evaluating a Mindset Training Program to Unleash the Enhancing Nature of Stress," *Academy of Management Proceedings*, Meeting Abstract Supplement (January 2011): 1-6; McGonigal, *The Upside of Stress*, 29-30; For more details on the three-step process used in the study to reappraising the stress mindset, see Alia Crum and Chris Lyddy, "De-stressing Stress: The Power of Mindsets and the Art of Stressing Mindfully" in *The Wiley Blackwell Handbook of Mindfulness*, vol. 1, eds. Christelle Ngnoumen, Amanda Ie, and Ellen Langer (UK: John Wiley & Sons, 2014), accessed April 2, 2016, https://mbl.stanford.edu/sites/default/files/crumlyddy_mindfulstresschapter_handbookofmindfulness_6.26.13.pdf.

[7] McGonigal, *The Upside of Stress*, 110.

[8] Ibid., 10.

[9] Ibid., 111-112.

[10] Committee on Women's Health Research, *Women's Health Research*, 59.

[11] Markus MacGill, "Oxytocin: What Is It and What Does It Do?" Medical News Today, September 21, 2015, accessed May 1, 2016, http://www.medicalnewstoday.com/articles/275795.php.

[12] McGonigal, *The Upside of Stress*, 52-53.

[13] M. J. Poulin and E. A. Holman, "Helping Hands, Healthy Body? Oxytocin Receptor Gene and Prosocial Behavior Interact to Buffer the Association between Stress and

Physical Health," *Hormones and Behavior* 63, no. 3 (March 2013): 510-17. doi: http://dx.doi.org/10.1016/j.yhbeh.2013.01.004; McGonigal, *The Upside of Stress,* 157-158.

14  Greg Bishop, "Who's Moved On? This Guy," *Sports Illustrated,* August 3, 2015, 42.

15  Jon Kabat-Zinn, *Full Catastrophe Living: Using the Wisdom of Your Body and Mind to Face Stress, Pain, and Illness* (New York: Bantam Dell, 1991).

16  A. Ellis, "Rational Psychotherapy and Individual Psychology," *Journal of Individual Psychology* 13 (1957): 38-44.

17  Dietrich, *How Creativity Happens,* 9, 116-126.

18  D. Rock, "Managing with the Brain in Mind," *Oxford Leadership Journal* 1, no. 1 (2009): 1-10.

19  Gross and John, "Individual Differences in Two Emotion Regulation Processes."

20  Ellis et al., "Rational Emotive Behavior Therapy."

21  Matt Schudel, "Albert Ellis; Pioneer in Behavioral Therapy," *The Washington Post,* July 25, 2007, accessed May 1, 2016, http://www.washingtonpost.com/wp-dyn/content/article/2007/07/24/AR2007072402199.html.

22  Modinos, Ormel, and Aleman, "Individual Differences in Dispositional Mindfulness and Brain Activity Involved in Reappraisal of Emotion."

## Chapter 7: Step 3: Cultivating Creativity

1  Yerkes and Dodson, "The Relation of Strength of Stimulus to Rapidity of Habit Formation."

2  W. Ng, E. Diener, R. Aurora, and J. Harter, "Affluence, Feelings of Stress, and Well-Being," *Social Indicators Research* 94, no. 2 (November 2008): 257-271. doi: http://dx.doi.org/10.1007/s11205-008-9422-5; McGonigal, The Upside of Stress, 63-64.

3  Seligman, *Flourish,* 16.

4  Quote Investigator, "The Great Use of a Life Is to Spend It for Something That Outlasts It," accessed April 27, 2016, http://quoteinvestigator.com/2012/11/28/great-life/.

5  Nancy Duarte, "The Secret Structure of Great Talks," TEDxEast, November 2011, accessed April 27, 2016, https://www.ted.com/talks/nancy_duarte_the_secret_structure_of_great_talks.

6  American Rhetoric, "Top 100 Speeches: Martin Luther King, Jr. *I Have a Dream*" (delivered August 28, 1963, at the Lincoln Memorial, Washington D.C.), accessed April 27, 2016, http://www.americanrhetoric.com/speeches/mlkihaveadream.htm.

7  Srinivasan S. Pillay, *Your Brain and Business: The Neuroscience of Great Leaders* (Upper Saddle River, N.J.: FT Press, 2011), 12, 171-172.

8  Gallup, "Understanding How Gallup Uses the Cantril Scale," accessed April 27, 2016, http://www.gallup.com/poll/122453/understanding-gallup-uses-cantril-scale.aspx.

9  McGonigal, *The Willpower Instinct.*

10  Michael Pollan, *In Defense of Food: An Eater's Manifesto* (London: Penguin Book, 2009), 1.

11  K. L. Olson and C. F. Emery, "Mindfulness and Weight Loss: A Systematic Review," *Psychosomatic Medicine* 77, no. 1 (January 2015): 59-67. doi: http://dx.doi.org/10.1097/PSY.0000000000000127; C. P. Earnest and T. S. Church, "Evaluation of a Voluntary Worksite Weight Loss Program on Metabolic Syndrome,"

*Metabolic Syndrome and Related Disorders* 13, no. 9 (November 2015): 406-14. doi: http://dx.doi.org/10.1089/met.2015.0075; Wally Gomaa, President ACAP Health, personal communication with the author about Naturally Slim weight loss program, April 2012.

12  National Institutes of Health, "Recommendations for Physical Activity," National Heart, Lung, and Blood Institute, accessed April 27, 2016, https://www.nhlbi.nih.gov/health/health-topics/topics/phys/recommend.

13  Max Hirshkowitz et al., "National Sleep Foundation's Sleep Time Duration Recommendations: Methodology and Results Summary," *Sleep Health* 1, no. 1 (2015): 40–43. doi: http://dx.doi.org/10.1016/j.sleh.2014.12.010.

14  B. Gardner, P. Lally, and J. Wardle, "Making Health Habitual: The Psychology of 'Habit-Formation' and General Practice," *The British Journal of General Practice* 62, no. 605 (December 2012): 664-6. doi: http://dx.doi.org/10.3399/bjgp12X659466.

15  Saddleback Church, "The Daniel Plan," accessed April 27, 2016, http://saddleback.com/connect/ministry/the-daniel-plan.

16  Charles Duhigg, *The Power of Habit: Why We Do What We Do In Life And Business* (New York: Random House, 2012).

17  P. Lally, C. H. M. van Jaarsveld, H. W. W. Potts, and J. Wardle, "How Are Habits Formed: Modelling Habit Formation in the Real World," *European Journal of Social Psychology* 40 (2010): 998–1009. doi: http://dx.doi.org/10.1002/ejsp.674.

18  *Wikipedia, The Free Encyclopedia*, s.v. "phubbing," accessed July 9, 2016, https://en.wikipedia.org/wiki/Phubbing.

19  Gary D. Chapman, *The Five Love Languages: How to Express Heartfelt Commitment to Your Mate* (Chicago: Northfield Publishing, 1995).

20  Stephen R. Covey, *The 7 Habits of Highly Effective People: Powerful Lessons in Personal Change* (New York: Simon & Schuster, 2013), 154-192.

21  William Ury, *The Power of a Positive No: Save the Deal Save the Relationship and Still Say No* (New York: Bantam Dell, 2007).

22  David Allen, *Getting Things Done: The Art of Stress-free Productivity* (New York: Penguin, 2015).

23  Jeffrey Victor Sutherland, *Scrum: The Art of Doing Twice the Work in Half the Time* (New York: Crown Business, 2014).

24  Tony Schwartz, "A 90-Minute Plan for Personal Effectiveness," *Harvard Business Review*, January 24, 2011, https://hbr.org/2011/01/the-most-important-practice-i.html; Tony Schwartz, "The 90-Minute Solution: How Building in Periods of Renewal Can Change Your Work and Your Life," *Huffpost Healthy Living*, November 17, 2011, http://www.huffingtonpost.com/tony-schwartz/work-life-balance-the-90_b_578671.html; Drake Baer, "Why You Need To Unplug Every 90 Minutes," *Fast Company*, June 19, 2013, http://www.fastcompany.com/3013188/unplug/why-you-need-to-unplug-every-90-minutes. (All accessed 28 April 2016.)

25  Nathaniel Kleitman, *Sleep and Wakefulness*, Midway Reprint (Chicago: University of Chicago, 1987).

26  P. Lavie, J. Zomer, and D. Gopher, "Ultradian Rhythms in Prolonged Human Performance" (ARI research note, Institute of Technology, Haifa, Israel, February 1995), accessed April 11, 2016, http://www.dtic.mil/cgi-bin/GetTRDoc?AD=ADA296199.

27 K. Anders Ericsson, Ralf Th. Krampe, and Clemens Tesch-Romer, "The Role of Deliberate Practice in the Acquisition of Expert Performance," *Psychological Review* 100, no. 3 (1993): 363-406.

28 Sophie Ellwood, Gerry Pallier, Allan Snyder, and Jason Gallate, "The Incubation Effect: Hatching a Solution?" *Creativity Research Journal* 21, no. 1 (2009): 6–14. doi: http://dx.doi.org/10.1080/10400410802633368.

29 G. Krampen, "Promotion of Creativity (Divergent Productions) and Convergent Productions by Systematic-Relaxation Exercises: Empirical Evidence from Five Experimental Studies with Children, Young Adults, and Elderly," *European Journal of Personality* 11 (1997): 83–99. doi: http://dx.doi.org/10.1002/(SICI)1099-0984(199706)11:2<83::AID-PER280>3.0.CO;2-5

30 M. Oppezzo and D. L. Schwartz, "Give Your Ideas Some Legs: The Positive Effect of Walking on Creative Thinking," *Journal of Experimental Psychology: Learning, Memory and Cognition* 40, no. 4 (July 2014): 1142-52. doi: http://dx.doi.org/10.1037/a0036577.

31 R. Stickgold, L. Scott, C. Rittenhouse, and J. A. Hobson, "Sleep-Induced Changes in Associative Memory," *Journal of Cognitive Neuroscience* 11 (1999): 182–193. doi: http://dx.doi.org/10.1162/089892999563319; S. M. Ritter and A. Dijksterhuis, "Creativity—the Unconscious Foundations of the Incubation Period," *Frontiers in Human Neuroscience* 8 (2014): 215. doi: http://dx.doi.org/10.3389/fnhum.2014.00215.

32 A. M Isen, K. A. Daubman, and G. P. Nowicki, "Positive Affect Facilitates Creative Problem Solving," *Journal of Personality and Social Psychology* 52, no. 6 (June 1987): 1122-31. doi: http://dx.doi.org/10.1037/0022-3514.52.6.1122; Susanne K. Vosburg, "The Effects of Positive and Negative Mood on Divergent-Thinking Performance," *Creativity Research Journal* 11, no. 2 (1998): 165-172. doi: http://dx.doi.org/10.1207/s15326934crj1102_6; Yohei Yamada and Masayoshi Nagai, "Positive Mood Enhances Divergent but Not Convergent Thinking," *Japanese Psychological Research* 57, no. 4 (2015): 281-7. doi: http://dx.doi.org/10.1111/jpr.12093.

33 J. N. Lieberman, "Playfulness and Divergent Thinking: An Investigation of Their Relationship at the Kindergarten Level," *Journal of Genetic Psychology* 107 (December 1965): 219-24.

34 Ravi Mehta and Rui (Juliet) Zhu, "Blue or Red? Exploring the Effect of Color on Cognitive Task Performances," *Science,* February 27, 2009: 1226-1229. doi: http://dx.doi.org/10.1126/science.1169144.

35 Geir Kaufmann and Suzanne K. Vosburg, "The Effects of Mood on Early and Late Idea Production," *Creativity Research Journal* 14, no. 3-4 (2002): 317-330. doi: http://dx.doi.org/10.1207/S15326934CRJ1434_3; S. Akbari Chermahini and B. Hommel, "Creative Mood Swings: Divergent and Convergent Thinking Affect Mood in Opposite Ways," *Psychological Research* 76, no. 5 (2012): 634-640. doi: http://dx.doi.org/10.1007/s00426-011-0358-z; Yamada and Nagai, "Positive Mood Enhances Divergent but Not Convergent Thinking."

36 Goodreads, "Rumi Quote," accessed June 28, 2016, http://www.goodreads.com/quotes/439208-you-were-born-with-potential-you-were-born-with-goodness. Author's note: All attempts were made to identify the current copyright holder of this poem excerpt, but we were not able to verify the original source.

## Chapter 8: Step 4: Catalyzing Growth

[1] Sharon E. Straus, W. Scott Richardson, Paul Glasziou, and R. Brian Haynes, *Evidence-Based Medicine: How to Practice and Teach Evidence-Based Medicine* (London: Churchill Livingstone, 4 ed., 2010); Daniel J. Friedland, Alan S. Go, J. Ben Davoren, Michael G. Shlipak, Stephen W. Bent, Leslee L. Subak, and Terrie Mendelson, *Evidence-Based Medicine: A Framework for Clinical Practice* (New York: McGraw-Hill, 1998).

[2] Edward Lorenz, "Predictability: Does the Flap of a Butterfly's Wings in Brazil Set off a Tornado in Texas?" (presentation for the American Association for the Advancement of Science, 139th Meeting, 1972), accessed April 10, 2016, http://eaps4.mit.edu/research/Lorenz/Butterfly_1972.pdf.

[3] The Human Memory, "Neurons & Synapses," accessed April 29, 2016, http://www.human-memory.net/brain_neurons.html.

[4] G. Fink, ed., *Stress Science: Neuroendocrinology* (Cleveland: Academic Press, 2009); Everly and Lating, *A Clinical Guide to the Treatment of the Human Stress Response,* 225-226; T. A. Eisenlohr-Moul, M. T. Fillmore, and S. C. Segerstrom, "'Pause and Plan' Includes the Liver: Self-Regulatory Effort Slows Alcohol Metabolism for Those Low in Self-Control," *Biological Psychology* 91, no. 2 (2012): 229-31. doi: http://dx.doi.org/10.1016/j.biopsycho.2012.06.006; S. C. Segerstrom, J. K. Hardy, D. R. Evans, N. F. Winters, R. A. Wright (ed.), and G. H. E. Gendolla (ed.), *Pause and Plan: Self-Regulation and the Heart* (Washington, DC: American Psychological Association Press, 2012), accessed July 9, 2016, http://psycnet.apa.org/index.cfm?fa=buy.optionToBuy&id=2011-09271-009.

[5] HeartMath, "The Science Behind the emWave and Inner Balance Technologies," accessed May 13, 2016, http://www.heartmath.com/science-behind-emwave/.

[6] McCraty, Atkinson, and Tomasino, "Impact of a Workplace Stress Reduction Program"; McCraty et al., "The Impact of an Emotional Self-Management Skills Course"; McCraty et al., "The Impact of a New Emotional Self-Management Program on Stress."

[7] Everly and Lating, *A Clinical Guide to the Treatment of the Human Stress Response,* 225-226.

[8] Dietrich, *How Creativity Happens in the Brain,* 48-49.

[9] McGonigal, *The Willpower Instinct,* 12-14, 36-37.

[10] McGonigal, *The Upside of Stress,* 52.

## Chapter 9: Cycles of Reactivity and Creativity

[1] N. I. Eisenberger, M. D. Lieberman, and K. D. Williams, "Does Rejection Hurt? An FMRI Study of Social Exclusion," *Science* 302, no. 5643 (October 10, 2003): 290-2. doi: http://dx.doi.org/10.1126/science.1089134.

[2] C. N. Dewall, G. Macdonald, G. D. Webster, C. L. Masten, R. F. Baumeister, C. Powell, D. Combs, D. R. Schurtz, T. F. Stillman, D. M. Tice, and N. I. Eisenberger, "Acetaminophen Reduces Social Pain: Behavioral and Neural Evidence," *Psychological Science* 21, no. 7 (July 2010): 931-7. doi: http://dx.doi.org/10.1177/0956797610374741.

[3] M. D. Lieberman and N. I. Eisenberger, "Neuroscience. Pains and Pleasures of Social Life," *Science* 323, no. 5916 (February 13, 2009): 890-1. doi: http://dx.doi.org/10.1126/science.1170008.

4   Ibid.

5   D. Lametti, "Mirroring Behavior: How Mirror Neurons Let Us Interact with Others," *Scientific American,* June 9, 2009, accessed May 15, 2016, http://www.scientificamerican.com/article.cfm?id=mirroring-behavior.

6   G. Rizzolatti and L. Craighero, "The Mirror-Neuron System," *Annual Review of Neuroscience* 27 (2004): 169-92. doi: http://dx.doi.org/10.1146/annurev.neuro.27.070203.144230.

7   V. S. Ramachandran, *The Tell-Tale Brain: A Neuroscientist's Quest for What Makes Us Human* (New York: W. W. Norton, 2012), 134.

8   C. Jarrett, "Mirror Neurons: The Most Hyped Concept in Neuroscience?" *Psychology Today,* December 10, 2012, accessed May 15, 2016, https://www.psychologytoday.com /blog/brain-myths/201212/mirror-neurons-the-most-hyped-concept-in-neuroscience.

9   Gregory Hickock, *The Myth of Mirror Neurons* (New York: W. W. Norton & Company, 2014), 24-25.

10  Ibid., 229

11  P. F. Ferrari and G. Rizzolatti, "Mirror Neuron Research: The Past and the Future," *Philosophical Transactions of the Royal Society London B: Biological Sciences* 369, no. 1644 (April 28, 2014): 20130169. doi: http://dx.doi.org/10.1098/rstb.2013.0169.

12  A. Lutz, L. L. Greischar, D. M. Perlman, and R. J. Davidson, "BOLD Signal in Insula is Differentially Related to Cardiac Function during Compassion Meditation in Experts vs. Novices," *Neuroimage* 47, no. 3 (2009): 1038-46. doi: http://dx.doi.org/10.1016/j. neuroimage.2009.04.081.

13  T. Singer, B. Seymour, J. O'Doherty, H. Kaube, R. J. Dolan, and C. D. Frith, "Empathy for Pain Involves the Affective but Not Sensory Components of Pain," *Science* 303, no. 5661 (February 20, 2004): 1157-62. doi: http://dx.doi.org/10.1126/science.1093535.

14  Gu et al., "Anterior Insular Cortex and Emotional Awareness."

15  Ibid.; Cacioppo et al., "The Common Neural Bases between Sexual Desire and Love."

16  Gu et al., "Anterior Insular Cortex and Emotional Awareness"; T. Singer, "The Neuronal Basis of Empathy and Fairness," *Novartis Found Symposia* 278 (2007): 20-30.

17  Singer, "The Neuronal Basis of Empathy and Fairness."

18  D. Perry, T. Hendler, and S. G. Shamay-Tsoory, "Can We Share the Joy of Others? Empathic Neural Responses to Distress vs Joy," *Social Cognitive & Affective Neuroscience* 7, no. 8 (November 2012): 909-16. doi: http://dx.doi.org/10.1093/scan/nsr073.

19  Ibid.

20  J. A. Coan, H. S. Schaefer, and R. J. Davidson, "Lending a Hand: Social Regulation of the Neural Response to Threat," *Psychological Science* 17, no. 12 (December 2006): 1032-9. doi: http://dx.doi.org/10.1111/j.1467-9280.2006.01832.x.

21  Lutz et al., "Regulation of the Neural Circuitry of Emotion by Compassion Meditation."

22  Lutz et al., "BOLD Signal in Insula is Differentially Related to Cardiac Function during Compassion Meditation in Experts vs. Novices."

23  Pillay, *Your Brain and Business,* 187.

24  A. A. Marsh, "Understanding Amygdala Responsiveness to Fearful Expressions through the Lens of Psychopathy and Altruism," *Journal of Neuroscience Research* (September 14, 2015): 513-25. doi: http://dx.doi.org/10.1002/jnr.23668; E. G. Bruneau, N. Jacoby,

and R. Saxe, "Empathic Control through Coordinated Interaction of Amygdala, Theory of Mind and Extended Pain Matrix Brain Regions," *NeuroImage* 114 (July 1, 2015): 105-19. doi: http://dx.doi.org/10.1016/j.neuroimage.2015.04.034.

25  Jonathan Dvash and Simone G. Shamay-Tsoory, "Theory of Mind and Empathy as Multidimensional Constructs: Neurological Foundations," *Topics in Language Disorders* 34, no. 4 (December 2014): 282–295. doi: http://dx.doi.org/10.1097/TLD.0000000000000040.

26  Ibid.

27  *Wikipedia: The Free Encyclopedia,* s.v. "Theory of Mind," accessed June 28, 2016, https://en.wikipedia.org/wiki/Theory_of_mind, citing D. G. Premack and G. Woodruff, "Does the Chimpanzee Have a Theory of Mind?" Behavioral and Brain Sciences 1, no. 4 (1978): 515–526. doi: http://dx.doi.org/10.1017/S0140525X00076512.

28  Dvash and Shamay-Tsoory, "Theory of Mind and Empathy as Multidimensional Constructs"; Helen L. Gallagher and Christopher D. Frith, "Functional Imaging of 'Theory of Mind,'" *Trends in Cognitive Sciences* 7, no. 2 (2003): 77–83. doi: http://dx.doi.org/10.1016/S1364-6613(02)00025-6.

29  Jessica R. Andrews-Hanna, "The Brain's Default Network and Its Adaptive Role in Internal Mentation," The Neuroscientist 18, no. 3 (June 1, 2012): 251–270. doi: http://dx.doi.org/10.1177/1073858411403316; Buckner, Andrews-Hanna, and Schacter, "The Brain's Default Network"; Philippi and Koenigs, "The Neuropsychology of Self-Reflection."

30  Matthew D. Lieberman, *Social: Why Our Brains Are Wired to Connect* (New York: Broadway Books, 2014), 181-202.

31  Ibid., 145-146.

32  J. M. Harlow, "Passage of an Iron Rod through the Head," *Boston Medical and Surgical Journal* 39 (1848): 389–393.

33  Ibid.

34  McGonigal, *The Willpower Instinct,* 14

35  R. M. Sapolsky, "The Frontal Cortex and the Criminal Justice System," *Philosophical Transactions of the Royal Society London B Biological Sciences* 359, no. 1451 (November 29, 2004): 1787–1796. doi: http://dx.doi.org/10.1098/rstb.2004.1547.

36  Daniel Goleman, "Three Kinds of Empathy: Cognitive, Emotional, Compassionate," June 12, 2007, accessed May 15, 2016, http://www.danielgoleman.info/three-kinds-of-empathy-cognitive-emotional-compassionate/.

37  O. FeldmanHall, T. Dalgleish, D. Evans, and D. Mobbs, "Empathic Concern Drives Costly Altruism," *NeuroImage* 105 (January 15, 2015): 347-56. doi: http://dx.doi.org/10.1016/j.neuroimage.2014.10.043.

38  C. L. Masten, S. A. Morelli, and N. I. Eisenberger, "An fMRI Investigation of Empathy for 'Social Pain' and Subsequent Prosocial Behavior," *NeuroImage* 55, no. 1 (March 1, 2011): 381-8. doi: http://dx.doi.org/10.1016/j.neuroimage.2010.11.060.

39  T. Tsukiura and R. Cabeza, "Shared Brain Activity for Aesthetic and Moral Judgments: Implications for the Beauty-Is-Good Stereotype," *Social Cognitive and Affective Neuroscience* 6, no. 1 (January 2011): 138-48. doi: http://dx.doi.org/10.1093/scan/nsq025.

40  T. Ishizu and S. Zeki, "Toward a Brain-Based Theory of Beauty," *PLOS ONE* 6, no. 7 (2011): e21852. doi: http://dx.doi.org/10.1371/journal.pone.0021852.

41  S. Zeki, J. P. Romaya, D. M. Benincasa, and M. F. Atiyah, "The Experience of Mathematical Beauty and Its Neural Correlates," *Fronters in Human Neuroscience* 8, no. 1 (February 13, 2014): 68. doi: http://dx.doi.org/10.3389/fnhum.2014.00068.

42  H. Plassmann, J. O'Doherty, B. Shiv, and A. Rangel, "Marketing Actions Can Modulate Neural Representations of Experienced Pleasantness," *Proceedings of the National Academy of Sciences USA* 105, no. 3 (January 22, 2008): 1050-4. doi: http://dx.doi.org /10.1073/pnas.0706929105.

43  Tsukiura and Cabeza, "Shared Brain Activity for Aesthetic and Moral Judgments."

44  L. K. Fellows and M. J. Farah, "The Role of Ventromedial Prefrontal Cortex in Decision Making: Judgment under Uncertainty or Judgment Per Se?" *Cerebral Cortex* 17, no. 11 (November 2007): 2669-74. doi: http://dx.doi.org/10.1093/cercor/bhl176.

45  H. Plassmann, J. O'Doherty, and A. Rangel, "Appetitive and Aversive Goal Values Are Encoded in the Medial Orbitofrontal Cortex at the Time of Decision Making," *The Journal of Neuroscience* 30, no. 32 (August 11, 2010): 10799-808. doi: http://dx.doi.org/10.1523/JNEUROSCI.0788-10.2010; Fellows and Farah, "The Role of Ventromedial Prefrontal Cortex in Decision Making."

46  E. F. Coccaro, M. S. McCloskey, D. A. Fitzgerald, and K. L. Phan, "Amygdala and Orbitofrontal Reactivity to Social Threat in Individuals with Impulsive Aggression," *Biological Psychiatry* 62, no. 2 (July 15, 2007): 168-78. doi: http://dx.doi.org/10.1016/j. biopsych.2006.08.024; Hänsel and von Känel, "The Ventro-Medial Prefrontal Cortex."

47  Ibid.

48  S. W. Porges, "The Polyvagal Theory: Phylogenetic Substrates of a Social Nervous System," *International Journal of Psychophysiology* 42, no. 2 (October 2001): 123-46. doi: http://dx.doi.org/10.1016/S0167-8760(01)00162-3; S. W. Porges, "Social Engagement and Attachment: A Phylogenetic Perspective," *Annals of the New York Academy of Sciences* 1008 (December 2003): 31-47. http://dx.doi.org/10.1196/annals.1301.004; S. W. Porges, "The Polyvagal Perspective," *Biological Psychology* 74, no. 2 (February 2007): 116-43. doi: http://dx.doi.org/10.1016/j.biopsycho.2006.06.009.

49  D. P. Rakel, B. P. Barrett, Z. Zhang, T. J. Hoeft, B. A. Chewning, L. Marchand, and J. Scheder, "Perception of Empathy in the Therapeutic Encounter: Effects on the Common Cold," *Patient Education and Counseling* 85, no. 3 (2011): 390-7. doi: http://dx.doi.org/10.1016/j.pec.2011.01.009; D. P. Rakel, T. J. Hoeft, B. P. Barrett, B. A. Chewning, B. M. Craig, and M. Niu, "Practitioner Empathy and the Duration of the Common Cold," *Family Medicine* 41, no. 7 (2009): 494-501.

50  Rakel, et al., "Perception of Empathy in the Therapeutic Encounter."

51  S. Lelorain, A. Brédart, S. Dolbeault, and S. Sultan, "A Systematic Review of the Associations between Empathy Measures and Patient Outcomes in Cancer Care," *Psycho-Oncology* 21, no. 12 (December, 2012): 1255-64. doi: http://dx.doi.org/10.1002/ pon.2115.

52  S. Dibbelt, M. Schaidhammer, C. Fleischer, and B. Greitemann, "Patient-Doctor Interaction in Rehabilitation: The Relationship between Perceived Interaction Quality and Long-Term Treatment Results," *Patient Education and Counseling* 76, no. 3 (2009): 328-35. doi: http://dx.doi.org/10.1055/s-0030-1263119.

53  R. Elliott, A. C. Bohart, J. C. Watson, and L. S. Greenberg, "Empathy," *Psychotherapy* 48, no. 1 (March 2011): 43-9. doi: http://dx.doi.org/10.1037/a0022187.

54  D. G. Safran, W. Miller, and H. Beckman, "Organizational Dimensions of Relationship-Centered Care: Theory, Evidence, and Practice," *Journal of General Internal Medicine* 21, suppl. 1 (January 2006): S9-15. doi: http://dx.doi.org/10.1111/j.1525-1497.2006.00303.x.

## Chapter 10: Resolving Conflicts and Nurturing Your Relationships

1  Covey, *The 7 Habits,* 247.

2  This practice is derived from the Buddhist practice of tonglen, which is Sanskrit for "sending and taking" (i.e., "giving and receiving"). Dictionary.com, s.v. "tonglen," accessed May 1, 2016, http://www.dictionary.com/browse/tonglen. For more on this practice, see Pema Chodron, "The Practice of Tonglen," accessed September 3, 2016, http://creationcoach.com/pdfs/tonglen.pdf.

3  Chapman, *The 5 Love Languages.*

4  David Marquand, "The Charisma Question: Disraeli and Gladstone Reappraised" (review of *The Great Rivalry: Disraeli and Gladstone* by Dick Leonard) New Statesman, July 25, 2013, accessed April 25, 2016, http://www.newstatesman.com/culture/2013/07/charisma-question-disraeli-and-gladstone-reappraised.

## Chapter 11: Cultures of Reactivity and Creativity

1  James M. Higgins, Craig Mcallaster, Samuel C. Certo, and James P. Gilbert, "Using Cultural Artifacts to Change and Perpetuate Strategy," *Journal of Change Management* 6, no. 4, (December 2006): 397-415. doi: http://dx.doi.org/10.1080/14697010601087057.

2  BRS, "Culture and High Performance Outcomes: An Introduction to the Human Synergistics Approach," accessed April 26, 2016, http://www.brsresults.com/assets/value_add/Culture_and_high_performance_outcomes_an_introduction_to_the_Human_Synergistics_approach.pdf.

3  Arthur Asa Berger, "The Meanings of Culture," *M/C: A Journal of Media and Culture* 3, no. 2 (May 2000), accessed April 26, 2016, http://journal.media-culture.org.au/0005/meaning.php.

4  S. Karpman, "Fairy Tales and Script Drama Analysis," *Transactional Analysis Bulletin* 7, no. 26 (1968): 39-43.

5  Patrick Lencioni, *The Five Dysfunctions of a Team: A Leadership Fable* (San Francisco: Jossey-Bass, 2002).

6  David Emerald, *The Power of TED\* (\*The Empowerment Dynamic)* (Bainbridge Island, WA: Polaris Publishing Group, 2009).

7  Robert Anderson, "The Leadership Circle and Organizational Performance."

8  Robert A. Cooke and J. Clayton Lafferty, "Organizational Culture Inventory," Human Synergistics International, accessed April 26, 2016, http://www.humansynergistics.com/Products/OrganizationDevelopment/OrganizationalCultureInventory; http://www.humansynergistics.com/ResourceCenter/ResearchandPublications.

9  Gallup, "Gallup Q12 Meta-Analysis," September 22, 2014, accessed April 26, 2016, http://www.gallup.com/services/177047/q12-meta-analysis.aspx.

10  Ibid.

11  Gallup, "Report: State of the American Workplace," September 22, 2014, accessed April 26, 2016, http://www.gallup.com/services/176708/state-american-workplace.aspx.

12  Raj Sisodia, David B. Wolf, and Jagdish Sheth, *Firms of Endearment: How World-Class Companies Profit from Passion and Purpose* (Upper Saddle River, NJ: Pearson Prentice Hall, 2007), 13.

13  Firms of Endearment, accessed July, 9, 2016, http://www.firmsofendearment.com/.

14  Ibid.

15  Tony Hsieh, *Delivering Happiness: A Path to Profits, Passion, and Purpose* (New York: Business Plus, 2010).

16  Ibid.

17  "How Zappos Creates Happy Customers and Employees," (summary of the talk given by Tony Hsieh at the 2011 Great Place to Work Conference), accessed May 16, 2016, https://s3.amazonaws.com/media.greatplacetowork.com/pdfs/Zappos_-_How_Zappos_Creates_Happy_Customers_and_Employees.pdf.

18  Zappos, "Meet Our Monkeys," accessed April 26, 2016, http://www.zappos.com/d/about-zappos-monkeys; Zappos, "CEO Letter," July 22, 2009, accessed May 14, 2016, http://www.zappos.com/c/ceoletter.

19  NQA, "What is Qigong?," accessed April 26, 2016, http://nqa.org/about-nqa/what-is-qigong/.

20  Centre for Bhutan Studies Under the Patronage of His Majesty the King, "Gross National Happiness Index Explained in Detail," accessed April 27, 2016, http://www.grossnationalhappiness.com/docs/GNH/PDFs/Sabina_Alkire_method.pdf.

21  Gross National Happiness, "GNH Index," accessed April 27, 2016, http://www.grossnationalhappiness.com/articles/.

22  United Nations, "UN Connects Well-Being and the Pursuit of Happiness," March 19, 2013, accessed April 27, 2016, https://www.un.org/development/desa/en/news/social/intl-day-happiness.html.

## Chapter 12: Transforming Families, Organizations, Communities, and the World

1   Yerkes and Dodson, "The Relation of Strength of Stimulus to Rapidity of Habit Formation."

2   The Leadership Circle, "Leadership Culture Survey," accessed April 28, 2016, https://leadershipcircle.com/assessment-tools/survey/.

3   Human Synergistics International, "The Circumplex," accessed April 28, 2016, http://www.humansynergistics.com/OurApproach/TheCircumplex.

4   ERIC, "California State Department of Education, Sacramento. Toward a State of Esteem: The Final Report of the California Task Force to Promote Self-esteem and Personal and Social Responsibility," accessed April 28, 2016, http://files.eric.ed.gov/fulltext/ED321170.pdf.

5   K. Lloyd Billingsley, "A CalWatchdog Retrospective: 20 years after the California Task Force to Promote Self-esteem and Personal and Social Responsibility," CalWatchdog.com, July 29, 2010, accessed May 1, 2016, http://calwatchdog.com/2010/07/29/retrospective-a-state-of-esteem/.

6    Nicholas Emler, *Self-Esteem: The Costs and Causes of Low Self Worth* (UK: Joseph Rowntree Foundation, 2001); Erica Goode, "Deflating Self-Esteem's Role in Society's Ills," *New York Times,* October 1, 2002, accessed April 28, 2016, http://www.nytimes.com/2002/10/01 /health/psychology/01ESTE.html?pagewanted=all.

7    "Feel Good about Failure" YouTube video, 5:45, John Stossel, ABC 20/20, January 8, 1999, accessed April 28, 2016, https://www.youtube.com/watch?v=KTfwH_DYWUo.

8    In Rosenberg's self-esteem questionnaire, participants indicate whether they strongly agree, agree, disagree, or strongly disagree with the following statements:

1.   On the whole, I am satisfied with myself.
2.   At times I think I am no good at all.
3.   I feel that I have a number of good qualities.
4.   I am able to do things as well as most other people.
5.   I feel I do not have much to be proud of.
6.   I certainly feel useless at times.
7.   I feel that I'm a person of worth, at least on an equal plane with others.
8.   I wish I could have more respect for myself.
9.   All in all, I am inclined to feel that I am a failure.
10.  I take a positive attitude toward myself.

Response to statements 1, 3, 4, 7, and 10 receive a score of 4, 3, 2, and 1 for Strongly Agree, Agree, Disagree, and Strongly Disagree respectively, and statements 2, 5, 6, 8, 9 receive 1, 2, 3, and 4 points for these answers respectively. M. Rosenberg, "Rosenberg Self Esteem Scale," taken from *Society and the Adolescent Self-Image* (Princeton: Princeton University Press, 1965), accessed July 9, 2016, http://fetzer.org/sites/default/ files/images/stories/pdf/selfmeasures/Self_Measures_for_Self-Esteem_ROSENBERG_ SELF-ESTEEM.pdf.

9    Daniel Friedland, "Findings from the SFO Self-Doubt Study, 2000. The Relationship of the Degree of Bother with Self-doubt and Self-esteem" (previously unpublished data). Spearman Correlation Coefficient = 0.565, P-value < 0.0001.

10   K. D. Neff, "The Science of Self-Compassion," in *Compassion and Wisdom in Psychotherapy,* eds. C. Germer and R. Siegel (New York: Guilford Press, 2012), 79-92.

11   Frederic Laloux, *Reinventing Organizations: A Guide to Creating Organizations Inspired by the Next Stage of Human Consciousness* (Brussels: Nelson Parker, 2014).

12   Ibid., 15-16.

13   Ibid., 17.

14   Ibid., 18-23.

15   Ibid., 23-30.

16   Shep Hyken, "Drucker Said 'Culture Eats Strategy for Breakfast' and Enterprise Rent-A-Car Proves It," *Forbes,* December 5, 2015, accessed April 28, 2016, http://www.forbes. com/sites/shephyken/2015/12/05/drucker-said-culture-eats-strategy-for-breakfast-and-enterprise-rent-a-car-proves-it/#52c2534574e0.

17   Peter F. Drucker, *Management: Tasks, Responsibilities, Practices* (New York: HarperBusiness, 1993), 125.

[18] "Herb Kelleher and his leadership at Southwest Airlines," YouTube video, 9:30, March18, 2012, accessed April 28, 2016, https://www.youtube.com/watch?v=UX1ZKHPiSZ8.

[19] Laloux, *Reinventing Organizations,* 30-35.

[20] Ibid., 315-317.

[21] Ibid., 55-56.

[22] Ibid., 43-51.

[23] Ibid., 56.

[24] Online Etymology Dictionary, s.v. "health," accessed May 12, 2016, http://www.etymonline.com/index.php?term=health.

[25] Laloux, *Reinventing Organizations,* 143-191.

[26] Ibid., 290-291.

[27] AES home page, accessed April 29, 2016, http://www.aes.com/about-us/mission-vision-values-and-culture/default.aspx.

[28] Laloux, Reinventing Organizations, 50.

[29] Ibid., 44.

[30] Ibid., 44.

[31] Warren Berger, *A More Beautiful Question: The Power of Inquiry to Spark Breakthrough Ideas* (New York: Bloomsbury USA, 2014).

[32] David Rock, *Your Brain at Work* (New York: HarperCollins, 2009), 206.

[33] Jerry Adler with Gretel C. Kovach, Julie Scelfo, Franco Ordonez, and Adam Piore, "The Spirit of America, September 2001, The Aftermath: Connecting in New York," *Newsweek,* Commemorative Issue, September 2001, 24-30.

## Conclusion: Lifelong Practice and Ongoing Transformation

[1] Lally et al., "How Are Habits Formed."

# Index